34.⁹⁵

D1557573

Arms Control Verification

Pergamon Titles of Related Interest

Art, Davis & Huntington REORGANIZING AMERICA'S DEFENSE

Kronenberg PLANNING U.S. SECURITY: DEFENSE
POLICY IN THE EIGHTIES

Record REVISING U.S. MILITARY STRATEGY

RUSI/BRASSEY'S DEFENCE YEARBOOK 1984

RUSI/BRASSEY'S DEFENCE YEARBOOK 1985

Schelling & Halperin STRATEGY AND ARMS CONTROL

Tsipis & Janeway REVIEW OF U.S. MILITARY RESEARCH
AND DEVELOPMENT: 1984

Tyroler ALERTING AMERICA: THE PAPERS OF THE COMMITTEE
ON THE PRESENT DANGER

Windass AVOIDING NUCLEAR WAR

Related Journals
(Free specimen copies available upon request)

DEFENSE ANALYSIS

Arms Control Verification
The Technologies That Make It Possible

Edited by
Kosta Tsipis
David W. Hafemeister
Penny Janeway

Published in cooperation with the
Program in Science and Technology
for International Security
Massachusetts Institute of Technology

PERGAMON·BRASSEY'S
International Defense Publishers

Washington New York Oxford Toronto Sydney Frankfurt

Pergamon Press Offices:

U.S.A.	Pergamon-Brassey's International Defense Publishers, 1340 Old Chain Bridge Road, McLean, Virginia 22101, U.S.A.
	Pergamon Press Inc., Maxwell House, Fairview Park, Elmsford, New York 10523, U.S.A.
U.K.	Pergamon Press Ltd., Headington Hill Hall, Oxford OX3 0BW, England
CANADA	Pergamon Press Canada Ltd., Suite 104, 150 Consumers Road, Willowdale, Ontario M2J 1P9, Canada
AUSTRALIA	Pergamon Press (Aust.) Pty. Ltd., P.O. Box 544, Potts Point, NSW 2011, Australia
FEDERAL REPUBLIC OF GERMANY	Pergamon Press GmbH, Hammerweg 6, D-6242 Kronberg-Taunus, Federal Republic of Germany
BRAZIL	Pergamon Editora Ltda., Rua Eça de Queiros, 346, CEP 04011, São Paulo, Brazil
JAPAN	Pergamon Press Ltd., 8th Floor, Matsuoka Central Building, 1-7-1 Nishishinjuku, Shinjuku, Tokyo 160, Japan
PEOPLE'S REPUBLIC OF CHINA	Pergamon Press, Qianmen Hotel, Beijing, People's Republic of China

---

Copyright © 1986 Pergamon-Brassey's International Defense Publishers

All rights reserved. No part of this publication may be reproduced, stored in a retrieval system or transmitted in any form or by any means: electronic, electrostatic, magnetic tape, mechanical, photocopying, recording or otherwise, without permission in writing from the publishers.

First printing 1986

Library of Congress Cataloging in Publication Data
Main entry under title:

Arms control verification.
    "Published in cooperation with the Program in Science and Technology for International Security, Massachusetts Institute of Technology."
    Papers presented at a conference held at M.I.T., Feb. 1984.
    Bibliography: p.
    1. Nuclear arms control--Verification--Congresses.
2. Arms control--Verification--Congresses. I. Tsipis, Kosta. II. Hafemeister, David W. III. Janeway, Penny. IV. Massachusetts Institute of Technology. Program in Science and Technology for International Security.
UA12.5.A76   1986   623.7'1   86-726
ISBN 0-08-033172-6

Printed in the United States of America

This book is dedicated to Pete Scoville,
who died before it was complete.
His wisdom, balance, generosity, compassion, and grace
lit the way
for two generations of people who have worked —
some as passionately as he did —
for peace.

Contents

Preface

The boundaries for nuclear arms control negotiations are set by what each negotiating party believes to be essential to its national security. What is the safe and proper balance between increasing some weapon systems and limiting others? Underlying that question is the issue of verification: If one side abides by agreed-upon limitations, how can they be sure the other side does not take advantage of their restraint by secretly violating the agreement? In the United States that issue is often phrased, "But what about the Russians?"

Views on the effectiveness of verification more often seem to be based on ideology than on information: "We" are good and do what we say we will do; "they" are untrustworthy cheaters. Most of the public debate on the issue has been unspecific, hortatory, and filled with worst-case assumptions. Little attention has been given to a detailed analysis of the technical capabilities available to the United States for monitoring compliance with nuclear arms control agreements. Because it is on these capabilities that objective judgments about the adequacy or inadequacy of our means of verification must be based, it seemed worthwhile to examine these technologies in a systematic way. Thus, the Program in Science and Technology for International Security of the Massachusetts Institute of Technology, with funds provided by the Levinson and Field Foundations, organized a conference of specialists to look at the technical means of verification of compliance with arms control treaties. It took place at the Massachusetts Institute of Technology on three days in early February of 1984.

The conference, and this, the resulting volume, aimed to examine the question of the adequacy of the technical means of nonintrusive inspection of activities in the Soviet Union, as well as technical advances, past and predicted, that could influence our judgments of what are referred to in the language of arms control treaties as "national technical means" (NTM). While there has been little disagreement on the performance characteristics of our means of collecting information about the production, deployment, and performance of Soviet military systems, and little disagreement on what types of information can and cannot be collected, there has been vigorous debate about what "adequate" verification is and how it can be defined in terms of specific instances of arms limitation agreements.

The organizers and participants of the conference were interested in putting this debate in context by first exploring the minimum requirements for information about Soviet activities and weapons systems dictated by the need to safeguard our national security and then comparing these requirements with existing and projected monitoring capabilities. No effort was made to do more than note the broader political, diplomatic, or compliance issues.

Some of the chapters in this book are quite general about the value and role of monitoring, some deal more specifically with particular verification missions, and some are quite technical and perhaps of interest chiefly to specialists. In their original form they were presented for discussion at the symposium. Many of the authors revised their original papers subsequently, and these have been further edited for clarity and accessibility for the non-specialist reader. In this connection, the editors particularly want to thank Matthew Bunn, research associate at PSTIS, for his help. Brief introductory notes summarize the more technical papers to help the non-technician understand where they fit in the overall picture. Philip Morrison's Afterword is a transcript of his remarks at the close of the symposium.

Most remarkable among the technical chapters in the book is the discussion of seismic detection of underground nuclear detonations. In it, Jack Evernden and Charles Archambeau present a novel way to treat the seismic signals from such detonations that permits the detection of distant nuclear explosions down to the level of a few hundred tons of TNT equivalent and can reliably distinguish between such explosions and natural phenomena such as earthquakes. This is a technological breakthrough of immense significance for the feasibility of a verifiable Complete Test Ban Treaty.

This volume does not contain two excellent papers on the verifiability of limitations on ICBMs, SLBMs, cruise missiles, and bombers delivered by Ray McCrory, who served as Chief of the Central Intelligence Agency's SALT Support Staff (redesignated the Arms Control Intelligence Staff in 1980) for most of the 1970s and early 1980s. Even though his presentation was unclassified, the CIA subsequently forbade Mr. McCrory to permit the papers, or even notes on the papers, to be published. We owe a debt of gratitude to Herbert Scoville, Jr., former CIA Deputy Director for Science and Technology, for agreeing to write the chapter on this subject. Mr. Scoville was a participant in the conference but did not expect also to be an author.

If a single conclusion can be distilled from the proceedings of the conference and of these chapters, it is that technology permits us to monitor with confidence much, although by no means all, of the weapons-related activities of the Soviet Union, and that the level at which the technology functions is higher than has generally been recognized. Many of the arms control specialists at the conference, familiar with the subject as they were, expressed surprise at the capabilities of some of the technologies discussed. The inquiry into what level of verification capability was necessary to prevent erosion of our national security through clandestine violations of treaties by the other side yielded a corollary conclusion, which is that the margin of United States security is very great. Violations of nuclear arms treaties that could seriously undermine it are well within the detection capabilities of our present verification technologies, to say nothing of expected improvements in these systems.

The verification question will be with us for a while, as we debate and negotiate our national arms control positions in Geneva, in Congress, in the news media, in seminars and think tanks, in town meetings, living rooms and kitchens, on the hustings, and at the ballot boxes. What limitations on our nuclear weapons are we safe in accepting? And how do we know what is safe? Our verification capabilities are an essential component of this debate. We hope that in providing specific and detailed information on the subject, this volume will be a valuable and lasting contribution to rational and responsible efforts to think through our nuclear weapons policies.

— The Editors

Introduction

Jerome B. Wiesner

One of the most important and one of the least well understood pieces of the arms control puzzle is the issue of verification. Understanding verification needs and capabilities is important because too often weapons reduction or elimination proposals are rejected with the argument that they cannot be adequately verified. It has been customary in arms control negotiations to insist on much more verification than is necessary.

A perfect verification system is impossible, even with quite intrusive means of inspection. For example, it is unlikely that one can verify to the exact number compliance with any agreements that set a numerical limit for missiles or aircraft. Fortunately, this is not the requirement for verification of arms-limitation agreements, any more than it is for monitoring an intense arms race. What really matters is whether or not the inspection system offers a high degree of confidence that it will provide a warning before a dangerous situation develops.

It was long ago agreed that a single clandestine test of a small nuclear weapon could not be detected with a high degree of probability, but it was concluded that this was not essential because, as both sides have had to conduct large numbers of tests to develop their nuclear arsenals, one test more or less would not make a significant difference in the quality of either stockpile. A major new development is not likely to be possible with a single test. Also, a nation that wants to carry out a clandestine series of nuclear explosions without detection, say a set of ten, must convince itself that not even one of them will be detected because, from the inspection viewpoint, a single unequivocal violation is sufficient to sound a warning or even destroy a treaty. Similarly, although it may be impossible to count accurately the exact number of missiles that have been deployed, there can be a high degree of confidence that changes in force size that could create a threatening situation would be detected by unilateral means long before the illegal increases could affect our national security.

It is not necessary to be familiar with all possible verification needs to understand that our present verification systems are adequate to do the job. In this volume, you will find chapters by people who are knowledgeable about many different aspects of verification. These chapters are the gleanings of a stimulating and, on the whole, encouraging conference sponsored by the Program in Science and Technology for International Security at the Massachusetts Institute of Technology in 1984. I say "on the whole, encouraging," because the general sense of the conference was that the technical people present were a group that, between them, had looked seriously at all the major verification needs and technologies. And the consensus was that our verification abilities are of a quality to permit confidence that neither violations of agreements nor unilateral declarations of limitations on testing or deployment of nuclear systems can become dangerous to our security.

One need only realize how effective the national systems of inspection and verification employed by the United States have been, especially since the late 1950s, to appreciate the participants' confidence in their potential value for the monitoring of arms reduction measures. The United States detected the first Soviet nuclear bomb explosion; it detected the earliest Soviet missile tests; it has unilaterally and with confidence reported on the size of the many components of the Soviet nuclear forces.

Many people fear that the certain-to-come reductions in the size of missile systems, the possibility of mobile rockets, and the deployment of the cruise missile will make verification less reliable. That is undoubtedly true. But if the purpose of the verification system or process is to assure discovery of violations and to provide warning of violations of agreements with sufficient lead time to avoid dangerous developments or deployments, the available systems are much more than adequate. Furthermore, as one looks to the future, one can also expect marked improvements on present verification capabilities (some of which are discussed in the chapters to follow). It should be expected also that the nations involved in arms reduction or control agreements would be prepared to permit an appropriate level of inspection when substantial progress has been made in reducing the size of nuclear arsenals.

Finally, it is important to realize that effective deterrents do not depend upon matching type for type or unit for unit in either delivery systems or nuclear weapons. Sea-based systems can deter land-based systems. Ballistic missiles can deter cruise missiles, aircraft can offset cruise missiles, etc. The important issue is that there exists a modest but secure retaliatory force, as long as deterrence must remain the peacekeeping strategy.

Everyone knows that there already exist enough nuclear weapons to wipe out most of life on our planet in a flash and convert it into a barren, poisoned wasteland. Not so well understood is the fact that there is no acceptable military use for these weapons. By acceptable military use I mean one in which the military advantage is sufficient to justify the disadvantages that appear to accompany their use. Studies of the possibility of carrying out a successful pre-emptive strike, for example, one that disarms the opponent's forces so completely that the retaliatory blow would not destroy the initiator's country, show that this option does not exist. In fact, many millions of people on both sides would die in any substantial nuclear exchange. The only role for nuclear weapons is as a deterrent to their use by others. The only meaningful question is how large a force is required to ensure confidence in the deterrent. And this is a matter of judgment and common sense. A very few nuclear weapons, certain of delivery, constitute an adequate deterrent, one so convincing that it will discourage any nuclear adventurism.

Unfortunately, the arms race has taken on a life of its own and has acquired so many supporters and beneficiaries that it dominates the lives of the two major nuclear powers, and especially their leaders, so that there is no time (at least in the United States) for serious and thoughtful study of the nature and consequences of the arms race. Perhaps this spell can be broken by a collective effort to understand the extent of the dangers, followed by a collective effort to work for a significant change in superpower behavior.

There are a few issues that, if widely understood and accepted generally, could give the leaders of the superpowers the confidence and courage to move unilaterally to halt the arms race and then reduce the number of nuclear weapons in their arsenals. Furthermore, if these points were clearly understood by most of the people who are basically opposed to the present directions, it would give them the confidence to demand a halt in the massive military commitments.

To start with, no one knows how to use nuclear weapons in warfare. There are hundreds of thousands of experts on technical matters and on military hardware. But on the critical issues of strategy, deterrence, war-winning, and damage effects of nuclear weapons on people, physical structures, and the environment, there are truly no experts. None. No one knows for sure about the field performance of nuclear weapons, their reliability, or accuracy. Because it is impossible to test nuclear weapon systems in realistic conditions, uncertainty about their performance in combat overrides the knowledge of the performance of individual components.

There has never been a war in which tactical or strategic nuclear weapons were used by both sides. Planners, therefore, are completely dependent on theory to support their strategies. All plans discussed with such solemnity by so-called experts are based entirely on speculation. That is why there is so little agreement among analysts after decades of thinking, writing, and debating about nuclear strategy.

The layperson who argues for a nuclear freeze or a test ban or some other arms-limitation measure is frequently dismissed because he or she lacks secret information on the matter. There are no secrets on the vital issues that determine the intensity and momentum of the arms race. Everyone should realize that on the critical issues of what is an adequate deterrent, whether humanity can recover from a nuclear war, and many other such questions, their studied judgments are as good as those of any political or military leader. In fact, they may be even better, because they will have more time to consider the matter and are not subjected to the pressures that impinge on people in high official positions.

It is important for people to realize that there is no monopoly on wisdom, no special knowledge that changes the commonsense conclusion that nuclear weapons have only one purpose—namely, to prevent their use— and that can be accomplished with a small number of secure weapons on both sides. Similarly, it should be obvious that if both sides believe that they can only get a fair hearing if they bargain from a position of strength, we will not only never stop the arms race, but we will have created conditions that ensure its growth. The determination by both sides to maintain even a five percent superiority will ensure a rapid growth in opposing forces, while a willingness to accept a lesser position of the same size by both would quickly begin the reduction of arsenals.

Neither secret information nor specialized knowledge is needed to understand the issues that really matter in shaping the arms race. And, furthermore, on those issues there are no experts whose views should be given special weight in decision making. To the extent that they can be understood at all, the significant facts of those issues can be understood by anyone who is willing to make a sustained effort to do so. A few hours of study and discussion a week can soon make a person knowledgeable if not expert, and a large body of knowledgeable people around the world could improve the dialogue in which the fate of the earth is discussed.

This is a volume in which a number of scientists and analysts put forth their special information, the fruits of their experience. They are experts, not on the use of nuclear weapons in war, but on particular technologies and political contexts that are relevant to verification. Though it may not be easy going for the layperson, despite the intent to be clear and to provide guides where the technical going is steepest, it is precisely the kind of reading that will equip people who are concerned about the urgency of reversing the arms race to arrive at and support their own views, as valid as any expert's, on the strategically important verification question. And to join in the dialogue of knowledgeable people, upon the outcome of which all our fates and those of our children and grandchildren depend.

Man is at a momentous crossroad. There is still time to stop the runaway arms race and to confront the other dangerous problems of survival, but the opportunity will soon pass. A nuclear war would certainly eliminate that opportunity. So will a few more years of continuing to prepare for one with the necessarily wrong priorities that this requires, which now determine national policies everywhere.

PART 1

VERIFICATION: THE PROCESS AND ITS USES

1.

Verification, Compliance, and the Intelligence Process

Noel Gayler

VERIFICATION EXAMINED

Nothing has impeded the negotiation of nuclear arms control agreements more than the vexed issues of verification. "What if the Soviets cheat?" marks at once a genuine concern on the American side and also a stick with which to beat any proposal for arms control. "Concealed espionage" and "affronts to our sovereignty" are the counter-slogans, genuine or otherwise, of the Soviets.

The issue is in fact little understood. Verification, strictly speaking, deals only with adherence to agreements. The term is often used, however, in reference to any adversary action, whether covered by agreement or not. Furthermore, most discussions fail to distinguish between three quite disparate kinds of verification:

- *Juridical verification*, which requires the ability to detect any departure, however insignificant, from the legal text of an agreement;
- *Political verification*, the aim of which is to give politically adequate assurance, both within our system and the Soviet, that adversary actions can be adequately detected; and
- *Military verification*, which must be able to detect violations or other adversary actions that make a significant difference in the chances of a nuclear war or its likely outcome or in the power positions of the adversaries.

Each of these has an importance of its own, but it is wise to avoid confusing them as we examine the technical bases for national means of verification.

Nor should we confuse issues of *verification*, the finding of fact and the resolution of questions, with issues of *compliance*, the enforcement of obligations.

Verification has at least four functions, all important. These functions are:

- *Insurance against significant surprise, or "breakout."* Breakout is the sudden unilateral abrogation of an existing agreement, followed by rapid progress in a new weapons technology or system formerly forbidden by the agreement, with the implication that much research had been done in preparation while the agreement was still in force. Most breakout scenarios are distinctly overdrawn: they are neither credible nor usually significant. They create a certain amount of disturbance in the political system, however. Insurance that there will be no undetected changes seems to be politically necessary.
- *Confidence-building between the adversaries.* Each must maintain high confidence that the other side continues to believe that arms control is in its best interest, that it continues to act in accordance with that interest, and that there are no covert actions at variance with agreed controls.
- *Creation of political support for arms control.* Both sides must believe that the risks of an arms control agreement are smaller than the risks of not having it.
- *Guidance for drafting treaties and agreements.* Many treaties and many agreements, both explicit and implicit, suffer from the fact that they were not drafted with an eye to facilitating verification. For example, an agreement specifying an upper limit on the size of underground nuclear explosions (the Partial Test Ban Treaty) is far harder to verify than a total ban would be. Knowledge of the strengths and weaknesses of verification methods produces better treaties.

COMPLIANCE AND STRATEGIES

The intelligence process is the basis for "national technical means of verification" (NTM), which is in turn the backbone of all strategic arms agreements. Stated another way: The images and transmissions provided by satellite-borne cameras and radios and other technical means would be of little use without the interpretive context provided by other kinds of information, gathered and analyzed without the cooperation of the observed party, that are the product of the intelligence process. Intelligence will always uncover various questionable activities by the adversary. Some findings are ambiguous as to fact but clearly relevant to a treaty or understanding. Some are the reverse: clear as to fact but uncertain in relevance or interpretation. Some are ambiguous as to both fact and interpretation. Still others seem clear-cut — at least to one of the adversaries. Some questionable activities may have military significance; to date, most have not.

Each side must develop a strategy to deal with this intelligence mix.

Among great powers there is no mechanism for enforcement by appeal to a court. There is little prospect for effective coercion by stick or carrot, or for appeals to international opinion. Effective compliance can come only from the self-interest of each adversary in the continued life of the agreement. This in turn requires assessment of the risks and gains from violations, whether covert or open. The role of verification is to ensure that violations are not likely to remain covert.

VERIFICATION AND THE INTELLIGENCE PROCESS

Verification of treaties and understandings is, of course, only one facet of the intelligence process, which operates continuously in all sovereign states and indeed within many other entities as well. This process has five dominant characteristics:

1. Intelligence is almost never positive or determinate. No one can say with total confidence that a given action will or will not be detected, or even what the probabilities of detection may be. There is some small probability that we have a "mole" in the Kremlin, so that all Soviet actions are open to us. There is a very high probability that if the Soviets build a replica of the Pentagon on the banks of the Moscow River, we will detect it. All other situations lie somewhere between those extremes of probability. But if advantage depends on not being found out, the side that cheats must be highly confident of remaining undetected. This is a very demanding requirement — far more demanding than that of the adversary, who needs only a fairly good chance of detecting an infraction to believe that cheating will seem unproductive to the other side.

2. Intelligence is interactive. Human intelligence brings counterintelligence. Signals intelligence evokes encryption, countermeasures, and suppression of signals. Industrial intelligence prompts controls. Political intelligence results in smokescreens and indirection. Challenge and response characterize the process.

3. Intelligence is highly synergistic. Different means of collection suggest to each other where to look and for what. Analysis is essentially putting together parts of a puzzle to find the best fit. In no other field is it more true that the whole is greater than the sum of the parts.

4. Much intelligence collection is vulnerable and necessarily secret, for the good reason that if the means of collection are known to the adversary, they will be lost. The agent will be shot or the communications encrypted. The full picture is not open to scrutiny, and this places a great burden on the public conduct of policy. Policy makers have not always resisted the temptation to invoke secret information to support policy, but the practice is unjustifiable.

5. Intelligence is much more than the amassing of information, or the direction of the interactive process of collection. In the end, it is expert

opinion based on careful analysis. It can never be absolute, nor better than the expertise and probity of the analyst.

SENSITIVITY ANALYSIS

To a first approximation, the consequences of a general nuclear exchange between the great powers at their present force levels appear generally unaffected by either numbers of weapons, reliability of weapons, or type of delivery technology. On the other hand, targeting policy, force application, fuzing policy, readiness states, force generation, circumstances of initiation, and tactics may make discernible differences in the outcome. These general findings need careful sensitivity analysis, to confirm and quantify the variables in the nuclear force equation that make a difference, and to distinguish them from those that do not. Only in this way can treaty designers understand which elements are important.

For example, if numbers are now so far above the saturation level that major increments or reductions make little difference, then preoccupation with numerical balance is misplaced. This would include, derivatively, concerns about stability of forces and about reliability. Verification requirements in turn would be affected, as would also requirements for stockpile reliability testing.

Sensitivity analysis can also show the extent, if any, to which the outcome of a nuclear exchange would be affected by new weapons developments. The analysis could therefore guide verification requirements in that area.

A major consideration in the design of national intelligence for verification is the need for convergence of legal verification, political verification, and military verification. Legal requirements of treaties should not be more restrictive and detailed than required for security and political acceptance. Political acceptance should be informed by realistic appraisal of the military and physical consequence of covert and undetected noncompliance. The education of politicians and the public in this area is a major and neglected need.

AGREEMENTS

Verification is an aspect of the total intelligence process, which goes on whether or not treaties are in force. But arms control treaties and agreements may, and generally do, contain provisions to facilitate the collection of information and the analysis of intention, by mutual consultation. These cooperative measures are major confidence builders, both a cause and a result of the perception of common interest in arms control.

Too much, however, can be made of the necessity for cooperative measures, such as on-site inspection. The Soviets, with characteristic paranoia about espionage and touchiness about sovereignty, have low tolerance for intrusive inspection. Nor is our own tolerance unlimited. It is difficult to imagine an American red carpet for Soviet technologists to come crawl around the Minuteman silos—though what the Soviets might have to gain from such a visit is unclear. The purported need for on-site inspections has in the past been made use of, somewhat disingenuously, to torpedo arms control agreements otherwise in the clear interest of both parties. It is therefore particularly important to focus verification efforts on improved technological means, such as seismic detection or high-resolution radar, that obviate requirements for intrusion.

TECHNICAL CONTRIBUTION

For these reasons, whereas cooperative measures are useful and desirable, confidence in compliance with arms control agreements must rest primarily on independent national intelligence. Capabilities that are totally under the control of the observing power and that involve the least intrusion on the sovereignty of the observed are to be preferred. Here is where improvement in the technical means of information collection can make real contributions to the cause of arms control.

For example, ongoing improvements in satellite photography such as increasing coverage, improving timeliness, or enhancing detail are useful. (These are discussed in Chapters 7 and 10 of this volume.) Synthetic aperture radar (Chapter 11) promises quasi-photographic coverage even at night and in bad weather. Enhanced seismic signal detection and analysis may yield assurance that underground events of low yield can be reliably detected and distinguished from earthquakes, even when decoupled. (An explanation of significant new conclusions in this field is in Chapter 16.) An unsolved technical problem is the analysis of ballistic missile tests, absent useful telemetry. Observables in the field of signals intelligence are less precisely defined but no less important, and technical progress in this area is very important.

National technical means of verification are accepted without question as a legitimate and inherent component of arms agreements. They are not the only component and may sometimes not be even the principal component of the capability of national intelligence to verify adherence. But they are visible, avowable, and understandable, and consequently important in sustaining political confidence.

Adequate support and technical improvement are therefore essential. In the intelligence field, as in many others, you tend to get what you pay for. The technical improvements, attained and potential, described elsewhere herein are examples of development that will pay off many times in confidence that we can safely negotiate agreements to reduce the risk of nuclear war.

2.

The Intelligence Process

William E. Colby

Understanding what the technical means of verification are capable of is essential to a balanced view of the possibilities for arms control. In order to put the technological factor into its proper position in the process of verification, however, it is essential to consider the spectrum of arms control and the intelligence processes which are necessary to verification.

Grossly simplified, the arms control process can be considered as having three basic elements. The first is the agreement, usually reached after long and agonizing detailed negotiations endeavoring to balance the requirements of the different parties, wrestle with the asymmetries of the weapons involved, and assure both sides that their welfare will be better served under the agreement than without it. The second element of the arms control process is verification, to determine whether the other side is complying with the agreement or is in violation. Verification, of course, depends heavily upon the intelligence process but, as we will see, it is not limited to that.

The third element of arms control is the decision as to the actions a nation should take if it finds the other side is not in compliance with the agreement. This can include various diplomatic actions, various sanctions imposed on the other party or the repudiation of the agreement. It is important to note that this third element is a clear and separate matter from the verification process. The administration is wrestling with whether certain Soviet actions are in violation of SALT II, but it is important to note that the basis of its concern is the information supplied by our intelligence machinery, and that the activities were identified in their early stages.

As noted above, the intelligence process is a major contributor to the second element of arms control, that is, determination of whether there is compliance with or violation of the agreements. Before going into details of technical means, however, it is essential to consider the intelligence process, so that the technical contribution can again be seen in proper proportion.

The intelligence process also can be divided into three major elements. First is the one commonly misunderstood as comprising the whole of the intelligence process, namely, *collection* of all relevant information on the question being examined. This is the explanation for the word "central" in the name of the American intelligence agency. The first and most obvious element of this process is overt collection, the assembly of all publicly available material, in the enormous volume in which this exists in our information age today. Collection of relevant press reporting, specialized journals, reporting services of various sorts, libraries, and other compilations all contribute to this information flow. In addition, a contribution is received from the official collection machinery of our government: the authorized activities of the foreign service, military attaches, and the various other overseas elements of our government that collect possible relevant information on such matters as crop situations abroad, commercial and trade problems, financial balances, and so forth. The key to this element of the process is that it is authorized by the government about which information is being collected, which is to say that the diplomat is not violating his function or going beyond his welcome when he interviews local sources of information and reports the results to his government. This obviously creates an enormous information flow toward the center and gives adequate coverage of many of the major problems that exist among nations today.

Technical means of collection are a relatively new development, although they also have their antecedents. Electronic collection has been under way since the last century and developed during World War II to include the interception of relevant communications. These communications are then subjected to sophisticated analysis to determine their content, although they may be protected in various ways by the nations using them. To these rather old-fashioned forms of technical collection, we have added in recent years a number of improvements, which will be discussed later in this volume, in electronics, acoustics and other forms of surveillance. A major step in this area occurred with the U-2 aircraft and its initiation of photographic collection, which opened up areas that had hitherto been hidden from external examination. This has expanded since the days of the U-2 to the area of satellite photography, on which much of arms control verification depends today. But photography is not the only source of such technical collection. Indeed, almost all the sciences today can contribute. Suffice it to say that the technological collection process has changed the nature of intelligence in these past thirty odd years. Areas from which we were totally excluded and of which we had no knowledge are now exposed to surveillance to determine whether activities incompatible with arms control agreements are proceeding.

A last, but by no means insignificant, element of collection is the centuries-old practice of clandestine collection. This played the major role in intelligence collection in previous centuries. It has been supplemented in enormous degree by the contributions of the overt and technological collection processes in these last years. But it is clear that clandestine collection can contribute certain unique elements to a total collection effort that can not be achieved by other means. To learn of the intangible area of intention, make an appreciation of the interrelationships between political forces, and to warn of plans for future weapons systems development, clandestine collection can make a unique contribution. Although on occasion the results will be less precise than the "harder" information that is derived from technical collection, they frequently can make a major contribution to the targeting of technical intelligence means, so that they can amplify, confirm or deny a hint or tip received clandestinely and transform it into specific and firm information about an arms control situation.

The collection of the information, however, is only the first step in the intelligence process. Since World War II, the true central element of American intelligence has resided in *analysis*. The raw information must be examined to determine its reliability, to resolve any contradictions it contains, refine any ambiguities that may be present. The word "central" was carefully chosen to reflect this central role of analysis of the myriad bits of data that overwhelm us in the modern world. It is through experienced and sophisticated analysts that we can hope to come to reliable conclusions as to the meaning of the many bits of information that surround us, particularly in resolving whether there is compliance or violation where an arms control agreement is concerned. A part of such analysis is to determine the motivations and forces that might lead in the direction of compliance or violation. As analysis proceeds, collection can focus on the more critical indicators of another nation's intentions or practices as they affect the United States. There have been great successes in this area in the past, and there have been some rather clamorous failures. The Pentagon Papers attest to a thoroughly objective and non-political analysis of the nature of North Vietnamese leadership and the strength with which it would resist the direct application of force through the bombing campaigns. On the other hand, the Cuban missile crisis came after an assessment by analysts that the Soviets had never placed, and consequently would never place, offensive nuclear weapons anywhere outside direct Soviet control on Soviet soil. The area of analysis is still under development to improve its disciplines and its procedures. But, however imperfect, it is a vast improvement over reliance upon raw reports suggesting one or another sensational potential conclusion, with decision-making based on these alone.

The third element of the intelligence process is the one least developed in our government, the *application* of the results of collection and analysis to the particular decision being faced by our leadership. In the early days this underdevelopment was perhaps a result of the excessively academic orientation of the analyst tradition, with the concept that its function was to provide a totally objective backdrop upon which decisions could then be taken.

In truth, however, the decision makers need the closest possible application of the collection and analytical process to the particular decision they face. Therefore, the increase in direct communication between decision maker and intelligence center in recent years is to be lauded, rather than suspected as placing intelligence under pressure to conform with predetermined policy. In arms control, it is plain that both the collectors and the analysts must be most intimately in contact with the key questions to be determined, namely, whether there is compliance with or violation of an arms control agreement by another nation.

Against this review of the arms control process and the intelligence contribution to it, a few general propositions about the verification problem can be postulated. The first is very simple. Our intelligence will be focused on the development and deployment of Soviet weapons and forces, whether there is an arms control agreement between us or not. This is for the simple reason that our national security demands that we have an understanding of the forces and weapons that could destroy our country so that we can take the requisite decisions to protect ourselves. It can be said in recent years that we do a good job in the intelligence process. The recent Defense Department publication, *Soviet Military Power*, is a graphic presentation of the scope of our intelligence about Soviet military forces, some of which are included under arms control agreements, some of which are not. From time to time, questions come up as to a loss of certain intelligence windows into Soviet forces. But the clear experience over the past fifteen to twenty years is that a loss of intelligence capabilities for local political reasons in a place like Turkey, say, or Iran, is compensated for so that our coverage continues. Information about Soviet military power is essential to the protection of the security of the United States, and we will devote such efforts and develop such techniques as necessary to enable us to have a satisfactory appreciation of it, whether there is an arms control agreement between us or not.

The second proposition is equally obvious, that most recent arms control agreements make this process easier. Thus, SALT I, SALT II, and other comparable treaties contain provisions against concealment, require declarations of forces, call for notification of weapons tests so that the other side's capabilities can be alerted to cover them, and provide counting rules to help resolve ambiguities where certain details cannot be resolved through technical means. Thus the difficulty of distinguishing a multiple-warhead from a single-warhead missile is solved by counting any missile of a type that has been tested with multiple warheads as having multiple warheads, whether a particular weapon has them or not. Some of the recent treaties or draft treaties have gone beyond these requirements and call for the exchange of geologic data, the implantation of sensors to reinforce the monitoring process, or even visits by inspection teams. The inspection team was once defined by Joseph Stalin as a form of American espionage, and his rejection of these teams led to the failure of the most dramatic arms control offer in history, by Bernard Baruch in 1946, which would have stopped the development of nuclear weaponry. In 1963, the Kennedy administration's consideration of a possible comprehensive test ban was stopped in part by a difference between the Soviet and the American negotiators as to how many inspection teams per year would be authorized — the Americans insisting on seven but the Soviets allowing only three. In the most recent comprehensive test ban proposal, inspection teams are called for. However, one should not be overly confident that the inspection team is the panacea of arms control, as it is the Russians who invented the Potemkin village, and their ability to put up false façades in the time of the Empress Catherine is certainly no less today under present Soviet management.

The third proposition is that the existence of an arms control treaty permits communication about the details of compliance or possible violation, which does not exist in its absence. If we see some suspicious activity in the Urals today, suggesting the possibility of some new form of Soviet weapon that is not included under an arms control agreement, our inquiries are likely to receive that warm and friendly "nyet" so familiar in our relations with the Soviets. On the other hand, the experience in the Standing Consultative Commission under SALT I has indicated that ambiguities can be raised and resolved, and that positive changes in Soviet behavior toward compliance can be obtained through such communication. On some occasions, the Soviets may not admit a violation, but we have seen their behavior change to compliance nonetheless.

The last proposition with respect to verification is that it not be allowed to control totally the arms control process. The usual way in which verification is debated is to ask whether there is any remote possibility that the Soviet Union could secretly violate a treaty in any degree. The question should rather be whether the Soviet Union could secretly violate an arms control agreement in any degree significant to our national security. This would permit an evaluation of whether a violation by the Soviet Union in a marginal way would be a smaller threat to our national security than the freedom of the Soviet Union in the absence of an agreement to go ahead and develop new weaponry in such quantity and quality as substantially to threaten the United States. Intelligence coverage of the Soviet Union is a continuing process and, as noted above, we do a fairly good job of it. We even cover weapons and forces that are inherently impossible to verify down to the last specific item or detail. Thus, we have perfectly reasonable and useful estimates of total Soviet tank forces, artillery, etc., although each of these could be subject to some degree of concealment. On the overall basis, however, as a result of the central intelligence process, knowledge of the strength of the forces in general is sufficient to allow us to be alert to the need to counter them in the fashions we need. It can be confidently said on the basis of our experience, especially since the development of satellite photography, that no Soviet weapon system or military force has risen to a state of development or power sufficiently to threaten the United States without being amply telegraphed in advance. The faster-than-expected Soviet development of thermonuclear weapons, the Sputnik, and even the increase in accuracy of their land-based missiles, all were to a degree surprises to American intelligence, but they were reported long before the development of forces or threats that could change the balance of power between our two nations.

Thus, I suggest as guidance for this volume on technical means of verification that we not allow ourselves to be dominated by the specifics of our capability of determining any one particular action by the Soviet Union in violation of an arms control agreement. Our focus should not be on whether we could identify the last fin on some missile, but on whether the Soviets could develop a utilizable force in secret to achieve the kind of surprise change in the balance of power Nikita Khrushchev sought in Cuba in 1962. The real contribution of this volume could be to ensure that all the stages of the intelligence process are understood, assisted and improved in their vital contribution to monitoring compliance or violation with respect to arms control agreements. But most of all, these descriptions of a wealth of sophisticated technical capabilities should lead to a resolute rejection of any conclusion that arms control is not feasible because the last detail of compliance is not possible to ascertain. Instead, the questions for our national security should be whether the degree of compliance that can be monitored is well within marginal levels and whether a contribution to our safety lies more in the limitation and reduction of these weapons than in continuing to build additional and more dangerous ones.

3.

Verification Issues from the Point of View of the Negotiator

Ralph Earle II

For exactly four months in 1979, from July 9 until November 9, various Senate committees focused on the SALT II Treaty and, in particular, upon the issue of its verifiability. Not only did the Senate Armed Services Committee and the Senate Committee on Foreign Relations address that issue, but the treaty was scrutinized at great length by the Senate Select Committee on Intelligence.

Basically, two questions were raised throughout those hearings: (a) Was the treaty as a whole "adequately verifiable?" and (b) Were particular and individual provisions of the treaty subject to adequate verification?

At one point in a closed hearing before the Intelligence Committee, when I was being interrogated regarding specific provisions of the treaty and their verifiability, I volunteered to the committee that I would take home that evening a copy of the treaty and cross out in red pencil all those provisions in it that would not have been included had the treaty been with another nation we trusted 100%. Even to my surprise, when I returned the next day I held a copy of the treaty in which somewhere between 85% and 95% of the verbiage had been deleted. In other words, only 5% to 15% of the treaty was substantive; the balance dealt directly or indirectly with the problem of verification. Moreover, in order to solve certain problems of verifiability, in some cases substantive prohibitions were adopted (e.g., to avoid the problem of compatibility between launchers of SS-20 IRBMs and SS-16 ICBMs, the Soviets formally agreed not to produce, test, or deploy the SS-16 or its third stage, reentry vehicle or post-boost vehicle).

However, the fact that the negotiators and drafters of the treaty had gone to such lengths to address verification did not satisfy all of the senators immediately and did not satisfy some of them eventually. Many seemed to have the impression that we, the negotiators, had drafted a treaty with a number of substantive provisions and *then* said to ourselves, "Here's the treaty—I wonder if it's verifiable."

However, as my colleagues and I attempted to demonstrate during those hearings, with one or two exceptions (which were to the potential or at least short-term advantage of the United States), there was never a proposal put on the table in Geneva that had not been determined to be adequately verifiable, from the point of view of the United States. That is a strong statement, and it deserves some supporting evidence. In fact, the support for that statement lies in a description of how negotiating proposals were developed in Washington, refined at the delegation level in Geneva, and presented to the representatives of the Soviet Union at the table. In fact, no instructions were sent to the delegation with regard to proposals, either general or specific, to be made to the Soviets that had not been cleared by, among others, the so-called "intelligence community" in Washington; this community was and is led by the Central Intelligence Agency and includes the Defense Intelligence Agency, the National Security Agency, and the Intelligence and Research Bureau of the Department of State. Frequently, in the development of a proposal within the United States bureaucracy, considerable negotiation was necessary when one or more of the members of the intelligence community were of the view that a specific treaty provision was not as verifiable as it should be. However, as noted, virtually no instruction reached Geneva without having gained an imprimatur as "verifiable" — at least so far as it impinged on the Soviet Union.

In that connection, one can gain considerable insight into the capabilities of U.S. intelligence collection methods when one examines certain provisions of the treaty itself. As an example, I would cite the provisions of Section 9 of Article IV and their accompanying Agreed Statements and Common Understandings, in which certain restrictions are placed on changes in existing types of ICBMs and on new types of ICBMs. In particular, it was proposed by the United States and eventually agreed by the Soviet Union that, among other things, percentage changes in excess of 5% of certain parameters, including length, diameter, launch weight, and throw weight would be prohibited. The mere fact of the United States' proposal of these limitations represented a clear, albeit implied, assertion on our part that our intelligence experts had concluded that changes in excess of the 5% permitted could indeed be monitored and detected by national technical means of verification; therefore, they were suitable proposals to make at the table in Geneva. In fact, there were a number of other limitations originally proposed to the Soviets in this context, including restrictions on changes in the total impulse of each stage and the initial weight and power of the post-boost vehicle; these were rejected by the Soviets on the ground that they were not verifiable. Whether this was a legitimate complaint on their part (which would imply that their national technical means were less effective than ours) or whether it was a disguise for an unwillingness to have those parameters monitored is not known. However, the point is that the United States had determined that it could monitor these additional parameters and were prepared to have limitations upon them written into the treaty.

A word should be said about the phrase "adequate verification." It was originated by President Nixon in the course of the discussions of SALT I and was used in the ratification of those agreements. Subsequently, it was adopted as the standard for the SALT II agreements, and the discussion in the course of the ratification hearings was based on that phrase. In a document submitted to the Senate together with the treaty, Secretary of State Vance presented it in the following fashion:

> (1) The anticipated SALT II agreement is adequately verifiable. (2) This judgment is based on assessment of the verifiability of the individual provisions of the agreement and the agreement as a whole. (3) Although the possibility of some undetected cheating in certain areas exists, such cheating would not alter the strategic balance in view of U.S. programs. (4) Any cheating on a scale large enough to alter the strategic balance would be discovered in time to make an appropriate response. (5) There will be areas of uncertainty, but they are not such as to permit the Soviets to produce a significant unanticipated threat to U.S. interests, and those uncertainties can, in any event, be compensated for with the flexibility inherent in our own programs.

In other words, items 3, 4, and 5 above are what constitute justification for the use of the word "adequate" — that the cheating would not go undetected for a sufficiently long period to affect the strategic balance, and that any such cheating could be compensated for in a timely fashion by changes in our own programs.

Obviously, the question of adequate verification was significant not only in a substantive sense from the point of view of the negotiations and the drafting of the treaty, but from a political sense. Unfortunately, those defending the SALT II Treaty (or any arms control treaty, for that matter) labor under a handicap. First, they must accurately acknowledge that no agreement of this sort is totally verifiable. Having made that concession, as it is viewed by some critics, they are then faced with the problem of finding a modifier for the absolute word "verifiable." In the case of the Nixon, Ford, and Carter administrations, the word was "adequate." Almost by definition, "adequate" is a subjective term, difficult to measure against any objective standards, except those already set forth in the Vance quotation above. But even those criteria are somewhat subjective. For instance, "would not alter the strategic balance," "would be discovered in time," and "a significant unanticipated threat" — each of those phrases can be interpreted in a subjective fashion, and therefore the solution remains elusive.

The present administration chooses to use the phrase "effective verification." It too is fraught with subjective interpretation, and, so far as I know, this administration has not attempted to define "effective" as did the previous administrations with respect to "adequate."

Another issue that arises under the question of verification, both in its terms of negotiation and political consequences, is the question of so-called "cooperative measures," a euphemism, although by no means a synonym, for "on-site inspection," as some people consider it. It is greatly troubling to read so frequently that various members of the Senate and, indeed, of this administration, claim that no present or future arms agreement can be monitored or verified effectively or adequately without some form of on-site inspection or cooperative measures. Flat statements such as this simply obscure the problem; they do not solve it. Moreover, with respect to SALT II, it had already been agreed by President Nixon and then by President Ford that the agreement should be verified by "national technical means."

Whether one is dealing with "adequate verification" or the desirability of on-site inspection, one cannot discuss an agreement as a whole in those terms — it is essential that the agreement be broken down into its individual articles and sections, and each one be tested against the appropriate means of verification currently available, either as a unilateral technical matter or as a matter of literal agreement. For instance, a ban on the construction of new fixed ICBM silos is one aspect of a treaty that can clearly be monitored and verified both adequately and effectively by national technical means, particularly by photographic satellites.

On the other hand, were the current freeze proposal to be put into effect, it would be difficult at best for a total prohibition of or limitation on the production of fissionable materials or nuclear warheads to be adequately monitored by any means, much less by national technical means. It is therefore essential that each individual limitation or prohibition be examined by itself and in the context of available verification methods. One can then make an overall judgment as to whether the agreement as a whole is satisfactorily verifiable.

This is not to say that cooperative measures or even on-site inspection could not in some cases be of assistance, or perhaps even be required, in verifying a provision. An example of such a limitation has not actually been conclusively addressed; however, one example that arose with respect to the provisions of the SALT II Treaty was the requirement that the Soviets give their thirty-one Bison tankers "functionally related observable differences which indicate that they cannot perform the mission of a heavy bomber." (Second Common Understanding to Paragraph 3 of Article II.) A superficial reading of that provision would indicate that it was less than totally verifiable because of the mobility of aircraft and the possibility of simply "FRODing" (creating "functionally related observable differences," such as eliminating bomb-bay doors) a portion of the number required to be altered and then moving them around in order to create the impression that their number equalled thirty-one.

Here, in the verification of compliance with this provision, cooperative measures could have played a considerable role — for instance, an agreed arrangement whereby the Soviets would have all the aircraft visible at one time, perhaps even in an airborne fly-by, through which we could determine that x number of Bison bombers had indeed been converted by viewing their underbellies and their absence of bomb bays. In short, one can go through the spectrum of provisions in the SALT I and SALT II agreements, and any potential strategic or intermediate range arms control agreement, and analyze it against available verification techniques through national technical means, to determine the possibility and advisability of cooperative measures and, perhaps, the very unverifiability of certain limitations.

And, in the context of cooperative measures and/or on-site inspection, one cannot exclude consideration of the concerns, real or exaggerated, of the United States military. For instance, in the course of SALT II negotiations, an American negotiator offered to the Soviets on-site inspection of our Minuteman fields in return for reciprocal arrangements at Soviet ICBM complexes; this was done without the approval or knowledge of the Joint Chiefs of Staff and resulted, to put it mildly, in their disapproval and disavowal.

So, when one goes beyond verification by national technical means and enters into consideration of cooperative measures and/or on-site inspection, one must consider not only monitoring capability from an intelligence viewpoint, but also acceptability to our military and desirability from the point of view of national security.

Finally, in the context of verification from the point of view of the negotiator and its political consequences, one must look at the Standing Consultative Commission (SCC) and its role. Mr. Michael Krepon has contributed a chapter to this volume entitled "The Politics of Treaty Verification and Compliance" (Chapter 4) in which he intelligently and accurately reviews the role and history of the Standing Consultative Commission. It is not my intention to repeat what Mr. Krepon has said there. However, I would add to his views that, again in the context of proposals approved by the United States government in Washington and put on the table to the Soviets in Geneva, the same personnel who are reviewing the SALT or START proposals for the U.S. government are those who are also backstopping the SCC. As a result, there is a total continuity and congruity of views with respect to proposals that are made and proposals that, subsequently accepted, come within the jurisdiction of the SCC. In other words, had the SALT II Treaty been ratified, the United States component of the SCC would have been in an educated position to challenge the Soviets regarding any "ambiguous situations" or possible violations of that treaty in the SCC, inasmuch as the personnel involved in supporting the SCC represent the same agencies and are, in most cases, the same people who initially approved, from an intelligence point of view, the proposals that were made and eventually accepted.

It is clear that the SCC has played a valuable and effective role in dealing with problems arising under the existing treaties, and should continue to do so. However, as the Soviets have recently complained, we are in breach of at least part of that commission's charter in that we have now gone public with allegations of violations. It is not helpful to be in breach of any part of an agreement of that sort, but when it entails bringing sensitive matters to the public's attention — matters which, as I understand it, have not been fully explored with the Soviets in Geneva — it can only serve at best to exacerbate the historically good and businesslike relations of the two sides in the SCC. At worst, it can terminate what appears to be the only line of communication we have at present with the Soviet Union regarding strategic and intermediate range nuclear forces.

4.

The Politics of Treaty Verification and Compliance

Michael Krepon

At the outset of the SALT I negotiations, President Richard Nixon vowed, "I am determined to avoid, within the government and in the country at large, divisive disputes regarding Soviet compliance or non-compliance with an understanding or agreement. Nor will I bequeath to a future president the seeds of such disputes."[1] Despite his intentions, the SALT I accords generated considerable controversy over Soviet compliance, contributing to President Jimmy Carter's failure to secure ratification of the SALT II Treaty. Subsequently, compliance problems have become progressively worse, as symbolized by United States and Soviet reports criticizing each other's compliance record. As a result of this turn of events, any president to the left of Ronald Reagan can expect verification and compliance issues to figure prominently in future ratification debates. More than ever before, progress in arms control will depend on an effective strategy to deal with verification and compliance issues.

THE POLITICS OF TREATY VERIFICATION

From the Limited Test Ban to the Salt II Treaty, American presidents supported a flexible approach to verification requirements: the United States had to be in a position to detect Soviet cheating of any consequence in time to take appropriate countermeasures. This operational principle became known as "adequate" verification during the Nixon, Ford, and Carter administrations. President Kennedy used a different terminology but a similar standard for verification during the Limited Test Ban Treaty debate.

During the SALT I and II debates, administration officials did not contend they could detect every instance of Soviet cheating; they asserted they could monitor any cheating that mattered. The risks of undetected cheating were acceptable because they were outweighed by the benefits of the agreement and because the United States would respond vigorously when cheating of military significance was detected. The ultimate United States sanction to non-compliance would be to abrogate the agreement in question.

President Reagan and most of his advisers rejected the standard of "adequate" verification as insufficient and concluded that political judgments as to adequacy in the past had not been rigorous. In addition, they claimed that previous arms control agreements had been poorly drafted, allowing the Kremlin to exploit ambiguities in ways they believed injured U.S. national security. Henceforth, a more exacting standard for verification would be required. To distinguish their standard from the previous one, Reagan administration officials referred to the need for "effective" verification.

How did effective verification differ from adequate verification? There was no clear answer from the president or his advisers, only inferences that U.S. monitoring had to be more intrusive and verification requirements tougher. For medium-range and strategic forces, administration spokesmen expressed concerns about stockpiled missiles, silo reloads, covert production, and the resulting possibilities of "breakout" against treaty constraints. Reagan administration officials could not agree, however, on what verification measures would be required to address these concerns. U.S. "Verification Annexes" had yet to be tabled at the START and INF talks when both were suspended in the late fall of 1983.

The implications of the Reagan administration's new verification standard were most apparent on the question of resuming anti-satellite negotiations. The administration resisted a ban on ASAT tests or limits on ASAT capabilities because such agreements couldn't be effectively verified and because of military requirements to place Soviet satellites at risk.

A March 1984 Reagan administration report explaining this position pointed to severe verification problems as well as to the impracticability of a comprehensive ban on ASAT capabilities, since anti-ballistic missile interceptors, ground-based lasers, manned space missions, or any intercontinental ballistic missile with a change in software could be applied to ASAT missions. More limited bans, such as a ban on flight-testing of dedicated ASAT systems, also posed verification problems for the Reagan administration. Just as the Nixon administration had argued with respect to MIRV flight tests, the Reagan administration asserted that ASAT tests could be concealed, allowing capabilities to be developed and deployed surreptitiously. The Reagan administration argued further that limited ASAT agreements could not adequately constrain the threat to U.S. assets in space.[2] This position on ASAT arms control mirrored the right-wing critique of previous nuclear arms control agreements: compacts of limited scope were insufficient, while those of an acceptable scope were unverifiable.

Behind the distinction between "adequate" and "effective" verification lie fundamental differences of view concerning Soviet objectives and the value of arms control. A more flexible standard for verification requirements makes sense for those who believe that the United States and the Soviet Union have common interests in maintaining the viability of agreements reached and in foreclosing destructive avenues of competition. The arms control community has repeatedly argued that the Kremlin does not sign agreements that, in its view, require cheating in order to protect its security. For the United States, therefore, such agreements do not require trusting the Kremlin to keep its commitments, but merely trusting it to act in its own best interests. In addition, there are bureaucratic reasons to expect Soviet compliance, once the Kremlin makes the necessary internal tradeoffs to reach agreement. With political commitments lined up to endorse agreements, bureaucratic inertia could be expected to buttress treaty compliance. Sophisticated national technical means of verification help assure U.S. officials and the American public that the Soviets are keeping up their end of the bargain and serve as a deterrent to Soviet cheating. Detection of cheating would be, at the very least, embarrassing, and could prompt unwanted reactions.

Holders of this view argue for flexible standards of verification, depending on the benefits of the agreement in question and the risks of undetected cheating. Since, for the arms control community, agreements are the essence of security and an unconstrained competition is not, "adequate" verification need not be overly stringent.

Skeptics of Soviet intentions and the value of arms control reject this calculus of benefits and risks. For them, arms control is more of a hindrance than a help to U.S. national security, because agreements are more likely to constrain U.S. weapons programs than malevolent Soviet ambitions. It follows that, at best, negotiated agreements have little bearing on U.S. security problems; at worst, they have a pernicious effect, lulling the West into a false sense of security while the Kremlin surpasses American strategic power, either by exploiting loopholes in treaty texts or by outright cheating. In its most extreme form, this view is reflected in reports like *A Quarter Century of Soviet Compliance Practices under Arms Control Commitments, 1958–1983*, prepared for President Reagan by the Arms Control and Disarmament Agency's General Advisory Committee. This report concludes that "the Soviets sign and ratify arms control treaties they are planning to violate." Moreover, "some of the apparent advantages gained by the recent breaches could have been obtained by 'legal' means" — in other words, the Soviets cheat even when they don't have to.[3]

A mindset most skeptical of Soviet intentions and the value of arms control naturally breeds a far different approach to verification issues, because failure to detect Soviet noncompliance does not necessarily mean that the

Kremlin is behaving itself; it means only that violations have not yet been detected. The best checks against nefarious Soviet practices, skeptics claim, are precisely drafted agreements, highly intrusive monitoring provisions, and a forceful policy of sanctions and unilateral actions once violations are perceived.

As a result of these contrasting viewpoints, congressional debates over verification issues have had a ritualistic quality. In every debate, critics called attention to problems of detection and the potential military significance of undetected Soviet cheating. During the Limited Test Ban Treaty debate, for example, critics pointed to the difficulties in detecting weapon tests in remote ocean areas, in space, behind the moon, adjacent to the Chinese border, under Lake Baikal, or even in the atmosphere during periods of heavy cloud cover. Another concern expressed in congressional testimony was that the Soviets could test "legally" under a few feet of soil, thereby gaining unfair advantages over the United States. Treaty opponents also pointed to important gaps in U.S. detection capabilities, since the first VELA satellites to monitor atmospheric testing had yet to be placed in orbit.

President Kennedy parried concerns over verification when he decided to forego a comprehensive treaty in favor of an agreement allowing underground tests. Thereafter, the Joint Chiefs reversed their opposition to an agreement. General Maxwell Taylor, speaking for the Chiefs, effectively argued that whatever clandestine progress the Soviets might make would be minor, especially with safeguards endorsed by congressional skeptics, which included a strong underground test program and improved monitoring capabilities. Harold Brown, then the Pentagon's chief scientist, persuasively assuaged concerns over Soviet cheating, noting the difficulty and expense of carrying out clandestine tests in remote areas, compared to the relative ease with which tests could be carried out underground. A reservation to the treaty making ratification contingent on a system of on-site inspections offered by Senator John Tower was easily defeated. Tower maintained that such inspections were necessary to ensure compliance; 76 of his colleagues felt otherwise.

One reason for Tower's overwhelming defeat was that public opinion strongly supported the treaty. One poll showed that four out of five Americans gave their "unqualified approval" to the Limited Test Ban Treaty before the Senate vote, up from 52% at the start of the Senate's deliberations. The treaty offered an end to radioactive fallout from U.S. and Soviet tests, as well as the promise of subsequent agreements. Concerns expressed by treaty opponents over verification appeared petty by comparison.

Verification concerns were similarly inconsequential during congressional debate over the SALT I accords. Secretary of Defense Melvin Laird and the Chairman of the Joint Chiefs, Admiral Thomas Moorer, flatly declared U.S. verification capabilities to be adequate, and little debate ensued on their assertion. Nixon administration spokesmen pointed out that, for the first time, the Soviet Union legitimized "national technical means of verification" (NTM) in the text of both the ABM Treaty and the Interim Agreement. Moreover, the Soviets agreed not to interfere with NTM and not to use deliberate concealment measures that impeded verification of treaty provisions. These provisions seemed more than sufficient for the kinds of controls embodied in the SALT I accords. With President Nixon's strong domestic political position and assurances from Pentagon officials, skeptics of the agreements were in a poor position to argue persuasively against the accords on verification grounds. As will be discussed in the following section, critics of SALT I were more concerned about unfavorable trends in the strategic balance than about our ability to verify them.

In stark contrast to preceding debates, verification issues were prominent during the SALT II hearings. The treaty's qualitative constraints placed more demands on United States monitoring capabilities, and compliance questions arising from the SALT I accords heightened sensitivities to the complexities of verification. Finally, events that occurred during the congressional review process, particularly the loss of Iranian monitoring stations and the "discovery" of the Soviet military brigade in Cuba, drew attention to our verification capabilities.

As in the Limited Test Ban Treaty debate, SALT II critics cited treaty provisions and Soviet activities that would be difficult to monitor. Carter administration officials provided the same assurances as their predecessors, but with considerably less success. Administration spokesmen could point to new treaty provisions that aided verification — such as counting rules, cooperative measures and a ban on encryption when it impeded verification of compliance with treaty provisions — but few were swayed by such arguments. Technical issues relating to verification became surrogates for broader political concerns during the SALT II debate, symbolized by Senator John Glenn's vote against the treaty in the Senate Foreign Relations Committee. Glenn withheld his support for the treaty until gaps in U.S. monitoring capabilities could be closed. Long before the Soviet invasion of Afghanistan, the treaty was in trouble because of perceptions of presidential weakness and apprehensions about disturbing trends in the superpowers' military capabilities.

THE POLITICS OF TREATY COMPLIANCE

When President John F. Kennedy assumed responsibility for negotiating a nuclear test ban and assuaging concerns over Soviet compliance, Fred Iklé, then a defense analyst with the RAND Corporation, wrote an important article entitled, "After Detection — What?"[4] Iklé was less concerned with treaty monitoring than with handling the problems of Soviet noncompliance once discovered. Despite evidence that compliance problems have become more troublesome over time, little has been written in response to Iklé's question since his essay first appeared in 1961.

As with the verification issue, congressional debates over treaty compliance have followed a discernible pattern. Critics have pointed out the dire implications of noncompliance and compiled lists of previous Soviet transgressions, whereas supporters dwelt on the benefits of the agreement at hand and the ultimate sanction of abrogation if the Kremlin did not fulfill treaty obligations.

During the Limited Test Ban Treaty debate, President Kennedy was in a strong position to defuse the compliance issue. Despite his reluctance to break the moratorium on atmospheric testing in place since 1958, he did so in 1961, following the example of France and the Soviet Union. In doing so, President Kennedy demonstrated that if the Soviets reneged on their treaty commitments, the possibility of U.S. abrogation was more than an idle threat. Moreover, the scenarios for possible compliance problems such as testing behind the moon or in deep space seemed far-fetched and the presumed value of clandestine cheating quite marginal. Critics published long lists of Soviet broken promises from the Bolshevik Revolution to Yalta, but with little effect. The perceived benefits of the Limited Test Ban Treaty clearly seemed worth the risk of Soviet noncompliance.

During the SALT I debate, congressional critics led by Senator Henry Jackson expressed concern not that the Kremlin would cheat, but that they could do so much harm under the terms of the Interim Agreement without resort to cheating. Senator Jackson and his allies were particularly concerned about ambiguities relating to the modernization of ICBM launchers that could be exploited by the Kremlin.

The Interim Agreement's provisions governing new ICBM launchers did not prohibit the replacement of existing Soviet ICBMs with new missile types of considerably greater size and capabilities. The United States had tried to do so without success, first by suggesting direct limits on missile volume and then by limiting increases in silo dimensions. Soviet negotiators consistently rejected U.S. formulations that would foreclose the deployment of their fourth generation of ICBMs — the SS-17, SS-18 and SS-19.

The Nixon administration's interest in selling the accomplishments of SALT I was totally compatible with the interests of congressional skeptics seeking favorable interpretation of the Interim Agreement's limitations on new Soviet ICBM launchers. Secretary Laird and Admiral Moorer were most explicit on this point: in their view, if the Soviets contravened a narrow interpretation relating to enlargements of ICBM launchers, this would constitute a violation of the Interim Agreement. The Soviets proceeded to deploy new ICBMs that did not conform to U.S. preferences.

Later, this issue would be a springboard for contentious debates over

Soviet SALT violations, but at that time, compliance questions did not loom large on the horizon. President Nixon did not need to defend his credentials as a staunch defender of U.S. interests in negotiations with the Soviet Union. Whatever criticism was levied at the SALT I accords was deflected by the president's acceptance and subsequent passage of the Jackson Amendment requiring follow-on agreements to provide for equal levels of intercontinental strategic forces. Moreover, Nixon was firmly committed to proceed with the B-1, Trident, and various other programs to strengthen his hand in subsequent negotiations. In addition, the SALT I accords established a special channel, the Standing Consultative Commission (SCC), to handle any compliance questions that might arise.

Later, the question of Soviet compliance with the SALT I accords figured prominently in the SALT II debate, where one-quarter to one-third of the Senate appeared irreconcilably opposed to the treaty. As in the past, committed treaty opponents compiled lists of Soviet transgressions. Unlike Presidents Kennedy and Nixon, President Carter was in a poor position to rebut these charges: the perceived benefits of the SALT II Treaty were not greatly appreciated, and the president's resolve in dealing with the Kremlin was widely questioned.

Occasionally, allegations of SALT I compliance problems were completely devoid of substance, such as reports in the fall of 1975 that the Soviets were blinding U.S. satellites. The source of this problem turned out to be fires along Soviet gas pipelines. Sometimes, however, allegations of Soviet wrongdoing provided some basis for concern requiring the attention of the SCC. Regardless of their veracity, reports of Soviet violations have had a damaging cumulative effect, leaving supporters of arms control in something of a bind, since it is difficult to rebut charges without focusing more attention on them and without seeming to defend Soviet behavior. Rebuttals must also be sanitized through the national security bureaucracy to protect intelligence sources and methods as well as the privacy of diplomatic communications. For these reasons, timely rebuttals are unlikely, while *ex post facto* summaries of how the SCC ironed out compliance questions rarely dispel built-up perceptions of Soviet wrongdoing.

The difficulties of defending the record of the Standing Consultative Commission in the political arena were apparent when, in 1978, the Carter administration released an unclassified report of U.S. and Soviet concerns raised in the SCC since its inception. The report provided little ammunition to committed treaty supporters and little consolation to treaty critics. Its findings did not dispute the claims of those who argued that the Kremlin repeatedly exploited definitional ambiguities and pressed at the margins of the SALT I accords. But the Carter administration's compliance report did refute assertions of violations, finding that in every instance of troublesome Soviet practices, after raising the issue in the SCC, "the activity has ceased or subsequent information has clarified the situation and allayed our concern."[5]

Presidents Nixon, Ford, and Carter studiously avoided a prosecutorial approach to these compliance issues, seeking instead to fence in problems by working out new common definitions to ambiguous treaty provisions. The clear objective for these presidents was to maintain the viability of the SALT I accords by halting Soviet practices that could, over time, undermine the worth of the agreements.

The process of fencing in Soviet testing at the margins was often an arduous one, as was evident in the compliance question relating to Soviet SA-5 radar tests "in an ABM mode." Article VI of the ABM Treaty barred such testing of air defense systems in order to prevent their effective utilization against strategic ballistic missiles. The picture was clouded, however, because there was no common agreement on what constituted tests "in an ABM mode" and because the United States maintained that tests for "range safety and instrumentation" were permitted.

In 1973, U.S. intelligence began to notice Soviet practices that could encroach upon treaty provisions when it became apparent that a radar, eventually identified as one associated with the SA-5 air defense system, had been turned on during the flight-testing of Soviet ballistic missiles. The reason the radar had been operating was unclear, requiring considerable evaluation by the U.S. intelligence community. When the Ford administration became convinced that SA-5 radar tests raised compliance problems, the United States made a rigorous presentation in the SCC about how such tests could undermine critically important treaty limitations. The SA-5 radar tests stopped within three weeks. It then required approximately two years of private diplomacy in the Carter administration to work out a common agreement on permissible uses of radars in conjunction with ABM tests and for range safety and instrumentation purposes.

For supporters of the SALT process and the SCC, this case study constituted a success story. For critics, it confirmed that Soviet violations had been swept under the rug by grandfathering the Kremlin's malpractices into the SCC's "solutions." In this view, the Kremlin had unfairly gained military advantages at the expense of negotiated agreements. In contrast, administration officials during this period took a more relaxed view toward Soviet practices, assuming that whatever tests were conducted with a radar associated with the SA-5 system did not provide Soviet air defense crews with much help to counter incoming strategic ballistic missiles. The bottom line appeared in Defense Department budget requests, where no compensating military initiatives were deemed necessary in response to Soviet crowding at the margins of the agreement.

Critics of the SALT process, including some former officials associated with the SALT I accords, rejected the Carter administration's conclusions about the work of the SCC and the record of Soviet compliance. During the bitter SALT II debate, these critics questioned the ability of the Carter administration to lodge future complaints due to loopholes within the treaty. For example, before he was appointed Assistant Secretary of Defense in the Reagan administration, Richard Perle asserted that the Kremlin could deploy a fifth generation of ICBMs then under development within the lax "new types" provision of the SALT II Treaty. Similarly, Perle claimed the United States could not verify compliance with a treaty provision barring the deployment of SS-16 missiles.[6] The Republican Party's campaign platform during the 1980 election formally pledged to end the "cover-up" of Soviet SALT violations.

Early in his administration, President Reagan declined to endorse a laundry list of violations compiled by critics during the Nixon, Ford, and Carter years. When new compliance issues arose, SALT II opponents within the Reagan administration argued against trying to resolve them in the SCC, since to do so would provide unwarranted standing for an agreement whose ratification they helped to block. Initially, a bureaucratic compromise was reached whereby the U.S. delegation was directed to express concern about SALT II compliance without entering into a discussion of specific issues. Typically, the commission will meet twice yearly, during the spring and fall. The United States began to discuss new ICBM compliance issues during the spring 1983 session of the SCC; U.S. concerns about construction of a large phased-array radar at Krasnoyarsk (instead of at the periphery of the Soviet Union, as the ABM Treaty requires for early-warning purposes) were raised in the fall 1983 session of the SCC. When administration officials were not satisfied with the Soviet explanations, President Reagan responded to a congressional initiative by publicly issuing his report of Soviet non-compliance. Included in the administration's findings were the "new types" and SS-16 citations previously considered by SALT critics to be either unverifiable or within the permissive boundaries of the SALT II Treaty.

The public release of the Reagan administration's findings was immediately questioned by those who felt it lengthened the odds against the commission's being able to resolve issues privately. There was also something incongruous about asserting violations of "political commitments" to agreements that the Reagan administration refused to ratify—as was the case with four of the seven citations in the president's report. The Reagan administration's findings on SALT II noncompliance also seemed premature, given the uncertainties associated with Soviet practices and the possibility of learning more about them, either by national technical means or by waiting for responses to U.S. inquiries made during the fall 1983 session of the commission. Although a report to Congress was mandated, the Congress did not set a date for its release, nor did it require findings of noncompliance in highly ambiguous cases.

The tentative language of the Reagan administration's report on Soviet noncompliance seemed to confirm the wisdom of those who had favored accumulating more evidence before going public with a report. The citations and conclusions in the report varied greatly in degree of importance and in kind, making generalizations difficult. SALT II citations dealt with definitional issues and problems with Soviet concealment practices—the hardy perennials of previous SCC exchanges.

In previous cases, however, Presidents Nixon, Ford, and Carter were able to hammer out common definitions of permitted activities and to curtail Soviet concealment practices at the SCC. The objective for these presidents was not necessarily to reestablish the *status quo ante*, but to maintain the viability of the SALT I accords. A second Reagan administration compliance report was issued in February 1985. Like its predecessor, it combined substantive compliance problems with questionable concerns, while confirming the administration's inability to resolve issues in the SCC.

The Reagan administration's compliance diplomacy operated from a different set of premises from those of its predecessors. To begin with, the president and his advisers were clearly ambivalent about maintaining the viability of nuclear arms control agreements negotiated by previous administrations. Moreover, administration officials could not agree on the nature of solutions deemed necessary to resolve outstanding compliance problems. For those who believed the Soviets gained advantage from noncompliance, the *status quo ante*, or something close to it, was an essential outcome of SCC deliberations. But the more Reagan administration officials telegraphed their ambivalence toward the SALT accords, the less likely they were to achieve success in the SCC.

PICKING UP THE PIECES

Although the Reagan administration has badly mismanaged compliance diplomacy, it has not invented problems of Soviet treaty compliance. These problems are not nearly as serious as ardent opponents of previous arms control agreements assert. Nevertheless, negotiated agreements clearly are unraveling, as the United States and the Soviet Union hedge their bets against an increasingly uncertain future. The value of the negotiating process has become more difficult to justify for supporters in both Washington and Moscow. The last nuclear arms control agreement to be ratified by both nations was signed in 1972, and prospects for new nuclear arms control agreements appear remote. In this political environment, compliance problems are unlikely to be resolved to the satisfaction of both parties.

The process of mutual hedging is most apparent with respect to the ABM Treaty. The Reagan administration has expressed concerns about how the Soviets are nibbling around the edges of treaty constraints by developing "rapidly deployable" ABM systems and anti-tactical-ballistic-missile defenses. In conjunction with these ongoing programs, the phased-array radar under construction at Krasnoyarsk is clearly worrisome — not because it projects a threat of imminent breakout from the ABM Treaty, but because it reflects a far more callous Soviet approach to treaty definitions than has previously been the case. Using the Soviet justification for the new radar, both sides could establish a territorial base for an ABM system, contrary to Article I of the treaty, by building more such radars within their interiors for "permitted" purposes.

Judging by the Kremlin's list of U.S. arms control violations and circumventions, Moscow is just as concerned about Washington's intentions toward the ABM Treaty. The Reagan administration is constructing large phased-array radars in Texas and Georgia for early warning against missile attacks. Each radar provides 240-degree coverage along southern arcs. By the administration's definition, these radars are "oriented outward," but they also provide coverage for a substantial portion of the continental United States. Additional large phased arrays are planned for Greenland and the United Kingdom, locations far from the periphery of the United States as required by the ABM Treaty. The administration contends these are modernization programs permitted by the treaty. The Strategic Defense Initiative announced by Reagan looks to the Soviets like explicit preparations for breaking out from the ABM Treaty. Current ABM developments are the clearest example of how military programs that may seem like prudent hedges are causing agreements in force to unravel. If both sides continue to exploit definitional ambiguities in the text of the agreement, the ABM Treaty can be badly eroded.

The more this pattern of hedging continues, the more difficult it will be to reverse the process of decontrol, particularly for a president predisposed to arms control. In a domestic political context, Soviet encroachment on treaty constraints inevitably erodes public and congressional support for arms control as well as confidence in our negotiating partner. Thus, a president who appears less than vigilant in providing for U.S. national security will find numerous conditions — including the negotiation of intrusive verification provisions and successful resolution of outstanding compliance controversies — imposed upon him before new arms control agreements are approved.

A moderate-to-liberal president inclined to take risks for arms control benefits will find it difficult to deflect unreasonable demands, particularly if he is perceived as lax in pursuing strategic modernization programs or unsteady in his handling of U.S.–Soviet relations. For these reasons, an arms control-oriented president would be wise to avoid epistemological disputes over effective or adequate verification. A far better strategy would be to stress new, improved monitoring capabilities and to select treaty provisions that constrain Soviet forces in ways that minimize monitoring difficulties and compliance questions.

Verification concerns can also be downplayed by avoiding difficult-to-monitor provisions that generate more problems than they solve. The SALT II provision governing modifications in ICBMs is a classic case in point. The Carter administration settled on provisions that allowed 5% leeway on certain ICBM parameters in order to distinguish between permitted modifications of existing missiles and "new types" of missiles, of which one was permitted. This was certainly better than allowing 50% improvements, but the SALT II "new types" provision proved exceedingly costly. It was difficult to negotiate, difficult to defend during ratification hearings, and politically damaging when Soviet missile designers and political leaders took up the challenge of shoehorning new missiles into the 5% rule. In addition, the "new types" provision required Soviet cooperation on encryption to be sure changes in the specified parameters did not exceed 5%. When the United States declined to ratify the treaty, the necessary cooperation was easily withheld.

Some controversies over treaty compliance are likely to ease with improved U.S.–Soviet relations, but the political dynamics of compliance diplomacy will continue to beset arms control-oriented presidents. Earlier citations of Soviet noncompliance endorsed by President Reagan simply will not go away. However, a president with Ronald Reagan's hardline, anticommunist credentials can break this vicious circle, if he and his Soviet counterpart can engineer an improvement in superpower relations. Like Richard Nixon before him, Reagan can defuse concerns over treaty verification and compliance by appealing for public trust in his judgment that the United States can monitor Soviet compliance and respond effectively to Soviet misbehavior. Irreconcilables in the Congress will bitterly contest the president's findings, but they can be isolated effectively by a conservative president in the White House. Congressional majorities in support of agreements reached under President Reagan's auspices will not be narrowed by unsatisfied concerns over verification or by outstanding compliance problems.

Compliance problems are essentially political, not technical, in nature. Compliance diplomacy can succeed when treaty signatories exercise care not to undermine the viability of previous agreements. When parties to an agreement question its worth or its future viability, compliance problems will multiply and not be resolved easily.

On the domestic front, the most effective way to outweigh concerns over verification and compliance is to bring home agreements that will generate widespread and enthusiastic public support. If the benefits of agreements are strongly appreciated, verification and compliance risks will not weigh so heavily in public debate, as was the case during the Limited Test Ban Treaty. If public support is not forthcoming, these issues will resonate strongly, as was the case during the SALT II debate. Future agreements do not need to yield immediate significant results to meet this criterion, but they must promise steady, progressive benefits over time. Otherwise, future presidents most inclined to reach arms control agreements with the Kremlin may find themselves unable to secure congressional support for them.

REFERENCES

1. Smith, Gerard C., *Doubletalk*. Garden City, N.Y.: Doubleday & Company, 1980, p. 99.
2. *Report to the Congress, U.S. Policy on ASAT Arms Control.* March 31, 1984.
3. Reproductions of vugraphs used by the General Advisory Committee in congressional briefings appeared in the *New York Tribune*, August 31, September 4 & 5, 1984.
4. *Foreign Affairs*, January 1961:208–220.
5. U.S. Department of State, Bureau of Public Affairs. *Verification of SALT II Agreements.* Special Report No. 56, August 1979, p. 3.
6. Perle, Richard. "SALT II: Who is Deceiving Whom?" in *Intelligence Policy and National Security*, edited by Robert L. Pfaltzgraff et al. Hamden, CT: Archon Books, 1981, pp. 151–154.

5.

Verification and National Security

Joseph J. Romm

The purpose of verification is not the accumulation of legal evidence for a court of law. It is to protect our nation against Soviet forces and weaponry.

William Colby, former CIA director, in 1982 Senate testimony.[1]

Because nuclear war is likely to be so catastrophic for both sides that neither side could win, the security of the United States rests on its ability to deter the Soviets from attacking in the first place. Exactly what deters the Soviets from attacking is hotly debated. Some feel that the way to deter a Soviet attack is with the threat that the United States could destroy their cities even after an attack on the United States; this is the doctrine of mutual assured destruction, commonly known as MAD. Others feel that the only realistic way to deter Soviet attack is with the threat to destroy the Soviet military forces—especially nuclear forces—they did not use up in their attack; this is the doctrine of counterforce. The degree of verifiability that one will demand of an arms control treaty to deem it worth signing is significantly dependent upon which doctrine one believes in—MAD or counterforce. This chapter examines the implications of each doctrine for treaty verification.

The deterrent capability of the United States or, indeed, of the Soviet Union rests on the survivability of its nuclear weapons. It is only the weapons that could survive an attack and remain ready for retaliation afterwards that serve to deter that attack. With survivability in mind, then, I will examine the strategic, or long-range, nuclear arsenals of the two superpowers.

The strategic nuclear bombs of each side are delivered in one of three ways: by submarine-launched ballistic missiles (SLBMs), by bombers, and by intercontinental ballistic missiles (ICBMs) stored in hardened silos in the ground. In the sea-based leg of its strategic "triad," the United States has about 5,000 warheads carried by 570 SLBMs on 35 submarines, while the U.S.S.R. has about 2,000 warheads on 950 SLBMs on 62 submarines.[2] Of these submarines, only those that are at sea have a significant probability of surviving an enemy attack. The United States has more than 20 submarines (with 3,000 warheads) at sea at all times, while the Soviet Union customarily has about 9 submarines (with 300 warheads) at sea. According to studies by the U.S. Navy, U.S. submarines at sea "are invulnerable as far into the future as we can project." These results are substantiated in studies by the CIA, the Defense Intelligence Agency, the RAND Corporation, and the Congressional Office of Technology Assessment.[3] During a period of tension, the United States (and, to a lesser extent, the Soviet Union) can improve the survivability of its submarines by moving more of them out to sea. The Soviets, however, would have to expect some attrition of their small and relatively noisy at-sea strategic submarine force in wartime because of the vastly superior U.S. anti-submarine warfare capability.

In the so-called "air-breathing" leg of the triad, the United States has roughly 3,000 warheads on 300 bombers, while the U.S.S.R. has about 300 warheads on 150 bombers. Of these bombers, only those on alert can be expected to take off quickly enough to survive an enemy attack and deliver their weapons. The United States has about 90 bombers, carrying some 900 nuclear warheads, on alert at all times, whereas the Soviet Union reportedly has none. The crucial issue for bombers that are not destroyed on the ground is their ability to penetrate enemy air space. Although the United States has not emphasized air defenses, the Soviet Union has. These defenses are not, however, impermeable. Large holes can be created in Soviet air defenses with a very few ballistic missiles (which can reach the Soviet Union hours before the bombers) or even the short-range attack missiles on U.S. bombers. The advent of the air-launched cruise missile (ALCM) — a small pilotless drone that is much more difficult to detect than a large bomber — should maintain the penetrating capability of the air-based leg of the U.S. triad for the foreseeable future, even without the B-1 bomber. In addition, during any period of tension that might precede war, the United States can improve the survivability of its bombers by raising their alert rate from 30% to 50% and even to 100%, given sufficient warning.

In the land-based leg of the triad, the United States has about 2,100 warheads on about 1,000 ICBMs, while the U.S.S.R. has more than 5,000 warheads on 1,400 ICBMs. The number of ICBM warheads that would survive an enemy first strike is difficult to predict. High accuracy and reliability, plus precision timing, are required to destroy any significant fraction of the other side's ICBM force. Such an attack against the other side's hardened ICBM silos is the so-called "counterforce" attack, which I will discuss in greater detail later. Depending on whether enemy weapons performed better or worse during wartime than expected from peacetime testing, the U.S. might have anywhere from 200 to 1,000 of its 2,100 ICBM warheads survive a counterforce attack by the current Soviet arsenal, while the Soviet

Union might have anywhere from 1,500 to 3,000 of its ICBM warheads survive a U.S. counterforce attack. (The technical problems that would plague a counterforce attack — including the "fratricidal" destruction of an incoming warhead by the one[s] preceding it — are detailed in an article by Bunn and Tsipis in the November 1983 issue of *Scientific American*.[4])

Tables 5.1 and 5.2 give an approximate assessment of the number of warheads that would survive an enemy first strike in 1984 for two separate cases — first, under conditions favorable to the defender (more warheads surviving) and second, under conditions unfavorable to the defender; these are the so-called "best" and "worst" cases.[5] These tables of estimates of survivable retaliatory (second-strike) weapons do not tell the whole story of U.S. security. The dispute over the best way to deter attack — MAD or counterforce — complicates the numbers.

What are the requirements of deterrence by mutual assured destruction (MAD)? Because nuclear weapons are so destructive, each nation can destroy a large fraction of the other side's population with a relatively small number of weapons. A common approximation is that a one-megaton nuclear bomb (which releases the energy equivalent of one million tons of TNT) will kill nearly everyone within a radius of 4.4 square miles (a circle covering 60 square miles). Over this 60-square-mile region, the blast wave overpressure of 5 pounds per square inch will destroy all houses, the winds at its outer rim will be over 160 miles an hour, and the heat there will be twice that needed to ignite standard building materials.

Table 5.1. U.S. Warheads That Could Survive a Soviet First Strike Today

	Favorable	Unfavorable
On SLBMs	3,000	2,700
On Bombers	900	600
On ICBMs	1,000	200
Total	4,900	3,500

Table 5.2. Soviet Warheads That Could Survive a U.S. First Strike Today

	Favorable	Unfavorable
On SLBMs	300	200
On Bombers	0	0
On ICBMs	3,000	1,500
Total	3,300	1,700

The total area destroyed, however, is not proportional to the total mega-tonnage of the attack. A number of smaller weapons whose yield adds up to one megaton would have a greater destructive effect than a single one-megaton weapon. To estimate the total destructive power of an attack involving weapons of various yields, it is common to use the measure of *equivalent megatons* (EMT), which is the yield of each weapon taken to the two-thirds power. The area destroyed by blast in an attack is roughly proportional to the number of equivalent megatons detonated.

The U.S. urban population of about 130 million people (60% of the total U.S. population) is concentrated in 17,000 square miles,[6] and therefore in theory can be killed by under 300 equivalent megatons (in the approximation that each equivalent megaton, properly targeted, kills everyone within a 60-square-mile region). Three hundred megatons is 5% of the 6,000 megatons in the Soviet strategic arsenal. The Soviet urban population of about 125 million people (50% of the total Soviet population) is concentrated in some 6,000 square miles, and therefore in theory can be killed with about 100 equivalent megatons — 2.5% of the United States's total of 4,000 megatons. The Soviet Union has such a high urban population density that more than 50 million Soviets live on 1,000 square miles and thus could be killed by about 16 equivalent megatons; 50 EMT could kill 100 million Soviets. Civil defense is not likely to make a significant difference. It offers relatively little protection against the radiation and massive fires from even these small attacks, and can be readily overcome by slightly larger attacks designed specifically to thwart any civil defense measures.

No one can know exactly what deters the superpowers from attacking each other. Nevertheless, it does not seem unreasonable to believe that the 40 to 100 EMT needed to kill 50 to 100 million Americans should be sufficient to deter the United States; in the early 1960s the United States was apparently deterred from using nuclear weapons by the prospect of a Soviet response that might have killed a few million Americans. As for the Soviets, according to President Reagan's Commission on Strategic Forces — the Scowcroft Commission — the United States can count on the Soviets acting cautiously: "Historically, the Soviets have not been noted for taking large risks."[7]

It seems unlikely that the Soviets would risk an action that would provoke a U.S. nuclear response of even 16 to 50 equivalent megatons, which might kill 50 to 100 million Soviets. Setting the requirement for deterrence at 50 EMT — though much lower than former Defense Secretary Robert McNamara's figure from the 1960s of 400 equivalent megatons — comes close to the more recent criterion of Harold Brown, Secretary of Defense during the Carter administration, of 200 Soviet cities destroyed. Three U.S. strategic submarines that can deliver a total of more than 50 equivalent megatons could destroy 200 or more Soviet cities with about 500 bombs, each at least three times the size of the one that leveled Hiroshima.

To those who believe that the Soviets are deterred from attacking the United States because of a U.S. threat to Soviet cities, both sides are very secure because, for the next several years at least, both sides have thousands of nuclear warheads capable of surviving a nuclear attack. Moreover, each side would seem to have far in excess of the number of warheads needed to deter the other from attacking its cities. Therefore, for believers in deterrence by MAD, it is not difficult to verify a nuclear treaty well enough to protect the United States from Soviet forces and weaponry. A conservative estimate of our abilities holds that we can verify the number of most Soviet strategic weapons to within about 10%. If so, with the weapon numbers given earlier, the United States should be able to verify limits to within a few submarines, 10 or so bombers, 100 SLBMs, and more than 100 ICBMs. For believers in MAD, these margins of uncertainty pose no threat to U.S. security.

It is easier to have confidence in verifying a total ban on a weapon system than in verifying limits on that weapon. If the Soviets are supposed to have none of a given weapon, the moment a U.S. monitoring system detects one, it becomes apparent that the Soviets have violated the agreement. Violating a treaty that banned an entire weapon system would be particularly difficult because of the large-scale activities involved in developing, testing, producing, and deploying a significant number of any large weapon. Indeed, any effort to conceal such activities would be handicapped by the fact that the Soviet Union does not know exactly what the United States can detect and what not. Therefore, they would not know what to attempt to hide and what not; to be certain that a clandestine weapon would be a surprise, they would have to hide *everything* to do with the laborious process that culminates with the weapon's deployment. And once again, even if the Soviets could somehow secretly violate a ban and build enough of a new type of weapon — a bomber, say — to increase their bomber force by 10%, it would not pose a significant threat to U.S. security for believers in deterrence by MAD. For them, the possibility of large-scale Soviet cheating going undetected is not catastrophic, and thus the verification of treaties limiting or banning a wide variety of nuclear weapons is not a significant problem.

Yet the United States targets no more than about 10% of its strategic weapons at Soviet civilian targets. Although this 10%, in terms of numbers, is far in excess of what is needed to devastate the Soviet Union, it does suggest that there may be reasons that explain why the United States directs some 90% of its weapons at the Soviet Union's military forces. One basic reason for this targeting plan is the doctrine of counterforce. This doctrine holds that a "credible" U.S. deterrent must be based on an ability to respond "in kind" to any Soviet attack, and that to deter the Soviets from an attack against U.S. military forces—a counterforce attack—the United States needs the ability to respond against Soviet military forces. According to this line of reasoning, the threat to destroy Soviet cities is not a credible deterrent against a Soviet counterforce attack.

The most effective counterforce weapons are ICBMs, because only land-based missiles are now accurate enough to threaten hardened targets, such as ICBM silos. The Soviets, because they have more ICBMs than the United States, possess the ability to destroy 50% to 90% of the U.S. ICBM force, using less than half their own force, in a counterforce first strike. Yet, as the Scowcroft Commission said, it would be a mistake to assume that ICBMs are the whole story: In their words, ". . . different components of our strategic forces should be assessed collectively and not in isolation."[8] The warheads on U.S. bombers and submarines, while not able to destroy the remaining Soviet ICBM silos rapidly, can be launched against other military targets and thus can respond "in kind" to the Soviet counterforce attack. For instance, the Soviets have about 400 army, navy, and air bases that contain the bulk of their conventional military forces, together with much of their air-based and sea-based nuclear forces. After a Soviet attack on U.S. ICBMs, it would still be possible for the United States to respond against Soviet military bases, keeping the attack countermilitary.

The Scowcroft Commission did not dismiss the importance of ICBMs (indeed they recommended building 100 MX missiles), but they did dismiss the idea of a surprise Soviet counterforce attack—the so-called "window of vulnerability" attack—saying,

> To deter such surprise attacks we can reasonably rely both on our other strategic forces and on the range of operational uncertainties that the Soviets would have to consider in planning such aggression.[9]

Accurate ICBMs still retain their special offensive ability to destroy hardened enemy ICBMs in their silos rapidly, but as the Scowcroft Commission says, they cannot be considered "in isolation" from bombers and submarines in assessing the strategic arsenals.

Bearing the Scowcroft Commission's caveat in mind, I will now examine verification issues as they apply to deterrence by counterforce, looking at the counterforce weapons and the question of ICBM vulnerability. The nuclear weapons that most threaten a nation geared to counterforce deterrence are those that can destroy its nuclear forces and its command and control facilities. Each side has far in excess of the number of (relatively inaccurate) nuclear weapons needed to destroy the other side's military bases and therefore their submarines in port and their bombers not on alert. Neither side, however, has the requisite combination of ICBM numbers and accuracy to be certain of destroying all of the other side's ICBMs.

Therefore, at present, the building of more ICBMs of higher accuracy represents a threat to destroy a larger number of enemy silos.

Yet there is a limit. Once your side has two extremely accurate warheads for each of your enemy's ICBM silos, then uncertainties are reduced to a minimum. You could then be fairly confident, for instance, that you could destroy nearly 95% of the enemy's silos, even if the reliability of each of your warheads were only 75%. Moreover, once you have enough extremely accurate weapons to destroy the other side's ICBM force, any additional extremely accurate warheads are of little value because the vast majority of hardened targets that high accuracy missiles are used for are ICBM silos. Such extreme accuracy will supposedly be attained by the MX missile and the Trident II submarine-launched missile, and perhaps by the next generation of Soviet ICBMs, if they improve their accuracy by about a factor of 2.

For these reasons, the first 2,800 warheads on the United States' MX and Trident II missiles represent a seriously increased threat to the Soviet Union's land-based forces. They would give us enough accurate warheads to target two against each of the 1,400 Soviet ICBM silos. Similarly, the first 2,000 of the Soviet Union's next generation of ICBMs would represent an increased threat to the U.S. ICBM force. On the other hand, increased deployments of less accurate SLBMs and bomber-delivered nuclear weapons—including ALCMs—do not represent a significant counterforce threat because they cannot destroy enemy ICBMs rapidly.

Although the Scowcroft Commission closed the "window of vulnerability," it is still clearly in the security interests of both sides to sign a treaty that maximizes the survivability of their strategic forces. Such a treaty is desirable because both sides face a drastic reduction in the number of survivable ICBMs. Tables 5.3 and 5.4 give an approximate assessment of the number of warheads on each side that would survive a projected enemy attack in 1990, assuming both sides go through with currently planned weapons deployment (which means assuming that the U.S. Trident II missile has not yet been deployed). Again both "best" and "worst" cases are given. Compare these numbers, especially the ICBM numbers, with the earlier tables.

The Soviet Union is particularly vulnerable because of its strong dependence on silo-based ICBMs. Yet a situation in which both sides have extremely vulnerable ICBM forces would be detrimental to the national security of each: The mutual vulnerability of ICBM forces might tempt one or both sides to adopt a dangerous "hair trigger" launch-on-warning policy whereby ICBMs are launched within minutes of computerized warning of enemy attack. This policy would leave little time to detect mistakes; for this reason, launch-on-warning tends to increase the chances for accidental nuclear war. Even without such policies, the improvement in counterforce capabilities might lead one side or the other to adopt a "use them or lose

Table 5.3. U.S. Warheads That Could Survive a Soviet First Strike in 1990

	Favorable	Unfavorable
On SLBMs	3,000	2,700
On Bombers	1,000	700
On ICBMs	400	100
Total	4,400	3,500

Table 5.4. Soviet Warheads That Could Survive a U.S. First Strike in 1990

	Favorable	Unfavorable
On SLBMs	1,000	350
On Bombers	0	0
On ICBMs	1,500	450
Total	2,500	800

them" philosophy during a crisis and strike first — which is one definition of crisis instability. Whether a nation bases its deterrence on MAD or counterforce, maintaining and increasing stability is paramount to its national security.

Therefore it is in the security interests of both sides to limit the counterforce capability of their arsenals with a treaty. Counterforce capabilities could be limited by either restricting the *number* of ballistic missiles, or by restricting their *accuracy*. In fact, believers in the doctrine of counterforce will find few other treaty provisions besides these two that would meaningfully increase U.S. security. But there is more to designing a useful treaty than just attempting to include these two provisions. Both sides have far in excess of the *number* of ballistic missiles needed to threaten the other side's ICBM forces (or will by the time U.S. SLBMs are improved to become potential counterforce weapons). Reductions in numbers would have to be extreme to make any difference. Moreover, purely numerical reductions are not necessarily a useful solution. Forcing the Soviet Union to reduce to significantly under 2,000 ICBM warheads (from its present 5,500 warheads) so as not to pose a threat to the 1,000 United States ICBMs would merely increase the Soviets' vulnerability to United States ICBMs, leaving them — in the counterforce scenario — with perhaps 200 to 400 survivable ICBM warheads. This would represent a significant drop from the 1,500 to 3,000 or so survivable ICBM warheads that they have today. The Soviet Union's past reluctance to accept drastic reductions in their ICBM force suggests that this type of arms control approach will not prove fruitful in the future.

Because limiting numbers alone will not maintain ICBM survivability, stability might be more advantageously improved by limiting missile accuracy. Verifying enemy accuracy by observing their ballistic missile testing is uncertain at best, however, and perhaps the only way to be sure accuracy is not improving significantly is to limit or ban entirely the flight-testing of ballistic missiles, including SLBMs. Banning all ballistic missile tests would also prevent re-testing of old ICBMs, thus gradually reducing confidence in their reliability and accuracy. Confidence in their ability to destroy enemy silos would decrease with time, increasing the security and survivability of both side's arsenals; eventually the old ICBMs themselves would devolve into purely second-strike deterrent weapons, rendered much more survivable by the other side's loss of confidence in its own ICBM capabilities. It is the extreme accuracy and precision that a 2,000-warhead counterforce attack requires coupled with the possibly devastating consequences of failure that make confidence in the counterforce missiles crucial to any decision to attack. As this confidence is eroded, so is the likelihood of first strike.

The superpowers currently require about 20 to 30 test flights to determine with confidence the accuracy of a new missile, and this figure helps set the constraint on verification of any treaty restricting ballistic missile testing. Because individual ballistic missile tests can be verified with high confidence, the chance that an enemy could secretly test as many as 20 times is extremely unlikely, and so neither side could expect to secretly test a new missile well enough to threaten the other side's forces with it. Therefore, a treaty banning ballistic missile testing could be adequately verified from the point of view of national security. The probability of the United States detecting a single Soviet flight test is doubtlessly higher than 90%, given the variety of means the United States has to detect these tests, such as satellites, listening stations, land- and sea-based radar arrays, and high altitude reconnaissance aircraft. Yet, even if the United States can be confident that it can detect the test of a Soviet ballistic missile only 90% of the time, then its chances of *not* detecting, say, one of six Soviets tests is only 1 in a million; the chances that not even one of 20 would be detected is one in 100 billion billion.

These considerations apply both to a complete ban on ballistic missile tests and to a limit on the number of tests. A treaty that allowed limited testing of old missiles, however, would also require the ability to distinguish between an old missile and a new missile, which can be difficult, as demonstrated by the arguments over the definition of "new types" of missiles in the SALT II treaty.

Even large-scale violations of a ban or limit on ballistic missile testing that resulted in the Soviets doubling their accuracy would only reduce the number of survivable United States ICBMs by a few hundred and would still leave more than 3,000 very survivable warheads on United States submarines and bombers as a deterrent to Soviet attack. Large-scale cheating by the United States on a test-restricting treaty would leave the Soviet Union much more vulnerable, though still with an awesome counter-city deterrent force. It is, however, hard to believe that the United States could cheat on a very large scale. The United States has a very open testing, production, and deployment process that would make even a few secret ICBM tests virtually impossible to cover up.

It has been argued that the Soviets might enter into a treaty like the ballistic missile test moratorium merely to restrict U.S. behavior while they conduct secret operations that would allow them to break out of the treaty suddenly and achieve a significant strategic advantage. This is the so-called "breakout" threat. Suppose that in the first ten years of a ballistic missile test ban the Soviets design a highly accurate new ICBM. Then suppose the Soviets quickly broke out of the treaty by building several of these new ICBMs and testing them for several months until they were sure they worked. The United States would no doubt be able to determine quickly that the Soviets had broken out of the treaty, but within a year it is at least conceivable that the Soviets might have enough of these new ICBMs to threaten 95% of U.S. ICBMs with very high confidence.

As I have argued above, the potential gain—if it can be called that—of such Soviet action would be a threat to destroy a few hundred more U.S. ICBMs (but no additional submarines and bombers). The potential risks, however, are very large. The treaty and the mutual enhancement of security that it brought would be ended. Future treaties would be less likely, the arms race would presumably accelerate, and the cold war would be intensified. In the short run, if the Soviets broke out of the ballistic missile test ban and began testing, the United States would put its strategic nuclear forces on alert and perhaps even threaten to adopt a launch-on-warning policy for its ICBMs if the Soviets did not discontinue testing. Such a dangerous launching policy would, as I have noted, diminish U.S. security by making accidental nuclear war more likely; nevertheless, as a threat to prevent breakout—as a deterrent—it can be useful. Soviet efforts to threaten U.S. ICBMs would be wasted if the United States adopted a launch-on-warning policy, because the Soviets would be unable to destroy U.S. ICBMs in a first strike if they had been launched by the time Soviet ICBMs arrive. This does not mean that the United States should ever prematurely adopt the risky launch-on-warning policy. What it does mean is that the United States could readily counter a Soviet breakout from a ballistic missile test ban treaty, or, in fact, from most treaties designed to limit ballistic missiles.

I have argued that *even large-scale enemy violations of a variety of security-enhancing treaties would not significantly diminish the other side's security.* Therefore, the benefits of cheating on those treaties are dubious at best. This conclusion will remain true until the superpowers' nuclear arsenals are reduced by about a factor of 10, which seems unlikely to occur in the foreseeable future. Until that time, the United States can monitor compliance with a variety of potentially useful treaty provisions, including a ban on ballistic missile testing as well as bans and limits on new submarines, bombers, SLBMs, and ICBMs, and therefore the United States can enter into treaties containing such provisions with confidence.

REFERENCES

1. United States. Congress. Senate. Foreign Relations Committee. Testimony before the Committee on May 13, 1982. "Nuclear Arms Reductions Proposals," p. 311.
2. The approximate numbers cited here for strategic weapons and readiness rates come from the following sources: *Report of the President's Commission on Strategic Forces* (hereafter referred to as the Scowcroft Commission Report), April 1983, pp. 4–5; *The New York Times*, May 22, 1984, p. A13, "White House Downplays Soviet Sub Threat" by Wayne Biddle; Cochran, Arkin, and Hoenig, *Nuclear Weapons Databook, Volume I, U.S. Nuclear Forces and Capabilities*, Cambridge, MA: Ballinger, 1984, pp. 100–106; *Challenges for U.S. Security, A Preliminary Report*, prepared by the Staff of the Carnegie Panel on U.S. Security and the Future of Arms Control, 1981, p. 60; and Senate hearings, "DoD Authorization for Appropriations for FY 1983," p. 4593.
3. United States. Congress. Senate. Rear Admiral William A. Williams, III, in 1981 Senate testimony. "Strategic Force Modernization Programs," p. 194.
4. Bunn, Matthew, and Kosta Tsipis. Uncertainties of a Preemptive Nuclear Attack. *Scientific American* (November 1983).
5. Neither the best nor worst case includes the possibility that increased tensions between the superpowers has led to higher rates of strategic readiness at the time of the attack.
6. Population densities for the U.S. and Soviet Union are from the U.S. Arms Control and Disarmament Agency's *An Analysis of Civil Defense in Nuclear War*. Washington, DC: ACDA, December 1978, p. 3, as cited in Arthur Katz's *Life After Nuclear War*. Cambridge, MA: Ballinger, 1982, p. 311.
7. The Scowcroft Commission Report, *op. cit.*, p. 4.
8. *Ibid.*, p. 8.
9. *Ibid.*, p. 17.

6.

Breakout from Arms Control Treaties: A Sensitivity Analysis of the Threat to National Security

David Hafemeister

INTRODUCTION

To sign and ratify a nuclear arms control treaty, a nation must know what it is risking. It must have confidence in its ability to verify the compliance of the other signatories with the provisions of the treaty, and it must have confidence that any violation of the treaty that could pose a decisive threat to its security would be detected — and detected early enough to take appropriate action in response.

In order for the leaders of a country to judge whether such confidence is justified, two questions must be answered. First, how good are the technical means of verifying compliance with the treaty (e.g., satellite reconnaissance, seismographic monitoring, and the like)? Verification can never be absolutely perfect, so this first question becomes: How large must a treaty violation be before one can have confidence of detecting it? Second, how large must a violation be before it constitutes a major security threat? If it would require 100 illegal ICBMs to significantly change the strategic balance, and the deployment of even ten such ICBMs could be easily detected, with enough lead time to take whatever action might be necessary in response, then U.S. verification technology is "adequate" for a limit on the number of ICBMs.

The chapters that follow in this book will discuss aspects of the first question, the technical capabilities of U.S. verification technologies. This chapter is directed toward answering the second: What possible treaty violations would constitute a threat to the security of the United States?

As the previous chapter by Joseph Romm has discussed, U.S. security rests on deterring the Soviet Union from nuclear attack; this in turn depends in part on the survivability of U.S. strategic forces against a disarming attack. Estimates of the precise number of surviving weapons necessary to deter various types of attack vary widely. As Romm has described, if all that is considered necessary to deterrence is the capability to launch a "mutual assured destruction" response against cities, then the number of surviving nuclear weapons necessary is small; 400 equivalent megatons (EMT) was the criterion used by Secretary of Defense McNamara in the 1960s, but it may be that as little as 10–50 equivalent megatons is a more "realistic" estimate of what is required. (Both the 400 EMT level and the 10–50 EMT level are indicated in the graphs of U.S. forces surviving a first strike, presented later in this chapter.) If more discriminating retaliation is called for, the number of surviving weapons required for deterrence may be somewhat larger. Such considerations apply only to offensive strategic nuclear weapons; we will not consider the effects of breakouts from other types of treaties.

This chapter will analyze how the number of U.S. weapons that would survive a Soviet attack might be affected by a possible Soviet "breakout" from an arms control treaty—that is, a sudden deployment of forbidden weapons intended to shift the strategic balance drastically. We will examine each of the numerical parameters of Soviet weapons that would affect the survivability of U.S. forces (accuracy, yield, reliability, number of warheads, degree of fratricide) and imagine that a treaty has been negotiated limiting that parameter—either directly, as in the case of a limit on total missile warheads as envisioned in START, or indirectly, as in the case of a limit on ballistic missile flight testing, intended to limit the accuracy or reliability of certain weapons. We will then go through a sensitivity analysis for each parameter, in order to evaluate how violations of such limits would affect the survivability of U.S. deterrent forces. Because the survivability of ICBM forces is more closely related to the technical characteristics of the opposing force than is the survivability of bombers, submarines, or strategic command and control, this chapter will concentrate primarily on issues concerning ICBM survivability. By assuming a severe Soviet preemptive attack with no warning and hence no increases in the alert level of U.S. forces, this chapter will estimate a "lower bound" on the number of U.S. forces that would survive a Soviet attack, given various possible changes in the Soviet strategic arsenal. This will provide a partial answer to the second question posed above: "How small a violation could pose a threat to U.S. security?"

THE VULNERABILITY OF SILOS TO A MISSILE ATTACK

The first step toward understanding this sensitivity analysis of U.S. strategic force survivability is to analyze attacks on a missile silo, first by one warhead and then by two warheads. The probability of destroying a missile silo depends on a number of parameters: Y = the yield of the weapon; CEP = its accuracy, or the so-called Circular Error Probable; H = the hardness of the silo; and R = the reliability of the missile and warhead combination.

The probability of a single warhead destroying a silo (assuming perfect reliability) is called the single shot kill probability (SSKP),[1] which is:

$$\text{SSKP} = 1 - \exp\left(\frac{-Y^{2/3}}{B(\text{CEP})^2 H^{2/3}}\right) \tag{1}$$

where B is 0.22 when Y is in megatons (MT), H is in psi, and CEP is in nautical miles (1 nmi = 1.115 miles = 1.852 kilometers). When the reliability of the system is included among the factors, the kill probability of one warhead (P_{1K}) is:

$$P_{1K} = R\,\text{SSKP} \tag{2}$$

where R varies from 0 to 1.

Consider the often-discussed scenarios of SS-18 warheads attacking Minuteman silos. A new modification of the SS-18 is now being deployed. The usual parameters given in the literature for the hardness of Minuteman silos and the characteristics of this new SS-18 are for Minuteman silos, H = 2,000 psi; and for the SS-18, Mod 5, Y = 0.75 MT; CEP = 0.15 nmi; and R = 0.75.

All of these numbers are rather uncertain; strategic weapons of necessity undergo only limited peacetime testing, and additional uncertainty in estimates of Soviet weapons results precisely from the imperfection of verification capabilities, especially in such areas as missile accuracy. The number given here for reliability is especially uncertain, as publicly available estimates of reliability vary widely.

Using these values in Eq. (2), we obtain P_{1K} = 0.49. That is the kill probability of one SS-18 Mod 5 warhead against a Minuteman silo, assuming that publicly available information is correct.

The yield of a weapon can be whatever its designer desires; ICBM accuracy increases over time with improvements in technology. Hence, very high SSKPs are achievable; within the next few years, weapons such as the MX will reach combinations of yield and accuracy sufficient to make their SSKP approximately 1, at least against targets in the hardness range of 2,000 psi. Thus, the limiting factor in determining the ultimate kill probability of nuclear warheads is likely to be their reliability. The reliability of any part of any weapon system (missile, reentry vehicle, warhead, etc.) is never 100%, and therefore an attacker would probably always want to target more than one warhead against each silo. Because the effects of the detonation of an exploding warhead upon another one arriving in its wake are not completely understood, there is considerable uncertainty about the effects of "fratricide" on the effectiveness of a two-warhead attack. In Appendix A of this chapter we have estimated the increased survivability of land-based missiles because of fratricide, but we will ignore these considerations in the body of the chapter. If one side has very lethal warheads, with an SSKP of about 1, fratricide effects can be ignored since the first warhead that explodes would destroy the silo.

Assuming statistical independence (and therefore ignoring fratricide), the probability of destruction of a silo by two warheads launched from separate missiles is:

$$P_{2K} = 1 - (1 - P_{1K})^2 \tag{3}$$

In the example of the SS-18 attack on the Minuteman silos, we obtained $P_{1K} = 0.49$. Using this value in Eq. (3), we obtain:

$$P_{2K} = 1 - (1 - 0.49)^2 = 1 - (.51)^2 = 0.74$$

If the reliability had been 0.85, then P_{2K} would have been 0.8. These results are similar to the results of Bunn and Tsipis, who have estimated[2] various uncertainties and found that P_{2K} ranged between 0.45 and 0.86. One could imagine an attack using more than two warheads against each silo, but unless the silo contained a large number of warheads, such an attack would expend more warheads than it would destroy; moreover, it would encounter even greater fratricide than a two-warhead attack. In this paper, we will use the common assumption that only two warheads would be targeted on each of the U.S. Minuteman silos.

NUMERICAL METHODS FOR A SENSITIVITY ANALYSIS OF A BREAKOUT

The preceding section presented the general ideas involved in calculating the percentage of the ICBM force that would survive a preemptive attack. In addition, Appendix B of this chapter, Differential Sensitivity Analysis, offers an approach developed to examine the effects of small changes in the parameters for reliability, hardness, yield and accuracy on the size of the surviving force after the attack.[3] Because we will be calculating the effect of *large* changes in these parameters that would represent a real breakout from an arms control treaty, however, the differential approach is inadequate, and it will be necessary to use the complete formulas (Eqs. 1, 2 and 3) to determine the results of various exchanges of weapons. By adjusting many of the parameters involved, we have determined the dependence of the size of the remaining U.S. strategic forces on changes in the Soviet attack parameters. We will now describe some of the details of this type of sensitivity analysis.

Each missile system will be described by six parameters:

Y = The yield of the weapon, in megatons,

M = The number of warheads per launcher (MIRVs),

L = The number of launchers per system,

CEP = The accuracy of the warhead, in nautical miles,

R = The reliability (0 to 1) of the warhead and system, and

H = The hardness of the silo, in psi.

If a spread of values has been published for a missile system characteristic, we have used an average value for the parameter. In the tabulation of the current balance, only ICBMs combine the accuracy and speed necessary to attack ICBM silos; for this reason, small changes in the data for ICBMs are more important to this analysis than are small differences in the data for bombers or SLBMs. Hence, when subclasses of ICBMs are significantly different, we have treated them as separate systems, while SLBMs and bombers have been aggregated into rough averages of the forces on each side. For example, the 65 kilotons (KT) for the submarine-launched ballistic missiles is an average of the 50 KT Poseidon and 100 KT Trident warheads; the 0.6 megaton value for the bombers is an average of the 1 MT bomb and the 0.2 MT short range attack missiles (SRAM) and air-launched cruise missile (ALCM). In addition to the above parameters, we varied the following parameters for both sides, when assessing possible breakouts from arms control treaties:

n = The number of warheads allotted to attack a silo,

DF = The duty factor for the submarines,

F(Bomber) = The fraction of bombers destroyed, and

F(ASW) = The fractional effectiveness of anti-submarine warfare.

Baseline Case

The current parameters for the sensitivity analysis have been drawn mostly from the *Military Balance: 1983–1984* of the International Institute for Strategic Studies (IISS),[4] with modifications from other sources.[5-9] For example, we did not list the 45 Titan missiles for the United States because they are in the process of being dismantled. This baseline case does not consider the future modernization of forces (see Table 6.1 and Table 6.2).

Table 6.1. American Matrix

Type	1 Y	2 M	3 L	4 CEP	5 R	6 H
1 = MMII	1.5	1	450	.2	.75	2,000
2 = MMIII	.17	3	250	.15	.75	2,000
3 = MMIIIA	.335	3	300	.12	.75	2,000
4 = SLBM	.065	9	568	.25	.75	na
5 = B-52	.6	8	272	na	.75	na

Table 6.2. Soviet Matrix

Type	1 Y	2 M	3 L	4 CEP	5 R	6 H
1 = SS-11(M1)	1	1	518	.75	.75	1,000
2 = SS-13(M1)	.75	1	60	1.1	.75	1,000
3 = SS-17(M1)	.75	4	120	.24	.75	2,500–4,000
4 = SS-17(M2)	6	1	32	.24	.75	2,500–4,000
5 = SS-18(M2)	.9	8	175	.24	.75	2,500–4,000
6 = SS-18(M3)	20	1	58	.19	.75	2,500–4,000
7 = SS-18(M5)	.75	10	75	.14	.75	2,500–4,000
8 = SS-19(M2)	5	1	60	.16	.75	2,500–4,000
9 = SS-19(M3)	.55	6	300	.16	.75	2,500–4,000
10 = SLBM	.39	2.7	950	.5	.75	na
11 = Bear/Bison	1	2	143	na	.75	na

As was described in the case of the SS-18, many of the numbers in Table 6.2 are uncertain; the reliability numbers are least well known. It is likely that U.S. missile reliabilities are actually higher than Soviet reliabilities, because of superior U.S. technology and Soviet reliance on liquid-fueled rockets.

This baseline case represents the present situation and hence ignores a number of future systems that will affect the strategic balance, such as MX, Midgetman, Trident II, and the Soviet SS-24, SS-25, SS-N-23, and so on. The most important improvements in these arsenals in the coming years will probably be in the accuracy of the missiles and in the number of ALCMs carried by each B-52. These possible changes in such parameters as accuracy and numbers of warheads will be modeled in the sensitivity analysis to follow (at least for the Soviet strategic force). Both the baseline case and the subsequent analysis also ignore factors such as intermediate-range and tactical systems, conventional and chemical forces, and possible new ballistic missile defense systems as envisioned in the Strategic Defense Initiative (SDI) program.

Survivability of Submarine-Launched Ballistic Missiles (SLBM)

Strategic submarines can be considered in two groups: those that are at sea at the moment of an attack, and those that are in port. Submarines in port are almost certain to be destroyed in a preemptive attack. Submarines at sea are considerably more survivable. Although a fraction of Soviet strategic submarines might be at some risk from U.S. anti-submarine warfare (ASW), Soviet ASW currently poses little threat to U.S. strategic submarines, for three reasons: (a) The geography of Soviet submarine bases is conducive to U.S. ASW surveillance; (b) Soviet ASW techniques are vastly inferior to ours; and (c) U.S. submarines are considerably less noisy and hence more difficult to locate. For our discussion, we will assume that Soviet ASW would have negligible effectiveness against U.S. strategic submarines; that is, $F(ASW) = 0$.

The most important number in considering strategic submarine survivability is therefore simply the percentage of those submarines that are at sea at any time, referred to here as the "duty-factor" (DF). For the United States, the current DF is about 60%, whereas for the Soviet Union it is only 20%. Hence, in the case of a Soviet preemptive attack with no warning, 60% of the U.S. SLBM force would be expected to survive; with warning, more submarines could be moved to sea, making that number substantially higher.

Strategic Bomber Survivability

Bombers continue to play an important role in the U.S. strategic triad. An effective bomber force must be able to survive an attack and then penetrate the air defenses of the other side. To ensure their survivability, the United States keeps roughly 30% of its bombers on alert at all times, at 19 bases. (The Soviet bomber force, by contrast, has traditionally not been kept on alert, although this could change in the future.) During an emergency the number of bases available to the planes can be increased to 45 (or more), and the percentage of bombers on alert can be drastically increased.

In a preemptive attack with no warning, the 70% of the U.S. bomber force not on alert would almost certainly be destroyed. It has been postulated that an even larger percentage might be destroyed if the attacker barraged the areas around the bomber bases, to destroy escaping bombers already in flight.[10] In this case, the number of surviving bombers, like the number of ICBMs that would survive an attack, would be closely dependent on the characteristics of the Soviet arsenal, specifically the flight time, number of warheads, and yields of Soviet SLBMs. Such an attack, however, would require a large number of submarines approaching very close to U.S. shores, which would surely be detected by U.S. ASW and other intelligence, providing strategic warning sufficient to alert and disperse the bombers. In this chapter, we will assume that only those bombers not on alert are destroyed in the initial attack.

The bombers that survive, however, must also penetrate Soviet air defenses. U.S. bombers are constantly upgraded to deal with these defenses; most important, perhaps, is the recent (and continuing) deployment of air-launched cruise missiles. Any estimate of the combined effect of a preemptive attack and Soviet air defenses is necessarily speculative, but for the purposes of this chapter, we will assume that roughly 25% of the total U.S. bomber force survives and penetrates, so that F(bomber) = 0.75.

RESULTS

The basic data and assumptions have been described in the last section. The size of the U.S. strategic triad before an attack is shown in Table 6.3 in terms of the number of warheads (W), the number of launchers (L), the total yield (YT) in MT, and the effective yield ($YEMT$) in EMT. The number of launchers is less than the SALT II limit of 2250 because about 300 B-52 bombers are presently in storage. Using these baseline data, and the other assumptions outlined previously, we have calculated the remaining U.S. forces after a Soviet attack. These are listed in Table 6.4 in the same format. Given this baseline estimate of the survivability of U.S. forces, it is now time to examine how that survivability would change in the face of

Table 6.3. IISS Data: Before

	W	L	YT (MT)	$YEMT$ (EMT)
Mman	2,100	1,000	1,103	1,253
SLBM	5,112	568	332	826
B-52	2,176	272	1,305	1,547
TOTAL	9,388	1,840	2,740	3,626

Table 6.4. IISS Data: After

	W	L	YT (MT)	$YEMT$ (EMT)
Mman	756	361	379	430
SLBM	3,067	340	199	495
B-52	544	68	326	386
TOTAL	4,367	769	904	1,311

changes in the numerical parameters of Soviet forces — accuracy, yield, reliability, and number of warheads.

Accuracy

In the baseline case, using IISS data, the most significant Soviet weapons (SS-17, SS-18, SS-19) have accuracies between 0.14 and 0.24 nautical miles. Figures 6.1 and 6.2 show the effect of possible improvements in this accuracy on U.S. force survivability. As the accuracy is increased from this spread of CEP values to a single value of 0.14 nmi, the size of the surviving U.S. triad would be decreased by about 10% to $W = 4086$ warheads, $L = 651$ launchers, $YT = 809$ MT, and $YEMT = 1,190$ EMT. As Soviet accuracy is improved further, reductions in the surviving force continue to take place until the accuracy is about CEP = 0.06 nmi; further improvements in accuracy do not make a substantial difference. The main parameter affecting the Minuteman missiles when the CEP is less than 0.06 nmi is the reliability of the SS-18 and SS-19 missiles. The size of the surviving forces under the condition of infinite accuracy (CEP = 0) is seen in Table 6.5.

Yield

The surviving U.S. triad is shown in Figures 6.3 and 6.4 as a function of the yield of Soviet warheads. To indicate the effect of changes in yield given likely future Soviet missile accuracies, we have used a single CEP of 0.15 nmi in this figure, rather than the baseline spread of 0.14–0.24 nmi. This improvement in accuracy reduces the U.S. surviving triad by about 10% to $W = 4,164$, $L = 690$, $YT = 852$ MT, and $YEMT = 1,240$ EMT.

Yields in the baseline case vary between 0.55 and 0.9 MT for the various SS-18 and SS-19 warheads, those most likely to be used in an attack on U.S. ICBMs. Additional increases in the yield reduce the surviving force, up to a limit of roughly 10 MT per warhead, beyond which further increases make little difference. At that point, the surviving U.S. force is substantially the same as in the "infinite accuracy" case above, for the same reason: the SSKP of Soviet ICBM warheads has reached unity.

Table 6.5. Size of Surviving Forces Under Condition of Infinite Accuracy

	W	L	YT (MT)	$YEMT$ (EMT)
Mman	131	63	70	79
SLBM/B-52	3,611	408	525	881
TOTAL	3,742	471	595	960

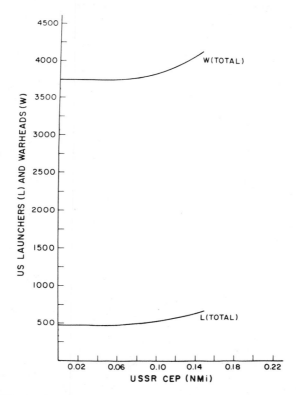

FIGURE 6.1. Effect of improvement in Soviet accuracy: U.S. launchers and warheads. The total number of surviving U.S. launchers (*L*) and warheads (*W*) has been calculated as a function of Soviet accuracy. Assuming no "breakout," the number is assumed to be 4,367 surviving warheads (*W* = 4,367) on 769 surviving launchers (*L* = 769). Included in this total are 3,067 surviving SLBM warheads in 340 submarine launch tubes and 544 surviving warheads, including ALCM and SRAM, on 68 surviving B-52s. Since the number of surviving submarines and B-52s is largely independent of improvements in Soviet ICBM accuracy, the SLBM and B-52 values were held constant in the calculations. The curves *L*(Total) and *W*(Total) indicate that the total number of surviving launchers and warheads is not greatly affected by the improvement of Soviet accuracy.

Reliability

Estimates of the overall reliability of the weapons in a preemptive attack must include a wide variety of factors that can never be tested, such as human errors in the heat of the moment and the like. To test the sensitivity of the result to uncertainties in reliability, we have calculated the survivability of U.S. forces for Soviet missile reliabilities between 0.6 and 0.9; the results are shown in Figures 6.5 and 6.6. In some cases, it may be possible

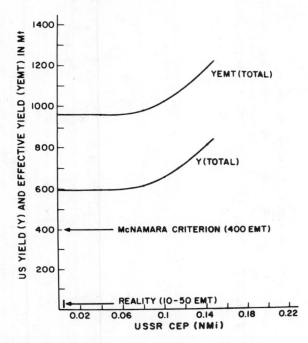

FIGURE 6.2. Effect of improvement in Soviet accuracy: U.S. yield. The surviving yield (*Y*) and effective yield (*Y*EMT) of the U.S. triad are calculated as a function of Soviet accuracy. Included in this total are, for the SLBMs $Y = 199$ megatons (MT) and $Y\text{EMT} = 495$ equivalent megatons (EMT), and for the B-52s $Y = 326$ MT and $Y\text{EMT} = 386$ EMT. As with Figure 6.1, the values for SLMBs and B-52s are held constant. The McNamara deterrence criterion of 400 EMT is indicated, as is the level of deterrence this chapter considers realistic (10 to 50 EMT).

to make up for imperfect reliabilities by reprogramming missiles to replace those missiles that fail on launch, but this would prolong the attack and make the attacker more vulnerable, and it might not be possible to correct for later failures such as those in timing, reentry, and weapons detonation, as those failures would be harder to observe in time. As in the last case, a single value of CEP = 0.15 nmi has been used, rather than the baseline spread. The U.S. forces surviving an attack in the two extreme reliability cases ($R = 0.6$ and $R = 0.9$) are shown in Table 6.6.

Numbers of Warheads

The Soviet Union currently has about 8,000 to 10,000 strategic warheads. For a preemptive attack on strategic forces and command and control, significantly fewer would be required. A 2-1 attack on the Minuteman silos

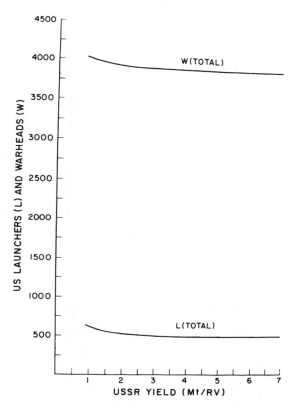

FIGURE 6.3. Effect of increase in Soviet yield: U.S. launchers and warheads. The curves L(Total) and W(Total) are the total number of surviving launchers and warheads in the U.S. triad as a function of increasing yield of Soviet weapons. The present yield of Soviet warheads ranges between 0.55 and 0.9 MT. For these calculations, Soviet accuracy is assumed to be CEP = 0.15 nmi.

would require 2,000 warheads, and attacks on SLBM ports, bomber bases, and command and control would probably consume at least 500 more. Figures 6.7 and 6.8 show how the size of the surviving U.S. force declines with the number of warheads the Soviets have available for preemptive attack. As can be seen, the first 500 warheads (the section of the curve labeled EMP/C^3I, B-52, SLBM) do much of the damage, with progressively less return for the first warhead on each Minuteman silo ($n = 1$) and the second warhead on each silo ($n = 2$). (This graph assumes that attacks on C^3I facilities do not actually prevent the launch of any surviving U.S. weapons.) As argued above, it is unlikely in most cases that more than two warheads would be used against each silo.

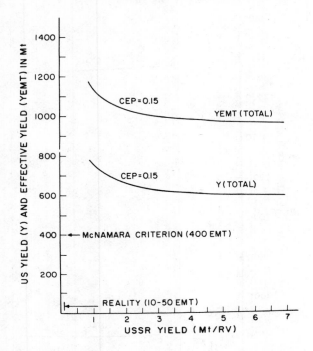

FIGURE 6.4. Effect of increase in Soviet yield: U.S. yield. The surviving yield (Y) and effective yield (YEMT) in the U.S. triad is calculated as a function of increasing Soviet yield. A Soviet accuracy of CEP = 0.15 has been assumed. The arrows indicate the McNamara deterrent level (400 EMT) and this chapter's (10–50 EMT).

These curves, approximate though they may be, indicate that beyond the point of roughly 2,500 Soviet warheads, further increases in the number of Soviet warheads have little effect on the survivability of the U.S. arsenal. The figure of 2,500 Soviet warheads is 50% of the 5,000 warheads called for by the build-down proposal and about 25% of the present Soviet strategic arsenal.

CONCLUSIONS

To put the results developed in the last section into perspective, we must return to the original question: "How small a violation could pose a threat to U.S. security?" Figures 6.1–6.8 suggest some answers. It is clear that small violations of possible limits on such parameters as the number, yield, accuracy, and reliability of Soviet warheads could do little to undermine deterrence; it would require a large change—a true "breakout"—from any of these parameters to significantly reduce the survivability of U.S. strate-

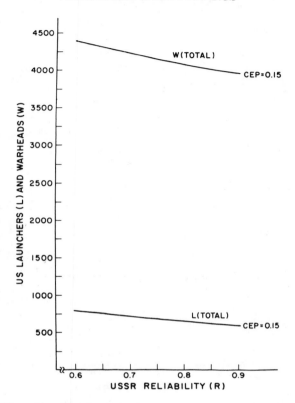

FIGURE 6.5. Effect of improvement in Soviet reliability: U.S. launchers and warheads. The curves L(Total) and W(Total) are the surviving launchers and warheads in the U.S. triad for Soviet weapon reliabilities of between 0.6 and 0.9. The current reliability of Soviet weapons is often given as 0.75. An accuracy of CEP = 0.15 nmi for all Soviet reentry vehicles has been assumed.

Table 6.6. U.S. Forces Surviving on Attack in Two Extreme Reliability Cases

	W	L	YT (MT)	YEMT (EMT)
$R = 0.9$	3,975	600	752	1,127
$R = 0.6$	4,393	798	970	1,375

gic forces. In the case of possible limits on the number, yield, or accuracy of Soviet weapons, there is a range in which major violations would have a significant impact on the number of surviving ICBMs, but beyond that range, the damage would already have been done, and further changes

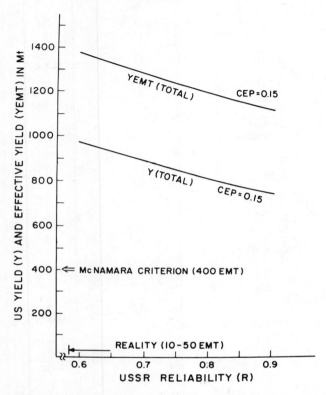

FIGURE 6.6. Effect of improvement in Soviet reliability: U.S. yield. The surviving yield (Y) and effective yield ($YEMT$) in the U.S. triad are estimated as a function of improvements in the reliability of Soviet weapons. The arrows indicate the McNamara (400 EMT) and this chapter's (10–50 EMT) deterrent levels. A Soviet CEP of 0.15 nmi has been assumed.

would have little effect. Improvements in the reliability of Soviet missiles, by contrast, would reduce the number of surviving ICBMs regardless of the range of values in which they occurred. In the range of current Soviet capabilities, the survivability of U.S. strategic forces is most sensitive to the accuracy and reliability of Soviet forces, and less so to their yield or numbers; it is unfortunate that accuracy and reliability are the least verifiable of the parameters of Soviet forces. It may be that the idea of a ban or strict limits on ballistic missile flight testing, discussed by Romm in the previous chapter, is the only means by which these parameters might be constrained.

More fundamentally, Figures 6.1–6.8 show that it would be difficult for the Soviets to come close to developing a disarming first-strike capability

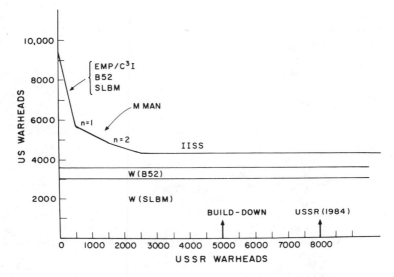

FIGURE 6.7. Effect of increase in number of Soviet warheads: U.S. warheads. The number of surviving warheads in the U.S. triad is estimated as a function of the number of attacking Soviet warheads. The first section of the curve indicates the approximate reductions from an attack by low numbers of Soviet weapons. The second section of the curve denotes the reduction in the Minuteman forces when one Soviet warhead has been targeted on each silo ($n = 1$). The third section of the curve indicates the continued reduction of the Minuteman forces when two Soviet warheads are targeted on each silo ($n = 2$). The fourth section has been drawn horizontally, on the assumption that more than two warheads per silo would not be likely. The lines represent the 3,067 surviving U.S. SLBM warheads and the 544 surviving U.S. B-52 warheads. The arrows indicate the number of warheads that would remain under the build-up proposal (5,000) and the number in the current Soviet strategic arsenal (8,000–10,000).

against the United States, even were they to "break out" of possible limits on the yield, number, accuracy, or reliability of their weapons; because the survivability of the bomber and SLBM forces are largely unaffected by changes in these parameters, the size of surviving U.S. nuclear forces is relatively insensitive to these types of breakouts. If the requirement is only to detect violations of a treaty that could seriously undermine deterrence, then "adequate" verification should be relatively easy to achieve.

APPENDIX A: FRATRICIDE

The detonation of an incoming nuclear warhead causes turbulent winds and shock waves, thermal radiation, neutron fluxes, an electromagnetic

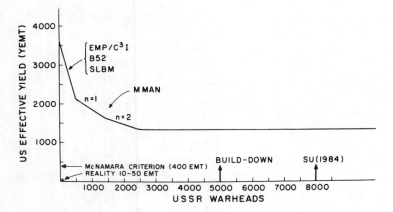

FIGURE 6.8. Effect of increase in number of Soviet warheads: U.S. yield. The surviving U.S. effective yield in the U.S. triad is estimated as a function of the number of attacking Soviet warheads. IISS accuracies have been assumed; a decrease in the CEP to 0.06 nmi would reduce the surviving yield to about 960 EMT. The arrows indicate the McNamara deterrent level (400 EMT) and this chapter's (10–50 EMT).

pulse, and dust and particles from ground bursts. These effects can destroy a nearby RV, but the severity of the effects are somewhat uncertain. For the case of no fratricide, the kill probability for two RVs from separate launchers attacking one silo is (from Eq. 3) $P_{2K} = 1 - (1 - R\,SSKP)^2 = 2R\,SSKP - R^2\,SSKP^2$.

For the case of complete fratricide, the kill probability is obtained from fault-free analysis, and it is $P_{2KF} = 2R\,SSKP - R^2\,SSKP$.

For the case of very lethal weapons (large yield, good accuracy with $SSKP = 1$), fratricide becomes irrelevant since it only takes one reliable warhead to destroy a silo ($P_{2K} = P_{2KF} = 2R - R^2$). In Figure A.1 we have plotted the number of surviving Minuteman launchers (1,000 launchers, $H = 2,000$ psi) as a function of the accuracy of the SS-18 RVs (0.75 MT, $R = 0.75$); we have considered both the cases of (a) no fratricide and (b) full fratricide. The curves coincide for accuracies better than about 0.06 nmi since the SSKP approaches one, and the two curves separate for greater values of CEP. The shaded area indicates that about 100 additional Minuteman launchers could survive because of fratricide for the present regime of SS-18 accuracy of CEP = 0.14 to 0.15 nmi. Because the remaining calculations in this paper will not consider these fratricide effects, the estimates for surviving land-based missiles should be increased since some of the attacking weapons will destroy each other.

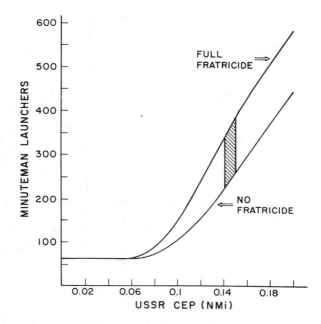

FIGURE A1. Fratricide. The number of surviving Minuteman launchers has been calculated as a function of Soviet accuracy for two situations: (a) no fratricide; and (b) total fratricide. The best accuracy estimates presently available for Soviet missiles is indicated by the cross-hatched area between 0.14 and 0.15 nmi. Totally effective fratricide would increase the number of surviving Minuteman launchers by about 100.

APPENDIX B: DIFFERENTIAL SENSITIVITY ANALYSIS

Let us consider small variations in the input parameters for reliability (R), yield (Y), hardness (H), and accuracy (CEP) in order to determine the variation in the kill probability

$$P = R(1 - e^{-V})$$

where $V = Y^{2/3}/0.22 \; \text{CEP}^2 \; H^{2/3}$. The base-case situation of an SS-18 RV attacking a Minuteman silo will be used with the parameters $H = 2{,}000$ psi, $Y = 0.75$ MT, CEP $= 0.15$ nmi, and $R = 0.75$.

By improving the reliability by 10% from 0.75 to $R = 0.825$, the kill probability is improved by 10% since

$$\Delta P_{1K}/P_{1K} = \Delta R/R = 0.075/0.75 = 10\% \; .$$

By increasing the yield by 10% from 0.75 MT to 0.825 MT, the kill probability is increased by

$$\Delta P_{1K}/P_{1K} = (2V/3)(\Delta Y/Y)/(e^V - 1) = 3.8\% \ .$$

By increasing the accuracy by 10% from CEP = 0.15 nmi to 0.135 nmi, the kill probability is decreased:

$$\Delta P_{1K}/P_{1K} = (2V)(\Delta\text{CEP}/\text{CEP})/(e^V - 1) = 11.3\% \ .$$

By increasing the hardness by 10% from 2,000 psi to 2,200 psi, the kill probability is increased by

$$\Delta P_{1K}/P_{1K} = (-2V/3)(\Delta H/H)(e^V - 1) = -3.8\% \ .$$

From these calculations, it is clear that reliability and CEP are the most critical variables affecting the kill probability. These formulas which deal with rates of change are accurate only for small changes; in the third section of this chapter (pp. 47–51) we have broadened this approach to include larger changes in the parameters.

REFERENCES

1. Tsipis, K. Appendix G in *Physics, Technology, and the Nuclear Arms Race*, edited by D. Hafemeister and D. Schroeer. *Amer. Instit. Physics Conference Series* 104 (1983): 353.
2. Bunn M. and K. Tsipis. *Sci. Amer.* 249 (November 1983): 38.
3. Hafemeister, D. *Amer. J. Physics* 51 (1983): 215.
4. *The Military Balance, 1983–1984.* London: The International Institute for Strategic Studies, 1983.
5. Scrowcroft, B. et al. *Report of the President's Commission on Strategic Forces*, Washington, DC: Government Printing Office, 1983.
6. Tinajero, A. A. *US-USSR Strategic Offensive Weapons: Projected Inventories Based on Carter Policies.* Washington, DC: U.S. Congressional Research Service, Report No. 81-238F, 1981.
7. Feiveson, H. and F. von Hippel. *Physics Today* 36 (1983): 36.
8. Schroeer, D. Appendix E in *Physics, Technology and the Nuclear Arms Race*, edited by D. Hafemeister and D. Schroeer. *Amer. Institute of Physics Conference Series* 104 (1983): 336.
9. Speed, R. *Strategic Deterrence in the 1980s.* Stanford, CA: Hoover Instit. Press, 1979.
10. Quanbeck, A. and A. Wood. *Modernizing the Strategic Bomber Force.* Washington, DC: Brookings Institution, 1976.

PART 2
IMAGING TECHNOLOGIES

7.

Imaging Technologies

Ronald J. Ondrejka

Introductory Note by Kosta Tsipis

Ongoing activities and events that cause visible permanent changes to the physical environment are most confidently detected by means of periodic photographing by optical systems carried on satellites in low orbit around the earth—that is to say, by photoreconnaissance. By photographing a scene repeatedly under the same conditions, one can see whether there have been changes. Given enough detail, it is possible to recognize the activity that caused the change.

To monitor activities and events within a country to which access is prohibited, the number of photoreconnaissance satellites must be sufficient to guarantee that one is over the particular scene to be monitored at all times. Each of the satellites is equipped with a camera of special design that collects the light reflected by the scene and forms an image that is a pattern of light and dark—or colored—dots on a photosensitive recording surface. Each of these dots is called a picture element, or pixel. The size of the pixels, the focal length of the camera, and the height of the satellite from the surface of the earth determine the resolution, which is the size of the smallest object on the ground that the system can distinguish. The smaller the size of the pixel and the longer the focal length, the higher the resolution will be. That is, the smaller the size of each patch of the ground scene that is distinguishable from its neighbors, the finer the detail of the scene that can be revealed by the photograph. The finer the detail available in a picture, the easier it is to detect changes from one picture to the next and the smaller the changes that can be detected. As a result, the higher the resolution, the greater the information content of these pictures.

This chapter first describes in some detail, based on unclassified information derived from experience with civilian photoreconnaissance systems, the important measures of quality of such systems. In the second section, it provides information on the working of the technologies and on the recent advances that have made photoreconnaissance a particularly important tool for the verification of arms control agreements. As the spatial, temporal, and spectral resolution of orbiting photographic systems improves, so does our ability to detect and identify activities inside the Soviet Union. So also, therefore, does the confidence with which we can enter into arms limitation agreements.

65

This discussion restricts itself to the technologies and systems for satellite surveys of the earth. It will include visible and reflective-infrared sensing and imaging systems expected to produce space-image data before 1990 that have a ground detail resolution applicable to verification of compliance with arms control agreements.

The relationship of these civilian technologies to verification application is obvious, simply because sensing and mapping of the earth from the air or space is a military as well as an economic planning necessity. Photointerpretation of the engineering layout and workings of a civil airport employs the same image information levels and analysis techniques as those needed for the monitoring of a similar military facility. Modern weapons systems depend upon precise digital geographic coordination data for targeting and navigation (see Table 7.1). This same photogrammetrically derived positional information is used for civil works such as highway construction, flood control projects, and property tax assessment. Multi-spectral crop surveys and subsequent forecasting can provide strategic international policy planning information as well as routine commodity stabilization and contingency planning data. Verification requirements are a category or "level" of information need that is served by the same imaging technologies suitable for many other military and civil needs.

BACKGROUND

Early in the space program, photography by means of television cameras began providing routine, repetitive images of world-wide weather patterns; through the years, these satellite sensor systems have become a mainstay in weather forecasting and global weather modeling. When humans ventured into space, they were equipped with better lenses, cameras, and films, and they took thousands of magnificent color photographs that showed much more than clouds and shorelines, but were primarily intended to show what they saw.

Unlike many other sciences to which "space" presented a new environment for experimentation that, in turn, might offer a new solution to sometimes undefined problems, the science of earth photography and recording of earth-related phenomena from a remote perspective saw "space" as a desirable *extension* of observation capabilities that had been developed and employed for decades. The "eye-in-the-sky" aerial photography of the earth is, and has been, for over fifty years, a principal means of operational inventory taking, assessing, and mapping of the earth and its structures and activities.

The principal civilian objective of earth photography and subsequent analysis is to monitor and assess the status of the living and nonliving

Table 7.1. Major Users of the Defense Mapping Agency: Mapping, Charting, and Geodesy Products and Data

	Precise Positions	Maps/ charts	Digitized Map (Terrain)	Information (Culture)	Gravity and Geophysical Data	Electronic Navigational Aids
Warships						
Aircraft Carriers	•	•			•	•
Submarine Systems	•	•			•	•
Other Surface Ships and Submarines		•				•
Aircraft						
AWACS (Airborne Warning and Control System)		•	•			
SAC: B-52, FB-111, KC-135	•	•	•	•		
TAC: F-15, F-16, A-7, A-10	•	•	•	•		
MAC: C-130, C-141, C5A	•	•	•	•	•	
Navy/Marine Corps:						
Attack: A-4, A-6, A-7	•	•	•	•		
Fighter: F-14, F-18	•	•	•	•		
Patrol: P-3	•	•	•	•		
Land Forces						
Infantry/Mechanized Units		•				
Tanks		•				
Attack Helicopters		•				
Artillery (supported by FIREFINDER System)	•	•	•			
Missiles						
Minuteman, MX	•	•			•	
PERSHING II	•	•	•	•		
SRAM (Short Range Attack Missile)	•	•				
Cruise Missiles	•		•	•		
Poseidon/Trident	•				•	
Merchant Marine						
U.S. Flag Vessels		•				•
Foreign Flag Vessels		•				•
Private Yachts		•				•

Source. MC&G, Published July 1982 by the Defense Mapping Agency.

resources of our planet. Without this routine capability, it is not possible to properly manage the location, allocation, and utilization of these resources for man's needs.

THE SPACE PLATFORM

The panoramic view afforded by space, complemented by improvements in camera systems, offers the very significant advantage of synoptic overviews of structures and activities on the earth. A space platform provides not only this advantage, but also a recording platform more stable and predictable than an aircraft. The resulting benefits are greater geometric accuracy and image data quality for any given sensor system; the possibility of world-wide, illumination-synchronized, systematic coverage in the shortest possible time; and the possibility of efficient temporal analysis of changing phenomena by repetitive recording of specific areas or locations.

When it comes to imaging the earth, however, orbital mechanics and atmospherics bring restrictions as well as advantages. For example, clouds obstruct imaging opportunities close to 75% of the time in tropical or semi-tropical regions. In the temperate zones we are faced with cloud problems 30% to 50% of the time that illumination conditions are suitable. Based on the planned angular and regional coverage of a sensor, we must also choose the proper orbital inclination, orbit altitude, and launch time. The consequences of these selections are illustrated with examples in Figures 7.1 and 7.2.

BASIC MEASURES OF SENSOR SYSTEM QUALITY

Sensor systems provide data that after skilled and coordinated analysis yield the required information. The data, however, are of marginal value or valueless unless their form and content meet the needs of the analyst, who must have certain kinds of information to provide the basis for his conclusions, measurements, or other end products. The basic measures of a system's suitability to an analyst's needs take a number of forms, which may apply individually or in groups to particular tasks.

Spatial Resolution

Spatial resolution (sometimes referred to as "detail" or "content") is determined by the ground resolution measured in meters per line pair for photographic systems or in meters per pixel for electro-optical systems (see Figures 7.3A and B). The relation between pixels and line pairs is not clearly established, but it is generally agreed by image analysts that about 2.0 to 2.5 pixels are required to present the same ground information content as one line pair. Additional content is provided by color, which helps in the differentiation of objects. Spatial resolution is, of course, dependent upon the focal length, light gathering ability, and quality of the sensor optical system; the granularity and response of film for photographic systems; the individual detector size for electro-optical systems; and the contrast ratio of the target object to its background. Equally important to maintaining spatial resolution are the compensation for dynamic effects of aircraft or spacecraft movement and providing the optimum environmental conditions for the sensor.

The specific spatial resolution requirements for military applications

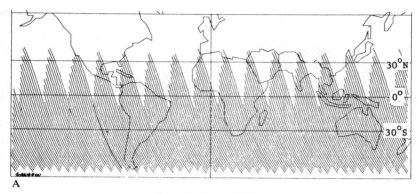

Launch time: 0900 hours

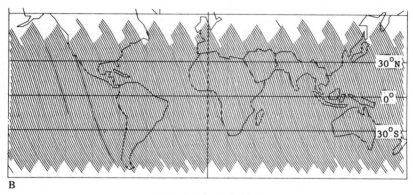

Launch time: 1200 hours

FIGURE 7.1. Launch-time sensitivity for a photographic mission. Progression of acceptable illumination conditions over the earth's surface. Launch site: West Coast. Orbit inclination: 70°. Orbit Altitude: 269.6 kilometers. Launch date: October 1.

deal with image study or interpretation functions, which in the visible and near infrared regions are commonly referred to as photointerpretation. Figure 7.4 graphically depicts the spatial resolution requirements. This is followed by Table 7.2, which provides detailed requirements for verification interpretation.

In Table 7.2, note the significantly increasing resolution requirements from the level of Detection to the levels of Identification and Description. Satellite sensor systems described in later paragraphs will indicate Detection level as meters per line pair or meters per pixel (IFOV). It is generally agreed that 3–5 resolution elements of pixels are required to recognize a

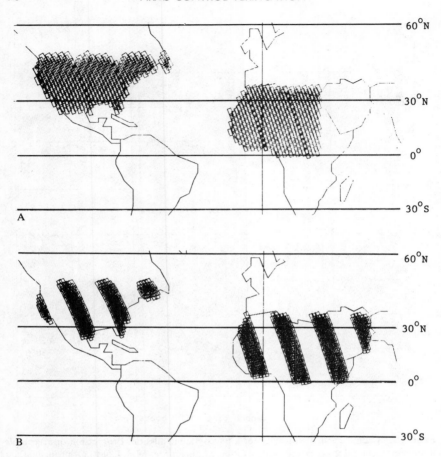

FIGURE 7.2. A, Orbit altitude: 269.6 kilometers; B, Orbit altitude: 257.4 kilometers. Orbit altitude sensitivity for a photographic mission. Cumulated area coverage with equal film supply for a 14-day mission. Launch site: West Coast. Orbit inclination: 70°. Launch date: October 1.

detected feature and up to 10 elements are required to describe a feature or object.

Spectral Resolution

Additional information can be provided by classification of ground features based upon their reflectivity of different parts of the electro-magnetic spectrum. Spectral resolution of optical sensors is expressed as the number of spectral bands in the visible and near-infrared atmospheric window, the

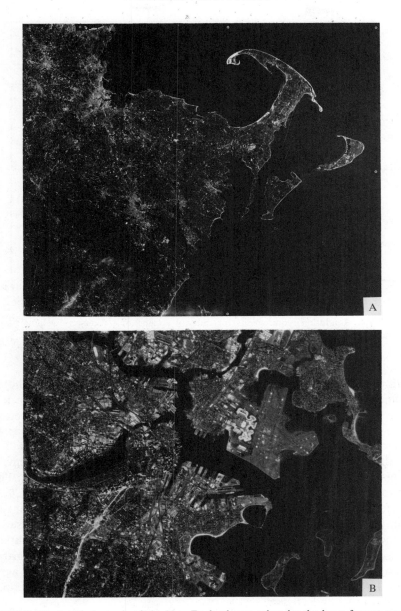

FIGURE 7.3. A, Photograph of the New England area taken by the large format camera (LFC) on its maiden engineering flight aboard the NASA space shuttle Challenger. The print shows the area of one photograph (originally 23×46 cm) of the original film imagery acquired on October 7, 1984 from an altitude of 148 statute miles. B shows an enlargement of a section of A, which is the city of Boston, as an example of the resolution obtainable from the original film.

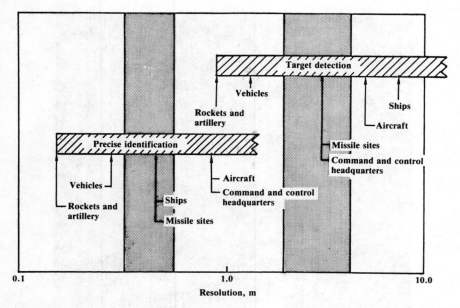

FIGURE 7.4. Resolution requirements for military applications. (Source: Reconnaissance Reference Manual, NAVAIR 10-1-789.)

width of each spectral band, and its exact location (see Figure 7.5). Photographic systems provide spectral data by selective use of films and optical filters. Electro-optical systems achieve multispectral capability by selection of the detector materials and by filtering of the light that reaches separate detectors on the spacecraft.

Perhaps the best known of space-imaging multispectral sensing systems is the NASA/NOAA Landsat series, which began operation in 1972. The spectral bands of the two present Landsat sensors are shown in Table 7.3.

Note that the spatial resolution of these spectral sensors is quite poor relative to the requirements previously identified. This is because Landsat is designed for thematic mapping rather than for cultural mapping or military photo-interpretation. The "themes" which benefit from multispectral recording are agriculture, land-use, geology, and hydrology. Generally, agricultural applications set the requirements for both the spectral and spatial resolution of Landsat.

Temporal Resolution

Dependent upon both the sensor (geographic coverage by optical field of view or pointability) and the flight parameters of the sensor platform, tem-

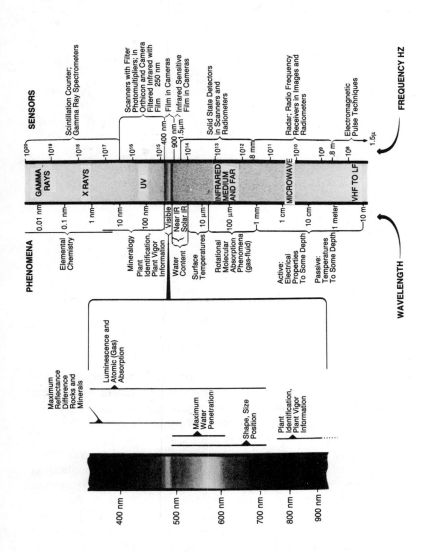

FIGURE 7.5. The electromagnetic spectrum, illustrating the possibilities of spectral resolution. Enlarged on the left is the visible and near-infrared portion of the spectrum where space cameras and earth resource scanners have been successfully employed.

Table 7.2. Ground Resolution Required for Treaty Verification
and Crisis Monitoring (in meters)

Object	Detection	Recognition	Identification	Description
Bridges	6	4.5	1.5	0.90
Radar	3	0.9	0.3	0.15
Radiocommunications	3	1.5	0.3	0.15
Material Depots	1.5	0.6	0.3	0.25
Troop Units or Bivouacs	6	2.1	1.2	0.30
Air Base Equipment	6	4.5	3	0.30
Artillery and Rockets	0.9	0.6	0.15	0.05
Aircraft	4.5	1.5	0.9	0.15
Headquarters	3	1.5	0.9	0.15
Ground-to-Ground Missile and Anti-Aircraft Sites	3	1.5	0.6	0.30
Medium-Sized Surface Vessels	7.5	4.5	0.6	0.30
Vehicles	1.5	0.6	0.3	0.05
Land Mine Fields	9	6	0.9	0.025
Ports	30	15	6	3
Coasts and Landing Beaches	30	4.5	3	1.5
Marshalling Yards and Railways Shops	30	15	6	1.5
Roads	9	6	1.8	0.6
Urban Areas	60	30	3	3
Military Airfields	—	90	4.5	1.5
Submarines on the Surface	30	6	1.5	0.9

Source. "Crisis Management Satellite," P.S.T.I.S., MIT Report #3, 1978.

poral resolution is critical to earth observation. It is a measure of the "revisit period" — the number of days elapsing before a satellite or system of satellites can take pictures over the same area, neglecting cloud cover but including suitable illumination conditions. "Revisit" is critical to many monitoring applications among which is military surveillance of dynamic activities. It is usually accomplished by employing sun-synchronous orbits or sensor pointing or a combination of the two. The altitude-inclination combination of the sun-synchronous orbit is such that the nodal motion caused by the earth's oblateness equals the mean rate at which the earth orbits the sun. The net result is that a spacecraft in such an orbit always passes over a given patch of the earth at the same local time. The revisit cycle of a single Landsat satellite with an altitude of 705 km and orbit inclination of 98.2° (near polar) is 16 days. The French SPOT system will be sun-synchronous but will increase revisit possibilities by means of the ability to point the sensor, as illustrated in Figure 7.6.

Table 7.3. Spectral Bands of Landsat Sensors

Wavelength (μm) Micrometers	Pixel Spatial Resolution
Multispectral Scanner (MSS)	
Band 1 0.50–0.60 (green)	80 m
Band 2 0.60–0.70 (red)	80 m
Band 3 0.70–0.80 (near infrared)	80 m
Band 4 0.80–1.1 (near infrared)	80 m
Thematic Mapper (TM)	
Band 1 0.45–0.52	30 m
Band 2 0.52–0.60	30 m
Band 3 0.63–0.69	30 m
Band 4 0.76–0.90	30 m
Band 5 1.55–1.75	30 m
Band 6 10.40–12.50	120 m
Band 7 2.08–2.35	30 m

Position

Position relates features shown on the map to the latitude and longitude reference systems on the earth. For most mapping systems, positional information is provided by referencing the images to known ground control points. However, in areas where ground control is not available, map position of surface features is derived from the location and attitude of the sensor recorded at the time the image is exposed.

The accuracy with which spacecraft position can be established depends upon the system employed. For most U.S. satellites, position data have been provided by the Spacecraft Tracking and Data Network (STDN). However, the STDN net is being phased out and is being replaced by the Tracking and Data Relay Satellite System (TDRSS). The Space Shuttle uses an inertial measuring unit (IMU) to establish the on-orbit position of the Orbiter vehicle. It is possible by postflight analysis of tracking data and spacecraft engine burns to greatly reduce the errors in computed spacecraft position. Within the next few years, the Navstar Global Positioning System (GPS) will be the principal means of establishing spacecraft position on orbit. The accuracies obtainable by these systems are shown in Table 7.4.

The accuracy with which attitude can be determined for spacecraft and their sensors also depends upon the system employed (Table 7.5). Landsat employs an inertial system with stellar control. The Space Shuttle depends primarily upon its Inertial Measuring Unit (IMU). The Shuttle Large For-

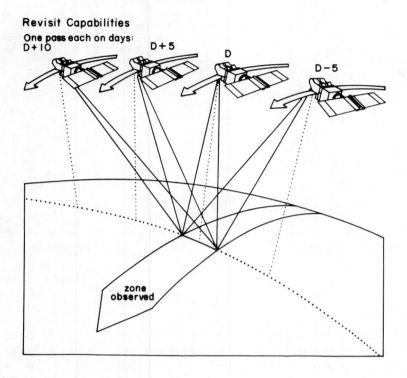

FIGURE 7.6. The French Spot system.

mat Camera (LFC) for mapping employs the stellar camera Attitude Reference System (ARS).

Elevation

Elevation data are derived fundamentally from stereoscopic coverage acquired by the sensor, although radar and laser altimetry are sometimes employed. The datum for topographic elevation is usually established by reference to ground control points whose elevation is known. However, just as in the case of positional data, elevation data can be derived in the absence of ground control from the position and attitude of the sensor known at the time the images are exposed. One of the most frequently used photographic interpretation aids/techniques is stereoscopic analysis. An image interpreter can create a three-dimensional, or stereoscopic, model of terrain by viewing overlapping imagery. The photographic basis for stereoscopy can be found in the principles of image displacement and stereo-

Table 7.4. Accuracy of Spacecraft Positioning

System	Along	Across	Altitude
Spacecraft Tracking and Data			
Network (STDN)	110 m	130 m	130 m
After 1 Revolution	260	130	150
Tracking and Data Relay			
Satellite System (TDRSS)	430	460	90
After 1 Revolution	610	460	90
Shuttle Inertial Measuring			
Unit (IMU)	1000	100	100
Post Flight Analysis	300	30	30
Navstar Global Positioning			
System (GPS)	10	10	15

Table 7.5. Accuracy of Spacecraft Attitude

Spacecraft	System	Tilts	Yaw
Landsat	Inertial & stellar	0.01°	0.01°
Shuttle	Inertial Measuring Unit	0.5°	0.5°
	Alignment	2°	2°
	Stellar Camera	5″	5″

scopic parallax. To illustrate stereoscopic overlapping photography, diagrams of the Space Shuttle Large Format Camera (LFC) are shown as Figure 7.7. The LFC is a NASA payload that began photographic missions for worldwide mapping in 1984.

SPACE SENSOR SYSTEMS OF THIS DECADE

Before we discuss the *imaging* system technologies used in earth sensing, we should identify current and near-future programs, specifically those of interest to this book. As mentioned before, we will restrict the discussion to:

- sensor systems in the visible and near-infrared portions of the electromagnetic spectrum;
- sensor systems that have a resolution level of interest;
- systems that have produced data or will produce data during the period of 1980 to 1990.

Tables 7.6 and 7.7 and Figures 7.8 and 7.9 provide selective characteristics of U.S. programs, foreign programs, resolution comparisons, and spectral resolutions of U.S. systems.

Table 7.6. U.S. Civilian Visible-Imaging Satellite Sensors Producing (or Planned) Data, 1980–1990

Selected Characteristics	Sensing Systems						Historical Reference	
	Landsat-2	Landsat-3	Landsat-4	Landsat-5	LFC/ARS	AEROS-A	S-190 A 6-Lens Camera	S-190 B Recon Camera
Sponsor	NASA	NASA	NASA	NOAA	NASA (SHUTTLE)	SPACE AMERICA	NASA (SKYLAB)	NASA (SKYLAB)
Launch	Jan. 75	Mar. 78	July 82	Mar. 84	Oct. 84	1986**	May 1973	May 1973
Status	Ended Feb. 82	Ended Mar. 83	Partial Use (See Text)	Expected Life 4-5 years	STS-17 7 days	Most Probable Commercial Venture	Ended February 1974 35,000 Photos Returned	
Coverage Potential	World	World	World	World	±60° Lat. Until 1986	World	±50° Lat.	±50° Lat.
Coverage Per Image	185 KM	185 KM 98 KM	185 KM	185 KM	200 × 400 KM	150 KM	160 × 160 KM	100 × 100 KM
Recording Method	Scanner & Vidicon	Scanner & Vidicon	Scanners (2)	Scanners (2)	Film	Solid-State CCD	Film	Film
Pointable	No	No	No	No	No	No	No	No
Revisit Cycle	18 Days	18 Days	16 Days	16 Days	Shuttle Launches	9 Days (Sidelap)	Various	None
Pixel Resolution (max. in terrain)	80 M	80 M & 30 M	30 M	30 M	5 M*	40 M	12 M*	6 M*
Terrain/Object Height Information	No	No	No	No	Yes	Yes	Some	No
Customers	Agri. Geology Hydrology	L-2 Plus Land-Use	Economic Intelligence & L-3	Same as L-4	Topographic & Geologic Mapping	Landsat Users (Foreign)	Experimenters	Experimenters
Users								

*Pixel Equivalents for Film Resolution (GRD ÷ 2.5 = IFOV).
**To be determined.

Table 7.7. Foreign Visible-Imaging Satellite Sensors Producing (or Planned) Data, 1980-1990

Selected Characteristics	Sensing Systems							
	M.O.M.S.	Atlas-A Atlas-B	Stereo M.O.M.S.	SPOT	Atlas-C	MOS-1 JERS-1	AERS	MRF-6
Sponsor	W. Ger.	W. Ger.	W. Ger.	France	W. Ger.	Japan	ESA	USSR
Launch	June 83	Nov. 83 Sprg. 86 Late 86	1986	Jan. 86	1987	1986 1987	1989	Various Soyuz Flts.
Status	Flown (Successful)	1-Flown 1-Assured 1-Probable	In Development	On Schedule	In Design	MOS (Devel.) JERS (Design)	Design	Flown (Successful)
Coverage Potential	±60° Lat. Until 1986	±60° Lat. Until 1986	±60° Lat. Until 1986	World	World (Shuttle or Free Flyer)	World	World	±82° Lat.
Coverage Per Image	140 KM	190 × 190 KM	70 KM	60 KM	150 × 150 KM	100 KM	175 KM	114 × 168 KM
Recording Method	Solid State CCD	Film	Solid State CCD	Solid State CCD	Film	MOS-Scanner JERS-CCD	CCD	Film
Pointable	No	No	No	Yes ±30°	No	No	Yes	No
Revisit Cycle	N/A	Shuttle Launches	N/A	1 to 4 Days	15 Days (Free Flyer)	30 Days	1 to 4 Days	Soyuz Operations
Pixel Resolution (max. in terrain)	20 M	4-6 M*	10 M	10 M	3-5 M*	50 M 30 M	15 M	6 M*
Terrain/Object Height Information	No	Limited	Yes	Yes	Yes	JERS-Yes	Yes	Yes
Customers / Users	Experiment	Europe Africa Mid-East Asia	Experiment Stereo Mapping	Mapping Geology Land-Use (LDCs)	Europe Mapping	Marine and Geology	Mapping Geology Land-Use	Land-Use and Topographic Mapping

*Pixel Equivalents for Film Resolution (GRD ÷ 2.5 = IFOV).

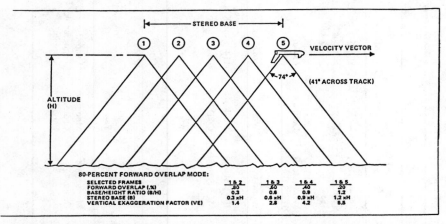

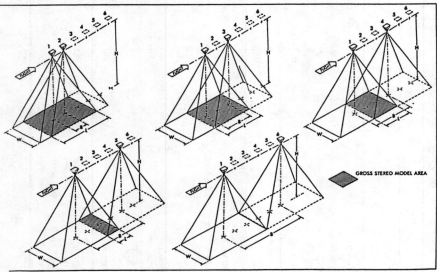

FIGURE 7.7. Large format camera (LFC) acquisition concept for 80% forward overlap (stereo) photography.

Camera Technology

The potential advantages of the panoramic view from space and the fulfillment of data needs are ultimately realized through camera system technology. The term "camera system" is used here to differentiate between the scientific earth recording camera and the hand-held astronaut/cosmonaut cameras that are still part of the space program for many other scientific

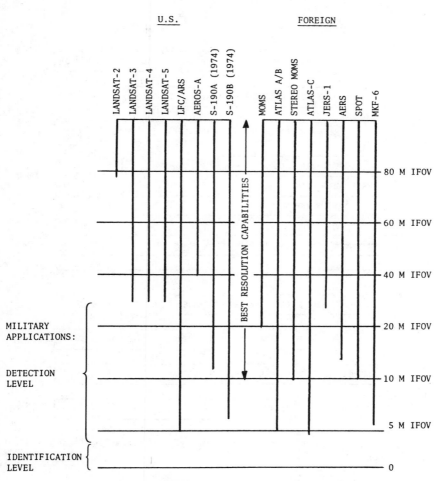

FIGURE 7.8. 1980–1990 early survey satellite imaging systems.

tasks such as solar astronomy, atmospheric studies, and space medicine. The word "system" indicates that the camera has several components and operational considerations such as:

- lenses
- filters
- films
- mechanics such as shutters, film transports, motion compensation, and structures insensitive to temperature, shock, vibration, etc.
- electronics

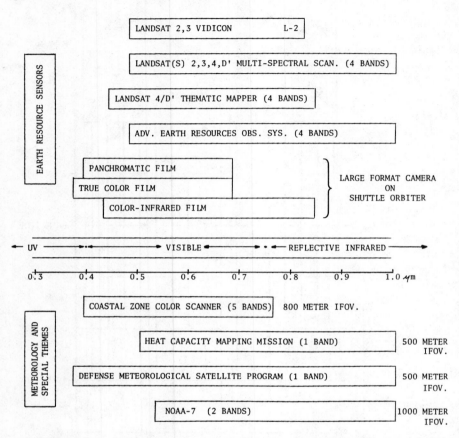

FIGURE 7.9. 1980–1990 U.S. earth observation satellite sensors for visible near-infrared spectral regions.

- thermal control and protection
- vacuum of deep space
- minimum power, weight, size
- reliability

The high-resolution "scientific" camera in many instances did not evolve through the demands of the space program but rather was available in some form as a result of developments for high-altitude military reconnaissance.

High Resolution Cameras. Aerial photographic reconnaissance is a peaceful yet hazardous military function. Whether it was a camera aboard a balloon during the American Civil War, cameras recording supply routes and trenches during World War I (see Figure 7.10 and Figure 7.11), RAF cameras over the German rocket base at Peenemünde during World War II, the camera-equipped U-2 over Russia and Cuba, or a camera aboard a military satellite monitoring arms control agreements today, the data the camera records sometimes become an undesirable factor to one side or the other in a hot or cold war. The obvious hazard-avoidance procedure is to fly higher, farther away (standoff photography), or faster (or all three if possible, as the SR-71 supersonic reconnaissance aircraft is presumed to be able to do (see Figure 7.12). The technologies involved in producing responsive camera capabilities are discussed next.

Films. During and following World War II, the aerial films for both military and civil purposes were generally identical: relatively fast but of coarse grain and, therefore, of moderate resolution. Offsetting the information limit of low-resolution film while staying at high altitudes required that the camera lens focal length be increased to permit an optical magnification of the required target objects prior to "presenting" them to the film to be recorded. The "no-substitute-for-focal-length" philosophy prevailed for many years in the United States and other military quarters to the extent that the U.S. Air Force Reconnaissance Laboratories at Boston University (the predecessor to Itek) developed a camera with a focal length of more than 6 meters. Aerial film technology was rapidly accelerated over the next thirty years and lenses (and therefore camera systems) could record the

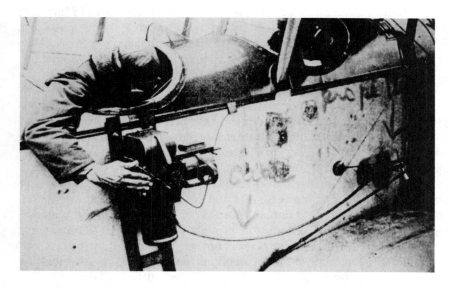

FIGURE 7.10. World War I aerial photography techniques. (Figures 7.10 and 7.11 are courtesy of Itek Optical Systems.)

FIGURE 7.11. Aerial photograph of World War I enemy trench complex.

same detail with more moderate focal lengths, and camera sizes and weights became more manageable for smaller and more efficient reconnaissance platforms. Today, Eastman Kodak lists commercial aerial films with a high-contrast recording capability of more than 800 line pairs per millimeter — a factor of more than 10 times improvement over World War II aerial films. The challenge for technical innovations was then returned to the optical/mechanical camera-component designers (see Figure 7.13).

Lenses. Optical lens design is centuries old. Development of the digital computer has brought older lens concepts to near perfection and has made possible radically new refractive and reflective lenses. Lens design is basically an iterative geometric process in which simulated light rays emanating from an object (at or near infinity for aerial camera lenses) are passed through various portions of powered glass elements and air spaces. The object is to adjust the surfaces and spaces so that all rays in image space converge to a common focal point. Additionally, focal "points" formed by rays incoming at angles to the lens axis must be brought into a plane — the focal plane where the film is placed. The process is further complicated by the fact that "white light" from natural objects contains the full spectrum of colors; by the proper selection of glass types, coatings, and surface relationships the individual colors, too, must be brought to a common focus.

FIGURE 7.12. SR-71 airplane.

The computer permits literally hundreds of iterations of a lens design where all the factors of glass refractive indices, surface shapes, air spaces, etc., can be sequentially adjusted to optimize the design in order to produce the desired result. The computer, however, is not the only recent innovation that permits high resolution lens development. A few of the other more significant related developments are as follows.

Glass types. Rare-earth materials are now used in the formation of glass "blanks," which permits the designer to select refractive indices for lens elements that will optimize design and, in some instances, provide a design possibility that was physically unachievable prior to this innovation. Glass composition and formation are now highly controlled, so that a specific glass can be made that is close to the design criteria. The lens manufacturer measures the refractive index before the lens design is finalized, and again the computer permits rapid final adjustments for any glass deviations before fabrication starts. *Raw* glass blanks of relatively exotic materials can cost as much as $20,000 to $30,000 for a piece one-third of a meter in diameter.

Aspheric elements. Traditionally lens surfaces were spherical (convex or

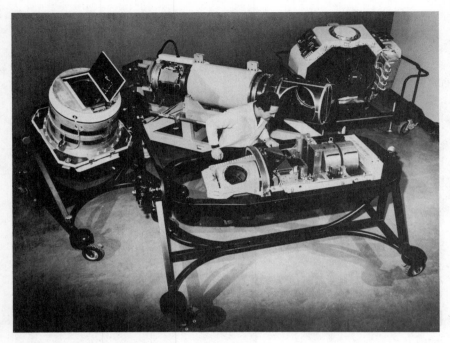

FIGURE 7.13. A sampling of modern high-resolution camera systems at the laboratories of Itek Optical Systems. The camera on the right is the Space Shuttle large format camera. The others are for high altitude airborne reconnaissance.

concave) or flat but again the flexibility of design provided by computers allows the manufacture and use of complex surface shapes in lenses. These are usually called aspherics and are used selectively in a lens system to correct unwanted effects of the other elements or to achieve an extended lens capability, such as higher resolution across a large field angle. The computer aids in the fabrication by physically positioning a grinding tool at the glass surface both in horizontal and vertical coordinates as directed by a digital contour map of the desired surface. Another recent innovation, the laser, permits the formation of optical interferograms from the measurement of the shape of the lens surface, which in turn provides the contour map of the existing surface. By comparing the existing lens contours to the digitally stored desired contours, the computer controls the position of the lens grinding tool and thereby achieves the desired surface.

Lens cell materials. Two of the potentially optically degrading effects of an uncontrolled environment such as outer space are high-temperature and large-temperature variations (see Figure 7.14). If the metallic lens enclo-

FIGURE 7.14. The lens cell and optical elements of the space-hardened Shuttle large format camera (LFC). The lens has a focal length of 305 mm and field-of-view of 80°.

sure, or cell, is expanding or contracting due to temperature changes, the resulting mechanical forces can be transmitted to the lens elements and can change their shape, magnifying power, and, therefore, the location of the focus and the shape of the focal plane. Modern metal alloys permit the selection of lens cell material whose thermal characteristics, such as the coefficient of expansion, match those of the materials of various glass-lens elements.

Insulation materials. The temperature of the lens and indeed of the entire camera can also be passively controlled with modern, thin, lightweight insulation materials. Layers of such material with air spaces between them become even more efficient in the environment of space where the layered air "outgasses" to leave a vacuum between the layers. It is not unusual to use up to 100 layers of metal-coated mylar as a passive insulation blanket in a space camera. Active thermal control materials and systems are equally advanced, lightweight, and reliable. It is quite common to maintain the camera at higher than ambient temperature in order to provide a more controllable and predictable temperature environment.

Electro-mechanical devices. Besides the obvious camera operations of driving a shutter and a film transport, a modern high-resolution camera has a myriad of electro-mechanical functions, such as operating thermal doors, changing filters, and compensating for aircraft or spacecraft forward motion during photo exposure. More complex cameras move film during the picture-taking process as well as between photos. These cameras, called panoramic, or strip, cameras, use very high-resolution, narrow-field lenses, but achieve wide area coverage by "sweeping" the lens while transporting the film under the precise control of electro-optical encoders. Advances in the technology of these devices permits the control of lens and film motion to be comparable to the lens-resolution capability, that is, a few micrometers at the focal planes.

As a result of these advances, the modern aerial camera has been able to match the challenges of aerial film development. It is quite reasonable to expect a reconnaissance lens system to resolve 300 to 400 line pairs per millimeter for high contrast objects and a lens film combination to resolve more than 250 lines/mm under the same conditions. Again, a factor of 10 times improvement over aerial camera technology during World War II.

A High Resolution Camera in Space

The first NASA high resolution camera to be put into orbit in space for systematic geologic and cartographic surveys was part of the Apollo program to map the moon, a fact that is technically ironic but politically understandable. Lunar geologic studies and maps of future landing sites created the demand. To this day, there are better, more accurate, larger-scale, and more complete topographic maps of the moon than there are of large areas of the planet earth.

In 1968 a military aerial reconnaissance camera developed by Itek was selected for the task of stereoscopically recording lunar surface objects of 1 to 2 meters (such as boulders, which would present spacecraft landing hazards) over as large an area as possible while orbiting 100 kilometers above the lunar surface. This task was formidable enough but theoretically possible for the camera. The additional constraints created the need for concern and innovation. A few of them are interesting enough to be discussed here.

1. *The camera would have to operate in hard vacuum.*

Concerns:
- bleeding of air in the lens and other camera locations
- breakdown of conventional lubricants
- no air for convection to disperse temperature traps
- electro-static discharge between moving surfaces causing fogging of film
- need to provide "air" for film transport cushions (no contacts with guides or rollers that might leave microscopic scratches on the film)

2. *The camera must operate in weightlessness.*

Concerns:

- need for 2,000-meter-capacity film supply spools to move freely to rotate and unravel the film
- inability to test camera components and operations in a gravity-free environment
- free-floating dust, chips, and mechanical parts able to disturb or destroy images or camera functions

3. *The camera must survive the shock of the launch environment and survive radiation and cosmic exposure.*

And, finally, of great concern because in many instances the manufacturer's profit is dependent upon it:

4. *The camera must work and meet performance criteria with better than 99% assurance. The million-dollar camera cannot be returned for repair or re-use. The flight and its ultimate mission are far more valuable than the cost of the camera.*

This experience with a high resolution camera in space was a complete success for three space missions and all goals were met or exceeded.

Multispectral Cameras

All objects at or near the surface of the earth either reflect or emit discrete electromagnetic energy, be it light, infrared radiation, or reflected microwaves, or else they display dynamic electrical properties. Remote detection and recording of these properties at different parts of the electromagnetic spectrum is commonly known as multispectral sensing. Within the visible and near-infrared portions of the spectrum these properties can be recorded on aerial film in a multispectral camera. As a result, objects with different spectral signatures are optimally recorded on a specific film and filter combination. A multispectral camera is simply a series of near-identical lenses, each covered with a filter that transmits energy of given frequencies and rejects the remainder. The film selected for each lens is that which will best record (is the most responsive to) the transmitted fraction of the received light.

This technique for aerial photoreconnaissance dates back to Germany in the 1920s; modern day uses began in 1960 with the development of the 9-Lens Multispectral Camera by Itek for the U.S. military (Figure 7.15). Its purpose was to detect signs of underground nuclear testing with the assumption that surface soil chemistry and porosity above the test would be changed, creating a pattern of vegetation with different spectral signatures

FIGURE 7.15. The 1960 9-lens multispectral camera used in U.S. experiments to determine earth surface effects of underground nuclear testing. (Courtesy of Itek Optical Systems.)

or soil with different reflectance characteristics. This experimental 9-lens camera was to determine which photo/optical "channel" would best detect and exaggerate the visible effects of phenomena. Similar multispectrum camera technology has been used for earth science study in the NASA Skylab program and also in the U.S.S.R. Soyuz program (see Figure 7.16).

Multispectral Films. To cover the spectral range from near-ultraviolet to near-infrared, a number of film types must be used in each of the nine separate camera channels. A conventional wide-range panchromatic black and white film can cover the visible region from the blue to the red portion of

FIGURE 7.16. The 6-lens Soyuz multispectral camera is a mainstay of the USSR earth resource survey program. Spatial resolution is said to be in the 15–20 meter/line pair range. (Courtesy of Jena-Optik.)

the spectrum. This region, when divided by filters into two or three bands, is optimal for maximum information on man-made objects such as road networks and utilities. It is also good for water penetration and all data requiring maximum spatial resolution.

Recording beyond the red region into the near-infrared requires a special infrared-sensitive film. Such a film was developed more than 40 years ago for military reconnaissance applications. Being insensitive to blue-haze rejection, it had improved penetration ability and provided maximum image contrast of distant horizon objects.

To record the shorter ultraviolet waves, special quartz lenses are required; to extend to longer wavelengths beyond the near-infrared to the thermal infrared, special all-reflective lenses are required. These regions therefore are not normally included in a multispectral film camera capability; they are detected and recorded electro-optically.

Perhaps the most significant recent innovations in spectral recording films are the new two- and three-layer color emulsions. Many multispectral cameras reserve extra channels for these films as they provide an immediate enhancement of certain spectral information.

Color infrared film (CIR) is a three-layer emulsion, again developed to fill a need of the military, and it has been in use since WW-II. The original purpose of CIR was camouflage detection, since it has the unique property of recording dead, dying, disturbed, or artificial vegetation.

The recent developments in both true color and color infrared films have resulted in significantly improved image quality. Today they are quite competitive in that respect to the black and white emulsions, and therefore they are prime candidates for space surveys where resolved detail is a factor that cannot be sacrificed for spectral enhancement.

Film manufacturers have also recently developed a two-layer color film with a spectral "window" at that part of the visible spectrum that permits penetration of water surface reflectance. This "water penetration" film is insensitive to sky, cloud, and water particulate disturbances and greatly simplifies the study and mapping of subsurface coastal features.

Electro-Optical (E-O) Space Photography

The principal advantages of E-O camera systems are:

1. The transmission of images with no film return, rapid data receipt, and reception anywhere in the world equipped with suitable receiver.

2. Provision of images in computer-compatible digital form, which offers convenient multispectral analysis and convenient temporal analysis (chance detection).

3. Spectral discrimination properties that allow narrow spectral bands (more discrete for resource reflectances), are not limited by film response, and have the ability to read thermal infrared.

Electro-optical cameras consist of a lens (either refractive or reflective) and a photosensitive detector (or detectors) at the focal plane in place of film. The brightness and/or spectral information of an area on the ground is focused on the detector, which records one brightness value for the area. This value can be stored on magnetic tape or transmitted to the earth for tape storage and/or photographic formation. Scanning of the lens across the orbital flight path and moving of the spacecraft along the flight path compile a photographed "area." A *series* of detectors, filtered for different spectral regions and simultaneously or serially recording the ground, make up a Multispectral Electro-Optical Camera. The present Landsat (since 1972) series of earth-resource cameras employ this scanning principle.

Emerging electro-optical multispectral cameras used a solid-state line array of as many as 10,000 detectors for cross-track coverage for each of the chosen spectral bands. The array will sweep along the line of flight to achieve continuous photographic coverage (the "pushbroom" technique). Figure 7.17 and Table 7.8 give information about the capabilities of this technique.

Solid-state line arrays are uniquely suited to satellite imaging of the earth. This is achieved by optically projecting the array to the ground so that the vehicle velocity causes it to "sweep" the earth's surface. The advantages of this technique over mechanical scanning are significant:

1. Because there are no mechanical devices needed for the imaging process, there is an opportunity to eliminate all mechanical disturbances, which is the ideal situation for high-resolution imaging.

2. The precise geometry of photoarrays, inherent in the photolithographic process by which they are made, as well as the stability of their silicon structure, provides the basis for registration from one spectral band to another and for the accurate location or mapping of terrain features.

3. Camera sensitivity is dramatically improved because of the longer "focus" time on the area of the focal plane from which the ground information is continuously gathered. For the same optical system parameters, the information is increased directly as the ratio of the number of detectors used. This greater power can be used to increase radiometric accuracy, to improve geometric resolution, or to provide narrower spectral bands, thereby increasing the precision of the information gathered.

IMAGE INTERPRETATION — MANUAL, MACHINE

Every person engages in image interpretation. Interpretation is the essential process through which information is obtained from images. Books, billboards, and television all offer images to the observer; each image conveys ideas or impressions. These ideas or impressions constitute interpretation. The interpretation may or may not be accurate and may be either conscious or unconscious, partial or complete. The degrees of accuracy and completeness are in large measure dependent upon the amount of experience the interpreter has in the particular purpose for which the interpreta-

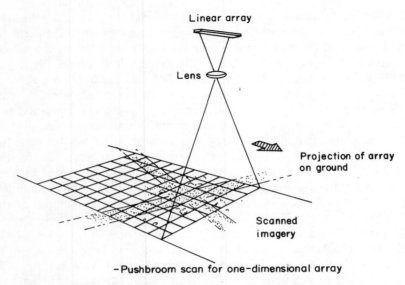

FIGURE 7.17. Pushbroom scan for one-dimensional array.

tion is occurring. Once the interpreter has gained experience in the field of image recording, the task of drawing accurate conclusions from the images observed can begin.

Image interpretation involves at least three mental acts that may or may not be performed simultaneously:

1. measurement of objects on the imagery,
2. identification of the objects imaged, and
3. appropriate use of this information in answering the question at hand.

Table 7.8. The Two Space Systems for Earth Surveys Employing
the Solid-State Linear Array Scanning Principle

	MOMS-01 (W. Germany) Shuttle Mission 7 1984	SPOT (France) 1986	
		Multispectral Mode	Panchromatic Mode
Spectral Channels	600 ± 25 nm; 900 ± 75 nm	0.50–0.59 μm 0.61–0.68 μm 0.79–0.89 μm	0.51–0.73 μm
Pixels Per Line	6912	3000	6000
Instrument Field of View	26.2°	4.13°	4.13°
Round Pixel Size (Resolution)	20 m × 20 m	20 m × 20 m	10 m × 10 m

It is not intended in this discussion to go into the detailed procedures or illustrate the instrument aids for image interpretation. Figure 7.18 illustrates the elements of interpretation and analysis. It is also very important to recognize the contributions of "collateral material" to image interpretation. This material can take many forms such as:

1. Material from the open literature (e.g., books, articles, reports, maps, census data, etc.),
2. Laboratory measurements,
3. Photo interpretation keys (e.g., elimination, selective, descriptive),
4. Field work, and
5. Other image sources (e.g., ground, aerial, space).

It is also equally important to recognize the ever-increasing contributions of computer-aided techniques as well as of complete computer interpretation of images. Digital image processing of remotely sensed images aids two principal applications:

1. Improvement of image information for human interpretation, and
2. Processing of scene data for computer-assisted interpretation.

Each of the elements of image interpretation is being addressed with varying degrees of success by computer techniques. A brief summary of these is found in Table 7.9. Some of these techniques can be incorporated on board the observing spacecraft to expedite analysis, to command a closer or sec-

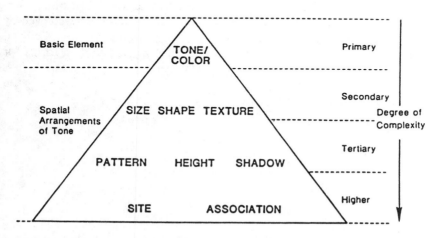

FIGURE 7.18. Primary ordering of image elements fundamental to the analysis process. (From: *Manual of Remote Sensing*, 2nd ed., 1983 by American Society for Photogrammetry and Remote Sensing. Copyright 1983 by ASPRS. Used with permission.)

Table 7.9. Computer Interpretation Techniques

Image Interpretation Elements	Domain	Examples of Computer Interpretation Techniques
Tone	Spectral	Density Slicing
Color	Spectral	Multispectral Classification
Texture	Spectral/Spatial	Texture Classification
Pattern	Spectral/Spatial	Spatial Transforms and Classification
Size	Spatial	Segmentation Algorithms and Size Feature Classification
Shape	Spatial	Syntactic Classification
Site	Spatial	A Priori, Modified
Association	Spatial	Contextual Classification Syntactic Classification

ond look at an interesting scene, or to detect changes from previous image acquisition.

CONCLUSION

To control costs, minimize data handling, and expedite analysis, image acquisition systems are designed for specific tasks. There appears to be no doubt that if an object on earth can be seen (unobstructed by clouds, smoke, poor illumination, or by a natural or man-made covering), an imaging system can be designed to record it down to the level of physical limits imposed by atmosphere, system dynamics, and sensor fabrication tolerances. As has been shown, verification information can be derived even by the analysis of data produced by the civilian imaging systems discussed here. This is explained by the similarities in data needs and data forms for military, civilian, academic, and industrial purposes. Imaging technologies, however, are continually advancing and will be available to serve an expanding scope of interests and purposes.

8.

Adaptive Optics:
Potential for Verification

J. Richard Vyce and John W. Hardy

Introductory Note by Kosta Tsipis

When the image of a scene is viewed in reflection from a distorted mirror or through a piece of uneven glass plate, it is itself distorted, as visitors to amusement parks with "fun house" mirrors can attest. The physical reason for the distortion of the image is that the bent mirror or the uneven glass causes the light waves reflected (or emitted) by the scene under observation to develop *phase errors* — that is, some of them lag behind the others in arriving at the observing sensor.

The layers of the atmosphere, like bent mirrors or uneven glass, distort images by causing phase errors. Because the effect of the distortion is greater the closer to the sensor the distortion occurs, these errors are more significant for sensors looking up from the earth towards space than for space-based sensors looking down. This paper describes the techniques and the equipment with which these phase errors can be measured and compensated for, thus restoring an undistorted image of the scene. The process is based on the availability of, first, very fast computers that can quickly sense the presence of a phase error and even more quickly decide how to eliminate it from the wavefront, and second, piezoelectric devices that can, when the distorting factors can be predicted, *predistort* a reflecting surface appropriately so that the wave form that leaves it is distortion-free.

This technique is useful for ground-based and air-based optical systems and for very large mirrors deployed in space. Although not necessary in current-size reconnaissance satellites, adaptive optics is essential in monitoring activities in space from earth.

The ability to examine things from a great distance is the basic requirement for what is referred to in the language of arms control as "national technical means." This long-range surveillance requires optical systems with large apertures, lenses, or mirrors that receive the light reflected or emitted from the scene under observation.

A problem common to most large-aperture optical systems is that the light wavefronts that reach them develop *phase errors*, which means that portions of the light wave lag behind the rest. These wavefront phase errors (WFE) are caused by imperfections in the optics and/or by atmospheric turbulence. The effects of atmospheric turbulence are familiar to us as the twinkling of stars and the shimmering of vistas over a hot surface. A correction for these effects in some cases is available from the technologies of adaptive optics, which can provide subsystems capable of measuring and compensating for wavefront phase errors everywhere over the area of the aperture to form a better-resolved image at the focal plane.

The mirrors and lenses used in ground-based and space-based imaging systems measure up to a few meters in diameter. They can be made precise enough to achieve diffraction-limited image angular resolution of approximately $(D/\lambda)^{-1}$ radians, or one over the number of wavelengths across the aperture. Indeed, space-based imaging systems can achieve this resolution in operation because there is no atmosphere to cause an effective wavefront phase error outside the optics. When the system is looking down from space, the atmospheric wavefront phase error is near the object being viewed and consequently has little effect on the optical path, so that ground resolution of a few centimeters is possible for sophisticated spaceborne optical systems.

But when the optical system is within the atmosphere, the scale of atmospheric turbulence, which is approximately 5 cm, limits angular resolution in the visible part of the spectrum to that of a 5 cm aperture, or 10 microradians, regardless of optical system size. As a result, a satellite potentially capable of imaging the earth to a resolution of a few centimeters can only itself be imaged from the ground with a resolution of several tens of centimeters. Thus, large ground-based telescopes are called "photon buckets," because they collect a great deal of light but fail to concentrate it into a diffraction-limited image.

The primary imaging application of adaptive optics is to compensate for atmospheric wavefront phase errors of endoatmospherically based imaging systems. Adaptive optics may also prove useful in compensating for wavefront phase errors associated with aircraft flight in large airborne cameras, as well as those in planned space-based optical systems some three to ten times larger than the Space Telescope that may suffer from waveform distortion caused by imperfections of the optics themselves (see Figure 8.1).

Adaptive optics systems use deformable mirrors, wavefront sensors, and wavefront processors as indicated in Figure 8.2. Part of the light from the object being observed is diverted to the wavefront sensor, shown in Figure 8.3, where it is brought to a focus, chopped by a moving grating and then observed by an array of detectors. In this way, the wavefront tilts in each zone of the aperture are converted into time displacements of the detector

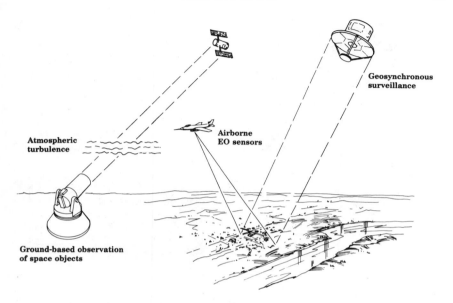

FIGURE 8.1. Artist's rendition of applications of adaptive optics for ground-based, airborne, and space-based surveillance systems.

output signals, which are then processed to obtain the data to drive the deformable mirror. To obtain good imaging, the rapidly changing wavefront aberrations caused by turbulence must be compensated by the deformable mirror to within a small fraction of the wavelength of light, which is about 0.5 micrometer.

Compact and efficient adaptive optics hardware designs are now available for optical systems of up to many meters diameter in the atmosphere and many tens-of-meters diameter in space.

LIMITATIONS OF ATMOSPHERIC COMPENSATION

One essential requirement for adaptive optics is a target or part of a target small and bright enough to allow measuring wavefront phase error with the necessary accuracy and speed. Adequate brightness for atmospheric compensation is available from typical sunlit targets, but the matter of size is more involved. Wavefront phase error caused by turbulence exists throughout the atmosphere, with a scale of a few centimeters at low altitude and a few tens of centimeters at high altitude. Adaptive optics systems sense the integrated atmospheric wavefront phase error from the target to the sensor and compensate it with the deformable mirror. While this com-

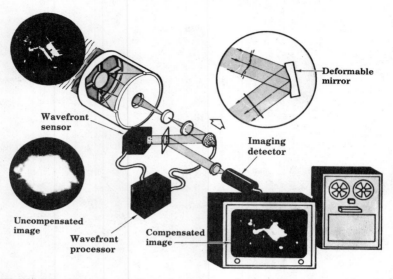

Wavefront
sensor

Deformable
mirror

Imaging
detector

Uncompensated
image

Wavefront
processor

Compensated
image

FIGURE 8.2. Adaptive optics can be used to improve the resolution of ground-based tele-scopes by removing the image distortions caused by atmospheric turbulence. Part of the light from the object being observed is diverted by a beamsplitter to the wavefront sensor which measures the instantaneous wavefront tilts produced by the turbulence, sending the data to the wavefront processor, which then instructs the deformable mirror to move in such a way as to remove the optical distortions. (Figure courtesy of Itek Optical Systems, a division of Litton Industries, Inc.)

pensation is excellent in the target direction, the compensated field of view is very small, and we do not know how to make it larger.

For uplooking systems, given the assumption of a 20 cm turbulence scale at an altitude of 10 km, then the angle over which wavefront phase-error compensation is valid, the so-called isoplanatic angle, is about 20 microradians, or 4 arc-seconds. For endoatmospheric imaging systems, the target size over which compensation is valid is approximately equal to the turbulence scale size, which decreases to a few centimeters at distances over one kilometer. These target size limitations severely restrict the utility of adaptive optics for imaging systems.

GROUND-BASED IMAGING

To date there has been no practical use for imaging endoatmospheric targets because of the small size of the compensated field of view.

Astronomical imaging is the most obvious exoatmospheric application of adaptive optics. The potentially resolvable objects of greatest interest are

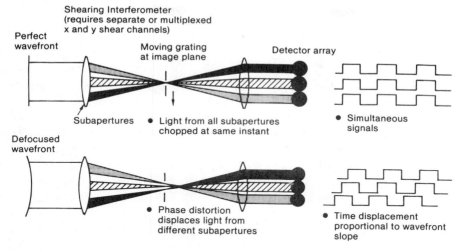

FIGURE 8.3. Wavefront sensor uses an array of optical detectors to measure the wavefront distortion. The incoming beam is first brought to a focus and then chopped by a rapidly moving grating that converts the image displacement produced by wavefront tilt in each zone of the aperture into a time displacement of the electrical signal at the output of the corresponding detector. This information is used to control the deformable mirror. (Figure courtesy of Itek Optical Systems, a division of Litton Industries, Inc.)

the nearby planets, but these are much larger than the isoplanatic angle, so their images cannot be effectively compensated.

Satellites are the one class of exoatmospheric target generally small enough to fall within the 20-microradian adaptive optics isoplanatic field of view. They can therefore be imaged from earth, but useful detail is obtainable only for satellites in low earth orbit, using adaptive optics telescopes limited to a few meters diameter.

Imaging of one low earth orbit satellite by another can, in principle, be done usefully with cameras up to Space Telescope size that should not require adaptive optics compensation. Useful imaging of satellites in geosynchronous orbits requires either a dedicated "inspector" in geosynchronous orbit, an exceptionally large (tens of meters in diameter) ground-based or low-earth-orbit telescope, or catching the satellite in low earth orbit before its injection to geosynchronous orbit.

Ground-based telescopes such as the Compensated Imaging System (CIS) require adaptive optics to obtain resolution better than 10 microradians; with adaptive optics they can be made as large as required to achieve a desired angular resolution, but only over the 20-microradian isoplanatic field of view. The CIS has already demonstrated that solar illumination provides enough light for fast and accurate wavefront phase error compensation and simultaneous imaging.

AIRBORNE IMAGING

An aircraft is frequently the preferred surveillance platform because of regularity of coverage and the good resolution allowed by proximity to the target. The combination of high-performance electro-optical imaging and adaptive optics compensation of local wavefront phase error offers greatly improved resolution over conventional airborne photography. Electro-optical imaging, using charge-coupled devices (CCDs) with a dynamic range remarkably greater than that of film, is essential to the recognition of targets in the presence of contrast attenuation at long slant range caused by air and haze scattering.

Although the uncompensated atmosphere at high altitude does allow something near to diffraction-limited imaging by cameras with apertures up to 0.5 m or larger, this is prevented in aircraft cameras by local wavefront phase error sources, including the boundary layer, thermal variations in the window and camera compartments, and vibration. There is reason to believe that adaptive optics can greatly reduce some of these wavefront phase errors, thereby significantly improving airborne camera resolution.

IMAGING FROM SPACE

It is well established that the atmosphere permits down-looking imaging of the earth surface with resolution of a few centimeters regardless of sensor altitude. For a satellite camera to achieve a given resolution, its aperture must grow directly with altitude. Thus, lower orbits allow smaller cameras. Because all low earth orbit satellites have about the same period and frequency of access to specific areas, lower orbits would seem preferable, but they do have drawbacks involving increased drag that limits a satellite's lifetime, and low coverage at a given obliquity. This leads to interesting trade-offs between camera size, number of satellites required for coverage, and lifetime. In any reasonable low earth orbit, the aperture required for very fine imaging falls in the range where high performance presumably can be built in and maintained without adaptive optics, as in the Space Telescope.

The two notably different cases are geosynchronous and Molniya orbits, in which one camera can provide full or almost full-time coverage of a large region on the earth. Here, the altitudes are enormous (20,000 to 40,000 km) and the camera aperture would have to be correspondingly large (several tens of meters) for reasonable resolution. Although systems of this class are overwhelming to contemplate they are probably feasible, but only with the aid of adaptive optics.

In the extremely large, active, segmented and lightweight optical systems required for surveillance from geosynchronous orbit, the function of adaptive optics is to compensate for wavefront phase error caused by optical surface perturbations and misalignment. In an orbiting surveillance system, the only disturbances are thermal variations and attitude changes, both of which occur slowly. Sufficiently fast wavefront measurement can be made using the earth image as a reference for the wavefront sensor, and compensation can be effected by controlling the active mirror segments and/or a separate deformable mirror.

CONCLUSIONS

Adaptive optics, although an interesting technology, currently has only a few applications of very high value. For verification purposes, adaptive optics may be of interest in the three imaging cases depicted in Figure 8.1:

- Satellite imaging from the ground, as with the Compensated Imaging System;
- Earth imaging from space with an ultralarge telescope parked at a geosynchronous orbit;
- Long-range oblique earth imaging with a large airborne camera from high altitude.

Of these, adaptive optics has been demonstrated only in the Compensated Imaging System, and development programs are required to prove its utility in the other applications.

BIBLIOGRAPHY

Papers covering many aspects of adaptive optics were published in the *Journal of the Optical Society of America* 67 (March 1977).

Hardy, J. W. Active Optics: A New Technology for the Control of Light. *Proceedings of the IEEE* 66 (1978): 651–697.

Adaptive Optical Components. *Proceedings of the SPIE* 141 (March 1978).

Adaptive Optical Components II. *Proceedings of the SPIE* 179 (April 1979).

Hardy, J. W. Adaptive Optical Systems Using Discrete Components. In *Conference Proceedings* No. 300, Conference on Special Topics in Optical Propagation. NATO Advisory Group for Aerospace Research and Development, 1981.

9.
Charge-Coupled Device Image Sensors

Morley M. Blouke and James R. Janesick

Introductory Note by Kosta Tsipis

One of the most useful applications of microelectronics has been the development of electro-optical devices that can transform light instantaneously into electric signals. These devices have found immediate use in photoreconnaissance from space.

Once the image of the ground scene is formed by the camera optics on board a reconnaissance satellite, it must be recorded and transmitted to a ground-based facility for analysis and interpretation. The recording can be done on photographic film, which must then be processed, either on board, in a manner similar to the way a Polaroid camera develops its film, for transmission via a system like a television camera, or else at a ground station after the film has been ejected and collected in mid-air by specially equipped retrieval aircraft. Both of these methods obviously cause delays in the reception of the pictures and limit the useful life of the satellite, since the cameras eventually run out of film. Now, because of this new microelectronic technology, there is an alternative method of transmission to the ground facilities in real time.

The recording can be done on a two-dimensional array of photo-sensitive electro-optical detectors called charge-coupled devices, or CCDs. An electro-optical detector transforms the amount of light it receives during a short, fixed period of time into a proportional amount of electric charge. Thus the pattern of light creates an electric charge replica of itself on the array of detectors. This pattern is converted to a sequence of numbers, which is then transmitted to a receiver on the ground. Equipment in the ground station transforms the charge replica of the light pattern recorded by the array on the satellite into a picture. Then this process is repeated and a new image is recorded.

When used with large focal length systems, electro-optical arrays can achieve pixel sizes comparable with the best photographic film. The pictures recreated on the ground are as accurate as those from photographic film and also have a much larger dynamic range, which means they do not get over- or under-exposed over a much larger variation of illumination intensity.

This chapter explains how these very useful devices work. It examines the physical reasons behind their remarkable performance characteristics and their advantages over photographic film.

INTRODUCTION

Charge-coupled devices (CCDs) are not new. They have been around for more than a decade. Initially, it was envisioned that their uses would run the gamut of electronic circuitry, from memories to signal processing and from logic circuits to imaging. And indeed, CCDs are capable of performing all these functions. Their memory applications, however, died when they missed the technological "window of opportunity" that existed for them. It simply was not possible at the crucial time to manufacture them cheaply enough to compete with dynamic random access memories (DRAMs).

CCDs are currently making their greatest contribution in the area of visible imaging. They will be used for the imaging sensors in the Wide Field/Planetary Camera on the Space Telescope, for the sensor in the navigation and imaging camera on the Galileo mission to Jupiter, and in the imaging camera on ESA's Giotto mission to Halley's Comet.[1] They are currently being used as the visible-imaging sensors of choice on the world's largest telescopes.

Recently there has been a great deal of interest in the idea of using CCDs for imaging in the soft X-ray part of the electromagnetic spectrum. Charge-coupled devices are being seriously considered as the detectors for the Advanced X-ray Astronomical Facility (AXAF) satellite to be launched within the decade.

The intent of this chapter is to describe the operation of a CCD, to discuss some of the performance parameters that might be expected, and to indicate possible future development of charge-coupled devices as image sensors.

CCD OPERATION

Taking a picture with a CCD can be compared to measuring the rainfall in a field.[2] First, distribute buckets in a rectangular array over a field. After it has rained, measure the quantity of water in each bucket by shifting the entire array of buckets towards a conveyor belt located at one end of the field, loading the buckets one row at a time onto the belt, which takes them to a metering station where the amount of rain collected in each bucket is measured. In this manner, the distribution of rain among the buckets can be evaluated and a detailed picture of the rainfall over the whole of the field be obtained.

The fundamental building block of the charge-coupled device, corresponding to the rain bucket, is the MOS capacitor. The MOS capacitor has a p-type silicon substrate; on top of the substrate a layer of silicon dioxide, on the order of 100 nm, is grown. This is followed by a metal or polysilicon gate deposition. If one now applies a negative potential to the gate, then holes, which are the majority carrier in the p-type silicon, will be attracted to the interface between the silicon and the oxide. If a small ac signal is now applied to the device, and one asks the question, "What is the capacitance of this structure?" the result is given by the expression

$$C_{ox} = k\epsilon_0 A/t \tag{1}$$

This is just the expression for the capacitance of two parallel plates of area A, separated by a dielectric of dielectric constant $k\epsilon_0$ and thickness t, and corresponds to the oxide capacitance of the device.[3]

If, on the other hand, one applies a positive bias to the gate, holes are driven away from the surface, leaving behind the uncompensated, negatively charged acceptor atoms that form a depletion region. If one again measures the capacitance of this structure, one finds that in this case the capacitance is given by the series combination of the oxide capacitor mentioned above, and the parallel plate capacitor whose plates are separated by the thickness of the depletion region. Thus,

$$C_T^{-1} = (1/C_{ox} + 1/C_{dep})$$

$$= (t/k\epsilon_0 + d/k\epsilon_{si})/A \tag{2}$$

As time increases, electrons will slowly be thermally generated in the various regions of the substrate, and at the surface. These electrons will collect in an inversion layer at the silicon dioxide interface. At the same time, the depletion region shrinks so that the total charge (electrons plus acceptors) remains constant. The exact number of electrons that can be accommodated in the inversion layer depends upon the details of the doping profile and the potential applied to the gate.

In well-formed MOS capacitors, the time it takes to generate the inversion layer thermally may be of the order of tens of seconds. It is this fact, along with the property of the device for storing charge, that makes the MOS capacitor useful for fabricating a CCD imager, since the device cannot tell the difference between an optically generated and a thermally generated electron.

To make a CCD, a number of these MOS capacitors are assembled in a linear array. There are several ways in which to fabricate the capacitors that form the CCD.[4] Conceptually simplest is the three-phase device, which is the manner in which the device was first implemented. In the three-phase device, a number of gates are arranged next to each other in a row and every third gate is connected to the same clock driver. The basic cell in the CCD, which corresponds to one pixel, consists of a triplet of these gates, each separately connected to a $\phi1$, $\phi2$, or $\phi3$ clock. If one now biases, for example, the phase $\phi1$ clock high (e.g., 10 V) then a depletion region will be created beneath each $\phi1$ gate (see Figure 9.1). These depletion regions beneath the $\phi1$ gates represent regions of lower electrostatic potential relative to the unbiased neighboring gates. Thus, potential wells are formed that collect the signal charge.

Figure 9.1 schematically shows how the charge can be moved in a three-phase CCD. At time t_0, the potential in the $\phi1$ clocks is held high and the wells are formed under the $\phi1$ gates. At t_1, the $\phi2$ clocks also go high, forming the same well under the $\phi2$ gates that exists under the $\phi1$ gates. The signal charge that has been collected now divides between the two wells. Note that a potential barrier between pixels still exists under the $\phi3$ gates. At time t_2, the $\phi1$ clock is returned to ground and this action transfers to the wells beneath the $\phi2$ gates. In the same way, the charge is transferred from the $\phi2$ to the $\phi3$ gates, and from there to the next $\phi1$ gate. Thus, the charge has been moved one entire pixel in one 3-phase clock cycle. The process involves the creation of wells and barriers, which are manipulated and maintained by applying the appropriate voltages to the gates at appropriately sequenced times. Note also that by interchanging any two of the clocks, the charge in the 3-phase device can be made to move in the opposite direction.

There exist other possible configurations by which to fabricate a CCD. These include a 4-phase process, a 2-phase and a single-phase or virtual-phase process. The operation of these devices is similar to that of the 3-phase device in that they all require the generation of potential barriers and wells, either internally during the fabrication process or externally with the gates.[4]

A CCD area imager can be thought of as an array of serial shift registers. The image-forming section is covered with closely spaced columns, called channels, in which the signal charge is collected. The channels are separated by channel stops which prevent the spread of the signal charge from one channel into another. The columns are subdivided into pixels (buckets) in the manner described above, by a series of parallel gates that run perpendicular to the array of channels. Each row of pixels (i.e., one pixel per column) is controlled by one set of these parallel gates.

The part of the conveyor belt is played by another serial shift register, a channel oriented at right angles to the channels of the imaging array. This register is isolated from the imaging array by a transfer gate and is located so that exactly one pixel in this serial register sits below one column of the imaging array. At the end of the serial shift register is an output amplifier

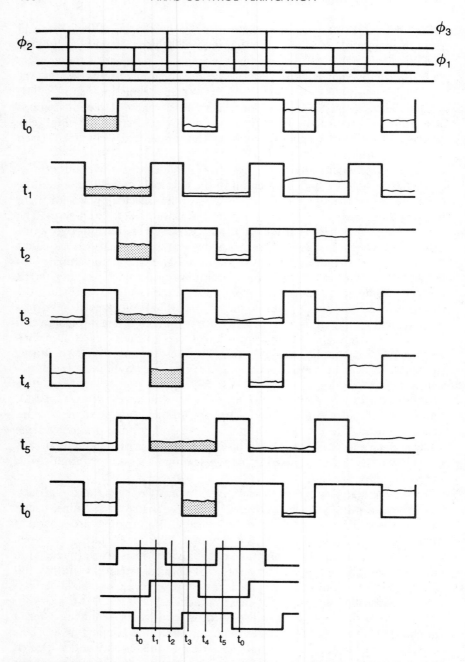

FIGURE 9.1. Schematic representation of the working principle of a CCD. The electrical charge is represented here as a free-flowing liquid (dotted areas).

(metering station), which is used to measure the charge collected in each pixel as it is delivered to it by the conveyor-belt-like shift register.

A picture is read out of the device by a succession of shifts through the imaging section. At each shift of the parallel section the last row of pixels passes through the transfer gate and into the serial register. Then, before the next row is shifted, the charge in the output shift register is transferred to the output amplifier. The output of the device is then a pixel-by-pixel, line-by-line serial representation of the scene incident on the device.

CCD PERFORMANCE

A number of criteria can be used to evaluate the performance of an optical sensor. Among these are quantum efficiency, spectral bandwidth, noise, dark current, geometric stability and fidelity, dynamic range, and linearity. For all of these criteria, the CCD is preferable to film. In this section, we will discuss some aspects of current CCD performance. The emphasis will be on data taken with the Texas Instruments 800×800 pixel 3-phase image.[1]

Spectral Response

One of the principal advantages of the CCD imager over many other optical sensors is the enormous spectral bandwidth over which the device can be operated. In this bandwidth, it is possible to achieve high quantum efficiencies (defined as the ratio of the number of signal electrons generated and collected to the number of incident photons). Figure 9.2 compares the spectral response of several common optical detectors with that of the CCD. As may be seen from the figure, the quantum efficiency of the CCD exceeds by more than an order of magnitude the quantum efficiencies of the other electronic sensors in the common regions of mutual sensitivity. The CCD is about 70 times more efficient, that is, more sensitive, in the visible region than film. In addition, the CCD is responsive to wavelengths in the region 750 to 1100 nm, where most of the other sensors are essentially blind.

At the short end of the spectrum (shortward of 400 nm), where the typical CCD loses sensitivity, there are two techniques used to improve the response. By thinning the substrate beneath the device to approximately 10 μm and illuminating the device from the backside, one can achieve reasonably high quantum efficiencies down to about 300 nm. In a technique developed for the devices to be used on the Space Telescope, it is possible to extend this response down to at least 58.4 nm. This technique involves the application of an ultraviolet sensitive phosphor to the backside of the thinned CCD. The phosphor, which fluoresces in the 500 nm range, converts the incident UV photons to a longer wavelength in which the CCD is much more efficient.

As mentioned in the introduction, recent work has been done on the use of CCDs for soft x-ray imaging. Indeed, experiments indicate that it is possible to image with the CCD from the XUV into the soft X-ray regime, that is, from about 15 eV (83 nm) to beyond 10 keV (0.12). In the soft X-ray region, from about 500 eV to 10 keV, not only can an image be formed, but the energy of the incident photon can be resolved. This provides the opportunity to construct a two-dimensional imaging spectrometer.

Thus, the useful spectral bandwidth of the charge-coupled device can be extended from the soft X-ray region (0.1 nm) through the XUV, UV, and visible regions to the near infrared (1,100 nm). This far exceeds the useful bandwidth for most other optical sensors.

Dark Current

One of the most important parameters of electronic image sensors is the dark current. This quantity is the "signal" that is measured by the device in the absence of any external signal. The dark current is usually due to thermally liberated electrons within the device structure and is an inherent limi-

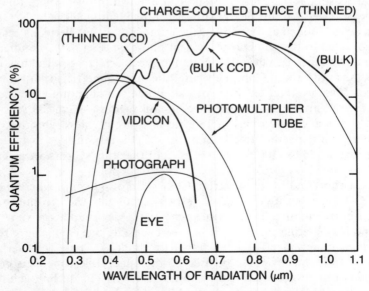

FIGURE 9.2. The spectral response, for example, the efficiency with which various optical devices detect radiation of different frequencies, is given by the various curves in this figure.

tation on the performance of the device. The principal concern with dark current is that this is equivalent to shot noise, which, when integrated over a long enough time, can dominate the background noise and ultimately limit the sensitivity of the device.

For CCD imagers there are basically three sources of dark current. These result from

1. thermal generation and diffusion of electrons from the neutral substrate;
2. thermal generation of electrons in the depletion region itself; and
3. thermal generation of electrons in the surface states at the silicon-silicon dioxide interface.

Of these sources, the contribution of the surface states is the largest at room temperature. This current can be expressed as

$$J_{SS} = CT^{3/2} \cdot \exp(-E_G/2kT) \tag{3}$$

where C is a constant, T is the absolute temperature, k is Boltzmann's constant, and E_G is the silicon energy bandgap.

Measurements of the dark current from room temperature to $-100°C$ have been performed on selected three-phase devices. The results of one set of such measurements are shown in Figure 9.3. The solid line is the calculated generation rate based on Eq. (3), given above, and the measured value of the dark current at room temperature. The integration times required to do the measurements below $-90°C$ are of 50-hours duration and illustrate the difficulty of the measurement. For example, the average time to collect, on the average, one electron per pixel at $-95°C$ is 200 seconds. The departure of the curve from a straight line below $-100°C$ is believed to be due to charge, stored in the oxide, being slowly but continuously released into the CCD wells.

At room temperature, typical values of the dark current are in the 1 to 10 nA/cm^2 for non-virtual phase devices. Virtual phase devices, because of the way in which they operate by sealing off the surface, can exhibit dark currents that are usually in the 100 to 300 pA/cm^2 range. For a 1 nA/cm^2 device with 20 μm pixels at room temperature, this corresponds to the generation of about 2.5×10^4 electrons/pixel/sec.

Noise

In addition to dark current, a second quantity of major importance in the evaluation of an imager is the fundamental noise floor of the device. Figure 9.4 presents a curve of RMS (root-mean-square) noise as a function of signal level for a 20 × 20 pixel array. The noise is defined as the standard

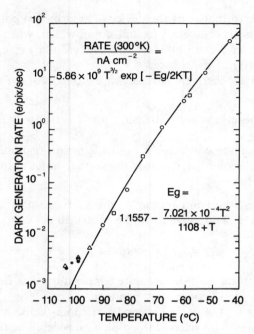

FIGURE 9.3. Variation of dark current, for example, unwanted and unavoidable noise of the detector, as a function of temperature.

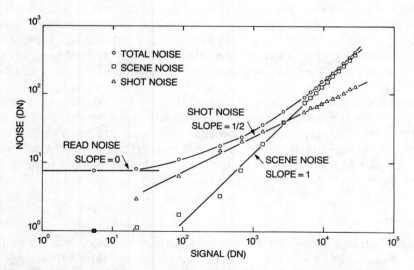

FIGURE 9.4. Contribution of various sources of noise to the total noise of the system as a function of signal intensity.

deviation of the signal from the mean value in the array. With the charge-coupled device there are three regions of interest in the noise curve, as is illustrated in Figure 9.4. These regions are

1. the read noise floor;
2. the shot noise regime; and
3. the pixel nonuniformity regime.

The read noise floor represents the noise associated with the readout circuitry, that is, the one-chip output amplifier. Typical values are in the range of 40 electrons for RCA chips, to near 10 electrons for the Space Telescope chips, to about 4 electrons with the new chips from the General Electric Company, Ltd., of Great Britain. This means that as the device is being read out under low light level or zero illumination conditions, there will be an uncertainty in the quantity of charge in each pixel given by this number of electrons. All these data are for a data rate of 50–100 kilopixels/sec. The noise can be expected to increase by the square root of the data bandwidth.

As the signal level increases, the noise becomes dominated by the shot noise on the signal itself. This is the middle regime of the curve in Figure 9.4 and is characterized by a slope of 1/2. The slope 1/2 arises because, in the case of shot noise, the noise is proportional to the square root of the signal level.

At high signal levels, the noise depends linearly on the signal. This is due to nonuniformities in the pixel response. During the chip fabrication, processing errors of photomask misalignment, etching variations, and, if thinned, variations in the thinning process will cause each pixel to have its own characteristic charge collection volume and its own characteristic quantum efficiency. When the device is uniformly illuminated, a scene noise results because of these pixel-to-pixel nonuniformities.

Linearity

In general, for imaging devices the output signal can be expressed in a power series involving the input signal. In the simplest cases this can take the form

$$S = KE^\gamma + K' \tag{4}$$

where S is the output signal, K is a constant, E is the input signal, raised to the γ power, and K' is the dark current, or system offset. Gamma (γ) is a measure of the linearity of the device. Because the photoelectric effect is an extremely linear process as a function of energy, CCDs are as a result also very linear devices.

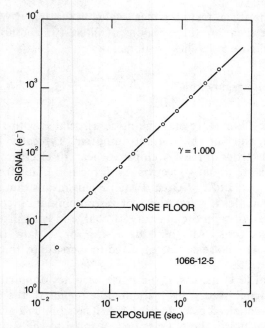

FIGURE 9.5. Illustration of the extraordinary linearity of CCD response to signals over an intensity range of three orders of magnitude.

Figure 9.5 illustrates the linearity of a CCD at low light levels. Detailed measurements of linearity using both point sources and diffuse sources have shown that the devices are linear over most of their useful range, that is, $\gamma = 1.000 \pm 0.002$, making them some of the most linear electro-optical transducers known.

The importance of the linearity of these devices cannot be overstated. This fact permits particularly simple computer algorithms to be used to remove pixel nonuniformities easily and accurately. For example, Figure 9.6A illustrates a raw CCD image of a uniform field, and B is the corresponding image with the nonuniformity removed.

The algorithm used to remove the nonuniformities is simply

$$Q_i = \mu_c (b_i / a_i) \tag{5}$$

Here Q_i is the corrected value of the signal in pixel i, μ_c is the mean value of the calibration frame, b_i is the value of the raw data for pixel i, and a_i is the value of the signal in the calibration frame. For CCD imagers that are

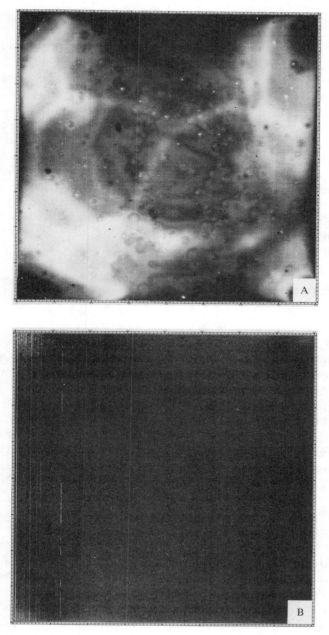

FIGURE 9.6. Illustration of the ability to "clean up" the picture obtained by a CCD by correcting for local nonuniformities of response across the array. This approach would not be possible if the response of the array were not as linear as shown in Figure 9.5.

blemish-free, the resultant corrected image contains only the random noise present in the raw and calibration frames.

Note in Figure 9.5 with the pixel-to-pixel nonuniformities removed, the signal-to-noise ratio of the device is limited by the shot noise on the input signal over most of the device's dynamic range. This is the best performance that one can expect to achieve, corresponding to the background-limited infrared performance (BLIP) of infrared detectors.

By comparison, photographic film has a logarithmic response above its threshold, while vidicons typically have a light transfer curve that must be approximated by a second- or third-order polynomial in the input signal. Reduction of such data and the extraction of accurate results are, of course, very expensive in computer time. With film, one can do photometry at the 5% level; with vidicons at the 1% level. With CCDs one can expect to do photometry at the 0.5% level.[5] The principal reasons for the CCD's ability to do photometry at that level are the linearity of the device and the accuracy of the calibration process.

Other Properties

One of the properties of CCDs that is held in common with all solid-state, self-scanned sensors is their geometric stability and fidelity. This is a result of the fact that the position and size of each pixel are fixed for all time when they are manufactured. Because the device utilizes a self-scan readout and the position of each pixel is fixed, there can be no pincushion or other nonlinear readout effects usually associated with an electron-beam-addressed device.

The fact that the pixels stay fixed in space and are all equal in size makes the CCD the most natural input device for computer analysis of data, where accurate spatial quantization of the input data is important.

One parameter that is peculiar to the CCD is the charge transfer efficiency (CTE). This parameter is a measure of the ability of the device to transfer charge from one well to the neighboring well. Typically, for well made, buried-channel devices, the CTE will be in the range of 0.99999/transfer or greater. This means that for a 2-phase device of, for example, 1,000 elements on a side, 96% of the charge collected in the pixel farthest removed from the output will remain in the pixel at the end of the process of transferring to the output (4,000 transfers). The rest is lost in the transfer process and dribbles out in the later, trailing pixels.

The well capacity of a CCD is the maximum quantity of charge that can be stored in a CCD pixel without spilling over into neighboring pixels. This quantity is dependent on the physical size of the pixel and varies for typical devices from 30 to 50,000 electrons for the Space Telescope devices with small pixels, to on the order of 0.5 to 1 million electrons for the larger pixel devices. Thus, the linear dynamic range of CCDs, expressed as the maximum well capacity divided by the noise floor, is from 3,000 to more than 10,000. For vidicons the dynamic range is about 1,000, whereas for film it is much less, on the order of 50 to 300.

THE FUTURE

The CCD is at a very exciting stage of its development and can offer to the user performance characteristics that only a few years ago would have seemed impossible. Of the performance parameters mentioned above, there are three that merit additional attention. These important parameters are the quantum efficiency, the read noise, and the charge transfer efficiency.

Quantum Efficiency

The use of the CCD as an imager outside of the visible region of the spectrum, has only recently begun to be appreciated. As mentioned above, preliminary results to date indicate that the device is capable of responding over the very large spectral bandwidth of from 0.1 nm to beyond 1,000 nm. This opens up new scientific opportunities in the fields of biology, medicine, laboratory plasma diagnostics, and a host of other physical and astronomical applications in the UV, XUV, and X-ray regimes.

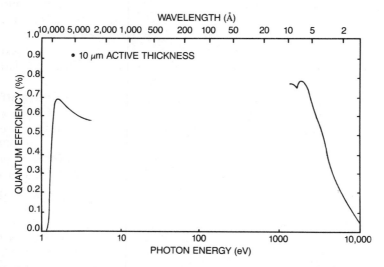

FIGURE 9.7. Quantum efficiency, for example, the fraction of energy of a photon that is transformed to electrical signal as a function of the photon energy (see text for missing portion of the curve between 6 and 1000 eV).

Figure 9.7 shows the present quantum efficiency capabilities of the 800 × 800, 3-phase CCD. Absolute quantum efficiency tests are now being performed from 6 eV to 1 keV in order to complete the figure. Theoretical absorption calculations in conjunction with spot quantum efficiency measurements indicate that these devices can achieve good response over this entire range if properly prepared. In particular, this means the proper preparation of the back surface of the thinned device.

Current research is also extending the quantum efficiency measurements at the high end of the X-ray spectrum, beyond 10 keV. Proper selection of the CCD thickness will enhance the quantum efficiency in this region, and make the devices potentially attractive as detectors for applications in nuclear medicine.

CCDs have also been considered as charged particle detectors in the area of high-energy physics. Any astronomer who has used such a device behind a telescope on a mountain top will testify to the ability of the device to detect cosmic rays. At least one proposal has been seriously forwarded to construct a particle detector for one of the high-energy accelerators.

Read Noise

As stated previously, the read noise is the pixel-to-pixel uncertainty in the measurement of the signal. It is typically expressed in RMS (root-mean-square) electrons and sets a lower limit on the dynamic range of the sensor. A low read noise floor allows the user to detect and accurately quantify smaller charge packets within a pixel. As mentioned above, low noise floors are typically around 10 e−, with lower noise floors being achievable if proper and careful signal processing is utilized. The noise floor is usually set by the noise characteristics of the on-chip output amplifier. Little work has been done in the past on the optimization of the signal-to-noise ratio of this output stage and future work in this area may succeed in driving the noise floor to the 1 e− level or below. This would be a major achievement and would be welcomed by all scientific users working with low level signals. At present, it is possible to resolve 6 keV X-ray lines with a resolution of about 200 eV, as shown in Figure 9.8. Thus, CCDs can both resolve in energy the individual X-ray transitions and define the spatial location of the source.

Charge Transfer

The charge transfer efficiency of the best available devices is very high, in the range of 0.999995 or better. However, even these devices, as with most others, exhibit a particular region of the device that traps more than the usual amount of charge. This charge comes out of the device in several

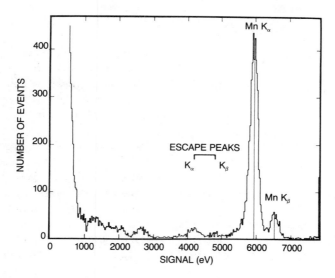

FIGURE 9.8. Example of the ability of CCDs to detect X-rays with good energy as well as spatial resolution.

trailing pixels. For example, the 800 × 800 device is capable of transferring the charge generated by a K_α photon (1,600 e−) over 4,800 transfers, leaving behind on the order of 30 e− in the form of a deferred charge tail, which is spread over several pixels. This problem can be eliminated by using a flat field exposure to prepare the CCD for readout. This, in essence, supplies a flat zero bias charge of 30 e− to the device. Unfortunately, this bias charge will degrade the noise floor of the device due to its own shot noise. A 30 e− bias charge will add a noise of 5.5 e−. When the read noise itself is 10 e−, the addition of 5.5 e−, in quadrature, is not particularly significant. However, if noise floors of 1 e− can be achieved, it becomes obvious that the addition of a bias charge of even 30 e− to the device cannot be tolerated. It therefore becomes a requirement that the charge transfer properties throughout all regions of the device be excellent. That such transfer efficiencies may be possible is illustrated by the CTE properties of the 800 × 800 device. In the serial register of this device, it is possible to transfer a signal over 2,500 transfers with a deferred charge of less than 10 e−. It will be interesting to see the ultimate limit of charge transfer properties of future devices.

SUMMARY

Charge-coupled devices are just now beginning to prove their value. Because of their extremely high quantum efficiencies and wide optical bandwidth, they have established themselves as the detector of choice on the major telescopes of the world.

The same properties that make these devices desirable as astronomical sensors make them attractive and useful as detectors for other systems. Their all-solid-state construction is suited to applications in which size and power constraints are important. Cameras using these devices have already been built with a volume of less than eight cubic inches. The fact that the devices have such a wide optical response means that the same scene can be imaged in several optical bands with the *same* sensor, eliminating the tedious task of geometrically scaling the data to force the images from several different sensors to match. In addition, the fact that the pixel size and position are fixed once and for all at the time of manufacture means that no correction of the data needs to be made for distortion in the detector, as with other electronic sensors.

Because the output of the CCD comes in spatially quantized charge packets, the data can be immediately digitized and stored for future use. This, coupled with the intrinsic linearity of the device, allows one to conceive easily of performing real-time, on-board data normalization and signal processing involving frame-to-frame differencing or edge enhancement using neighborhood operators on the data. These are real advantages that are not available to film.

The one advantage that still accrues to film is that of large area coverage. However, techniques are currently being examined and developed to create mosaics of these devices using optics, fiber optics, and simple physical abutment.

REFERENCES

1. Blouke, M. M., J. R. Janesick, J. E. Hall, M. W. Cowens, and P. J. May. 800 × 800 Charge-coupled Device Image Sensor. *Optical Engineering* 22 (1983): 640.
2. This analogy was originally conceived by J. Kristian and presented in the article, Kristian, J., and M. M. Blouke. Charge-coupled Devices in Astronomy. *Scientific American* 247 (October 1982): 67.
3. Sze, S. M. *Physics of Semiconductor Devices.* New York: John Wiley & Sons, 1969.
4. General references to CCD operation are: Sequin, C. H., and M. F. Tompsett. *Charge Transfer Devices.* New York: Academic Press, 1975. Melen, R., and D. D. Buss. *Charge-Coupled Devices: Technology and Applications.* New York: IEEE Press, John Wiley & Sons, 1977.
5. Westphal, J. A. California Institute of Technology, Pasadena, CA, private communication.

10.

Image Enhancement by Digital Computer

B. R. Hunt

Introductory Note by Kosta Tsipis

In the past fifteen years, digital computers have made possible significant improvements in the quality of photographic pictures, increasing the amount of information that can be extracted from the images. This chapter reviews and discusses a number of techniques for the enhancement of imagery by digital computer. The *resolution* of an image cannot be improved by such techniques, but blurring, obscuration and poor contrast can all be remedied. As a result, pictures, be they of the moons of Jupiter or a Soviet shipyard, can be made "crisper," making recognition of the features of a scene easier or more assured. By itself, digital image processing (DIP) is an interesting technique, but when it is combined with the intrinsically digital output of charge-coupled devices and with improvements in the resolution and multispectral images of a scene, it makes extraction of information from pictures practical where it otherwise would be impossible.

INTRODUCTION

During the past fifteen years it would have been difficult (perhaps impossible) to have been a regular reader of newspapers and magazines and not to have seen remarkable pictures of the Moon, Mars, Saturn, Jupiter, and a score of their satellites. The pictures released by NASA were obtained by remote satellite spacecraft, and they are remarkable in their quality and depiction of detail on our planetary neighbors. What the casual viewer of these images does not know, however, is that these pictures are the product of substantial amounts of computing. A variety of digital image processing techniques are often applied by NASA to the images received from the spacecraft. The finished or "enhanced" images are often a dramatic improvement over the original or "raw" images. It is these improved images of which the public is aware, rather than the original unprocessed images.

Technology is ubiquitous. What can be done to improve the imagery from Mars can also be done to the images acquired by a military reconnaissance sensor. Thus, the questions arise: what is digital image processing, and how is it to be applied to imagery? Answering these questions is the purpose of this article.

It is an element of open public discussion in the news media that the United States possesses various reconnaissance systems that are capable of obtaining images of regions to which free access is denied. The exact nature of the reconnaissance systems is also widely speculated upon in the news media. However, the government of the United States does not formally admit to any of the various speculations, nor does it offer information at any open official level about the nature of the sensor systems, nor does it make any official admission concerning the quality and nature of the images obtained by any possible sensor system. Therefore, there are no openly available *hard data* concerning the utility or applicability of any such sensors in general, or the utility and applicability of such sensors in verification of arms control in particular.

In arms control, the applicability of digital image enhancement is to verification. If one knows that NASA can improve the quality of spacecraft images from Jupiter, then one can speculate about applications to improve the quality of images produced by sensor systems employed for the purposes of arms control. Because the U.S. government does not officially acknowledge any such sensors or their operating characteristics, it is important to note that any discussion of this general area can only be speculation — albeit intelligent speculation guided by basic principles of optics, engineering, and computing. All the material in this chapter is based on publicly available basic research in methods of image processing.

SOURCES OF DEGRADATION IN IMAGERY

We begin by defining more precisely what we mean by image enhancement and image restoration. By *image enhancement* we mean any process that leads to an improvement in the visual quality of an image. The key words are "visual quality," because they imply a subjective judgment that the image has been improved. On the other hand, *image restoration* is more specific. In image restoration we are concerned first with identifying a specific class (or classes) of degradation effects in the image formation process that created the image and second with removing those degradation effects. Thus, we "restore" the image from effects of degradation.

Image enhancement often reduces to a "bag of tricks," that is, the development of a repertoire of processes that can be applied to an image and that are known generally or usually to have a beneficial effect on image quality. However, image restoration is much more precise. To carry out image restoration, a mathematical model or description of image degradation effects is created. The creation of an algorithm for image restoration can then be posed as the solution of the equations of the degradation model for the values of the restored image.

Image restoration is a much more scientific process than image enhancement. The usage of digital image processing to improve imagery is usually carried out by implementation of various schemes of image restoration.[1] However, the term "image enhancement" is more widespread in both technical and general literature and is often applied to situations that are more accurately described as image restoration. Certainly processing of the highest quality to produce an image with the greatest fidelity to the original objects being imaged represents tasks in image restoration. In the remainder of this chapter we will follow the popular (but erroneous) practice of using "image enhancement" all-inclusively to refer even to what would more accurately be described as "image restoration."

Before attempting to remove sources of degradation in images obtained by a sensor system, it is first necessary to describe the processes that occur in image formation that can degrade an image and thereby make the process of image enhancement (restoration) desirable. There are three broad classes of image degradation effects:

1. Object and scene radiometry,
2. Optical image formation mechanisms in the sensor, and
3. Image detector mechanisms in the sensor focal plane.

Object and Scene Radiometry

Observed objects are described as a two-dimensional pattern of reflectivity $r(x,y)$. This pattern is illuminated by a solar flux, I_0, which for simplicity we assume to be constant but which can also be a spatial distribution in the case of complex haze or cloud cover. The product $I_0 r(x,y)$ is attenuated by scattering in suspended aerosols in the atmosphere (water, vapor, dust). In addition, aerosols directly scatter some fraction of the solar flux back into the optical axis of the sensor. Thus the total flux observed by a sensor system is:

$$s(x,y) = \alpha_1 I_0 + \alpha_2 \alpha_3 I_0 r(x,y) \tag{1}$$

where α_1 is the scattering fraction of solar flux into the sensor, α_2 is the coefficient that accounts for attenuation of the reflected flux, and α_3 represents attenuation of incident solar flux.

Detection of objects is strongly dependent upon the *visible contrast*, that is, the relative change in shades of gray at the boundaries between two objects. When the change between two shades of gray at an object boundary approaches 1% to 2% of the maximum image brightness, the human visual system loses the ability to distinguish the boundary and, hence, to detect or perceive the object.

The importance of contrast in radiometry can be understood in terms of Eq. (1). Suppose that the magnitude of the $r(x,y)$ term is small compared to the term $\alpha_1 I_0$. The control of exposure* for image formation in the sensor must be based upon the maximum visible flux, which is controlled by the term $\alpha_1 I_0$ under our above supposition. If the exposure is set to accommodate $\alpha_1 I_0$ the result will be to capture an image that has little variation in contrast. The term $\alpha_2 \alpha_3 I_0 r(x,y)$ being small compared to $\alpha_1 I_0$, its dynamic range of contrast is compressed relative to the $\alpha_1 I_0$ term. The result is a *low-contrast* image. If the contrast compression is severe enough, the object details in $r(x,y)$ may become invisible to the unaided eye.

Inherent photon noise also becomes a problem in low contrast imaging. Since photons obey a Poisson law, then the standard deviation of photons at the sensor is:

$$\sigma_{\text{sensor}} = \overline{(\alpha_1 I_0 + \alpha_2 \alpha_3 I_0 r(x,y))}^{1/2} \tag{2}$$

where the overbar represents ensemble flux average and the square-root is usual for Poisson statistics. Obviously if σ_{sensor} is of the same order of magnitude as the $r(x,y)$ term, then the low-contrast image is further corrupted by noise. Image noise is visible as "salt and pepper" flecks overlaying the visible scene. The "snow" affecting TV reception in a fringe broadcast area is a fine example of image noise.

Low contrast imaging is a degradation associated with three major phenomena. First, the inherent reflectivity variations may be small. Second, the incident flux I_0 may be small, for example, objects within the shadow of a cloud or in the shadow of another larger object. Third, the transmission coefficients α_2 and α_3 may be small and/or the aerosol scattering coefficient, α_1 may be large (relative to α_2 and α_3).

Image Formation Mechanisms in the Sensor

The flux that propagates from the scene to the sensor is collected by an optical system and brought to concentration in a focal plane. The image within the focal plane can be described by a specific two-dimensional convolution, which we do not prove here. The resulting equation is:

---

*"exposure" is a term that is valid for both film-based imaging or imaging by electro-optical sensors such as charge-coupled devices.[2]

$$g(x,y) = \int_{-\infty}^{\infty} \int_{-\infty}^{\infty} h(x - x_1, y - y_1)s(x_1, y_1)dx_1 dy_1 \tag{3}$$

where $s(x,y)$ is as described in Eq. (1), $g(x,y)$ is the image observed in the focal plane, and $h(x,y)$ is the image formation point-spread-function of the optical system. (See Reference 3 for details in the derivation of Eq. 3). It is possible to prove that Eq. (3) has an equivalent description in the Fourier frequency domain,

$$G(u,v) = H(u,v)S(u,v) \;, \tag{4}$$

where G, H, S are the two-dimensional Fourier transforms of the corresponding quantities.[3]

The important effects in image formation are obviously embodied by the *point-spread-function* $h(x,y)$ or its Fourier transform, $H(u,v)$. If $H(u,v)$ approaches zero for any values of (u,v), then for those values of (u,v) no information from the objects of the scene, $S(u,v)$, are transferred to the image $G(u,v)$. Even when $H(u,v)$ does not approach zero, if it becomes small relative to other values, the loss of contrast at those spatial frequencies represents an inability to detect object structure, as discussed above. Image degradations which can be present either singly or in combinations in the image formation process are:

1. Diffraction optical effects. Every optical aperture has a cut-off beyond which no finer object resolution is possible. At spatial frequencies below that cutoff, the magnitude of $H(u,v)$ can be so small as to cause an effective loss of information.[1,3]

2. Optical aberrations, such as an out-of-focus lens, can cause attenuation of spatial frequency structure and effective loss of information.

3. Relative motion during the period of exposure between objects being imaged and the focal plane can cause a loss of object structure in the image.

Image Detector Mechanisms in the Image Focal Plane

A detector is a mechanism that intercepts the flux concentrated in the focal plane by the optics. The detector is itself a source of degradations that are similar to the types of degradations previously discussed. The degradations are:

Detector Transfer Function. The detection mechanism, whether film or semiconductor, integrates a finite area of the image to produce a response. This integration can be described by an equation similar to Eq. (3) above, but with a different function h. The Fourier transform of the detector function that replaces h in Eq. (3) is referred to as the Detector Transfer Function.

Detector Sensitivity. Detectors are not devices with perfect sensitivity to photons. Most imaging detectors require more than one photon to produce a unit of detector response, for example, a photo electron or a developed grain of silver in a film. The *detector quantum efficiency* (DQE) measures this sensitivity, and if the DQE is small, then the loss of contrast occurs, particularly in the presence of detector noise.

Detector Noise. No detector is perfect. The capturing of image information is always accompanied by random uncertainty in the image information. In detectors that capture image information the noise is usually due to electronic thermal noise (for electronic or semi-conductor image detectors) or the random size and shape of silver grains in a photographic emulsion.

For general reading and references of the modeling of image degradation effects the reader should consult Andrews and Hunt.[1]

The basic equation of the image formation can be summarized as:

$$g(x,y) = \int_{-\infty}^{\infty} \int_{-\infty}^{\infty} h_c(x - x_1, y - y_1)s(x_1, y_1)dx_1 dy_1 + n(x,y) \qquad (5)$$

where h_c is a composite spread function of a number of effects (optics, motion, detector), $s(x,y)$ is as given in Eq. (1), and $n(x,y)$ encompasses all noise sources. Equation (4) assumes the image detector is linear in response. If the detector is nonlinear (photographic film is the most prominent example of a nonlinear detector), then the equation for the image recorded on the detector becomes:

$$g(x,y) = \phi\left[\int_{-\infty}^{\infty} \int_{-\infty}^{\infty} h_c(x - x_1, y - y_1)s(x_1, y_1)dx_1 dy_1\right] + n(x,y) \qquad (6)$$

where $\phi[\cdot]$ is a function that describes the nonlinear detector response.

Equations (1), (5), and/or (6) describe mathematically the image restoration (enhancement) problem. Given the image $g(x,y)$ we must infer $s(x,y)$, which in turn must be used to infer $r(x,y)$. This is *not* an easy problem. Students in mathematics recognize Eq. (5) as a Fredholm integral equation of the first kind, and such equations are notoriously difficult to solve. It is this problem, as well as the even more difficult problem in Eq. (6), which represents the challenge in image restoration.

TECHNIQUES OF DIGITAL IMAGE RESTORATION AND ENHANCEMENT

The employment of a computer for image restoration/enhancement must begin with conversion of the image onto a form suitable for digital computation.* This conversion consists of two steps: scanning the image and extracting samples from the image, each sample representing the image intensity at a particular point; and quantizing the extracted samples into a digital number which can be entered directly into a computer or recorded on a computer storage medium such as magnetic tape.

The extraction and conversion of image information into digital form is governed by some basic constraints. There is an upperbound or maximum spacing between samples which must be adhered to, or the sampling process will lose information. Likewise, each sample must be quantized to a minimum number of bits in a binary computer representation or the quantization process will introduce an unacceptable amount of error.[4]

The computer operations that can be applied for image enhancement can be divided into two broad classes: *point operations* and *neighborhood operations*. (The dividing line is not precise. It is possible to modify a point operator with neighborhood statistics.) A single sample from an image is usually referred to as a picture element, or *pixel* in the common technical vernacular. Point operations can be characterized as operating upon a single pixel to produce an altered value of the pixel, that is, a single spatial picture sample has its value changed without reference to any other picture sample. By contrast, a neighborhood operation will alter the value of each pixel as a function of the pixels which surround each pixel within some neighborhood or spatial region.

To understand some simple bases for point operations, consider the radiometry in Eq. (1). Because $r(x,y)$ is the desired object reflectivity that may be obscured by atmospheric conditions, then solving Eq. (1) for $r(x,y)$ yields:

$$r(x,y) = \frac{s(x,y) - \alpha_1 I_0}{\alpha_2 \alpha_3 I_0} \tag{7}$$

This equation states that to obtain an estimate of $r(x,y)$ we would subtract an estimate of the reflected flux and then divide by the incident flux times the attenuation coefficients. What makes this a point operation is obvious in this equation. The value of the image in pixel $s(x,y)$ is the input to a calculation that does not require any other pixels neighboring to $s(x,y)$. In fact, because the denominator is fixed by atmospheric conditions, the operation is obviously *linear*.

Point operations need not be linear, of course. Given a pixel at location

---

*Conversion to digital form is required for film imagery. Modern electro-optical sensors, such as CCDs, can be engineered so that their output is intrinsically digital, and no digital conversion is necessary.

(x, y), it is legitimate to consider an arbitrary transformation of the pixel value. Thus, mathematically we express the enhancement as:

$$g_e(x, y) = p[g(x, y)] \ , \tag{8}$$

where $p[\cdot]$ is an arbitrary linear or nonlinear operator and g_e is the pixel value after enhancement. What matters is that the operator $p[\cdot]$ accomplish some desired objective with respect to making scene detail more useful visually. The choice of $p[\cdot]$, therefore, may be closely associated with the nature of the degradation which afflicts the imagery. Point operators are often referred to as *contrast operators* or *contrast alterations* because they function, in a generalized mathematical way, like the contrast adjustments that can be implemented by darkroom photographic technique.

Important categories of point operator processes and the type of degradation they correct are as follows:

Linear Scalings. Operators, similar in form to Eq. (7), can be realized by combinations of additions/subtractions and multiplications by a constant. The correction of degradations such as radiometry errors is obvious, but is also applicable to any type of degradation involving an equation of the type of Eq. (1), for instance, attenuation of the information, plus an added bias term. The actual enhancement need not be recomputed for every pixel. Since pixel intensities are usually quantized at a small number of bits, say 8 bits, the actual results of Eq. (7) can be precomputed, stored in a table, and looked-up from the table for a given pixel intensity.

Non-linear Scalings. The more general point operator $p[\cdot]$ in Eq. (8) has to be chosen to match the type of degradation, which must be corrected. For example, in an overexposed picture a statistical histogram of pixel intensities would be dominated by the largest pixel intensities. Any operation that increases the magnitude of small numbers more in proportion than large numbers would be useful to correct for the overexposure. A logarithm function for $p[\cdot]$, followed by a linear rescaling to preserve dynamic range, would be valid. For an underexposed image, the opposite operation, such as an exponential, would be useful. The actual utility of any nonlinear operation is determined by the extent to which the functional form of $p[\cdot]$ matches a particular form of degradation. For example, if the nonlinear function ϕ in Eq. (6) is known, then it may be removed from the imagery by choosing a function ϕ^{-1} for the operator $p[\cdot]$.

Histogram-Derived Transformations. The discussion in the previous paragraph accentuates the usage of statistics for determining the point operator. The final refinement of this is the histogram equalization operation. A histogram of pixel intensities is accumulated, from which it is always possible to determine a transformation that distributes pixel intensities over the entire dynamic range of intensities in such a way that the transformed intensities occur with equal probability, that is, the histogram of the transformed image is uniform or "flat." The result is an image with very strong accentuation of minor contrast differences.[5]

Human Interaction. Recent developments in computer hardware make it possible to implement any point-operation with a look-up table. The table can be referenced so fast that imagery can be enhanced at the video refresh rate of a conventional color CRT. This in turn means that any operator interaction device can be linked — for example via microprocessor — to mathematical models of enhancement, and the parameters of the enhancement adjusted in real-time. The resultant enhanced image is instantly visible, since the operator adjustment can be used, via the enhancement model, to alter the contents of the look-up table. Thus, the human operator can adjust "knobs" and see the enhanced picture instantly. The knobs may be physically real or only a linkage to a mathematical enhancement model of substantial complexity. However, the ability to instantly view the results of adjusting knobs allows the human operator to optimize visible image quality. A completely mathematical optimization of visible image quality is not possible, of course, because no complete model of human visual response is known. Using the interaction by human and computer enhancement model, no human visual system is needed. Instead, the operator directly optimizes visual quality for the particular enhancement model employed.

As stated above, the second broad class of enhancement is by *neighborhood operations.* The broadest analytical model of a neighborhood operator is given as:

$$g_e(x,y) = \rho[g(x,y)] \quad \text{for } (x,y) \in R \tag{9}$$

where $\rho[\cdot]$ is the functional form defining the neighborhood operator and R is the actual dimension of the neighborhood itself.

The most common neighborhood operation is that of convolution, or weighted averaging. For a set of pixels, we have:

$$g_e(x,y) = \sum_{s=1}^{M} \sum_{r=1}^{N} h(r,s)g(x-r,y-s) \tag{10}$$

where h is a set of MN weights in the average. For the simplest case, $h(r,s) = 1/MN$ for s; thus, we see that Eq. (10) is a moving average. In general, there is a well-developed theory corresponding to Eq. (10), and one can show that it is the sampled-image version of Eq. (3) and that a discrete Fourier transform of Eq. (10) exists which is the discrete (sampled) analogy of the continuous transform seen in Eq. (4).[1,5]

Given the simplicity of the operator in Eq. (10), it is not surprising that what makes the difference is the specification and design of the weights

$h(r,s)$. Equivalently, from the discrete analogy mentioned above we have that:

$$G_e(m,n) = H(m,n)G(m,n) \tag{11}$$

where m,n are discrete frequency indices; in discrete Fourier space, the problem is the design of the Fourier transfer function $H(m,n)$. If the transfer function is appropriately chosen, then a variety of degradations in the imagery may be corrected. The processes that are invoked to design either $h(r,s)$ or $H(m,n)$ belong to the study of the theory of optimal filtering, which we will not attempt to explicate here. (See, for example, the books by Andrews and Hunt[1] or Pratt[5] or Oppenheim and Schafer.[4]) However, for an appropriate optimality criterion in the design of the filter, there exists the implementation of a linear neighborhood operator in the form of either Eq. (10) or (11).

It is important to note that because certain image degradations are expressible in the form of Eq. (3) (or in Eq. 4, which is the Fourier analogy to Eq. 3), the correction for degradations of the form of Eq. (3) is to apply a digital version of a neighborhood operator that is identical in form to the original degradation. The only difference between the h in Eq. (3) and the h in Eq. (10) is the following: Because Eq. (3) describes a degradation process, then the enhancement is achieved by choosing h values for Eq. (10), which are the inverse, *with respect to the moving average operator*, of the h values in Eq. (3). In terms of Fourier descriptions, the $H(m,n)$ values in Eq. (10) must be $1/H(u,v)$ from Eq. (4).

The following types of degradations have been removed from imagery by the simple linear operator of the form of Eq. (10):

Diffraction limit. Although information cannot be obtained beyond the optical diffraction limit of an aperture, substantial loss of image quality occurs for objects that approach in scale the smallest spatial frequency details visible through the aperture. Substantial improvement in image quality is achievable by using a filter which attempts restoration, out to the optical cutoff, of the diffraction limited optical transfer function of an optical system.

Optical aberrations. Many optical aberrations can be described as an equation such as (3). A common example is when the optical system is out of focus. Again, if the optical transfer function of the aberration process is known, it is possible to find a processing by neighborhood operation in the form of Eq. (10) that will correct for the aberration.

Motion. If the optical focal plane and the object are in relative motion and if the motion of the image in the focal plane is rapid during the time the image is being exposed, then the focal plane image will be blurred by the motion. Depending on the complexity of the motion, a transfer function can be written to describe the motion blur. This transfer function can then be used in the form of either Eq. (10) or (11) to restore the image from motion degradation.

Noise filtering. As seen in Eq. (5), noise is present in any real image. The magnitude of the noise is the issue. The noise magnitude is usually quantified by the signal-to-noise ratio (SNR). A typical measure of SNR is the variation in image signal divided by image noise. Using statistical variance as our measure of variation, then:

$$\text{SNR} = \frac{\sigma^2_{\text{image}}}{\sigma^2_{\text{noise}}} \tag{12}$$

When the SNR is large enough, no visible noise effects are perceived. As the SNR drops, the noise becomes visible and objectionable. To reduce the noise effects, a filter of the form of Eq. (10) can be used to average the noise in spatial neighborhood and reduce its visible effects.

Neighborhood operators need not be linear. Again, it is the type of degradation that is most important in choosing and specifying the type of *nonlinear* enhancement operator. One very prominent nonlinear neighborhood operator is the moving median filter. Instead of computing an average of pixels in a moving neighborhood, the median of the pixels in the moving neighborhood is computed. The resulting filter has been shown to be very powerful for removal of certain types of noise. Noise due to isolated defects, such as a scratch in the emulsion of a film, can be removed by a median filter. The median filter has little effect on edge sharpness if properly designed, so that isolated streaks, scratches, or spot flaws can be almost magically removed without affecting other visual properties of the image. This is quite important, because a more conventional noise filter using a moving average will tend to reduce visual sharpness of objects in the image as it smooths out the visible noise.

Other nonlinear filters are based on the nonlinear model of Eq. (6). If the degree of image blur caused by h in Eq. (6) is too great and if the response characteristic ϕ in Eq. (6) is too nonlinear, then the optimum solution of (6) for the undegraded images must be made by a nonlinear operator. The actual rationale for solution involves Bayesian probability analysis, but the actual computation can be shown to be equivalent to linear neighborhood operators combined with nonlinear point operators.[1]

This latter point indicates a more general aspect of image enhancement. Frequently the best improvement of the imagery can not be obtained by a single step. Instead, to produce the optimum results it is necessary to combine several linear and nonlinear operators of both the point and neighborhood type. Again, modern computing technology is quite important, because it is possible to build economical but quite powerful special purpose computers in which a human can interact with the image enhancement processes, choosing and applying the appropriate one at each step. Again, in lieu of a general theory of visual image quality on which to base comprehensive enhancement models, the availability of interactive image computers is essential for optimum improvement of image quality.

THE NECESSITY FOR MORE IMAGE ENHANCEMENT RESEARCH

When the visible improvements in image quality from image enhancement are seen, it is sometimes natural for the non-expert to believe that image enhancement is magic and that there are no limits to the degree of improvement that can be achieved. There are, however, very distinct and basic limits to the degree of improvement in image quality possible. The fundamental limit lies in our ability to deal with an unfavorable SNR. In Eq. (5), as noted above, we are faced with solving a Fredholm integral equation of the first kind in order to restore the image from the degradations. Such equations are ill-conditioned, which means that small errors or uncertainties in the data can be translated into very large errors in the solution. Noise, as in Eq. (5), represents such a source of errors. It is possible to show that many enhancement processes have the effect of amplifying whatever noise is present in the degraded image. If noise amplification is too great, then the enhanced image quality is suppressed by the visually objectionable aspects of the amplified noise.

Noise is a fundamental limit, like that of entropy in thermodynamics. (Indeed, there is legitimate justification for considering any kind of noise in a measurement process as a manifestation in various ways of the Second Law.) Reduction of the uncertainty that noise represents can only be done by the injection of other information into the enhancement paradigm. For example, if one knows the image being enhanced is that of an airplane, then the knowledge about the object represents considerable a priori information that can be added into the enhancement process. But the exact mechanism by which to do this is uncertain. The research necessary to achieve this a priori constraining of restoration options has not been carried out.

Image enhancement/restoration has not been adequately discussed in this short article. Indeed, entire books have been written on the topic.[1] Nevertheless, the discussion has been complete enough to make clear the following points:

1. Image enhancement/restoration is based upon the physics and mathematics of image formation processes. The understanding of these models is the most complete aspect of our theory of image enhancement.

2. Much of image enhancement must be characterized as a "bag of tricks," that is, a selection of techniques that must be applied by a human

analyst. Hopefully, the analyst may have available an interactive image processing computer that will make it possible to optimize the quality of the enhanced image by allowing the analyst to instantly see the results of his enhancement process. However, there is one *great* deficiency to the "bag of tricks" approach. Not all human operators are equally clever or resourceful in using the tricks at their disposal. Consequently, an image that causes one analyst to conclude no enhancement is possible may be treated with great success by another analyst. For images with great significance, such as those which might be used in weapons verification monitoring, it is disturbing to think of the consequences if an analyst failed to produce the optimum visual quality from a given image.

3. The frontiers of image enhancement lie in trying to make better use of marginal imagery, that is, images in which the SNR is so low that current enhancement technology will fail. It is most unfortunate that little research is going on currently in this area. The remarkable successes of image enhancement/restoration have led many to believe that image enhancement is a "solved problem," when only the easiest parts of the problem have been solved as of yet. It is ironic that research on enhancement/restoration is declining at a time when the discussions about weapons control and verification are emphasizing the virtues of obtaining maximum information from an image.

The decline of image enhancement research is a natural consequence of the successes of this technology as well as the perception that perhaps enhancement is not needed. The engineers who specify, design, and build sensor systems always have plans to create a bigger and better sensor, one that produces images of an even higher quality than anything seen so far. In this environment, image enhancement seems of secondary importance. Nonetheless, image enhancement remains of importance. True, each new and improved sensor creates higher quality imagery than its predecessor. Yet no complex sensor system always operates exactly as designed and programmed. Occasionally, it fails in some major or minor way and the resulting image, be it underexposed or out-of-focus or whatever, will be a candidate for image restoration or enhancement. If that particular failure is associated with an image of critical importance to a specific weapons verification problem, then do we not want available the best enhancement technology?

REFERENCES

1. Andrews, H. C. and B. R. Hunt. *Digital Image Restoration.* Englewood Cliffs, NJ: Prentice-Hall, 1977.
2. Hall, J. E. *et al.* A CCD imager for image processing applications, *Proceedings 1978 IEEE Electron Device Meeting*, Washington, DC, Dec. 1978, pp. 415–418.

ARMS CONTROL VERIFICATION

3. Goodman, J. W. *Introduction to Fourier Optics*. New York: McGraw-Hill, 1968.
4. Oppenheim, A. V. and R. Schafer. *Digital Signal Processing*. Englewood Cliffs, NJ: Prentice-Hall, 1972.
5. Pratt, W. K. *Digital Image Processing*. New York: Wiley, 1978.
6. Gonzalez, R. and P. Wintz. *Digital Image Processing*. Reading, MA: Addison-Wesley, 1977.
7. Rosenfeld, A. and A. Kak. *Digital Picture Processing*. New York: Academic Press, 1979.
8. Hall, E. *Digital Image Processing and Recognition*. New York: Academic Press, 1982.

11.
Radar Imaging for Arms Control

Eli Brookner

Introductory Note by Kosta Tsipis

Although photoreconnaissance is an important means of obtaining detailed information about activities inside the Soviet Union (and other countries), it is not sufficient, because there are times when cloud cover and darkness prevent the imaging of ground scenes by the cameras on orbiting satellites.

This gap in our monitoring capabilities is, to a great extent, filled by the imaging properties of specially configured radars carried by satellites. Radar images need no solar illumination of the scene, so they can be made in darkness and through clouds. On the other hand, because the wavelength of radar waves is large compared to that of light waves, the resolution of images made by means of radar waves returned from the reflecting scene is quite poor compared with photoreconnaissance.

Because the resolution of a system is proportional to the ratio of the wavelength divided by the optical aperture or antenna of the receiver, the way to improve the resolution of a radar wave system is to increase the size of the aperture. Radar resolution can in fact be dramatically improved by use of a very large antenna, several hundred meters long. Clearly it is not possible or practical to have a physical antenna of that size on a satellite. But by making use of the satellite's motion with respect to the earth, it is possible to make a physically small antenna appear to the returning radar signals to be an antenna as long as the distance the satellite has travelled during the time it took each wave to travel from the satellite to the ground and back.

This chapter explains the ingenious techniques by which this imaging method can achieve resolutions comparable to those obtained by photographic cameras. The importance to arms control of "synthetic aperture radar" (SAR), as this method is known, and of its inverse, namely the detailed imaging of rapidly moving objects from a stationary radar using similar processing techniques, cannot be overemphasized. SAR permits the monitoring of activities in the Soviet Union in the darkness of the polar night and in the presence of persistent cloud cover. Its inverse, ISAR, allows the detailed imaging of reentry vehicles, satellites and aircraft by stationary radars providing us with valuable information about Soviet tests and activities in space.

135

FIGURE 11.1. TR-1 reconnaissance aircraft (the U-2 replacement).

INTRODUCTION

It is possible to obtain very high resolution maps of Russian ground facilities with a radar on a satellite. The resolution of such maps is not as good as that obtainable with optical cameras, but radar mapping has the advantage of being able to provide maps during nighttime conditions, when there is cloud cover, and even when it is raining. Furthermore, since radar electromagnetic energy can penetrate foliage, with some radar systems it is possible to obtain maps of ground facilities that are obscured by trees. To achieve this, a low-frequency radar with a carrier-wave frequency of 1.25 GHz (1.25×10^9 cycles per second) or lower is used. (For a carrier frequency of 1.25 GHz, the depth of penetration through mature green crops can typically be several meters, whereas at a carrier frequency of 10 GHz it is one meter or less.[1]) For mapping ground facilities (such as in Cuba), the radar could be mounted on an aircraft platform, such as the TR-1 or the SR-71; see Figure 11.1 for an example.

Figure 11.2 shows a high-resolution image obtained with an airborne radar from the Oakland Bay Bridge and adjacent areas.[2] The system used to obtain this map is capable of a 2 m resolution. Figure 11.3 shows a high-resolution radar map obtained of Los Angeles International Airport. This map has a 25×25 meter resolution. The radar operated at a carrier frequency of 1.275 GHz called L-band. A resolution about four times as good (6 m, in the along-track direction) has been achieved with the Seasat system.[3-5] To obtain a still higher resolution, the space radar should use a higher carrier frequency. Figure 11.4 shows typical resolutions theoretically achievable as a function of frequency. The figure indicates that resolutions of about 6.1 m, 2.3 m, 1.4 m, and 0.8 m are theoretically achievable at car-

FIGURE 11.2. SAR image of Oakland Bay Bridge and adjacent areas. Radar data digitally processed on the Synthetic Aperture Precision Processor-High Reliability (SAPPHIRE) System. (Courtesy of Goodyear and from "Synthetic Aperture Radar Improves Reconnaissance" by J. H. Jolley and C. Dotson, 1981, *Defense Electronics*, September 1981, p. 111. Used with permission.)

rier frequencies of respectively 1.25, 3.3, 5.5, and 10 GHz.* The finest resolution that is achievable practically is limited by the radar system instabilities and the atmospheric inhomogeneities.

The ability of a radar mapper to obtain maps during cloud cover is illustrated in Figure 11.5. This figure gives a map of the planet Venus obtained by an orbiting radar satellite. The frequency for the radar was 1.757 GHz. The planet Venus is always covered by clouds and hence no maps were available of its surface until radar maps were made. Figure 11.6 gives the attenuation, that is, the diminution of the size (or amplitude) of the wave as a result of rain when mapping the earth's surface from a satellite. The results are given for the carrier frequencies of 1.25, 3.3, 5.5, and 10 GHz.

---

*The same processing time was assumed for all the carrier frequencies in Figure 11.4, this being about the same as that used by the Seasat L-band SAR system to achieve the resolution of 6 meters.

FIGURE 11.3. 25 meter high resolution SAR map obtained August 12, 1978 of Los Angeles with Seasat.

Figure 11.6 indicates the percentage of time that the attenuation because of rain is greater than a specified amount. The results are given for the case where the signal intercepts the ground surface being mapped at an incident, or grazing, angle of 20°. At a carrier frequency of 10 GHz, the attenuation is less than 2 dB (equivalent to a 37% reduction in the received signal power) 99.9% of the time and less than 4 dB (equivalent to a 60% reduction in the received signal power level) 99.98% of the time over central Russia at a latitude of about 55°N. In addition to attenuating the signal, rain can present another problem. The radar signal can be reflected from the rain drops. If the echo from the rain is greater than the echo from the ground, the rain echo masks the ground that is being imaged. This occurs only a very small percentage of the time, as indicated in Table 11.1.

In addition to penetrating clouds, rain, and foliage, it is possible for a radar signal to penetrate dry sand and to map what is below the sand. This

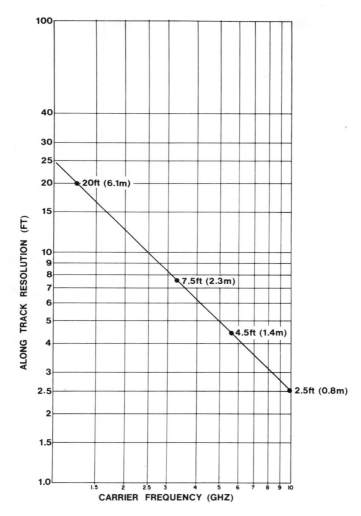

FIGURE 11.4. SAR along-track resolution versus carrier frequency.

was done with the Seasat radar over the Sahara Desert. Figure 11.7A shows a map of the Sahara Desert obtained with the Landsat optical imager operating in the visible and infrared region. Figure 11.7B shows a map obtained of the same region with the Seasat radar. Whereas the optical wavelengths cannot penetrate the sand, the microwave L-band wavelengths penetrate through the sand to show prehistoric river beds up to 5 meters below the surface of the sand.[6,7]

FIGURE 11.5. Pioneer 12 Venus Orbitor Radar Mapper map of Venus. The highland region (Ishtar Terra) is about the size of the U.S. continent, which is overlaid on the map. The flat plateau region is 3,300 m high; the highest point of the mountain Maxwell Montes on the right is 10.8 km above "sea level," higher than Mount Everest.

The difficulty with radar imaging for mapping and verification was that to obtain a high-resolution radar map from an airborne or satellite platform would require a very long antenna, too long to actually be carried by an aircraft or deployed in space. This problem is circumvented by synthesizing a very long antenna by motion of the platform. The synthesized antenna length is equal to the distance the platform moves during a coherent processing interval of the radar. Thus, although the real antenna on board the platform may only be a few meters long, the synthesized antenna may be kilometers long. This type of radar is called a synthetic aperture radar or SAR.[8,9,10,11] There are two types of SARs. One is the strip-map type, which provides long strip maps of the ground, as does the Seasat radar in mapping the Sahara Desert. (See Figure 11.7B.) The other type of synthetic aperture radar is called the spotlight SAR.[10,11,12] This type of radar provides a map only of a small region, a region smaller than the footprint of the real antenna beam on the ground. This latter type of SAR has the potential to provide higher resolution than the strip-map type of radar.

Figure 11.8 gives the geometry for a high-resolution strip-map SAR system. For this type of system, the real antenna on the airplane or spacecraft forms a narrow beam looking out to the side and downward to the ground,

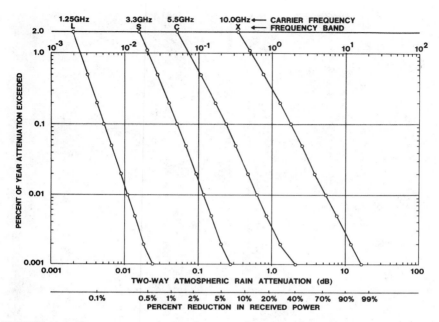

FIGURE 11.6. Two-way atmospheric rain attenuation. Central Russia, approximately 55°
north latitude.

as illustrated. This beam is fixed relative to the aircraft or satellite platform. The scanning of the ground to form the strip map is achieved because
the motion of the platform causes the beam footprint to scan out a strip
along the ground, as illustrated. Resolution in the across-track direction
(perpendicular to the motion of the platform) is achieved by transmitting a
very short pulse. Resolution in the along-track direction (the direction the
platform is moving) is achieved by the synthesis of a very long antenna, as
indicated above. For the strip-mapper, the maximum map resolution
achieved in the along-track direction is equal to one-half the real antenna
length L_R in the along-track direction, that is, it is equal to $L_R/2$.[9] Hence,
if the real antenna length is 11 meters, the along-track resolution would be
5.5 meters, or about 18 feet. Actually this result only applies for an aircraft
platform at a height at which the earth can be considered flat. For a spaceborne platform, the curvature of the earth must be taken into account, with
the result that the resolution will be slightly better than $L_R/2$. For an
11-meter antenna, the resolution will be about 4.9 meters for a satellite at
an altitude of 800 kilometers (432 nmi, the altitude of the Seasat satellite)
when mapping a ground region for which the elevation above the horizon
to the satellite is 20°. As indicated above, for a spotlight mapper, resolutions smaller than one-half the real antenna length can be achieved.

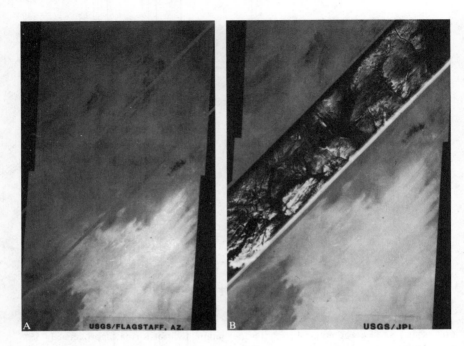

FIGURE 11.7. A, Landsat picture of Sahara Desert in Egypt. B, Synthetic aperture radar picture obtained with the Space Shuttle. (From: "Spaceborne Imaging Radars Probe 'In Depth'" by C. Elachi and J. Granger, 1982, *IEEE Spectrum*, 19, p. 24. Copyright 1982 by The Institute of Electrical and Electronics Engineers, Inc. Used with permission.)

By using two antennas on an aircraft or satellite it is possible to obtain three-dimensional surface mapping information.[13,14,15]

Maps obtained from two successive passes over a region can also provide three-dimensional image information if the passes are displaced from one another. Such stereo maps have been obtained with the Seasat system.

These are the methods for obtaining radar images from aircraft or satellite platforms looking down on the earth. It is possible also to obtain images of space or airborne objects from a fixed, ground-based radar looking up. In this case the radar is stationary; however, a large antenna can be synthesized by making use of the target motion instead of the radar motion. Things are relative, so if one imagines sitting on the moving target and thinking of it as stationary, with the world moving around it, then one has in effect a moving radar with a stationary target, and hence a long antenna is synthesized as described above. This technique is the inverse of the SAR technique for a moving airborne or spaceborne radar and hence is called an inverse SAR, or ISAR. As with the standard SAR technique, it is possible

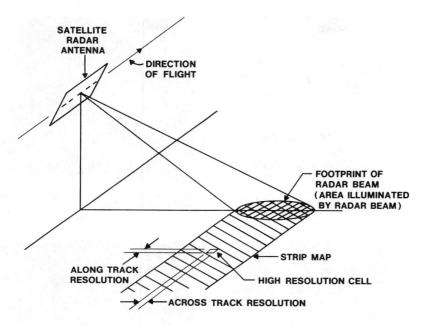

FIGURE 11.8. Geometry of high resolution strip mapper.

with the ISAR to obtain images through cloud cover and through rain. This technique would permit obtaining images of foreign reentry vehicles, post-boost vehicles, and tank boosters. It also permits the imaging of foreign satellites in space. Figure 11.9 shows measured ISAR images of aircraft;[16] simulated ISAR images of aircraft are given in Ref. 17. Figures 11.10 and

Table 11.1. Percentage of Year Rain Echo Masks Echo from Areas over U.S.S.R. Being Mapped. Results Given for Areas at About 55° North Latitude

Carrier Frequency (GHz)	1.25	3.3	5.5	10
Type Area Mapped				
City	*	*	*	0.0048
Rural Area	*	*	0.0031	0.085
Asphalt	*	0.0012	0.02	0.46
Concrete	*	0.015	0.24	4.2

*Much less than 0.001% of the year, or equivalently much less than 5 minutes out of the year.
Note. Area being mapped is assumed to be masked if rain echo equals or exceeds echo from area being mapped. Assumptions: Satellite altitude = 800 km; elevation angle to satellite at area being mapped = 20°; antenna length = 11 m; slant range resolution equals along track resolution given in Figure 11.4.

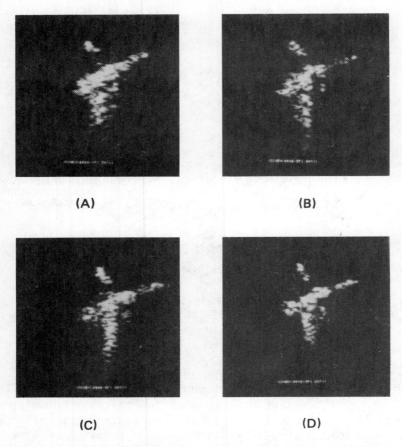

FIGURE 11.9. ISAR aircraft images obtained from adjacent coherent intervals, each 20 seconds long. Approximately 2.5 degree aspect change. (From: "Target-Motion-Induced Radar Imaging" by C. Chen and H. C. Andrews, 1980, *IEEE Trans. on Aerospace and Electronic Systems*, 16, p. 2. Copyright 1980 by The Institute of Electrical and Electronics Engineers, Inc. Used with permission.)

11.11 show ISAR images obtained of B-52 and Space Shuttle models using microwave tomography imaging techniques.[12,18-25]

Many future space SARs now being planned could be used for arms control.[26] West Germany has developed an X-band sensor for use on the Shuttle.[6] Studies have been done on the possibility of flying systems capable of mapping simultaneously at L, C and X-band on future shuttles. Canada plans a free-flying SAR in a polar orbit to monitor iceberg movements.[27,28] Japan is planning an L-band free-flying SAR to map earth resources. The European Space Agency (ESA) has authorized the construction of its first

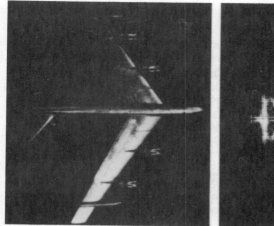

FIGURE 11.10. ISAR images obtained of model of B-52 using microwave tomography. (Model on left side; image on right side). (Figures 11.10 and 11.11 are from: "High Resolution Wideband Radar Adds New Dimension to Imaging" by B. E. Manz, 1983, *Microwaves and RF*, 22, pp. 35–38. Used with permission.)

Remote Sensing Satellite, ERS-1. It will carry a C-band SAR mapper to obtain all-weather high resolution images of coastal zones, open oceans, ice areas and land areas. Finally, NASA plans to fly an SAR around the planet Venus in 1988. The radar is to operate at a carrier frequency of 2,385 MHz and provide a resolution down to 220 m. This SAR will provide the first high resolution maps of the surface of Venus, more than one hundred times finer than previous images. (The Pioneer 12 spacecraft provided radar maps of the surface of Venus from 1978 to 1980 with a resolution of only 30 km.) At present, to process the radar data in order to obtain the map shown in Figure 11.3 takes 600 times the actual time it took the radar to

FIGURE 11.11. ISAR image obtained of model of Space Shuttle using microwave tomography. (Model on left side; image on right side).

collect these data.[25] However, in the near future real-time digital processing of satellite SAR data should be available. Jet Propulsion Laboratory (JPL) for example is presently developing such a processor.[29]

In the next sections the principles of the strip-map SAR, spotlight SAR and ISAR techniques are described in detail.

STRIP-MAP SAR[8,9,10]

Refer again to Figure 11.8, which gives the geometry of a strip-map SAR. As mentioned before, to obtain high resolution in the across-track direction, a short pulse is transmitted. As an example, say a 6-foot range resolution is desired in the across-track direction. A resolution of 6 ft would be obtained if the echoes from two objects 6 ft apart can be seen as separately resolved echoes in the receiver. Figure 11.12 illustrates this situation with two telephone poles 6 ft apart in the across-range direction. The echo from the second telephone pole will arrive after the echo from the first telephone pole by an amount equal to the time it takes for the second echo to propagate past the first telephone pole, go to the second telephone pole, and then come back to the first telephone pole, a distance of twice the separation between the telephones, or 12 ft. The velocity of light is equal to 1 ns per ft (equivalent to 3×10^8 meters per second). Thus the leading edge of the second echo will trail the leading edge of the first echo by 12 ns. Conse-

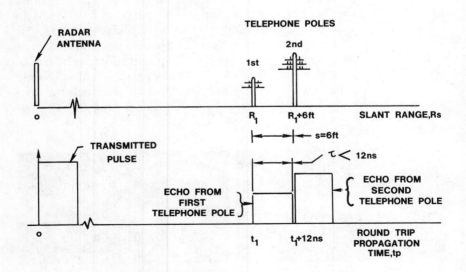

τ =TRANSMITTED PULSE WIDTH

FIGURE 11.12. Principle of across-track range resolution.

quently, the maximum pulsewidth that can be transmitted and still have the two echoes show up in the receiver as two separable distinct echoes is slightly less than 12 ns, as illustrated in Figure 11.12. In general, the resolution ΔR_C in the across-range direction is equal to one-half the transmitted pulsewidth converted to the distance, specifically, the distance light travels in half the pulsewidth time. Thus

$$\Delta R_C = \frac{\tau}{2c} \tag{1}$$

where τ is the pulsewidth, and c is the velocity of light, which is essentially the same as the velocity of radar waves.

For an airborne or satellite SAR system, the rays to the region being mapped make an angle γ with the ground as shown in Figure 11.13. Equation (1) above gives the resolution along the line of sight. The resolution for two scatterers along the ground will actually be less. Specifically, it is equal to the projection of half the pulsewidth onto the ground as shown in Figure 11.13. Consequently for an elevated platform the across-range resolution along the ground is given by

$$\Delta R_C = \frac{\tau}{2c \cos \gamma} \tag{2}$$

By way of an example, if the grazing angle at the region being mapped is $60°$, the resolution instead of being 6 ft for the 12 ns pulse will be twice as much or 12 ft. Thus the SAR mapping resolution in the across-range direc-

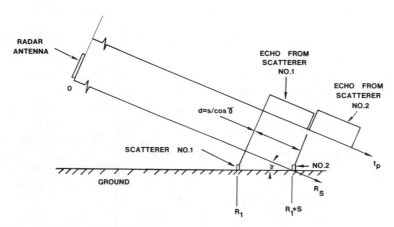

FIGURE 11.13. Across-track range resolution for non-zero grazing angle.

tion decreases as one maps regions at higher and higher grazing angles closer to the ground track of the airborne platform.

As indicated previously, one way to obtain a high resolution in the along-track direction is to use a very long real antenna. The beamwidth of a real array antenna of length L_R is approximately given by

$$\theta_{3R} = \frac{\lambda}{L_R} \tag{3}$$

where λ is the wavelength of the microwave radar signal; see Appendix A for a derivation of (3). The attenna width θ_{3R} is the half-power width, that is, the angular width at the points where the antenna beam power is one half that at the beam peak. Again assume a satellite altitude of 800 km (432 nmi). Assume that the slant range to the region being mapped is 956 nmi. At this slant range, the line-of-sight grazing angle with the ground is 20°. Assume a carrier frequency f of 5.5 GHz so that $\lambda = c/f = 0.055$ meters. The along-track range resolution ΔR_A is given by

$$\Delta R_A = R_S \theta_{3R} = R_S \frac{\lambda}{L_R} \ . \tag{4}$$

Consequently, in order to obtain an along-track resolution of 4.9 meters it is necessary that the antenna length L_R be 19,940 meters (10.8 nmi). Obviously it is not practical to deploy an array antenna that big in space. As indicated previously, what is done to circumvent this problem is to synthesize a very long antenna whose length is equal to the distance the platform moves during the coherent receiver processing interval. For such a synthesized antenna the half-power beamwidth is not given by (3) but instead is given by

$$\theta_{3S} = \frac{\lambda}{2L_S} \tag{5}$$

where L_S is the distance traveled by the platform during the coherent receiver processing interval, that is, L_S is the length of the synthetic array antenna. (See Appendix B for a derivation of Eq. 5.) Equation (5) indicates that the synthesized antenna has a beamwidth equal to a real antenna twice the synthetic antenna length. Thus to achieve the 4.9 meter along-track range resolution, the synthetic antenna length has to be half that of the real antenna length required of 19,940 meters, or equivalently 9,970 meters. The satellite velocity at the altitude of 800 km is 4.01 nmi/sec. Hence the received processing interval needed is 1.34 seconds.

The maximum antenna length that can be synthesized is determined by the maximum time any region being mapped is illuminated. This in turn is equal to the time it takes for the real beam to cross over any scatterer being mapped. For simplicity, assume a flat earth. For this case the distance moved by the platform during the time it takes for the antenna beam to sweep over the target is equal to the width of the antenna beam at the point being mapped. The resulting along-track resolution is then given by

$$\Delta R_S = \frac{L_R}{2} \tag{6}$$

where L_R is the width of the real antenna in the along-track direction. (See Appendix B for a derivation of Eq. 6.) Thus, the maximum along-track range resolution is equal to one-half the real antenna's along-track length. This along-track resolution is independent of the slant range to the target. By way of an example, assume that the along-track antenna length is 11 meters. Then the maximum range resolution achievable with a strip-map SAR is 5.5 meters. If the earth's curvature is taken into account, then a resolution slightly less than that given by Eq. (6) is obtained. Specifically, for the example given above the resolution is 4.9 meters instead of 5.5 meters.

Equation (6) implies that a resolution as small as desired can be obtained by making the real antenna length in the along-track direction correspondingly smaller. However, this is not true. When the real satellite antenna length is made too small, the antenna beamwidth along the ground in the along-track direction becomes large. This can result in a problem of multiple synthetic antenna beams being formed in azimuth. (See Appendix C and the figures referred to there.) Specifically, there will be two additional antenna beams, one at an angle θ_G to the left and one at an angle θ_G to the right of the main synthetic antenna beam as illustrated in Figure C.1 of Appendix C. As a result, at the same time that a return is being obtained from the main synthetic array beam, returns are also being obtained from the two additional beams, called grating lobe beams. These two additional returns are ambiguous with the return from the main synthetic array beam, thus corrupting the map obtained by the main synthetic array beam. Another way to look at this is that three maps are being made simultaneously and overlaid on each other with a misregistration of plus and minus θ_G. To eliminate these grating lobes of the synthetic array antenna it is necessary that the real antenna length be large enough to produce a narrow beam which suppresses the grating lobes. (See Appendix C.)

A similar ambiguity can arise in the across-range direction if the height of the antenna is too small. The length of the beam spot illuminated on the ground in the across-track direction becomes very large, with the result that range ambiguities in the along-track direction can occur. (See Appendix C.) To eliminate these ambiguities, it is necessary that the real antenna area not

Table 11.2. Minimum Antenna Area and Dimensions Required
to Avoid Range and Doppler Ambiguities

Frequency (GHz)	Minimum Area (M^2)	Minimum Height and Width for Square Aperture (M)
1.25	186	13.7
3.3	71	8.4
5.5	42	6.5
10.0	23	4.8

Note. Assumptions: Satellite altitude = 432 nmi = 800 km; Signal from satellite intercepts ground surface being mapped at a 20° grazing angle.

be less than a specified amount. Table 11.2 indicates the minimum antenna area needed to eliminate the possibility of ambiguities in both the along-track and across-track range directions. Table 11.2 also gives the minimum antenna width and height needed to eliminate these ambiguities, assuming that the length and height of the antenna are equal. At the higher carrier frequencies indicated in the table (like 5.5 GHz and 10 GHz), the dimensions of an antenna for a satellite system may actually have to be larger than the minimum specified in Table 11.2. This is because a larger antenna may be needed for the system to achieve sufficient sensitivity for mapping the ground without requiring excessive transmitter power on the satellite.

SPOTLIGHT MAPPER[10]

Figure 11.14 shows the geometry for a spotlight mapper aboard an aircraft. For this system the real antenna beam is pointed either electronically or mechanically toward the region of the ground where a high-resolution map is desired. The size of the region being mapped is smaller than the area illuminated by the real beam. In the past the coherent processing time used for this mode was generally much less than for a strip mapper. As a result, the resolution obtained with this mode was poorer than obtained by a strip mapper. For simplicity in discussion, assume that a spot map is being made at a region abeam to the platform velocity vector. The processing time for the synthetic antenna array is made equal to much less than the time it takes for the beam footprint to pass over a scatterer being mapped. This is done in order that all the points in the region being mapped remain in the footprint of the real antenna during the whole processing interval. To achieve this the antenna beam might typically move only one tenth of the antenna beamwidth in the along-track direction during the coherent processing interval. As a result, the synthetic array antenna length will be one-tenth the maximum achievable with a strip mapper, and consequently the resolu-

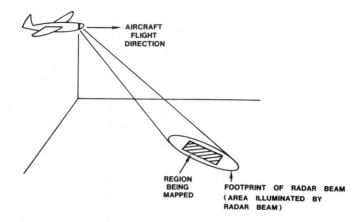

FIGURE 11.14. Spotlight mapper geometry.

tion obtained with the spotlight mapper will be ten times that of the strip mapper in the along-track direction.

It is potentially possible, however, to achieve a better resolution with the spotlight mapper mode than with the strip mapper mode. To do this the real beam is not held fixed during the coherent processing interval, but is instead re-steered so that the beam can dwell on the region being mapped for a time longer than obtainable with a strip mapper.[11,12,24,30,32] Thus, for the satellite example given above, if the beam is re-steered so that the region being mapped is illuminated for a time of 4 seconds instead of the 1.34 seconds maximum achievable with a strip mapper, the spotlight mapper resolution becomes above $(1.34/4) \times 4.9$ m $= 1.6$ m or equivalently 5.4 feet. With this technique the antenna can be made large enough to eliminate the range ambiguity problems described above while at the same time providing for the ability to achieve higher resolution.

INVERSE SAR[11,24]

For the ISAR system the target is moving instead of the radar. Figure 11.15A depicts this situation for a tumbling reentry vehicle (RV). Let us situate ourselves on the RV with a fixed coordinate system relative to the RV. It would appear to us as if the radar is moving rather than the RV. Consequently, a long antenna can be synthesized through this apparent motion of the radar relative to the RV. For example, assume that the tumbling rate of the RV is ω and that the coherent processing time is T_C. Then the distance traversed by the ground radar relative to the RV due to its tumbling is given by

$$L_S = R_S \omega T_C \tag{7}$$

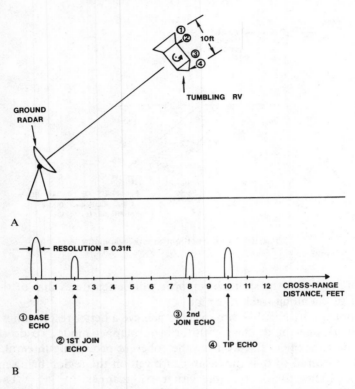

FIGURE 11.15. Tumbling reentry vehicle (RV): Broadside view. A, geometry. B, radar image.

where R_S is the slant range to the RV from the radar. Thus for a processing time of T_C an antenna of length L_S is synthesized. The resolution in the direction perpendicular to the line of sight (which formerly was called the along-track direction and here for the ISAR is called the cross-range direction, not to be confused with the across-track direction of the strip mapper of Figure 11.8) is thus given by

$$\Delta R_A = \frac{\lambda R_S}{2L_S} = \frac{\lambda R_S}{2R_S \omega T_C} = \frac{\lambda}{2\theta_R} \tag{8}$$

where θ_R equals the angle rotated by the RV during the coherent processing interval. By way of example, assume a slant range of 1000 nmi, a tumbling period of 2 seconds, a 10 ft long RV, a coherent processing time of 0.05

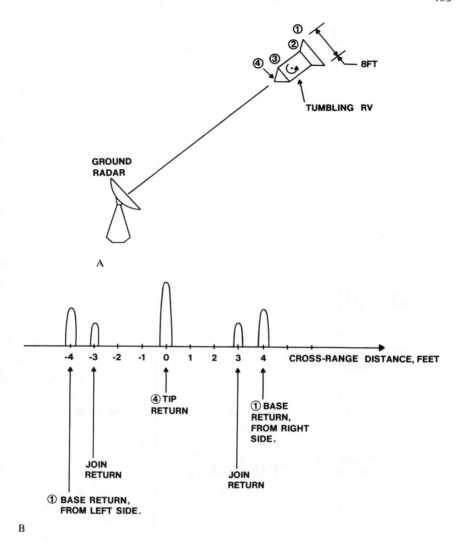

FIGURE 11.16. Tumbling reentry vehicle (RV): Nose-on view. A, geometry. B, radar image.

seconds, and a carrier frequency of 10 GHz, then $L_S = 291$ km and the cross-range resolution is $\Delta R_A = 0.31$ ft. If a 1.25 GHz carrier frequency had been used instead of 10 GHz, this resolution would be 2.5 ft. However, increasing the processing time by a factor of 2 would improve this resolu-

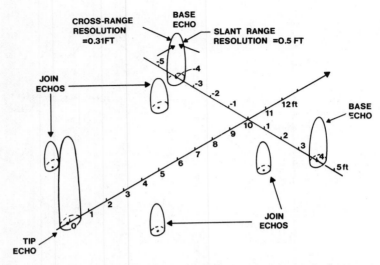

FIGURE 11.17. Two-dimensional image of tumbling RV: Nose-on viewing aspect.

tion to 1.25 ft. Figure 11.15B shows the map obtained of the RV with a 10 GHz radar for the assumption given above. The picture clearly shows the scattering from the base, tip and joins of the RV. One-half second after the time depicted in Figure 11.15A the RV will have tumbled 90° so that the situation depicted in Figure 11.16A prevails for the 10 GHz radar. The corresponding map obtained is shown in Figure 11.16B, the same coherent processing time being assumed. From this image the base diameter of the reentry vehicle and the diameter of the cylindrical section of the reentry vehicle is obtained. The image of Figure 11.16B (and for Figure 11.15B) assumed that the scatterers of the RV were not resolved in the slant range direction, that is, the slant range resolution was poorer than the 10 ft length of the RV. If instead a 1 ns pulse is assumed to be transmitted a slant range resolution of $\frac{1}{2}$ ft is achieved and the returns from the scatterers in the slant range direction will be separated out and separate images obtained for resolvable $\frac{1}{2}$ ft cells. A two-dimensional image of the RV is then obtained as illustrated in Figure 11.17.

APPENDIX A
REAL ANTENNA BEAM RESOLUTION

Assume a real antenna consisting of an array of $N = 8$ elements as shown in Figure A.1. The N array element signals arriving from a point on the mechanical boresite of the antenna will all arrive with essentially the same

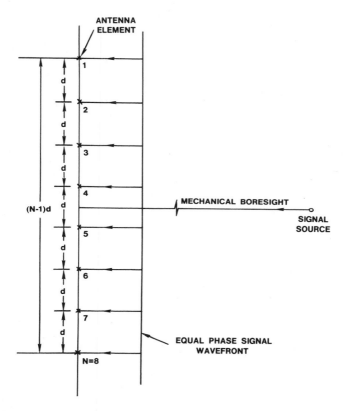

FIGURE A.1. Real antenna array of $N = 8$ elements; signal source on boresight.

phase. When these N signals are added up in the receiver, they produce a sum signal N times the strength of each component signal. For a signal emanating from a point at an angle θ away from boresite as in Figure A.2, the phases of the signals received by the various phased-array elements will not be the same and hence the N signals will not add up in phase. The signals will not be in phase because the path length distance to the different phased array elements are different. There is an angle θ for which the N signals have phases uniformly distributed from 0 to 360° so as to add up to 0. This situation is depicted in Figure A.3. This will occur when the phase of the signal to radiating element #2 lags behind that of radiating element #1 by an amount $360°/N = 360°/8$. (This is also the phase between any other two adjacent elements.) If the spacing between elements is d, then the extra distance that the signal has to go to reach element #2 over that required to reach element #1 is $D_2 = d \sin \theta$ (see Figure A.2). Consequently, the phase

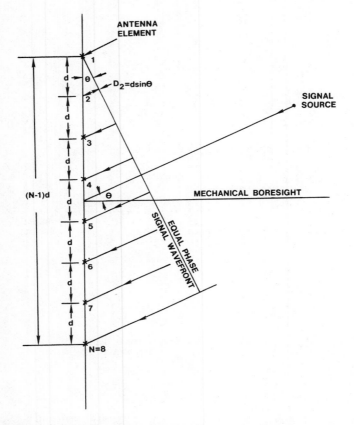

FIGURE A.2. Real antenna array of $N = 8$ elements; signal source off boresight.

of the signal arriving at element #2 will lag that of element #1 by the angle ϕ_2, given in radians by

$$\phi_2 = \frac{2\pi d \sin \theta}{\lambda} \tag{A.1}$$

Letting ϕ_2 of (A.1) equal $360°/N = 2\pi/N$ radians and solving for θ gives the angle at which N signals add up to zero. This represents the angle at which the antenna pattern goes through its first null (see Figure A.4). Designate the null-to-null width of the antenna pattern as θ_n. Then it follows from the above that

$$\sin(\theta_n/2) = \frac{\lambda}{Nd} \tag{A.2}$$

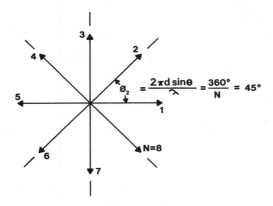

FIGURE A.3. Phasers of received signals for $N = 8$ array elements. Depicted is the situation for which they add up to zero.

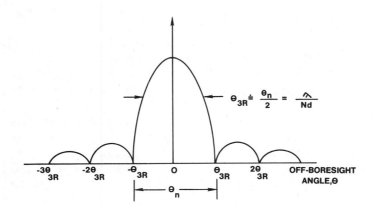

$\theta_n \equiv$ ANTENNA PATTERN NULL-TO-NULL WIDTH$= \dfrac{\lambda}{Nd}$

$\theta_{3R} \equiv$ ANTENNA HALF-POWER WIDTH

$\dot{=} \lambda/Nd$

FIGURE A.4. Real antenna pattern.

Since θ_n is very small, $\sin(\theta_n/2)$ can be approximated by $\theta_n/2$ so that (A.2) becomes

$$\frac{\theta_n}{2} = \frac{\lambda}{Nd} \tag{A.3}$$

The antenna half-power width approximately equals $\theta_n/2$ (see Figure A.4), and the effective antenna length L_R equals Nd. Hence

$$\theta_{3R} = \frac{\lambda}{Nd} = \frac{\lambda}{L_R} \tag{A.4}$$

This is identical to Eq. (3) which we set out to derive. For further reading, see Reference 31.

APPENDIX B
SYNTHETIC ARRAY RADAR

Figure B.1 depicts a synthetic array antenna consisting of N array elements. In contrast to the real antenna array, these array elements do not exist simultaneously. Instead, they represent the positions of the platform at successive time instants. These are the time instants that the successive transmitter pulses are sent out. For example, at time zero the platform is at the position of array element #1 and a pulse is transmitted and its echo received. At time 2 the platform has moved from position #1 to position #2 and the second pulse is transmitted and its echo received, etc. (The antenna actually moves between the time the pulse is transmitted and its echo is received. For simplicity, though, it is assumed that this round-trip time for the pulse is negligible, so that the platform essentially does not move during this time. To account for the motion, it is possible to replace the positions of the platform at the instant the pulse is transmitted and at the instant its echo is received by an equivalent position from which the pulse can be considered to be transmitted and received. This equivalent position is the actual position of the array elements formed by the platform motion. The equivalent positions are given by the midpoint between the positions of the platform on transmit and receive.) The situation for the synthetic array antenna is thus distinctly different from that of the real antenna where on receive all the signals arriving at the different radiating elements result from a single pulse transmission. For the case of the synthetic array antenna, the signal arriving at the ith radiating element results from the ith pulse transmission. Because of this difference, the synthetic antenna pattern is determined by a two-way propagation of the N transmitted pulses rather than a one-way propagation resulting from a single transmitted pulse as it backscatters from a point scatterer to the real antenna radiating elements. The pulse transmitted from radiating element #1 goes a distance R_S to the target and another distance R_S back to the radiating element #1 for a total round-trip distance of $2R_S$. For radiating element #2, the pulse goes an

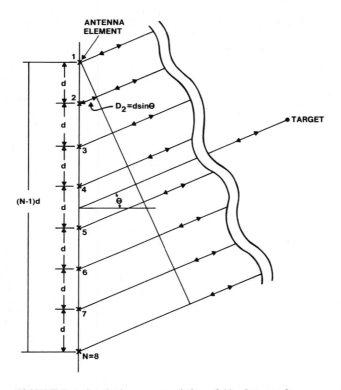

FIGURE B.1. Synthetic array consisting of $N = 8$ array elements.

extra distance $d \sin \theta$ to reach the target and an extra distance again $d \sin \theta$ on returning to the radiating element. Consequently, the signal from radiating element #2 to the target and back goes an extra distance to $2d \sin \theta$. Thus, the signal to element #2 lags that from element #1 by

$$\phi_2 = \frac{2\pi \cdot 2d \sin \theta}{\lambda} \tag{B.1}$$

(This is in contrast to a real antenna, where this lag is half as much; see A.1. Because of this, the angle to the first null, $\theta_n/2$, for the synthetic array is half that for the real antenna as given in Eq. A.3. This shall be shown in Eq. B.3 below.) For a scatterer on boresite, that is, for $\theta = 0$, ϕ_2 is zero, so that the two signals are in phase. Moreover, all the signals received are in phase for this case. Thus, the sum of the N signals will add in phase, the peak of the synthetic beam being formed at mechanical boresight. The first null in the synthetic antenna pattern occurs when the N signals add up to zero. This occurs when the signals are phased relative to each other as depicted in Figure A.3 — that is, if the phases between successive radiating element signals are given by $360°/N$. Setting ϕ_2 equal to this value and solving for θ in (B.1) yields the angle at which the first null occurs, which is equal to half the null-to-null width, or equivalently $\theta_n/2$. Thus

$$\sin\frac{\theta_n}{2} = \frac{\lambda}{2Nd} \tag{B.2}$$

which for small θ becomes

$$\frac{\theta_n}{2} = \frac{\lambda}{2Nd} \tag{B.3}$$

The half-power beamwidth of the synthetic array is approximately equal to $\theta_n/2$ and the synthetic aperture effective length L_S equals Nd. Consequently, the half-power beamwidth of the synthetic array θ_{3S} is given by

$$\theta_{3S} \doteq \frac{\lambda}{2Nd} = \frac{\lambda}{2L_S} \; ; \tag{B.4}$$

see Figure B.2. Equation (B.4) is identical to Eq. (5), which we set out to prove.

As indicated previously, the maximum length L_S synthetic aperture that can be synthesized with a strip map SAR is equal to the width of the antenna beam in the along-track direction at the region being mapped. If the slant range to the point being mapped is R_S, then this distance is given by

$$L_S = R_S\theta_{3R} \tag{B.5}$$

where θ_{3R} is the real antenna half-power beamwidth, which is given by (3). Substituting (3) for θ_{3R} into (B.5) and in turn substituting (B.5) into (B.4) yields that

$$\theta_{3S} = \frac{L_R}{2R_S} \tag{B.6}$$

The along-track resolution is obtained from (B.6) by multiplying by the slant range, which results in

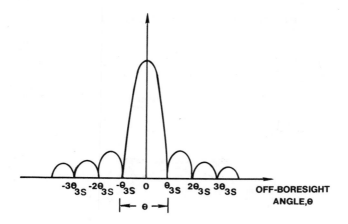

$\theta_{3S} \equiv$ ANTENNA HALF-POWER WIDTH

$\doteq \lambda/2Nd = \lambda/2L_S$

FIGURE B.2. Synthetic antenna pattern.

$$\Delta R_S = \frac{L_R}{2} \qquad \text{(B.7)}$$

which is identical to Eq. (6) as was desired to show.

APPENDIX C
AMBIGUITY PROBLEM

As the angle θ in (B.1) is increased beyond the angle $\theta_n/2$ at which the first null occurs an angle θ_G is reached at which the N signals add up in phase again. This will occur when $d \sin \theta = \lambda$. For this condition the phase between any two adjacent radiating elements is 360° so that in effect all elements are in phase and will add up in phase. At this angle a beam like the main boresight beam is formed which has essentially the same gain and width as the boresight beam; see Figure C.1A. This beam is called a grating lobe. The angle θ_G is easily found by setting (B.1) equal to 2π and solving for θ, which becomes θ_G. Doing this yields that

$$\theta_G = \sin^{-1}\frac{\lambda}{2d} \qquad \text{(C.1)}$$

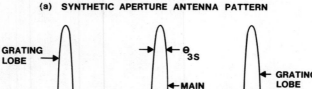

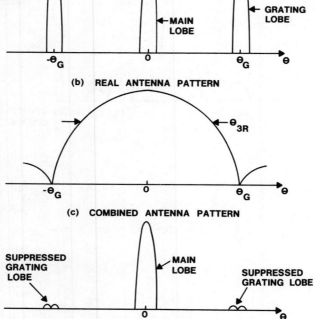

FIGURE C.1. Grating lobe removal.

$$\theta_G \doteq \frac{\lambda}{2d} \ \text{for} \ \lambda/2d \ll 1 \tag{C.1a}$$

A grating lobe will exist at $-\theta_G$ as well as $+\theta_G$. Because of these two grating lobes, regions of the ground observed simultaneously by the two grating lobes are superimposed on the regions observed by the main synthetic aperture lobe at boresight ($\theta = 0$), thus resulting in a corrupted map. To eliminate this problem, the real antenna pattern should be narrow enough so as to suppress these grating lobes. For example, if the nulls of the real antenna occur at the angle $\pm\theta_G$ as indicated in Figure C.1B, then the combined antenna pattern consisting of the cascade of the synthetic array pattern and the real array pattern should result in the array pattern shown in Figure C.1C which has no grating lobes.

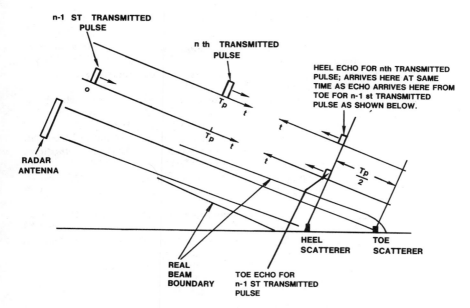

FIGURE C.2. Across-track ambiguity problem.

If the real antenna pattern is too wide to eliminate these grating lobes, that is, the grating lobes fall within the main lobe of the real antenna pattern, then it is possible to eliminate the grating lobes by shifting them out in angle so they do fall at the nulls of the real antenna pattern. This is done by reducing the spacing d between the synthetic aperture array elements. To do this, the time between successive pulse transmissions is reduced. A potential problem, however, can result from this solution. Specifically, range ambiguities can arise instead in the across-track direction. This would occur if the footprint size in the across track direction is too large. Specifically, if the time it takes for the signal to travel from the heel of the footprint on the ground to the toe of the footprint on the ground and back is equal to or greater than the time between successive pulses transmitted. If it is just equal to this time, then it turns out that the echo from the toe of the beam resulting from the n-1st pulse will arrive at the same time as the echo from the heel of the beam resulting from the n-th pulse (see Figure C.2). To prevent this from happening, the height of the beam must be large enough to keep the footprint length in the across-track direction less than one-half the time between pulses converted to distance. To eliminate both angle and range ambiguities, the real antenna area is constrained as indicated in Table 11.2.

REFERENCES

1. Ulaby, F. T., R. K. Moore, and A. K. Fung. *Microwave Remote Sensing, Active and Passive, vol. 2,* chapter 11. Reading, MA: Addison-Wesley, 1982.
2. Jolley, J. H. and C. Dotson. Synthetic Aperture Radar Improves Reconnaissance. *Defense Electronics* (September 1981):111–118.
3. Held, D. N., J. R. Bennet, and R. A. Shuchman. The Seasat Synthetic Aperture Radar: Engineering Performance Evaluation. 1982 International Geoscience and Remote Sensing Symposium in Munich, June 1982.
4. Li, F. and H. Zebker. A Digital Seasat SAR Correlation-Simulation Program. *Proceedings of the International Geoscience and Remote Sensing Symposium.* Washington, D.C., 8–10 June 1981, IEEE 81CH1656-8.
5. Wu, C. et al. Modelling and a Correlation Algorithm for Spaceborne SAR Signals. *IEEE Transactions on Aerospace Electronic Systems* 18, 5 (September 1982):563–575.
6. Elachi, C. and J. Granger. Spaceborne Imaging Radars Probe 'In Depth.' *IEEE Spectrum* 19, 11 (November 1982):24–29.
7. McCauley, J. F. et al. Subsurface Valleys and Geoarcheology of the Eastern Sahara Revealed by Shuttle Radar. *Science* 218:1004–1019.
8. Curtis, W. C. Synthetic Aperture Fundamentals. In *Radar Technology,* edited by E. Brookner. Artech House, 1977.
9. Kovaly, J. J. High Resolution Radar Fundamentals. In *Radar Technology,* edited by E. Brookner. Artech House, 1977.
10. Brookner, E. Synthetic Aperture Radar Spotlight Mapper. In *Radar Technology,* edited by E. Brookner. Artech House, 1977.
11. Ausherman, D. A., et al. Developments in Radar Imaging. *IEEE Transactions on Aerospace and Electronic Systems* AES-20, 4 (July 1984):363–400.
12. Munson, Jr., D. C., J. D. O'Brien, and W. K. Jenkins. A Tomographic Formulation of Spotlight-Mode Synthetic Aperture Radar. *Proceedings of the IEEE* 71, 8 (August 1983):917–925.
13. Graham, L. C. Synthetic Interferometer Radar for Topographic Mapping. *Proceedings of the IEEE* 62, 6 (June 1974):763–768.
14. Brookner, E. Present and Future Trends in Synthetic Aperture Radar Systems and Techniques. In *Radar Technology,* edited by E. Brookner. Artech House, 1977.
15. Elachi, C. Radar Images of the Earth from Space. *Scientific American* 247, 6 (December 1982):54–61.
16. Chen, C. and H. C. Andrews. Target-Motion-Induced Radar Imaging. *IEEE Transactions on Aerospace and Electronic Systems* AES-16, 1 (January 1980):2–14.
17. Dike, G., et al. Inverse SAR and Its Application to Aircraft Classification. IEEE 1980 International Radar Conference, Arlington, Virginia, 1980, pp. 161–167.
18. Manz, B. E. High Resolution Wideband Radar Adds New Dimension to Imaging. *Microwaves and RF* 22, 4 (April 1983):35–38.
19. Chan, C. K. and N. H. Farhat. Frequency Swept Tomographic Imaging of Three-Dimensional Perfectly Conducting Objects. *IEEE Transactions on Antennas and Propagation* AP-29, 2 (March 1981):312–319.
20. Lewis, R. M. Physical Optics Inverse Diffraction. *IEEE Transactions on Antennas and Propagation* AP-17, 3 (May 1969):308–314.
21. Farhat, N. H. and T. H. Chu. Projection Imaging of 3-D Microwave Scatterers

with Near Optical Resolution. *URSI/IAU Symposium on Indirect Imaging*, Sydney, Australia, August 30–September 2, 1983.

22. Farhat, N. H., T. H. Chu, and C. L. Werner. Tomographic and Projective Reconstruction of 3-D Image Detail in Inverse Scattering. *Proceedings of the IEEE 10th International Optical Computing Conference* (1983):82–88.

23. Farhat, N. H., C. L. Werner and T. H. Chu. Prospects for 3-D Tomographic Imaging Radar Networks. *URSI Symposium on Electromagnetic Theory* (1983):297–301.

24. Walker, J. L. Range-Doppler Imaging of Rotating Objects. *IEEE Transactions on Aerospace and Electronic Systems* AES-16, 1 (January 1980):23–52.

25. Brookner, E. and B. R. Hunt. Synthetic Aperture Radar Processing. *Trends and Perspectives in Signal Processing* 2, 1 (January 1982):2–4.

26. Brookner, E. Radar of the 80's and Beyond. *IEEE Electro/84 Conference Proceedings*, May 15–17, 1984, Session 4.

27. Spaceborne Imaging Radar Symposium, January 17–20, 1983, Jet Propulsion Laboratory Publication. JPL Publication 83-11.

28. Elachi, C., et al. Spaceborne Synthetic Aperture Imaging Radars: Applications, Techniques, and Technology. *Proceedings of the IEEE* 70, 10 (October 1982):1174–1209.

29. Bicknell, T. Real-Time Digital Processing of SAR Data. Spaceborne Imaging Radar Symposium, January 17–20, 1983, Jet Propulsion Laboratory. JPL Publication 83-11.

30. Swiger, J. M. Principles of Synthetic Array Radar. Hughes Aircraft Company Report, Culver City, CA, July 1978.

31. Brookner, E. Phased-Array Radars. *Scientific American* 252, 2 (February 1985):94–102.

32. Ausherman, D. A. SAR Digital Image-Formation Processing. *Proceedings of the International Society for Optical Engineering*, vol. 528, pp. 118–133.

12.
Infrared Surveillance and Detectors

James C. Fraser

INTRODUCTION

Infrared (IR) detection is particularly useful for the verification of arms control treaties because it produces images without visible light, and it can be used at night. Infrared capabilities for surveillance are expanding rapidly as new technologies in optics, detector arrays, and signal processors mature. NASA and DoD investments in new IR technologies are expected to pay off in operational systems of higher performance within the next decade. Improvements currently under development will extend the spectral bands and increase the ground swath coverage per system in space. Remote sensing and discrimination of natural and artificial earth features will be improved several times over current Landsat series capabilities.

Some specific examples of maturing technology area payoffs will be touched on lightly here.

New optical technologies to produce lightweight mirrors will enable telescopes with ten times greater sensitivity and field-of-views to be launched into space. Advances in infrared mosaic detector technology will increase the affordable number of detectors in the optical focal plane to several hundred thousand, using the new optics more efficiently. Advanced onboard satellite signal processors will be capable of handling greater data rates from these sensors and will provide faster and more sophisticated screening of data before transmission to the ground receiving network.

The combined potential of these emerging technologies to improve both civilian and military surveillance is enormous. The opportunity to apply advanced, unique infrared surveillance systems from space as technical tools for verification of arms control agreements must be seriously considered in future agreements.

BASICS OF THE INFRARED SPECTRUM

Infrared energy is a form of light energy that we cannot see but normally can feel as radiant heat. It occupies that portion of the electromagnetic

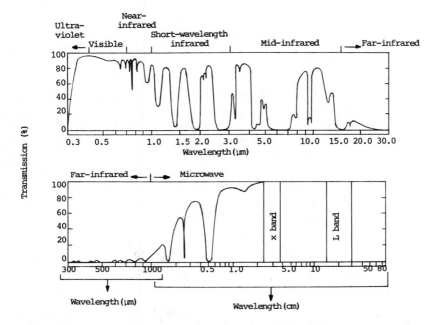

FIGURE 12.1. Generalized absorption spectrum of the atmosphere at the zenith with the named spectral regions outlined. (From: "Geologic Remote Sensing" by A.F.H. Goetz and L.C. Rowan, 1981, *Science*, 211, p. 781. Copyright 1981 by The American Association for the Advancement of Science. Used with permission.)

spectrum just beyond the red end of the visible spectrum, from about 0.7 microns* to about 1,000 microns wavelength. This total spectral span is divided into three general IR window regimes by the earth atmospheric absorption spectrum, shown in Figure 12.1.

The first regime, the near-infrared, extends from 0.7 to about 2 microns. It is like an extension of the visible region in that detection and discrimination of an object in this regime depend on that object's reflectance or absorption of natural solar radiation in these wavelengths. In fact, the output of near-infrared sensors is taken in a series of narrow spectral bands of the regime, which—like visible colors—can be displayed by using various arbitrarily assigned colors to construct a false color image of the scene in the near-infrared. The assignment of false colors to portions of the near-infrared regime can be used to emphasize various specific features in the imagery.

---

*1 micron = 10^{-6} meters

An example of the ability of near-infrared imaging sensor data is well known today because of success of the NASA Landsat satellite data, and its widespread use in agriculture, land management, and geologic exploration throughout the world.

The second important infrared regime extends from about 2 to 14 microns, where thermal radiation from objects at room temperature (20 Celsius or 300 Kelvin) peaks. The atmosphere, with help from vapor and CO_2, absorbs most of the infrared spectrum beyond 14 microns. Fortunately, there are two transmission windows at 3–5 and 8–14 microns through which thermal radiation in these bands can be detected over distances of several kilometers at sea level. From outer space the atmosphere transmission in these windows is great enough so that the surface of the earth can be observed. In general, an object emits a broad spectrum of wavelengths whose relative and absolute strengths depend on the temperature of the object. The detailed physics will not be covered here, but it is useful to understand two fundamental physical principles of these infrared emissions.

The first is that, although thermal emissions occur over a broad band of wavelength, the emittance from any object at room temperature (300 K) peaks at about 10 microns wavelength, and the position of the peak wavelength shifts inversely with the absolute temperature. Thus, it can be quickly determined that the solar thermal spectrum from the sun's photosphere at a temperature of 6000 K peaks at 0.5 microns. Hot objects like the sun (6000 K) or quartz halogen lamps (3400 K) appear white because of the dominant emittance in the visible spectrum (0.4 to 0.6 microns).

The second useful principle is that an object emits a total thermal energy proportion to the fourth power of the absolute temperature ($\propto T^4$). Thus, very hot objects emit vastly greater amounts of energy than colder objects. Even though the peak emittance shifts to shorter wavelengths as an object gets hotter, its emittance at any given fixed wavelength increases.

Because of this behavior of thermal emission with temperature as expressed by these simple principles, the 8–14 micron window band is better than 3–5 micron window band for remote thermal imaging. Also, solar reflected energy is very low compared to thermal self-emissions in the 8–14 band, and thus much less reflected sunlight clutter is present in the 8–14 micron image. For these reasons, the 8–14 micron is the most preferred and most commonly used thermal imaging band.

A third significant regime is the far-infrared, extending from about 14 to 1,000 microns. Because of the reasons discussed previously, this regime is most useful for detecting objects at temperatures much colder than room temperature. This is often the case for objects that exist in space at only a few degrees above absolute zero. The techniques and technology of detection in this regime have been developed mostly by a few specialists in infrared astronomy. This regime is generally limited to space surveillance and detection of very cold bodies in space. For this reason, and because of the special technology requirements, most of this regime is not considered practical for general surveillance.

In summary, the near-infrared (0.7 to 2 microns) and the thermal infrared (3–5 and 8–14 microns) are proven to be practical infrared spectral regimes for remote sensing from space and terrestrial thermal imaging. The near-infrared is dominated by solar energy, and remote sensing must be done under solar illumination. The thermal bands are used to sense self-emissions in the absence of solar illumination, that is, in the dark.

Special infrared emissions due to intense spectral lines of gaseous combustion products give these events characteristic infrared signatures that may be detectable at any wavelength, usually from visible to about 14 microns. In other cases, characteristic absorption signatures of small amounts of gaseous contaminants may be detectable as a decrease in observed emittance from a remote object. Some examples are infrared emissions from rocket plumes or explosions, measurement of chemical pollutants, and the determination of the amount of water vapor in a local region of the atmosphere. The signatures can be used to determine the chemical constituents of the event or the type of pollutant present.

INFRARED SENSOR TECHNOLOGY

An infrared sensor converts infrared energy into electrical signals as illustrated in Figure 12.2. It consists of (a) a telescopic system that uses mirrors to gather the energy and focus it on the detector array, (b) a detector or focal plane array to sense the energy and convert it to electrical signals, and (c) a signal processor to amplify, condition, and multiplex the detector signal to form a data stream. An infrared scene is thus converted into an electrical signal output which can be used to sound an alarm or reconstruct an image of the scene. In order to cover fully the optical field-of-view (FOV), a scanning system must be used to scan a detector sequentially over every picture element (pixel) in the FOV. Most sensors in use today have a complex mechanical scanning mirror to move the FOV periodically over one or a few detectors in the focal plane. Some common scanning schemes are illustrated in Figure 12.3.

Another type of sensor uses a mosaic of millions of detectors to simultaneously detect and electronically scan out the image by staring continuously at the scene. This mosaic focal plane array technology is the object of a very intensive research and development program today in NASA and DoD.

Sophisticated data processing can also be applied to perform a complex task of discriminating against unwanted data to reduce the net output to

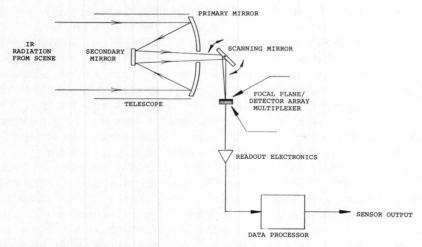

FIGURE 12.2. A generic infrared sensor system consists of an optical telescope, a scanning system and a focal plane detector array with electronics and data processor.

only the desired information, or to provide merely a simple warning indication.

Optics

The optical telescope fixes the field-of-view or coverage of the sensor. Ordinary optical glass cannot be used for infrared telescopes because it

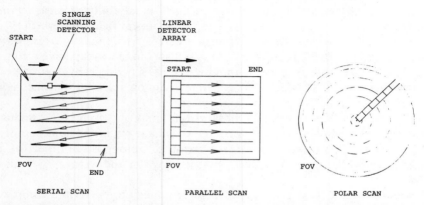

FIGURE 12.3. Some forms of scanning systems used to fill the optical field-of-view (FOV).

does not transmit in the long wavelengths. Although there are a fairly large number of IR lens materials to choose from, the difficulty of fabricating a sophisticated refracting lens such as used on 35mm cameras is so great that reflecting, or mirror, telescopes are generally preferred. The refracting elements are limited to flat windows or corrector plates. Even these are fabricated with difficulty because a visual test through the generally opaque IR transmitting material cannot be made. The most common type of telescope is the two-mirror Cassegrain system (as shown in Figure 12.4) which has a typical FOV of about 1 degree, and is limited to a speed of about f/16 for diffraction limited performance across the field. However, variants on this basic design using aspheric mirrors can achieve high performance up to FOVs of about 3.0 degrees and speeds of f/5. Normally, these telescopes would be considered "long lens" by a 35mm camera user. However, for most IR imaging applications such as night vision, weapon targeting, or civilian remote sensing, these narrow FOVs are perfectly adequate.

A useful reference on FOV is to realize that the earth sublends about 18 degrees from a synchronous orbit. Thus, a full earth, non-scanning sensor placed in geosynchronous orbit would require an 18° FOV optical system. Wide FOV telescopes, greater than about 3.5 degrees, require deep aspheric mirrors, corrector plates, or unusual mirror arrangements. Such an exam-

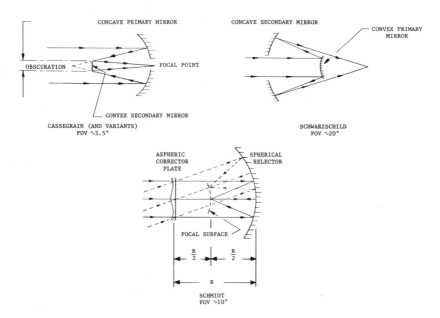

FIGURE 12.4. Typical infrared optical telescope designs using reflective mirror elements.

ple, useful to about 10 degrees, is the Schmidt design shown in Figure 12.4. Another potential wide-FOV design is the Schwarzschild arrangement, also illustrated in Figure 12.4. Both of these telescopes use spherical mirrors (easiest to make), but require mirror diameters about two times greater than the effective aperture diameter or light gathering entrance to the telescope. Advanced IR surveillance concepts from space with high sensitivity and resolution will require aperture diameters of at least 1 meter or greater. The mirrors for these advanced sensor telescopes will have to be several meters in diameter.

Mirror fabrication techniques and weight have become the key technology issues for these advanced wide FOV sensors. The excess weight, high cost, and a fabrication time cycle of several years could prohibit such sensors from ever being launched. Generally, the time needed to fabricate a mirror goes up roughly as the cube of its size, which means that mirrors 2 or 3 meters in diameter would require several years to fabricate. Glass is the most common material used for mirrors today. No better substitute has yet been found to match its stability and workability, although a lot of research on substitute materials has been done. The technology now exists to construct lightweight glass mirrors up to about 2 meters in diameter, but years of fabrication time are still needed to complete them. The future surveillance sensor engineer will be forced into a weight–size tradeoff between coverage (FOV) and sensitivity (aperture) in deciding how to use the maximum practical mirror diameter orbits available to him. Meanwhile, sensors requiring full-earth FOV from geosynchronous must settle for either polar-axis scan (see Figure 12.3) or a refractive optical system with a very small aperture.

Focal Plane Detector Technology

The earliest forms of infrared detectors were highly sensitive heat detectors (bolometers) which would sense an imperceptible excess of incident thermal radiation against the normal temperature background. The modern form of the infrared detector, developed since the 1940s, is a solid-state device which converts the infrared photons to electrons by a quantum interaction in a semiconducting material. This type of detector is known as a quantum detector and is characterized by its quantum efficiency, or the ratio of the number of electrons generated per photon absorbed in the material.

The practical quantum detector comes in two forms: the photoconductive and the photovoltaic, as illustrated in Figure 12.5. A photoconductive detector behaves like a variable resistor in which an increase in absorbed photons increases the conductivity of the material. An external circuit with a battery and load resistor is used to sense the change in conductivity. In the photovoltaic form, an electric field across a *p-n* junction separated by an absorbed photon causes a self-generated current of photons to flow in an external circuit, just like a battery. There is a minimum energy and wavelength threshold for this interaction given by λ (microns) $= 1.24/E(\text{eV})$, where $E(\text{eV})$ is the gap energy in electron-volts. For example, in pure silicon where $E \cong 1.1$ eV, the threshold wavelength $\lambda \cong 1.1$ microns. In this case, the threshold wavelength for detection is set by the band gap energy of silicon. Germanium has a slightly narrower band gap ($\cong 0.73$ eV) and thus a longer wavelength threshold of 1.7 microns. Silicon is the preferred semiconductor for detection in the visible and near-infrared spectral regions. It has the advantage of being integrated directly with electronics for readout and multiplexing on a single chip. Band gap detectors of this type are known as intrinsic detectors.

To detect at 3–5 and 8–14 microns for thermal imaging, the energy gap must be about 0.1 eV, or 1/10 that of pure silicon. One approach is to dope silicon with an element which forms an impurity energy level at less than the band gap near 0.1 eV. The element gallium in dosages of about 10^{16} atoms per cm^3, or approximately 2 parts in 10 million, converts the silicon material to a very sensitive long-wavelength, infrared photonconductive detector. This type of detector is known as an extrinsic (silicon) detector. Its properties can be tailored for specific wavelength thresholds by doping with a suitable impurity. Figure 12.6 shows the spectral response and quantum efficiency (the fraction of photons that develop an electronic charge in one detector) of silicon doped with gallium ($E = 0.063$ eV) and with indium ($E = 0.11$ eV). Dozens of elements from the periodic table have been inves-

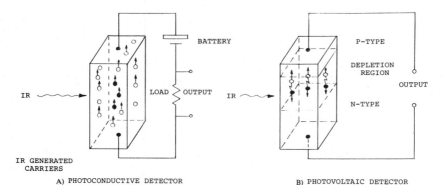

FIGURE 12.5. Two basic semiconductor infrared detectors are illustrated. An IR signal is produced at the output of photoconductive Type A because of varying conductivity with intensity of the radiation. In the photovoltaic Type B, current is produced at the output by electron–hole pairs generated in the carrier depletion region of a *p-n* junction.

tigated as dopants for silicon. Only a few of these dopants have proven practical for reasons of material and electronic compatibility with silicon.

Other semiconductor materials commonly used for both photoconductive and photovoltaic detectors are indium antimonide (InSb), lead sulfide (PbS), lead selenide (PbSe), and lead telluride (PbTe). Considerable effort is required to fabricate detectors with high quantum efficiency and low intrinsic noise characteristics.

Repeatability and yield in manufacture, always an issue with detectors, is stressed by a demand for large arrays of several hundred and more detectors per system. For surveillance sensors having large coverage, silicon would seem to be the preferred choice for producibility.

The application of silicon detectors in full mosaic focal plane arrays has been retarded because the physics of silicon devices requires a much lower operating temperature, approximately one-half of that needed for the compound semiconductors. To achieve maximum theoretical performance, detectors of threshold wavelengths greater than 2 microns require some cooling below room temperature. The operating characteristics of some of the detectors require extreme cryogenic cooling to 4 Kelvin. All thermal imaging sensing devices incorporate some form of cryostat or cryo-refrigerator to cool the detectors.

Cryogenic cooling is an especially important issue for space satellite operation because up to several hundred watts of electrical power may be needed onboard the space platform for every watt of cryogenic cooling for the focal plane.

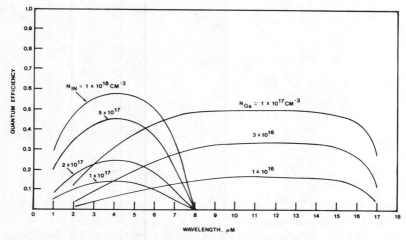

FIGURE 12.6. The quantum efficiency of Si:In and Si:Ga detectors as a function of wavelength for several impurity concentrations (N).

Mercury cadmium telluride (HgCdTe) comes as close to satisfying nearly all of these needs as can a single type of semiconductor compound. Advances in materials science make it possible to fabricate very high-quality crystalline mercury cadmium telluride (HgCdTe) in bulk crystalline and thin film crystalline forms compatible with large detector arrays. HgCdTe material research for detector applications is receiving substantial attention internationally. This material has the unique advantage of being adjustable in threshold wavelength, while being very electrically and mechanically compatible with silicon electronic readout devices. The wavelength adjustment is made by changing the ratio of HgTe to CdTe during growth to fix the band gap of the resultant crystal. The ability to tailor the threshold wavelength is important because the detector wavelength response can be selected for the application to avoid cooling to temperatures lower than needed for proper operation.

Lead tin telluride (PbSnTe) material has this same threshold wavelength flexibility in compositional variation (PbTe-SnTe) and is somewhat easier to grow than HgCdTe. However, HgCdTe has been favored over PbSnTe because of its much lower dielectric constant and its closer match in thermal expansion coefficient with silicon. These qualities make it more suitable for electrical and mechanical integration with silicon readout electronics to construct a mosaic focal plane.

Typical Detector Performance

The sensitivity of a detector is often described by a quantity known as the detectivity. It is referred to in a normalized figure-of-merit form as D^* (dee-star). It is given by the relation:

$$D^* = \frac{(S/N)}{P} (A\Delta f)^{1/2} \tag{1}$$

where S is the detector signal when an incoming radiation of power, P, is applied to it, and N is the detector noise when the radiation is shut off.

The normalization assumes the detector noise will vary with detector area, A, and noise measurement bandwidth, Δf. D^* may also be expressed as a function of wavelength, λ, and a maximum D^*_λ can be theoretically calculated. The maximum D^*_λ depends on the natural thermal background radiation incident on the detector. A standard measurement condition useful for comparing the measured or theoretical performance of detectors is to expose them to normal 300 K (room temperature) thermal background without shading or restricting their FOV, that is, measuring with an 180° FOV.

Under these conditions, the spectral D^* for several typical commercially available detectors is shown in Figure 12.7. Note that the uppermost solid curve and the short dashed curve are the maximum theoretical D^* of photoconductive and photovoltaic types, respectively.

Advanced Focal Plane Configurations

As described previously, future advanced concepts for IR focal planes anticipate fabricating thousands of detectors per chip, like integrated circuits for electronics. There are very general configurations for IR detectors: (a) the planar, and (b) Z-configurations. Each type of configuration has its practical and potential advantages. The planar type is very simple and easy to fabricate but provides a limited amount of area per detector for readout circuit. If a large area for electronic circuitry per detector channel is needed, the Z-configuration, which has considerable space in the vertical direction, must be used, since it is desirable to keep the readout circuity in the shadow of the detector array to allow butting or close spacing of chips with a large focal plane.

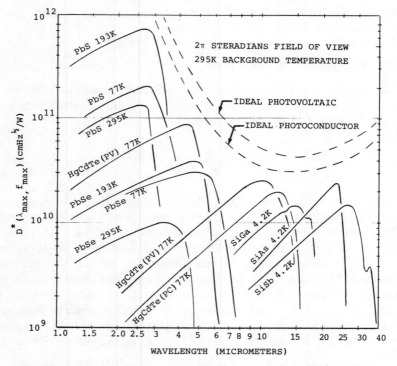

FIGURE 12.7. Spectral D^* for a number of commercially available detectors.

The planar format also creates some problems for the designer in accessing the silicon chip leads under the detector array. The Z-format, on the other hand, demands precision construction techniques in order to have up to 128 matching layers with edge lead access. With considerable industrial ingenuity, working versions of both types have been made. The planar format has received much more attention in development and has produced the most successful variety of results and data to date. However, as the Z-format matures it will provide a high payoff in versatility of application, detector materials, and built-in signal processing for future sensors.

Detector/CCD Coupling

Charge-coupled devices (CCDs) were first applied to the problem of low-noise IR detector readout for linear focal planes by Nummedal at Hughes Aircraft Company in 1972, only 2 years after their invention at Bell Laboratories. Because CCDs are described by Blouke and Janesick in Chapter 9, only a brief description of the IR/CCD interface will be given here. The single significant advantage of a CCD over all other forms of readout electronics is that it has a very compact periodic structure that operates to perform self-scanning charge transfer over a 2-dimensional path. Fabricated on silicon, a planar CCD matches the normally small detector geometries of only a few microns in dimensions and can self-scan several thousand elements of an array in a TV-like raster pattern. More sophisticated circuitry can now outperform CCDs for a lot of critical applications, but a Z-format is required to provide the area for the electronics.

A substrate material like silicon is a natural choice because it can be impurity-doped to operate as an extrinsic detector with the CCD fabricated directly on top of the detector array to form a monolithic focal plane array of a single material.

The input circuits can integrate the detector signal continuously into an integrating storage potential well, to be periodically transferred to the readout CCD. This means there will be no loss of signal or detector sensitivity due to the readout process interval.

Focal Plane Examples

Some examples of the types of focal planes that have been developed and demonstrated will be presented here. This represents only a very small sampling of a great number of focal planes demonstrated or reported on or actually used in various types of NASA and DoD sensors.

Scanning Array. A single, staggered, linear, 180-element HgCdTe array with silicon electronic readout devices is shown in Figure 12.8. In the photograph, the focal plane assembly is mounted on the cold plate of a dewar so we can view the array in the same direction as that of the incoming IR radiation. In operation, a scanning mirror placed in front of the array would allow the entire FOV to be scanned electronically in vertical columns at each instantaneous horizontal position of the scan mirror. This array and the readout electronics (3 chips arranged vertically on each side of the linear array) was especially designed to operate in the 8–14 window band for thermal imaging. A unique readout circuit is used in the silicon chips to preserve high uniformity of response between elements across the detector array. The array is operated at about 80 Kelvin. This focal plane was developed in 1983 and represents the state of the art.

Two-Dimensional Arrays. Figure 12.9 is a photograph of one of the first successfully demonstrated large mosaic chips. It consists of 1,024 detector elements of gallium-doped extrinsic silicon, which are read out by a CCD processed directly on the silicon detector substrate.

Since this chip was designed, more sophisticated detector coupling circuitry has been developed to improve noise, saturation and dynamic characteristics of the readout electronics. Recently, a new, higher-performance

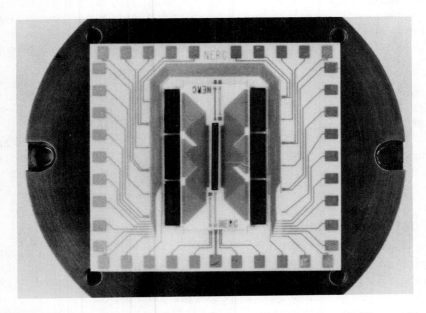

FIGURE 12.8. An example of a long linear 180-element HgCdTe array with silicon readout electronics. A scanning mirror is used to move the image across the linear array. The devices are mounted on a ceramic substrate assembled for easy insertion into a cryogenic dewar.

device has been demonstrated using several different dopants in a hybrid-like extrinsic silicon-on-silicon (SOXS) device, which is assembled like the planar configuration focal plane. This does not require electronic device fabrication directly on the detector array chip, and it preserves the normal high performance of the detector material by avoiding exposure to contam-

FIGURE 12.9. An example of a two-dimensional mosaic of 32×32 detector elements in a monolithic focal plan array format. This was one of the first mosaic devices successfully fabricated using extrinsic silicon (1974).

inants during the high temperature steps used in fabrication of the readout electronics. A unique 16,000-detector mosaic version of the SOXS developed by Pommerrenig at Rockwell International has been used to generate planetary imagery with a resolution of 20 seconds of arc in the 3–5 micron band.

Intrinsic Hybrids. An intrinsic semiconductor used in a planar hybrid configuration with a silicon CCD is the most common form of mosaic focal plane under development. Detector materials used in this format include InSb, In AsSb, PbSnTe and HgCdTe (short and long wavelength versions). HgCdTe is the most versatile form because a common set of electrical/mechanical interface technologies can be used with this one detector material to cover the entire region from 2 to 14 microns.

The Z-technology has been demonstrated using PbS and HgCdTe detectors by Grumman Aerospace. In front illumination, the active face of the detector is on top of the array. Special ion-milling HgCdTe delineation technology was developed at New England Research Center for this purpose. In back illumination, the detector array is flipped over to make a soft-solder bump bond from each detector to the readout electronics. The detector material must be very thin or on a transparent substrate for this approach.

Some Examples of Sensors

The most widely known examples of infrared sensors are the NASA Landsat remote-sensing series of satellites which have produced spectacular false-color earth imagery with the multispectral scanner (MSS). Infrared remote sensing (from high-altitude aircraft and space satellites) techniques are used routinely for agriculture, forestry, and demographic monitoring. Recently, new sensor technologies are being used routinely as techniques for geologic remote sensing in mineral and energy exploration, plant siting, and tectonic modeling.

The spectral region from 3 to 15 microns is especially useful for geologic mapping. Goetz and Rowan (*Science*, Feb. 1981) have described the use of the electromagnetic radiation spectrum from wavelengths from visible (0.4 micron) to L-band (30 cm) for these purposes. Using multispectral data provided by the NASA Thematic Mapper, the major geologic features of the Las Vegas, Nevada, area are clearly delineated in the false-color image shown in Figure 12.10. Roads and other artificial surface features can be seen (in the original). The resolution of this sensor is about 30 meters on the ground from an altitude of 700 kilometers. Analysis of these Landsat multispectral scanner images have resulted in the discovery of previously unmapped geologic features. The potential application of this technology to verification can be inferred from this NASA capability.

The Thematic Mapper sensor is shown in Figure 12.11. The sensor characteristics are summarized in Table 12.1. The aperture of this sensor is 0.4 meters, providing about 2.5 times greater resolution over previous sensors. It is capable of detecting temperature differences as small as 0.25°C in the scenes.

Another example of infrared imagery is shown in Figure 12.12. This image was made at night from an aircraft flying at 1,000 feet, using a Daedalus Enterprises DS-1220 terrain surveillance scanner. The sensor param-

FIGURE 12.10. Landsat-4 Thematic Mapper Image of Las Vegas, Nevada, December 12, 1982, 9:30 A.M. in spectral bands 2.22, 0.66 and 0.83 microns. Total scene covers a region of 180 km sq. Taken from an altitude of 700 km. (Courtesy of Santa Barbara Research Center.)

Table 12.1. Design Parameters

	Visible and Near-Infrared	Thermal
Spectral bands, microns	(6) from 0.45 to 2.35	10.4 to 12.5 (1)
Detectors	Silicon (64), InSb (32)	HgCdTe (4 at 95K)
Resolution, meters	30	120
NE T at 320 K, K		0.25

Orbit: 705 km, 99 min, polar, sun synchronous (9:15 am)
Scan: 7.0 Hz linear cross-course
Telescope: 40.6 cm diameter, f/6 Ritchey-Chretien
Size: 71 × 109 × 200 cm
Weight: 243 kg

ters are given in Table 12.2. The sensor detects in both the 3–5 micron and 8–13 micron bands. The imagery shows bright spots representing the detection and pointing of several small, hot targets, including open and camouflaged charcoal fires in a typical forest campground environment. A number of the small targets are identified in the figure. Although the temperature sensitivity is about the same as the Thematic Mapper, the ground

FIGURE 12.11. The NASA Landsat Thematic Mapper. This sensor provides imagery in seven spectral bands from the visible, near-infrared, and thermal infrared regimes. Specifications are given in Table 12.1. (Courtesy of Santa Barbara Research Center.)

Table 12.2. Daedalus Sensor Model No. DS = 1220 Parameters

Operating Wavelengths	3.0–5.5 and 8.0–13.0 Micrometers
Aperture	5 Inches
Focal Length	6 Inches
Optical Aperture (effective)	f/2
Scan Rate	160 Scans Per Second
Total Field of View	87° 20′
Gated Field of View	77° 20′
Instantaneous Field of View	1.7 Milliradians
Temperature Resolution	0.2°C
V/H	0.26 Radians/Second
Roll Correction	Total: ±10°; Unvignetted ±5°
Weight	112 Kg
Size	50 × 50 × 160 cm

FIGURE 12.12. A Daedalus Enterprises, Inc. dual channel terrain surveillance scanner, DS-1220 infrared image at night from a height of 1,000 ft. The figure is dual channel, 3–5 microns and 8–13 microns IR image. Several small targets are seen as hot (bright) spots in a wooded area representing a variety of terrain and vegetation. Targets were charcoal fires, bonfires, vehicles, and people. The large bright spot in the upper-left corner is a bonfire surrounded by people and vehicles (warm). The cluster in the middle-upper right represents warm vehicles including one covered by a canvas tent. The cluster at the lower center represents several small charcoal fires adjacent to four aluminum strips. The aluminum strips are cold (black) because they are reflecting the cold night sky.

FIGURE 12.13. High altitude thermal image of the United States at night. (Courtesy of RCA.)

resolution is approximately 0.5 meters. However, this is actually about 40 times worse in angular resolution than the Thematic Mapper. This decrease in resolution in this case is due to the smaller aperture of the Daedalus system and a somewhat larger detector than the Thematic Mapper. The much shorter range from the sensor to the scene for the Daedalus example makes up for the lower performance of the sensor.

A final example of an IR image is presented in Figure 12.13. This may be recognizable as a view of the continental United States. The image is a two-pass composite taken in the long wavelength thermal infrared band from a high-altitude meteorological satellite. The densely populated areas in the East, Midwest, South Gulf areas, and the West Coast are readily seen.

Each of these sensors represents a particular design solution tailored to the application. Continued improvements in detector and optical technologies will increase sensitivity and resolution of future sensors.

13.

Fourier Transform Spectroscopy Measurements at Infrared and Millimeter Wavelengths

Robert J. Bell

Introductory Note by Kosta Tsipis

Light reflected or emitted from atoms or molecules of various substances has a spectrum of characteristic frequencies unique to each substance. Thus, if one can scan rapidly and precisely the light emitted or reflected from even very distant objects, substances or gasses, one can identify the particular physical or chemical composition of the reflected or emitted light. The implications of this fact for the monitoring of activities inside another country without physically intruding on it are enormous.

The Fourier transform spectroscopy described in this paper provides precisely this capability. It is a thousand times more efficient than older conventional (or traditional) spectrographic techniques. Because the Fourier transform spectrometer has a wide aperture rather than a small slit, it receives much more light, and as a consequence can be much more sensitive than ordinary instruments. Equally important, this new type of spectrometer can process signals in real time, something not possible in the past. Fourier transform spectrometers, and the associated computers that process the data they obtain, can be carried on aircraft, satellites, sounding rockets, and balloons, as well as on land and sea surface vehicles. It is possible, then, utilizing the immutable physical properties of atoms, to identify the presence of given materials or chemicals in the gaseous effluents of Soviet plants or to determine the material that coats Soviet ICBM reentry vehicles, to give two examples. In the case of the first example, such information can be used to deduce operations within the plants, to monitor the production of potential chemical or biological warfare agents, and to verify the absence of activity in plutonium- and tritium-producing reactors and processing plants (thus monitoring a ban on the production of nuclear materials). In the case of the second example, information about reentry vehicle coating is useful for monitoring the sophistication of Soviet ICBM technology in the testing stage.

There is a very large number of other uses of this little-mentioned monitoring technology that are now routine practice in civilian scientific applications as well as in other intelligence-gathering operations. Its precision and certainty provide an exciting step forward in many areas, but none more promisingly than verification.

INTRODUCTION

Over the last few years Fourier transform spectroscopy[1,2] (FTS) has been developed for infrared to millimeter wavelength studies of remote objects. Trace gas detection studies; temperature and pressure measurements of the atmosphere and of effluent gases from many different types of sources; dust and aerosol studies; atmospheric turbulence avoidance techniques; very high spectral resolution infrared and millimeter wavelength measurements of many sources—the planets, stars, and deep space; and surveillance of agriculture production and diseases have been among the uses made of FTS. Vehicles such as satellites, rockets, balloons, airplanes, and vans have been used as platforms for the FTS equipment and computers. Data recording and computer analysis times as short as a few milliseconds to seconds have been realized in practice.

As seen in practice at the infrared and longer wavelengths, there are many advantages to FTS, with techniques for rapid scanning, background discrimination, simultaneous observation of many radiation frequencies at the same time (multiplexing), high spectral resolution, excellent throughput efficiencies, very accurately determined wave numbers, small and light packaging of instruments, and very rapid data analysis. On the other hand, the instruments are delicate, and finding very sensitive detectors and strong sources is difficult. In many cases cryogenics are required for detectors, and at very long wavelengths the entire instruments sometimes must be cooled.

Compared to grating instruments, the principal advantage of Fourier transform spectrometers are[1]:

1. One multiplexes the radiation signal received by recording optical signals at *all* frequencies during a scan (the FTS can be up to 10^3 times more efficient than is possible with grating instruments).
2. The resolution of FTS is primarily determined by the maximum optical path difference in the interferometer. Thus, the source aperture can be very large (and circular) compared to narrow slit widths in grating instruments. This results in an FTS signal-to-noise advantage of the order of one hundred over older instruments and is sometimes called the "throughput" advantage.

3. With small HeNe laser beams tracking the movable mirror position in the interferometer, the frequency determination of radiation spectral lines can be made very precise.
4. Because the fast Fourier transform ("Cooley-Tukey algorithm") is so extraordinarily fast, computer manipulation of signals can be done on-line or off in fractions of a second on modern small computers such as the IBM-PC.

OBTAINING THE RADIATION SPECTRUM
FROM THE RECEIVED SIGNAL

If one has a Michelson interferometer,[1,2] as shown in Figure 13.1, and a monochromatic (σ = wave number) source, the signal recorded (the "interferogram," $I(\delta)$) as a function of the optical path difference, δ, between the mirror arms is a cosine function. The magnitude of the interferogram is proportional to the intensity of the source at frequency f. If there are many sources each of differing frequency f and each of magnitude $B(f)$, one then observes in $I(\delta)$ the sum of the many intensities from each of the frequencies. That is, $I(\delta)$ is the sum of cosines, each of different magnitudes and frequencies. Fourier's basic idea can be invoked to transform $I(\delta)$ versus optical path difference, δ, into the magnitude components of the spectrum at each wave number K with

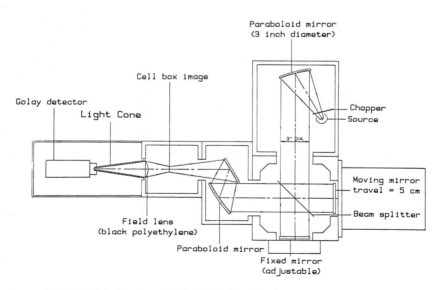

FIGURE 13.1. Diagram of RIIC Michelson Fourier transform spectrometer.

$$B(f) = \int_0^\infty [I(\delta) - I(\delta = \infty)]\cos(2\pi f\delta)d\delta \tag{1}$$

where proportionality constants have been dropped. All one need do is record $I(\delta)$ (δ is equal to twice the movable mirror displacement) and perform the Fourier transform on a computer to find $B(f) =$ (intensity versus wave number, or frequency).

RAPID-SCAN FOURIER TRANSFORM SPECTROSCOPY

In usual practice the interferogram is recorded by moving the mirror in steps through the maximum drive distance, $L/2$. However, one may move the mirror very rapidly at constant velocity and record the interferogram on magnetic media.[1] Rapid scanning also means moving the mirror at a rate such that the interferometric fringes suppress themselves. The modulation in the interferogram furnishes an alternating current signal that can be processed for electronic spectral filtering, electronic noise reduction, and for avoiding some low frequency atmospheric turbulence. The technique of rapid-scan Fourier spectroscopy makes it possible to record single interferograms in under one second (sometimes in a millisecond).[3] Repetition is used to improve the signal-to-noise ratio whenever necessary.

Rapid-scan Fourier transform spectroscopy was developed by Mertz[4] and described in an article, "Rapid Scanning Fourier Transform Spectrometry," and in his book, *Transformations in Optics*.

If one has a spectral signal $B(K)$ for a monochromatic source at a given wave number K and optical path difference δ, it may be expressed in

$$I(\delta) = B(K)[1 + \cos(2\pi K\delta)] \tag{2}$$

with δ given by

$$\delta = 2vt \tag{3}$$

where v is the velocity of the movable mirror and t is the instantaneous scan time. For a source of many Ks the interferogram, $I'(v,t)$, as a function of movable mirror velocity and time is

$$I'(v,t) \equiv I(\delta) - I(\infty) = \int_0^\infty B(K)\cos(4\pi vKt)dK \tag{4}$$

with the modulation frequency of the interferogram given by

$$f = 2Kv . \tag{5}$$

For v of 10^{-2} to 10 cm/s, one has f of the order of 1 to 10^3 Hz in the near IR. A moderately fast detector is needed.

If one wants to compute a spectrum between wave numbers K_1 and K_2, electronic band-pass filters can be used to isolate the spectral range in the interferogram. The desired range of frequencies in the interferogram is determined by

$$2vK_1 \leq f \leq 2vK_2 \ . \qquad\qquad (6)$$

One can reduce or eliminate electronic noise by accepting only ac signal voltages above a certain level. The voltage level is set low enough to pass spectral information but too high for noise. Because the rapid-scan system requires no mechanical suppression of fringes, one has the entire signal on the detector all the time. Therefore, it is twice as efficient as spectrometers with choppers.

The experimentalist can choose the exact frequencies he wishes to receive by choosing v for a given spectral range. In astronomy, the fringe frequency is set above atmospheric gaseous turbulence frequencies.

Weak spectral signals in a rapid-scan Fourier transform spectrometer require that the interferogram be recorded repetitiously. One can average the interferograms or the computed spectra to obtain the required signal-to-noise ratio in the final averaged spectrum. The Cooley-Tukey algorithm[1] keeps computation times negligible for many situations except for very high resolution scans not often done using rapid-scan techniques.

HIGH SPECTRAL RESOLUTION OF FTS

With movable mirror displacements up to one meter ($\delta_{max} = 2$ m), FTS in ground-based use has been extended to resolving powers of 0.005 cm^{-1} at the Air Force Geophysics Laboratory at Bedford, Massachusetts, the Université Pierre and Marie Curie in Paris, and the Centre National de la Récherche Scientifique in Paris. By triple passing (using retroreflectors), G. Guelachvili[5] extended δ_{max} to 6 m yielding resolution of about 0.002 cm^{-1}.

Referring to Figure 13.2, one may see how the resolution of laboratory or laboratory-telescope FTS has improved by about three orders of magnitude over the last 20 years to the present state of the art. Of course, these capabilities developed in the laboratories assist "in-the-field" use.

ATMOSPHERIC GASES AND PARTICLES

FTS can be used to obtain at a distance information (molecular identity, temperature, and pressure parameters plus some limited information about particle sizes, shapes, orientation, concentration, etc.) about some sources of radiation and about the transmittance of radiation through the relevant atmospheric regions.

The contents of the earth's atmosphere are documented[7-9] under many different circumstances, with variables such as time of day, season, lati-

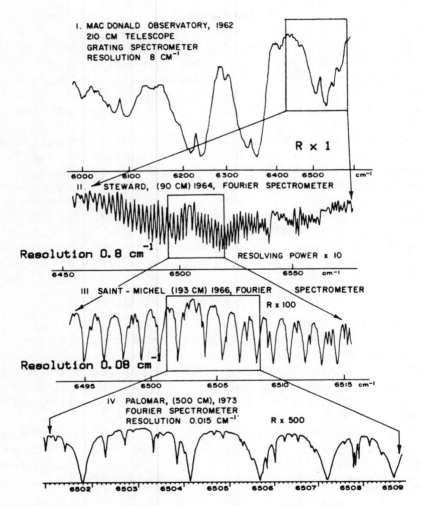

FIGURE 13.2. Spectra of Venus taken with ground-based telescopes showing the improvements of the resolution of the Fourier spectrometers over the years. Laboratory measurements of higher resolution, 0.002 cm^{-1}, are cited in reference 6. (Figures 13.2 and 13.3 are from: "Astronomical Fourier Spectrometer" by P. Connes and G. Michel, 1975, *Applied Optics*, 14, p. 2067. Copyright 1975 by Optical Society of America. Used with permission.)

tude, geography, relevant distances, altitude, temperature, pressure, and albedo, among others. The mixing ratios of the gases[7] CO_2, N_2O, CH_3, CO, N_2 and O_2 remain relatively constant at all altitudes at the following values: 330, 0.28, 1.6, 0.075, 7.905×10^5, and 2.095×10^5 parts per million respectively. O_3 relative concentrations are variable. In the atmospheric window region from 9.5 to 12 micrometers wavelengths, nitric acid has been shown to be a significant source of stratospheric emission. For computer output, refer to the LOWTRAN code[10] which calculates atmospheric transmittance and radiance averaged over 20 cm^{-1} intervals in steps of 5 cm^{-1} from 350 to 40,000 cm^{-1} (28.5 to 0.25 μm).

Figure 13.3 indicates the trace gases in the lower atmosphere. In laboratory studies of atmospheric gases, Hanst[11] reports detectability limits for NH_3, CO, CH_3 and HNO_3 of 0.2, 0.6, 0.6, and 0.3 in billionths of an atmosphere, respectively.

FTS is concerned with atomic, molecular, and particulate absorption.[12] It has been used to gather some data on particles in the atmosphere so that this contribution can be subtracted from the measurements. By using the rapid scan FTS technique, it has been possible to obtain complete spectral data "in-the-field" in scan times of the order of 100 seconds down to milliseconds. With ground, water, air, rocket, and satellite platforms, FTS has been employed with discrimination against various backgrounds. The major component of the normal upper atmosphere is considered to be meteoric dust.

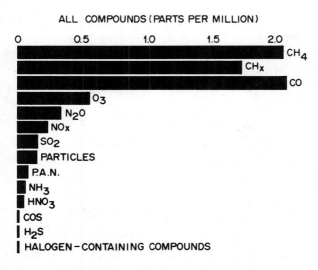

FIGURE 13.3. Atmospheric trace gases.

ELIMINATING BACKGROUND RADIATION
FROM THE RECEIVED SIGNAL

An important technique for picking an emission signal out of the background has been developed by George A. Vanasse, et al.[13] The method is called BOSS (background optical suppression system).

In a dual-beam Michelson FTS, there are two radiation beams simultaneously passing through the interferometer — one is the radiation signal plus background and the other radiation beam comes from the background nearby the signal source. In real-time the background radiation is *optically cancelled at the beamsplitter*, and one sees only the wanted signal (modulated) from some distant source. That is, as the interferogram is recorded the modulated signal does not have any background contribution (see Figure 13.4). The instrument is compact and has already been field-tested on the ground. The BOSS will work in either the "step-and-record" FTS technique or the "rapid-scan" FTS technique.

The bandwidth, or dynamic range advantage, of a double-beam interferometer is illustrated by the spectra of Figure 13.4A, which shows the spectra of smokestack emissions plus background obtained with the interferometer operated as a single-beam interferometer. Figure 13.4B is the single-beam spectra of the background only, and Figure 13.4C is the resultant spectra obtained by the intensity subtraction of the two single-beam spectra of Figures 13.4A and 13.4B. Figure 13.4D is the BOSS, or double-beam spectra, of the same scene. To obtain these spectra, the interferograms were converted to digital words with an amplitude resolution of 10 bits.

The CO_2 spike is readily identifiable in the double-beam spectra, Figure 13.4D, whereas in the subtracted single-beam spectra it is obscured by quantization noise. These spectra show in a dramatic way the bandwidth advantage of the BOSS scheme. See Table 13.1 for the experimental parameters of design for the BOSS of Vanasse.

SPACECRAFT SPECTRA USING FTS

The FTS spectra of the earth taken by the Nimbus III[1,2,7,14] satellite are shown in Figure 13.5. These data have been called "the best thermal emission spectra of the earth available as of this writing."[15]

INFRARED AND MILLIMETER WAVELENGTH FTS FROM
BALLOONS WITH COOLED SYSTEMS

In monitoring the residual radiant flux from the "Big Bang" creation of the universe, a group under P. L. Richards at the University of California-

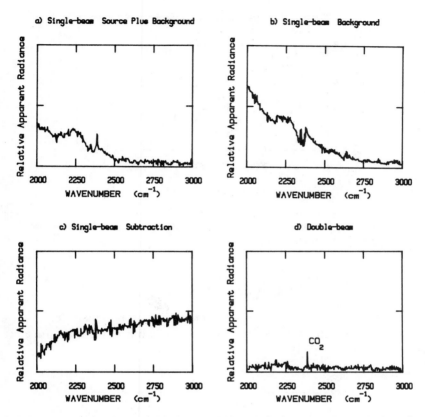

FIGURE 13.4. Comparison of dual-beam BOSS and single-beam spectra obtained from interferograms focused on and nearby the plume above a smoke stack of a natural gas heating plant at a distance of 350 meters. Parts c and d of the figure tell the story in noting the CO_2 spike left in the BOSS spectra. (From: "Double-Beaming Techniques in Fourier Spectroscopy" by G. Vanasse, R. Murphy and F. Cook, 1976, *Applied Optics*, 15, p. 290. Copyright 1976 by Optical Society of America. Used with permission.)

Berkeley[14] flew a cooled millimeter λ FTS in a balloon. Their results are shown in Figure 13.6. (The entire instrument was cooled for increased sensitivity.)

In balloon experiments flown on 23 October 1983, one interferogram was taken every 25 seconds, yielding resolution of 0.12 cm^{-1}. The spectral range was 2 to 24 μm wavelength. The instrument "would be very efficient for down-looking measurements for various emissions."[14]

For some upcoming infrared "shuttle flights," over 500 liters of liquid helium will be put onboard to cool the infrared instrumentation including the associated telescope.

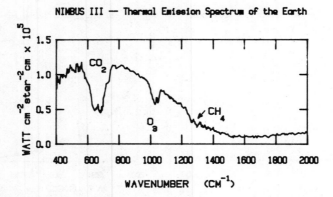

FIGURE 13.5. Emission from the earth's atmosphere as measured aboard Nimbus III using FTS. (Adapted from: Chapter 2 by R. Hanel, 1983, in G. Vanasse, ed., *Spectrometric Techniques*. New York: Academic Press.)

$^{235}UF_6$ AND $^{238}UF_6$ SPECTRA

Several different ways of obtaining uranium isotope separation involve the gases of UF_6; the infrared spectra[16] for the two isotopic gases are given in Figure 13.7.

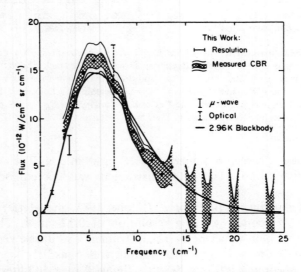

FIGURE 13.6. FTS measurements from a balloon of the cosmic background radiation. (From: "Near-millimeter Spectrum of the Microwave Background" by P. Woody and P. Richards, 1981, *Astrophysical Journal*, 278, p. 18. Used with permission.)

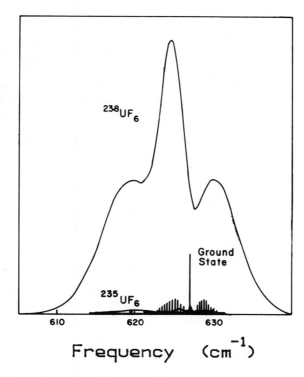

FIGURE 13.7. Infrared spectra of $^{238}UF_6$ and $^{235}UF_6$ at room temperature obtained with an FT spectrometer. (From: "Prospects for Uranium Enrichment" by R. Jensen, J. Marinuzzi, C. Robinson and S. Rockwood, 1976, *Laser Focus*, 12, p. 51. Reprinted from Laser Focus © 1976 with permission of PennWell Publishing Co., Littleton MA.)

Table 13.1. BOSS Interferometer System Specifications

Spectral Range	1820–7900 cm^{-1}
Spectral Resolution	3.86 cm^{-1}
Aperture	22-mm diam
Lens f/No.	f/2
AΩ	7.1×10^{-5} cm^2 sr
Spectral Transmission (Single Beam)	0.4
Detector Type	InSb (PV)
Detector Size	0.025-cm diam
$D^*(\lambda_{pk}, 900, 1)$	3.5×10^{11} cm Hz$^{1/2}$ W^{-1}
Scan Rate	1 sec/scan
Sampling Rate	8 kHz
Data Bandwidth (Maximum)	2.5 kHz
NESR* (at 2000 cm^{-1})	3.2×10^{-8} W/cm^2 sr cm^{-1}

*NESR ≡ (Noise Equivalent Spectral Radiance, at some wave number)

REFERENCES

1. See, for example, *Aspen Int. Conf. on Fourier Spectrosc.*, G. A. Vanasse, A. T. Stair, Jr., and D. J. Baker, Eds. AFCRL (now AFGL)-71-00195, Jan. 1971, Spec. Rep. No. 114; Bell, R. J. and R. W. Alexander, Jr. *Introductory Fourier Transform Spectroscopy.* New York: Academic Press, 1972; and Vanasse, G. A., Ed. *Spectrometric Techniques.* New York: Academic Press, Vol. I in 1977, Vol. II in 1981 and Vol. III in 1984, among others.

2. Bell, R. J. Applications of Fourier Transform Spectroscopy. In *Spectrometric Techniques*, Vol. 1, Chap. 3, edited by G. A. Vanasse. New York: Academic Press, 1977; Griffiths, P. R., *Science* 222 (1983): 297; and Vanasse, G. A. *Appl. Opt.* 21 (1982): 189.

3. Schildkraut, E. R. Block Engineering, private communication.

4. Mertz, L. *Transformations in Optics.* New York: Wiley 1965, p. 44.

5. Connes, P. and G. Michel. *Appl. Opt.* 14 (1975): 2067; Guelachvili, G. *Appl. Opt.* 16 (1977): 2097.

6. Loete, M. *et al. Journal of Molecular Spectroscopy* 99 (1983): 63.

7. Kneizys, K. X. *et al.* Air Force Geophysics Laboratory, Hanscom AFB, Bedford, MA 01731.

8. Rothman, L. S. *Appl. Opt.* 20 (1981): 791.

9. Goldman, A. *et al. Appl. Opt.* 21 (1982): 1163.

10. Kneizys, F. X. AFGL/OPI, Hanscomb AFB, Bedford, MA 01731.

11. Hanst, P. L. Chap. 2. In *Fourier Transform Spectroscopy*, Vol. 2, edited by J. R. Ferraro, L. G. Basile, and L. J. Easile, New York: Academic Press, 1979.

12. Bohren, C. F. and D. R. Huffman. *Absorption and Scattering of Light by Small Particles.* New York: Wiley, 1983, p. 438.

13. Vanasse, G. A., R. E. Murphy, and F. H. Cook. *Appl. Opt.* 15 (1976): 290.

14. Woody, D. P. and P. L. Richards. *Astrophysical Journal* 248 (1981): 18.

15. Hanel, R. Chap. 2. In *Spectrometric Techniques*, Vol. 3, edited by G. A. Vanasse. New York: Academic Press, 1983.

16. Jensen, R. J., J. C. Marinuzzi, C. P. Robinson, and S. D. Rockwood. *Laser Focus*, 12(5) (May 1976): 51.

PART 3
MONITORING

14.
The Application of Verification Tools to Control of Offensive Strategic Missiles

Herbert Scoville, Jr.

Land- and submarine-based intercontinental ballistic missiles, long-range bombers, and long-range cruise missiles were the key offensive strategic weapons that the SALT I, SALT II and START negotiations attempted to control. These will also occupy the primary attention of the negotiations that began in Geneva on March 13, 1985. The monitoring of such strategic delivery systems by non-intrusive means provides useful examples of techniques of verification that can be applied to other arms control areas. Therefore, it is pertinent to see how the various verification techniques described in the foregoing chapters can be integrated so as to provide confidence that non-compliance with any treaty would not significantly affect the security of either signatory party. In many cases, the language in a treaty itself can become an important tool to make the available technologies more effective.

In the negotiations to date, primary attention has been directed toward the numbers of weapons deployed, but the characteristics of the new weapons that might displace the older ones are of equal if not greater importance. The key goal of arms control is reduction of the probability that a nuclear conflict will break out, and the *types* of weapons are here much more critical than the *numbers*. Weapon characteristics are only susceptible to verification when a weapons system reaches the test stage, because the monitoring of laboratory research and, more significantly, the determination of its purpose are unreliable. Data from the tests can be correlated with observations of the missiles when they are deployed. Production of delivery vehicles is also an important phase of any weapons program for monitoring purposes, even though verification of controls on production is more difficult than prohibitions regarding testing or deployment. Despite lower reliability of production verification, controls here can add an important element to the overall objective of limiting an offensive strategic weapons system.

LAND-BASED INTERCONTINENTAL BALLISTIC MISSILES

The deployment of fixed intercontinental ballistic missiles (ICBMs) can be easily observed by satellite photography because the launchers and associated logistic support are readily identifiable. Furthermore, they require several years to build, so that even were satellite photography unavailable for protracted periods because of cloud cover or other factors, any new launcher would almost certainly be detected well in advance of becoming operational. Attempts to camouflage such launchers as oil tank farms or other installations would almost certainly not escape notice. As a general rule, the United States has obtained one- to two-years advance notice of new Soviet missile deployments.

The fear that the number of launchers does not accurately represent the number of missiles available for attack is not realistic. To deal with this concern, however, the SALT II Treaty actually banned the acquisition of rapid reload missiles. These would require testing to assure the necessary reliability. Such testing could be observed by satellites and other means. If the extra missiles were to be stored nearby, they would require special hardened facilities whose construction would be observable by satellite. If they were stored at considerable distances in order to make them more survivable in the event of an attack on the launcher itself, then they would have to be moved after the attack and installed in the launch silo. This would require, especially in the case of liquid-fueled missiles, several days at least during which the missile would be visible and vulnerable to destruction by even small, inaccurate warheads. Furthermore, the area in which such an operation would have to be conducted would be highly radioactive if the launch complex had been attacked already. The acquisition of a rapid reload capability would be particularly difficult for the Soviets, because almost all of their current operational missiles are liquid fueled and thus require fueling in the launcher itself. Future generation Soviet missiles may employ solid fuels, but, even so, rapid reload is not a serious military threat.

It would be more difficult to verify the number of deployed mobile ICBMs, because continuous coverage of all such missiles might not be feasible. Long-term concealment of a significant number of mobile missiles would nevertheless be subject to observation. They would still require logistic support and special security arrangements, all of which would provide clues to our national intelligence. No truly mobile ICBM has yet been tested or designed, but it seems that important violations in the total number available are not likely to escape detection. The Soviet intermediate-range SS-20 missile is movable (a more accurate description of the missile's capability than "mobile"), and yet the U.S. Defense Department has announced the deployment of every additional missile. A mobile intercontinental-range missile, because of its larger size, would be even easier to detect. Thus, while some uncertainty might exist as to the total number of mobile missiles deployed, this uncertainty would not be large enough to provide a major security risk. A total ban on such systems would offer the maximum reliability of verification.

The testing of new land-based ICBMs is readily detectable by a wide range of the verification techniques discussed elsewhere in this volume. Monitoring of the Soviet test ranges both from surface stations outside the borders of the Soviet Union and from satellites has provided high confidence that every Soviet test can be observed. A launch from a new test range could be detected by infrared satellites in a geosynchronous orbit. There is no reason to believe that any Soviet ICBM test since the beginning of their program in 1957 has occurred without our knowledge.

The acquisition of telemetry from ground stations on the periphery of the Soviet Union provides a wealth of information on the characteristics of the missile tested. Encryption of such telemetry makes it more difficult to obtain this type of data. Therefore the SALT II Treaty specifically banned encryption that impeded the verification of compliance with the limitations in the treaty. Both countries have, however, encrypted telemetry data. When accused of violating the treaty, they have claimed that the special data encrypted were not relevant to the treaty limitations. This has, however, become a source of considerable international controversy, and sweeping provisions banning encryption of all telemetry would be useful in any future situations. Such broad restrictions could probably not be agreed upon, unless the treaty also banned all new weapons testing.

Observations of ICBM test programs are not limited to the launch part of the trajectory. Much valuable data can be obtained by instruments placed at the reentry end of the range. Surface instruments on both land and sea can obtain data on the numbers of reentry vehicles and their capabilities. Infrared instrumentation, radars, and other electronic devices provide detailed information on the characteristics of these reentry vehicles.

All changes in weapons characteristics cannot, however, be verified by national technical means (or NTM, the all-inclusive term for a country's non-intrusive, legal surveillance capabilities). For example, the SALT II Treaty did not ban improvements in missile accuracy since the characteristics of the guidance systems on tested missiles cannot be reliably verified by national technical means. Observation of where a missile lands will not tell its accuracy, but telemetry can provide data on the operational characteristics of a guidance system from which estimates can be made of the potential accuracy. Telemetry will also indicate whether significant changes have been made in the system from previous tests. As long as some replacement of older missiles by new missiles is allowed, it will always be very difficult to verify that no changes have been made in all of the important characteristics of the new missiles. If the ban were more sweeping, however, and called for a halt to any changes from previously tested missiles, as well as forbidding the encryption of telemetry, then our national technical means would have a high probability of detecting a violation that could result in the development of a reliable and significantly improved new missile for deployment.

The production of ICBMs is the most difficult phase of a weapons program to verify. However, national technical means do provide some tools for this purpose. Any facility producing a significant number of such big missiles must be large and therefore easily detectable. The most difficult problem results from confusion of other large production sites with those for missiles. But even here there are many potential clues for an alert intelligence to locate a clandestine production. Senior Defense Department officials have testified that we know where such sites are today. If a production ban were agreed to, then these would have to be closed down and the construction of new ones or renewed operation of a declared one would have a high probability of being spotted by satellite photography. Any production site must have the logistic support for materials to be brought in and the finished parts to be brought out and assembled. Even though the probabilities are lower than for monitoring testing and deployment, the probability of detecting secret production would add to the capability for verifying a total ban on the acquisition of new and more advanced ICBM capabilities.

The destruction of ballistic missiles, both land- and submarine-based, as a part of an arms reduction agreement, can be verified by agreeing on procedures for such destruction to make it easily observable by satellites. Methods for doing this were worked out in the Standing Consultative Commission (SCC) set up by SALT I, and no serious question has been raised over the adequacy of such procedures in the more than ten years that the Interim Agreement has been in force. These procedures are still classified, because the actions of the SCC are not made public, but there is no doubt about their efficacy. Thus, one has already in place the verification capabilities for reductions in ballistic missiles and ten years of experience in applying them.

SUBMARINE-LAUNCHED BALLISTIC MISSILES

The numbers of deployed submarine-launched ballistic missiles (SLBMs) can be verified by observation of the submarines designed to carry such missiles. The construction facilities in which the submarines are built are readily identifiable, and the number of launch tubes in each submarine can be determined by satellite surveillance. By the time a submarine begins sea trials, the number of missiles that are deployed or deployable can be counted. Therefore, it is not necessary to locate all the submarines in the ocean at any particular time. The size of the launch tubes gives information on which types of missiles can be deployed, and this can be correlated with information on those that have been tested.

The testing of SLBMs is usually started from land test ranges and can be monitored by the same methods used for ICBMs. When the missile is nearly operational, the tests might be launched from the submarines themselves, but such tests can be detected by infrared satellites. These can spot launches not only from land but from any of the possible ocean areas that might be used for testing. Furthermore, because any test is carried out to provide information on the performance of the missile, it is necessary for the testing nation to have instrumentation to observe the reentry and probably other parts of the trajectory. This provides many opportunities for getting information on the characteristics of the missile that is being tested in much the same way as is done for land launches.

The verification of production of SLBMs is no different from that of land-based missiles. However, in this case the availability of extra missiles is not very significant, since before they can be launched, the submarine would have to return to port and reload. This would be a time-consuming process and, of course, the submarine itself will be vulnerable as long as it is in port.

LONG-RANGE BOMBERS

The number of long-range bombers in the arsenal of either the United States or the Soviet Union can be readily determined by national technical means, primarily by satellites, but with the very useful assistance of communications and other intelligence techniques. Bombers must fly if they are to have any operational capability. They cannot be stored in a hangar or mountainside and then wheeled out for a surprise attack. For large aircraft, even the production would be very hard to conceal. If some production were allowed, then it might be more difficult to determine the rate at which they were being built. However, since any plane must be transported to and operated from some air base, it is most unlikely that any significant uncertainty would exist about the number of aircraft available. As a part of a reduction agreement, procedures for observing the destruction of any aircraft could be worked out.

The biggest difficulty with bombers, as with missiles, is not the numbers but the characteristics of the plane itself. Is it long range or intermediate range? And what type and number of bombs and missiles can it carry?

These characteristics vary according to plans for the operational use of the particular aircraft, since reduction in the fuel load will reduce the range and permit more payload. Conversely, reduction in payload permits extension of the range. The planned speed and altitude at which the plane would fly on a mission can also have a tremendous effect on its range and on the payload that it could carry to this distance. There is also the question of whether the aircraft would have a one-way capability or the ability to return to a secure base. Aerial refueling capabilities can usually be determined by looking at the plane and at the availability of tankers, and by the electronic monitoring of test and training flights in which such refueling must be practiced. Many of the characteristics of a bomber force can be estimated by analysis of the plane's configuration, but there will always be some uncertainties and differences of view, even among experts.

For example, during the SALT II negotiations there were many arguments within the U.S. security community as to whether the Soviet Backfire bomber was an intercontinental or medium-range aircraft. Its primary design purpose was clearly for shorter range missions, but nevertheless it could reach targets in the United States on one-way missions by flying at subsonic speeds at high altitudes. Those who wished to count it as part of the Soviet strategic force insisted that it was an intercontinental bomber, while others did not believe that its intercontinental capabilities were sufficiently great to warrant its inclusion in the overall strategic delivery vehicle totals. In the end this controversial issue was papered over by getting Secretary General Brezhnev to sign a separate letter stating that the Soviets would limit the production of Backfire bombers.

The other verification problem with bombers involves the question of what types of armament they can or would be allowed to deliver. This became quite critical in connection with cruise missiles in SALT II and will be discussed in the next section, which deals with cruise missiles.

LONG-RANGE CRUISE MISSILES

Cruise missiles present many new and different problems for verification. They are relatively small and mobile vehicles (about 20 feet in length), and the logistics support required for them is not nearly as extensive as for ballistic missiles. Furthermore, cruise missiles are being designed to carry conventional as well as nuclear warheads, and there is no ready means of distinguishing by visual observation between a conventional and a nuclear-armed missile. The same cruise missiles can also be delivered by aircraft, launched from the ground, or fired from submarines or other ships. But even a fully developed ground-launched cruise missile would probably have to be tested from an aircraft or a submarine before it could be operationally reliable in these other delivery modes.

Verification of a ceiling on the numbers of long-range cruise missiles once they have been tested and produced would be difficult. There are no available technical means for accurately counting the total number of such missiles deployed at any one time. Counting would have to be done in the production phase. This would be much more difficult than in the case of ballistic missiles because of the cruise missile's smaller size and its indistinguishability from other types of tactical weapons. These other weapons would create a lot of confusion in the verification system and lead to many false alarms or uncertainties as to the actual number produced. Perhaps on-site inspections of some sort could be developed to assist in this verification, but it may be difficult to agree on procedures that would not be considered too intrusive by either the Soviet Union or the United States. Declarations of the location and production rate of production facilities existing at the time the agreement is signed could assist subsequent verification.

A total ban or perhaps a freeze on testing, production, and deployment of long-range cruise missiles would be very much easier to verify, because it would then only be necessary to detect a single new cruise missile in any of these phases in order to have evidence of a violation. Any extensive secret deployment of either ground- or sea-launched strategic cruise missiles would almost certainly be detected before it could be significant. Satellites as well as other national technical means would have a high probability of providing such evidence. If production of conventional-warhead cruise missiles is allowed, then verification would be extremely unreliable. The only obvious way to deal with this problem would be to ban conventional long-range cruise missiles as well as nuclear ones. This should not be a major military loss, however, since an expensive cruise missile, sent 2,000 or more miles with a few hundred pounds of TNT, does not seem like a very efficient conventional delivery system, regardless of the accuracy that it could achieve.

Some handle on cruise missile verification can be obtained by observation of the carrier vehicles. For example, in SALT II the problem of monitoring air-launched cruise missiles was dealt with by an agreement that all aircraft modified to carry cruise missiles must have "functionally related observable differences" from other strategic aircraft. Limitations on the number of cruise missiles that a given type of aircraft could carry were also included. Counting such aircraft would then permit calculation of the number of possible air-launched cruise missiles that could be deployed. Whether such provisions would stand up for long in an atmosphere of suspicion of violations is not certain. It might be difficult to detect that an aircraft carried cruise missiles internally in the absence of any external differences observable by satellites. Opportunities for spotting such a violation would, however, always exist in the testing and training phases, particularly if a significant capability were being acquired.

Some of the loopholes in the possibilities of cruise missile verification can be narrowed by observation of their testing. But this too is much more difficult than in the case of ballistic missiles. The actual test ranges might be located by satellites, although some uncertainty might develop as to whether cruise or other types of military hardware were being tested. Cruise missiles fly at relatively low altitude, so that they cannot be monitored confidently from the surface outside the Soviet Union. This concealment might be easier for the Soviet Union, because testing even at full range could occur well within its boundaries. It might be more difficult for the United States because of the more limited (and populated) area of its land mass. While national technical means might pick up evidences of testing—and we obviously have been doing this in the past—such capabilities might be unreliable or inadequate in an arms control situation. It would also be even more unreliable if some types of cruise missiles are allowed to be developed, produced, and deployed.

One other problem raised by cruise missiles is how to determine their operational range. Just as with aircraft, the range can be extended by reducing the payload. If one assumes a certain payload, then one can calculate the possible range based on visual observations of the missile's configuration. Testing during a large part of the development of a cruise missile system can be done at reduced ranges or by reversing the direction in midcourse. At some point, however, a military planner would want some full-range testing before the missile could be reliably deployed. Therefore, there would be some opportunities to determine the potential range of a given cruise missile type, but it is likely that there always will be considerable uncertainty here.

In sum, long-range cruise missiles present a major new problem, which is rapidly making the possibility of verification of controls on their number very difficult. At the moment the numbers deployed and the state of the development programs probably make this manageable, particularly for verifying compliance by the Soviets, since they are considerably behind the United States. Nevertheless it will not be long before it gets out of hand. A total ban on all long-range cruise missiles could, however, be readily verifiable, but the achievement of such a total ban may be a very difficult negotiating job unless both nations start exercising restraint in this area.

CONCLUSION

Even this abbreviated analysis shows that national technical means of verification can now provide assurance that any significant non-compliance with limitations on offensive strategic nuclear delivery vehicles would be detected. Future weapons developments could reduce this assurance. The more complete a ban, the more reliable and easy will be the verification.

Some types of restrictions are easier to verify than others, but much is gained by including in an agreement many individual limitations, even though they may be more difficult to monitor. The fact that these limitations are complementary creates a helpful network of corroboration, given that the basic goal is the control of an overall weapons program. Verification is greatly enhanced where redundant techniques are available to check on any specific violation. Properly crafted treaty provisions can be of great assistance to national technical means of verification. Consultation provisions, such as those that established the Standing Consultative Commission in SALT I, are also essential in order to deal with inevitable ambiguities and new technological and political situations. On-site inspections rarely add to national technical means, but sometimes as a last resort they can add confidence in compliance after the consultation process on an ambiguous event has been exhausted.

15.
ASAT Treaty Verification

Richard L. Garwin

I define verification of limitations on anti-satellite (ASAT) capabilities as timely warning, with appropriate confidence, of violations of formal provisions of a treaty limiting ASAT acts, capabilities and preparations. The feasibility and cost of verification is highly dependent on the form of the treaty that one has to verify. There are always (and there should be) cost and resource constraints, so that if a treaty is perfectly verifiable at infinite cost, one will choose not to do it perfectly. The optimum allocation of resources should give high confidence of observing violations that are significant for the near term or that represent severe threats and lesser confidence of observing violations of parts of the agreement that are not so significant.

It is fundamental that the ability to detect noncompliance with a treaty ("verify the treaty") depends strongly on what is banned under the treaty. I believe that important restrictions on Soviet activity can be imposed and verified.

First, verification cannot be and need not be absolute. A treaty is a contract, very much like a contract for buying or selling a house. Certain things are of primary importance — getting the money (to the one selling the house) or not being committed to go through with the purchase if the house burns down before final transfer (to the buyer). Such provisions are important, and it is appropriate that they be spelled out and that compliance be ensured.

Somewhat closer to the enhancement of national security by arms control constraint is the example of "verification" of the ban on carrying weapons into the cabin of civil aircraft in the United States. Verification (in part) is by x-ray inspection of carry-on baggage and by screening the passengers themselves with a magnetometer capable of detecting metallic guns, knives, and other substantial objects. There is an optimum threshold for the sensitivity of the magnetometer; it is easy enough technically to make a magnetometer which will detect a single dime or earring, but under those circumstances one need not have a magnetometer — a red light and buzzer would do, because almost everyone would be stopped for failing the test. At present, with a reasonable threshold, those who fail the "verification" instrument are subject to "on-site inspection," and the question of compliance is resolved. It is possible to argue that even small coins could be used to injure the cockpit crew, short out the aircraft electrical system, and the like, but a rule of reason has prevailed in the limitation on behavior of passengers on aircraft. There is value in aircraft travel, and the constraint on behavior and the verification requirements imposed must not eliminate that value.

Similarly, there is great value to the United States in limiting Soviet activities by arms control treaties, and the limitations and verification requirements should not be so onerous that they either eliminate any incentive the Soviet Union may have to participate in such accords or delay the impositions of the restraints.

Verifiability depends on the nature of the accord. Of course, there are treaties (or wish lists) that would not be verifiable. The Reagan administration report to Congress maintains that a "comprehensive treaty" is not verifiable. Indeed, some in and close to that administration, who are avowedly totally opposed to space arms control, include in their "comprehensive" description of ASAT activity, interference with the communication link from the satellite ground station to Washington, and they maintain that a pair of wire cutters or a charge of explosives constitutes a capability for such interference and, thus, ASAT activity. This is an extreme and non-serious definition of "ASAT activity." One can also interfere with the utility of satellites (in a system which is not designed for wartime operation) by attack on the ground-station receivers, by jamming of the satellite sensors themselves, and the like.

What is and is not to be banned by a treaty must be carefully considered, with the significance of the capability to be prohibited weighed against the practicality of verifying compliance. In an attempt to approximate a "real world" ASAT treaty, a panel for the Union of Concerned Scientists (UCS), chaired by Kurt Gottfried of Cornell University, on which I served, produced a document called "The Union of Concerned Scientists Draft Treaty: A Treaty Limiting Anti-Satellite Weapons."

Our draft, which was presented to a subcommittee of the Senate Foreign Relations Committee on May 18, 1983, was prompted by the fact that the U.S. government had not responded to a Soviet draft treaty of August, 1981, which was introduced in the U.N. We hoped to advance the understanding of the advantages of ASAT treaty limitation by remedying some glaring deficiencies in the 1981 Soviet draft.

The Soviet Union responded in August, 1983 by introducing, once again in the U.N., a draft treaty: "Banning the Use of Force in Space . . . ," which incorporated almost all of the improvements of our draft and retained none of the deficiencies of the 1981 Soviet draft, except for the clause that denied any military role (solely) to manned reusable spacecraft, while allowing a military (but not "weapons carrying") role to unmanned spacecraft. We continue to find this clause unacceptable. To say that we cannot use our space shuttle for military purposes, for which we are allowed to use (and the Soviets can use) unmanned satellites, is to have a non-negotiable treaty. Also in August, 1983, Yuri Andropov committed the Soviet Union to a moratorium on launching ASAT weapons into orbit as long as the United States did not test its ASAT.

On March 31, 1984, President Reagan transmitted to Congress a report dealing with verification of ASAT limitations, which seemed to conclude that one could not verify a treaty that would impose militarily significant limitations on Soviet ASAT activities. Unfortunately, the report had no specifics as to what limitations of Soviet ASAT programs would be required to maintain and improve U.S. security, nor even a definition of a "comprehensive" ASAT ban, which it judged unverifiable.

It is difficult, even pointless, to discuss verification in the abstract, without saying what you are trying to verify. In order to provide a concrete basis for discussion, I will take the UCS Draft Treaty and look at it in terms of how each of its provisions might be verified.

Article I

Each Party undertakes not to destroy, damage, render inoperable or change the flight trajectory of space objects of other States.

How should we monitor that the other side is not violating Article I of this draft? We are most interested, of course, in preserving our satellites. That is, after all, the purpose of an ASAT agreement; it bans anti-satellite weapons because we're interested in keeping our satellites operating in peacetime and as far into national conflict as possible. These satellites are, among other functions, a mainstay of our capabilities to monitor and verify other arms control treaties. It is bizarre to imagine that we could have the United States destroying the Soviet Union on the ground (or vice versa) and believe that either would then obey a treaty limiting ASAT warfare. However, the satellites might survive a little longer because some of the provisions of the treaty make it less likely that either side could have highly capable, instantaneous ASAT weapons.

To monitor compliance with Article I on behalf of our military space systems (and our civil systems too, if we care), we could have sensors on board the satellites themselves to verify that they were not being destroyed, damaged, rendered permanently inoperable (which is what that phrase really means) or having their flight trajectories changed when we don't want them changed. It would be relatively easy to see whether a satellite is surviving or whether its own rocket thrusters are firing whenever its flight trajectory is changed and to report that to the ground. It could be done with a little hardened box that would survive even if the main satellite power systems went out. But to do this, you would have to care a little bit about it.

How would you know who was violating the treaty? How would you know whether it was just a meteor, for instance, which by bad luck struck your satellite, or a little bit of space debris? You will never really know with 100% confidence; on the other hand, you do know that it doesn't do the other side much good to destroy only one of your satellites in a time of crisis. The more you want to be sure, the more it will cost you: in multiple on-board sensors; in little radars to see the velocity of what it was that struck you, if you really want to do that; or in light beams.

You could also have external sensors — shepherds that look after your satellites. These could have radars in space and could scan continuously or at random the vicinity of your satellites, focusing on whatever might be coming up to them. However, the treaty also forbids each party to destroy, damage, render inoperable, or change the flight trajectory of space objects of any state. If we really cared about the Soviet Union's not destroying other countries' satellites, we would need appropriate monitoring capability, either unilateral or collaborative, on those other satellites.

What are the threats addressed by this first article of the treaty? Threats of collision with large satellites. Space mines, for instance, which could follow the quarry satellite around and explode on command, destroying the quarry satellite in a few milliseconds. Pellets that could be put, more or less permanently, into orbit. Aluminum foil that can cover its antennas. Black paint to cover its lenses.

Non-damaging electronic countermeasures we explicitly permitted, except where banned for certain satellites by other arms control agreements, and this would be in the negotiating record. If the Soviets have a radar ocean reconnaissance satellite that looks at our aircraft carriers, it is entirely permissible under this treaty to jam that sensor by sending high-power microwaves up so it can't see anything or to have decoys that look like aircraft carriers or to interfere with reception of its downlink, so that it cannot report at a time of crisis. But it is not permissible for us to seize the command link of that satellite, under this treaty, and tell it to de-orbit or to go to a higher orbit. That's not allowed; we're giving that up. If they cared, the Soviet Union, of course, would be able to know if we actually had exercised any of these forbidden capabilities against their satellites, but they may be less certain that we do not have such capabilities.

Incidentally, although jamming is easy, it is very difficult to damage a well-designed satellite with microwaves. Satellites (especially radar satellites) are rather thoroughly protected against high power right in-band (at the frequency at which the satellite also needs to be most sensitive). You really have to make an effort to injure a satellite. You could have such a clandestine capability, but you don't need it. You don't need to destroy a satellite in order to defeat it, and so you wouldn't do it. You wouldn't take the risk of having somebody "rat" on you.

Article II

1. Each Party undertakes not to place in orbit around the earth weapons for destroying, damaging, rendering inoperable, or changing the flight trajectory of space objects, or for damaging objects in the atmosphere or on the ground.

2. Each Party undertakes not to install such weapons on celestial bodies, or station such weapons in outer space in any other manner.

3. Each Party undertakes not to test such weapons in space or against space objects.

Article II broadly forbids possession and testing of the means to carry out the acts banned in Article I. The first provision of Article II says: " . . . not to place in orbit . . . weapons for destroying, damaging . . . etc." What does "weapons for" mean? It does not say "weapons capable of," because any satellite is capable of destroying any other satellite; you just have to maneuver it into contact and it is "capable." It does not say "weapons intended to," because how are you going to prove that it is "intended to?" As "weapons for," it is something in between. You don't have to prove intent and you don't have to prove lack of capability.

To take the provisions in reverse order, Article II.3 bans the testing (or use) of the banned activities against one's own satellites, which would otherwise not be forbidden by Article I. In this way, one prevents a state from practicing to perform an act that is banned by the treaty. The tests that the Soviets have made in which they send up a satellite to intercept a target satellite would have been illegal under this treaty. It says, "Each Party undertakes not to test such weapons in space or against space objects." "Such" is a very important word there, and it refers to II.1. It means "weapons for destroying, damaging, rendering inoperable or changing flight trajectory, or for damaging objects in the atmosphere or on the ground." Something new. Even though this treaty is titled "Treaty Limiting Antisatellite Weapons," here we introduce a ban on placing in orbit weapons for damaging objects in the atmosphere or on the ground.

Article II.3 contains the only ban on ground-based or air-based ASATs. Otherwise the treaty specifies "not to place in orbit" and "not to install on celestial bodies" and so on. So "not to test such weapons" (weapons for doing those things to space objects) "in space or against space objects" means you can't put them up there and test them (you can't put them up there in the first place); and you can't test against space objects even if they're on the ground.

To test our ASAT, in space or against space objects, would be illegal. It is a quibble as to whether it is an ASAT at all if you launch only the two booster stages without a homing sensor and warhead. As for the altitude at which space begins, that will be in the negotiating record. Item II.3 is a ban on testing, not on possession, and if we are verifying the complex of Article II we are verifying the absence of testing, not the absence of possession.

The threats against which this article is aimed are similar to the ones I mentioned before: collisions, pellets, space-based lasers, ground-based lasers, particle beams on the ground, particle beams in space, miniature homing vehicles (like the U.S. MHV), co-orbital ASATs (like the Soviet ASAT), third-generation nuclear weapons, space mines—all of these are banned as acts under Article I, and their testing is banned under Article II.

How will we monitor non-compliance with Article II, and with Article II.3 specifically? The Soviet Union might test their "such weapons" against their space objects. (They cannot test them against ours, or those of other states, without violating Article I.) Or they could test them "in space," that is, not against a space object at all. A ground-based laser beam sent upward but not against a space object is also, in my view, tested in space.

Can we be sure that we could see any test of these things? For instance, can the Soyuz be classified as a space mine because it approaches close to other satellites? Sometimes it docks, sometimes it doesn't. How can the Soviets operate their Soyuz at all under this treaty? You have to have a rule of reason. If every ASAT were as big as Soyuz, I would be happy to have them build lots of ASATs. But the kind of homing system that you would need for an ASAT is very different from one that makes a close approach and docking maneuver. For instance, our miniature homing vehicle will have some 10 km/s crossing velocity, and it has to arrive at exactly the right point within a meter or so and at exactly the right time, which is very different from the successive-approximation close approach with Soyuz.

A space mine gets closer to what Soyuz does than does our ASAT, but space mines are to be banned under "installation." Their testing is also banned, but we could not be positive that they were not testing with Soyuz the homing and station-keeping device for a space mine. A space mine will only be useful if it is repeatedly tested and if there are a lot of them. We have to observe events in monitoring, and then we have to interpret events. Those are two very different things. The Soviets might launch something from their launch sites at Tyuratam, where they usually launch their ASATs, and we would be faced with a question of what this was. If it went up and looked like an ASAT, sounded like an ASAT, maneuvered like an ASAT, then another item in the treaty allows us to talk to the Soviet Union and puts the onus on them to explain what they are doing.

We can observe a large booster, for instance, by the large flame associated with its launch. We could focus whatever kind of specific verification measures or other intelligence-gathering systems we have on what would happen to the thing that was launched by this booster. At the Kettering School in England they do this quite well most of the time. We could see a big thing in space or on the ground. We would follow it very carefully. We could look at satellites, if we cared about this, to see whether they are producing large clouds of hydrogen fluoride gas, and if the Soviets say "that's just the atmosphere we breathe these days, that's no laser," then we might complain about that.

We don't have to tell them exactly how we're going to do all this. For ground-based systems, lasers, particle beams, or whatever, we could observe potential target satellites or candidate ground installations — "SATs or sites," so to speak. That is, their finite number of satellites that could be instrumented to report back what is happening to them — that they're being warmed by ground-based lasers, for example — might be monitored by our reconnaissance satellites. We could observe those same satellites ourselves, or we could observe the sites. There are a finite number of sites on the ground. One might postulate an airborne-laser laboratory, but there are a finite number of those possible, too. We could look at the approach of space objects to one another and we could require (we have done this under another provision of the draft treaty) prior notification of close approach, or of anything that might be ambiguous. Ultimately you have to remember the "1% likelihood" suggested by Admiral Noel Gayler that there is a "mole" or ordinary spy who will inform us of violations (and give full details).

What are the capabilities for performing these monitoring tasks? A lot of these things we haven't had to "verify" before because they haven't been banned, although we've had a great deal of interest. So we may or may not have targeted the systems that we have on such activities. We may very well have information that the Soviets aren't doing anything in ASAT except their conventional — since 1968 — co-orbital interceptor.

Visitors to the Soviet Space Research Institute ("IKI") in Moscow have been shown plans for a liquid-helium-cooled multi-year-lifetime millimeter-wave space telescope. The United States has a similar technology on its IRAS satellite. Although you would not have to use millimeter-wave sensors for verification, you could use infrared observation from a satellite to monitor whether laser ASATs were being tested. You could look at satellites to see that they don't suddenly break out into a fever while they're passing over suspected Soviet ground-based laser sites. You could use the same kind of multi-spectral analysis under development at IKI to look for laser light, which, after all, is not perfectly absorbed by a satellite and can be distinguished from other kinds of light. If you care, you can do that; it depends on the number of targets, on how much you care, and on how much notice you would be getting of such activities.

I want to discuss one bit of technology here. There is an enormous range between, for instance, ground-based laser power required to destroy a satellite by overheating and the ground-based laser power required to impair the operation of an imaging satellite. Consider a laser on the ground with a 20-cm diameter telescope, approximately diffraction-limited. At visible wavelengths this has about three microradian divergence. So, on a satellite at 200-km range, this would yield a spot about 60 cm in diameter; a satellite with a 60-cm lens would have 1-microradian angular resolution. If the ground-based laser could track the satellite well enough and point accurately enough to put all the laser light into the satellite lens, how much laser energy would be safe? Suppose you have 50 line-pairs per millimeter resolution on your film, and you want to get 100 times the intensity of sunlight on the photographic film; that's likely to do a little bit of damage — 10 watts per square centimeter for some time on a pixel of a millionth of a square centimeter requires a total of 10 microwatts. So a sub-milliwatt laser on the ground for a reasonable fraction of a millisecond into a 20-cm diameter telescope illuminating a satellite with a 2-foot diameter lens will overheat a very small portion of the focal plane.

What does it take to overheat the satellite itself? You have to put 10 watts per square centimeter on the whole 60-cm diameter — almost a square meter. It takes about 100 kilowatts acting for some seconds to overheat the satellite itself with that kind of ground-based telescope; a bigger ground-based telescope would produce a smaller spot only with adaptive optics to compensate for atmospheric inhomogeneity. In this case, there is a factor of a billion between the damaging of the film and the damaging of the satellite itself. So when people ask, "Can you be sure that the people on the ground do not have the capability to interfere with national technical means or to damage your imaging satellites?" the answer is, "No, you can't." But could you observe that they were damaging, could you do something about this threat if you really cared? The answer is, "Yes, you can. There are a lot of things that you can do." And if you care, you will do it.

However, there would be no difficulty in my opinion in observing the relatively few places from which megawatt lasers could project for a considerable time (or where ground-based lasers could project 10 to 100 kilojoules) against satellites, and that's the kind of verification systems that you would be talking about.

Now, let me backtrack to Article II.2, "installing such weapons on celestial bodies. . . ." A space mine could be carried into space concealed in another working satellite. Much good it would do anybody to have an untested space mine, far from the quarry satellite, but you cannot be absolutely certain that the Soviets don't have some of these capabilities in space. You may have been quite certain they have not been tested, but possession is much more difficult to detect, especially of some of these little things like space mines, which don't even have to be bigger than a miniature homing vehicle, which is only about a foot in diameter by a foot long. Those who are real enthusiasts about progress in science and technology making it possible to have defense against ballistic missiles in space (because you "will have computers as small as your head which do billions of operations per second") ought to be enthusiastic about what they can pack into a 5-kg space mine that only has to tag along—having been helped into position within a few hundred meters of its quarry satellite by a lot of ground-based radars and commands from the ground—and just stay there without damaging itself against the kind of maneuvers that a solar-cell-powered satellite can make.

Article II.1 is more difficult to monitor than Article II.3 (testing). In II.1 we are "not to place in orbit" these damaging things. Placing in orbit untested systems is likely to be of very little utility, and this article also bans placing in orbit those weapons which could damage objects in the atmosphere or on the ground. That includes orbiting nuclear weapons, which are already banned by the 1967 Outer Space Treaty and for which we presumably have verification capability already; if we don't, we could imagine how to do that, if we cared. It bans the orbiting darts and deep-space battle stations that people like to talk about at the Military Space Thought Symposium—you base non-nuclear weapons 100,000 km out in space and by very good guidance bring the non-nuclear projectiles down to the ground and stick one through a transformer on a power pole near Moscow.

It is not desirable to allow all acts that are not militarily significant or to ban even insignificant acts that may be difficult to verify. If the treaty permits the installation in space of all kinds of things that look suspicious and which you therefore do not have any right to bring up in the Standing Consultative Commission (SCC), you weaken your position.

How about the ASAT capability of existing systems? Assume the Soviet ASAT has been tested and works quite well (which, as we have seen, is not true). Without Article II.1, under this treaty the Soviets could fill space with these ASATs and have a ready capability already tested. With Article II.1, even if they were successful in testing a new ASAT clandestinely, they are still banned from deploying it.

Article III

1. For the purpose of providing assurance of compliance with the provisions of this treaty, each Party shall use national technical means of verification at its disposal in a manner consistent with generally recognized principles of international law.

2. Verification by national technical means shall be supplemented, as appropriate, by such cooperative measures for contributing to the effectiveness of verification by national technical means as the Parties shall agree upon in the Standing Consultative Commission.

3. Each Party undertakes not to interfere with the national technical means of verification of the other Party operating in accordance with paragraph 1 of this Article.

4. Each Party undertakes not to use deliberate concealment measures which impede verification by national technical means of compliance with this treaty.

Articles III.1 and III.2 do not need to be verified; those are just permissions. Article III.3 means that those systems that are used for verifying these provisions cannot even be temporarily jammed or blinded, unlike all the other systems, such as broadcast satellites, that have nothing to do with treaty verification. Article III.4 would ban, for instance, Stealth launches of the SRAM-ALTAIR combination for the U.S. MHV. If we have stealthy missiles and stealthy aircraft, then the other side may say, "you have a capability to evade these commitments," but we would not wish to ban separately Stealth aircraft or Stealth missiles simply because the use of the combination for this purpose is banned.

Some maintain that every detail must be a matter of negotiation, included as part of the treaty, because it is felt that if you leave it for discussion in the SCC, it will always be deemed inappropriate to consider. There is something to be said for not attempting to wring all flexibility out of an agreement. I think treaties become more complicated when you try to permit things. For instance, in the ABM treaty the United States was very much interested in permitting a future development of the anti-tactical ballistic missile capability of the SAM-D system (now "Patriot"), and so the treaty was carefully drawn not to ban such capabilities. We have now developed Patriot, which unfortunately does not have anti-tactical ballistic missile capability, and the Soviets have marched into that loophole and developed a system with considerably greater capability. There's no difference between the range of a submarine-launched ballistic missile launched into the perimeter of the Soviet Union from close to shore and the range of a tactical ballistic missile. So if they were to deploy this capability widely around their periphery they would have the makings of some kind of defensive system — a strategic defensive system that is explicitly permitted, I guess, by the ABM treaty. We would complain about where these things were located — where there aren't any tactical ballistic missiles to counter. But that would weaken our position in some other arms control agreements.

Nevertheless, I think the ABM treaty is a better treaty than the Limited Offensive Agreement or the much longer SALT II treaty. There is something to be said for not attempting to wring all flexibility out of an agreement.

Article IV

1. To promote the objectives and implementation of the provisions of this treaty, the Parties shall use the Standing Consultative Commission, established

by the Memorandum of Understanding Between the Government of the United States of America and the Government of the Union of Soviet Socialist Republics regarding the Establishment of a Standing Consultative Commission of December 21, 1972.

2. Within the framework of the Standing Consultative Commission, with respect to this treaty, the Parties will:

a) consider questions concerning compliance with the obligations assumed and related situations which may be considered ambiguous;

b) provide on a voluntary basis such information as either Party considers necessary to assure confidence in compliance with the obligations assumed;

c) consider questions involving unintended interference with national technical means of verification, and questions involving unintended impeding of verification by national technical means of compliance with the provisions of this treaty;

d) consider, as appropriate, cooperative measures contributing to the effectiveness of verification by national technical means;

e) consider possible changes in the strategic situation which have a bearing on the provisions of this treaty, including the activities of other States;

f) consider, as appropriate, possible proposals for further increasing the viability of this treaty, including proposals for amendments in accordance with the provisions of this treaty.

The forum of the SCC permits more detailed commitments—some of which can be kept not totally public—as to how the parties will assure one another that they are not violating the treaty, thus allowing the treaty to avoid defining specifically "fences-around-fences," that is, every banned act, every banned test, every banned capability.

Article V

The Parties undertake to begin, promptly after the entry into force of this treaty, active negotiations with the objective of achieving, as soon as possible, agreement on further measures for the limitation and reduction of weapons subject to limitation in Article II of this treaty.

This seems self-verifying, although it may not be taken seriously.

Article VI

In order to ensure the viability and effectiveness of this treaty, each Party undertakes not to circumvent the provisions of this treaty, through any other State or States, in any other manner.

This treaty would be open for accession by anybody. But there might be nonsignatories, and Article VI is there to prohibit any party to the treaty from circumventing it by encouraging and exploiting banned acts by a nonsignatory nation. It is a lot easier to monitor the behavior of nonsuperpowers in this regard, if you care.

Article VII

Each Party undertakes not to assume any international obligation which would conflict with this treaty.

Article VIII

1. Each Party may propose amendments to this treaty.
2. Agreed amendments shall enter into force in accordance with the procedures governing the entry into force of this treaty.

Article IX

This treaty shall be of unlimited duration.

Article X

Each Party shall, in exercising its national sovereignty, have the right to withdraw from this treaty if it decides that extraordinary events related to the subject matter of this treaty have jeopardized its supreme interests. It shall give notice of its decisions to the other Party six months prior to withdrawal from the treaty. Such notice shall include a statement of the extraordinary events the notifying Party regards as having jeopardized its supreme interests.

Article X is about withdrawal. If compliance with such a treaty is found to be onerous in the future because you discover that it would be in your interest (or in both your interests) to deploy a space-based ballistic missile defense system, you could withdraw. After all, what is more important to the supreme national interest than to survive?

To complete the treaty, here are the last two articles:

Article XI

1. This treaty shall be subject to ratification in accordance with the constitutional procedures of each Party.
2. This treaty shall enter into force on the day of the exchange of instruments of ratification.

Article XII

1. Done in two copies, each in the English and Russian languages, both texts being equally authentic.
2. This treaty shall be registered pursuant to Article 102 of the Charter of the United Nations.

There are a lot of technical questions; there are a lot of cost questions; but if you found a national benefit in preserving your satellites and you thought that an ASAT limitation contributed to that national benefit, as do those of us who helped present this treaty, in my opinion, having looked at this, such a treaty is adequately verifiable.

Ultimately an ASAT ban is in our interest because it would reduce the threat to our valuable peace-keeping and military-support capabilities in orbit. It is valuable to us because by reducing the threat to Soviet satellites that continue to assure the Soviet Union that the United States is not launching a strike against them, we reduce the Soviet propensity to ready their weapons against us. An ASAT ban:

1. helps preserve our satellites in peacetime;

2. helps preserve our satellites in non-nuclear war; and
3. gains time before satellites are vulnerable in the event of abrogation of an ASAT ban.

On the other hand, without an ASAT ban we could have our own ASAT. It has been claimed that a U.S. ASAT would confer the following benefits:

1. Supposedly, it would deter the use of a Soviet ASAT by allowing us to respond "in kind" to Soviet destruction of a low-altitude U.S. satellite.
2. Supposedly, whether or not the Soviets have an ASAT we "need" an ASAT in order to be able to destroy Soviet military-support satellites during non-nuclear war—particularly the Soviet Radar Ocean Reconnaissance Satellites (RORSAT), which can locate and provide targeting information about U.S. aircraft carriers.
3. Supposedly, our ASAT can counter (destroy) the Soviet co-orbital ASAT and thus protect U.S. low-altitude satellites.

I will take these one at a time.

A typical U.S. low-altitude satellite has a mission life of several years, and it must be a very expensive and very capable vehicle in contrast with a Soviet satellite of a few-weeks lifetime. How much would it deter Soviet attack on our valuable satellite (on which we depend very greatly) to be able to destroy one of their less valuable ones? Deterrence of Soviet attack on U.S. satellites can be achieved by threatening to impose comparable total damage on the Soviet Union, and that cannot be done by destroying one of their satellites if they destroy one of ours.

Next, the ability to destroy the Soviet RORSAT is unnecessary to protect our fleet. We can deny its utility by jamming, deception, and by other means. In fact, as has been put very perceptively by Admiral Noel Gayler (former Commander-in-Chief of U.S. forces in the Pacific, former Director of the National Security Agency), U.S. carriers and other major ships can survive with only the aid of our own satellites, by the use of low probability of intercept (LPI) communications from the ships to the satellites, so that the ships are not vulnerable to location by other means. Thus, countering Soviet RORSAT by non-damaging electronic warfare means and countering EORSAT by "silent communication" to our own satellites would be a positive benefit and does not depend in any way upon our possession of an ASAT capability.

And finally, the ability to protect U.S. satellites by destroying the Soviet co-orbital interceptor before it strikes is just technically not there. If the Soviets cooperated in not maneuvering their ASAT during the one or two orbits during which it is accompanying its quarry, then we might be able to attack the ASAT. But the Soviet ASAT is maneuverable, and the U.S. ASAT has obviously a very small allowable "basket" in which the quarry satellite must appear if we are to be able to home on it and destroy it.

If there is no ban on ASAT, obviously the Soviet Union will not stop with their crude and unreliable existing ASAT. They will mimic the United States to find a capability that will be far more usable in terms of instantaneous flexible destruction of U.S. satellites. Furthermore, nations that are constrained in their access to nuclear weapons have no such impediment in regard to non-nuclear ASAT capability, and we can be confident of seeing Japanese and German as well as British and French ASATs on the scene.

A particular instability arises in the presence of a program to provide a highly reliable space defense against nuclear weapons. Under these circumstances (which Secretary Weinberger has dubbed a "strategic nightmare" if the Soviet Union begins to deploy such a system), ASATs could well be used immediately to destroy such a nascent defensive capability.

If you think that some time in the future you are going to have a space-based ballistic missile defense and that it is going to work perfectly (as our president seemed to think on March 23, 1983, and maybe some people still think), well, I as your opponent am going to counter that system. If the Soviet Union began to develop and deploy that system, I would counter it with space mines. Every one of those satellites up there in the ocean of space is going to have next to it (within a lethal radius) a non-nuclear space mine, and if effective countermeasures are deployed against non-nuclear space mines, I will have a nuclear space mine, because the survival of the United States is more important to me than the sanctity of the 1967 Outer Space Treaty.

I fear that if we don't ban ASATs and we develop and deploy space-based weapons, we are going to have a proliferation of space mines; one side or the other is then going to tell the other side, "My defense in space is important to me. It's not going to work if you keep putting those space mines up. You may not launch anything further into space in peacetime without my permission." You may think this is fantasy, but recently proponents of space-based defense have admitted, "Yes, that's how it will have to go — if you believe in Star Wars."

Then you are going to have a war in peacetime. A big war. As a result of destroying the other side's satellite launches, he is going to punish you in return. As the assassination of Archduke Franz Ferdinand was the proximate cause of World War I, this might very well be the cause of the outbreak of World War III.

But, some ask, how about "residual" ASAT capabilities, even if all ASAT tests and use are banned? We have already mentioned docking practice, and one might imagine a possibility that some of the Soviet ASAT interceptors would be hidden instead of destroyed. Furthermore, newly capable ASATs might have been developed secretly, although not tested in space, and these would have some (even if negligible) capability.

More important is a capability against low-altitude satellites posed by nuclear-armed ABM interceptors, such as those around Moscow. Most important (and a capability available to both the United States and the Soviet Union) would be the use of ICBMs (with their nuclear warheads) for point-in-space intercept. The United States has long assumed that the Soviets could put their ICBMs on silo targets in the United States with an accuracy of a small fraction of a second. Using the same ICBM against a target that is a point along the orbit of a quarry satellite would provide a highly flexible nuclear-wartime ASAT capability. There is no way in which this capability could be eliminated by any ban on ASAT possession or testing, and every test of an ICBM against a ground target is effectively a test of this ASAT capability.

Nevertheless, it would be unreasonable to assume that any ASAT treaty would protect satellites in nuclear war, at a time in which the United States and the Soviet Union were exploding nuclear weapons on one another's territory.

Note that the UCS draft treaty did not propose to ban possession of ASAT capabilities — only use and test. We made this choice in order to be able to verify everything that we required. Nevertheless, Yuri Andropov offered in August, 1983, to destroy existing ASATs, and the Soviet draft treaty of August, 1983 contains this provision. In a negotiation, we ought to accept the Soviet offer and request of them the detailed assurances as to how we can be certain that they have destroyed their existing ASATs.

In considering verifiability of an ASAT treaty (called into question in large part by those who enthusiastically support President Reagan's Strategic Defense Initiative), one should compare the verification requirements for an ASAT treaty with the observation requirement for the effective defense called for in the SDI.

In my opinion it is both feasible and urgent to negotiate a ban on weapons in space, and I believe that it could be concluded in a month. I do believe that there is considerable support from high-level active military officials for such an ASAT treaty; it should certainly not be taken for granted that our military leaders oppose it.

ASATs threaten to interfere with treaty monitoring. Furthermore, they can destroy our ability to understand what's going on in the Soviet Union and to assure ourselves minute-by-minute, day-by-day, that they are not threatening an attack on us. Space could be a place to deploy weapons to damage things on the ground. Space-based antiaircraft capability is a lot easier than ballistic missile defense; there will be space mines against those, and the beneficial satellites on both sides will be the easiest things to destroy. These are my reasons for wanting an ASAT treaty.

16.

Some Seismological Aspects of Monitoring a CTBT

Jack F. Evernden and Charles B. Archambeau

Introductory Note by Kosta Tsipis

This chapter makes a major original contribution to the science of detecting seismic waves generated by even minute underground nuclear detonations and, more important, to our ability to discriminate seismic waves from detonations from those caused by earthquakes.

In the first part of the chapter, Evernden and Archambeau review the empirical data on which discrimination has been based, setting them in a theoretical framework. The non-technical reader may wish to skip to the second part of the chapter in which the new possibilities of detection and discrimination are discussed.

There has been little doubt in the scientific community for the past ten years or so that underground nuclear detonations with an energy yield equivalent to more than 5,000 or 10,000 tons of TNT can be detected and distinguished as explosions rather than as earthquakes with great confidence. In principle at least, such capability would allow the verifiable ban of underground detonations since there is little to be gained in terms of new and useful information from underground nuclear tests of yields smaller than a few kilotons equivalent. But since total verification of all underground testing could not be assured, a complete test ban treaty was not acceptable, and the Partial Test Ban Treaty (1963), which banned testing in the atmosphere but not underground, was the result.

Those in the United States who opposed an underground test ban raised two possible situations in which testing of nuclear explosives with substantial yields could go undetected by distant seismic monitoring stations. One possibility they foresaw was that a very large cavity in which to detonate a nuclear weapon might be excavated deep underground. Such an arrangement would "decouple" the blast wave generated by the detonation from the surrounding soil, resulting in a seismic pulse of much smaller amplitude than a detonation of that level would ordinarily send out. The small pulse could escape detection altogether, or if detected might not be recognized as the signature of a forbidden test.

The other possibility raised by opponents of a complete test ban was that a nuclear device could be prepared for detonation ahead of time and triggered to explode when a major earthquake occurred in its vicinity. The signal of the detonation would thus be obscured by the presumably larger pulse generated by the earthquake. Therefore, the opponents of a complete test ban treaty have argued, it would be possible for the Soviet Union to test new nuclear explosives in violation of such a treaty without being detected by the United States.

A pulse generated either by an earthquake or an underground detonation consists of the superposition of a very large number of individual waves of varying wavelengths (i.e., frequencies) and amplitudes all generated at the same time. Discrimination between pulses generated by earthquakes and those caused by explosions has been based until now primarily on the relative size of the signals generated by an event as they arrive at a detection station via different paths. Thus, the amplitude of the detected pulse was the crucial parameter on which discrimination was based.

In the second part of this chapter, Evernden and Archambeau show that the largest portion of the energy emitted into the surrounding soil by an earthquake is carried away by waves of low frequency, while energy from detonations is carried away by waves of much higher frequency. Thus, if one "tunes" the distant seismic detectors to higher frequencies only, they can "hear" only the waves from detonations while ignoring the earthquake waves. This eliminates the ubiquitous noise of earthquake and other earth movements and permits the detection of extremely weak seismic pulses from detonations.

This new method removes the very last scientific objection to a complete test ban and opens the way for the verification of a Complete Test Ban Treaty already agreed upon, but not signed as yet, by the United States, the U.S.S.R., and the U.K.

INTRODUCTION

This chapter is divided into two sections. The first section is intended to demonstrate that sound theoretical bases exist for all discrimination criteria found useful for differentiating the seismic signals of explosions and earthquakes. Discrimination has been discussed largely in terms of empirical data; in the first section all of these empirical data are placed within a thoroughly developed theoretical context. In other words, seismological studies in this area are mature.

The second section presents data that indicate that a seismic network internal to the U.S.S.R. will have a much greater monitoring capability than suggested by all previous studies. It gives an update of the network analyses based on the theoretical models and observations of the high frequency spectra of explosions and earthquakes (discussed in the first section) and from recent observations on the ambient amplitudes of high frequency microseismic noise. These observations in particular suggest that earthquakes can be distinguished from explosions down to quite low levels and at considerable distances by seismic means.

This chapter is a sequel to work published in two articles co-authored by one of us (Evernden): "The Verification of a Comprehensive Test Ban"[1] and "Seismic Methods for Verifying Nuclear Test Ban Treaties."[2] Topics discussed in detail in those articles are only referred to as necessary for continuity in this chapter.

SEISMIC DISCRIMINATION OF EARTHQUAKES AND EXPLOSIONS

The first part of this chapter constitutes a rapid journey through a body of seismological data and theoretical predictions, the purpose of the journey being to display the fact that observations and theory relative to seismic discrimination are now in near-total agreement.

Figure 16.1 is to remind the reader of a set of seismological definitions and concepts that are important to the following discussion. The only one requiring a few words is related to the basis of the theoretical calculations for an earthquake source, that is, a large volume relaxation source. It is, of course, true that a dislocation source[3] can be constructed to be equivalent to a relaxation source[4] as regards far-field radiation. However, all variations in the characteristics of radiated waves of earthquakes are clearly expressed in terms of physical parameters of the failure process[5,6] in relaxation theory, while being generally impossible of meaningful investigation via the largely ad hoc dislocation theory.

Generally used identification criteria are of three types: location, depth, and spectral contrasts. In the operation of a seismic network in a Comprehensive Test Ban Treaty (CTBT) context, maximum exploitation of location and depth criteria will be done in order to minimize spectral analysis. Table 16.1 illustrates the utility of location and depth in such a screening process. The values are based upon analysis of world-wide earthquakes for the years 1967 through 1971. Location is expressed in terms of the epicenter being in water-covered (W) areas at or more than 0, at or more than 15, and at or more than 25 kilometers from shore, and in land (L) areas. One third of all earthquakes have depths of 50 kilometers or greater, a depth easily established in areas of interest. Only 11% are at depths of less than 50 kilometers and under land. Most of these will be in areas with no potential as sites of clandestine nuclear tests. Only 1% or so of all earthquakes are at depths of less than 50 kilometers and in areas of potential nuclear explosions, thus possibly requiring analysis via spectral discriminants. It should not be concluded that determination of depth of focus as greater or less

DEFINITIONS

Body waves — P and S

Surface waves — Rayleigh and Love

Magnitude — m_b and M_S (M_L)

Depth of focus

Source mechanism:
Explosion — radial pressure
Earthquake — shear strain release

Relaxation source

Location — W,S,L and Area of Interest

Identification Criteria:
1 — Location
2 — Depth of Focus
3 — Spectral Criteria

FIGURE 16.1. Seismological terminology pertinent to the paper.

than 50 kilometers is a measure of seismological capabilities. In areas of especial interest, careful research and modeling, using data from earthquakes in or near the area, allow depth estimates within a few kilometers when using data of only a few stations. Thus, many or most of the 1% mentioned will actually be classed as earthquakes via depth criteria after a surveillance network has been in operation for two or more years.

The next figures illustrate some of the empirical facts of spectral behavior of earthquakes and explosions that require explanation. Figure 16.2 illustrates the $M_S:m_b$ values (magnitude values based upon 20-second Rayleigh surface waves and 1-second P body waves, respectively) for all shallow focus earthquakes (depths of 30 kilometers or less) of m_b 4.5 or greater that occurred in the world during the first 162 days of 1972,[7] the $M_S:m_b$ values for 24 U.S. and 24 U.S.S.R. explosions,[8] and the $M_S:m_b$ values for a specially investigated set of earthquakes between m_b 4 and m_b 4.5.[9] M_S values are in nearly all cases based upon 20-second Rayleigh

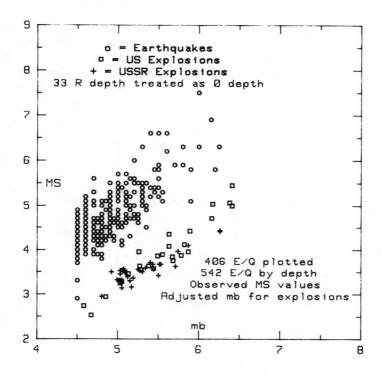

W/W E/Q(30 >=DEPTH>= 0 KM) & US & USSR XP

FIGURE 16.2. M_S versus m_b values for earthquakes and explosions. See text for sources of data. All m_b values have been adjusted for regional bias, the normalization region being central continental (eastern U.S. or central U.S.S.R.). Earthquakes have depths of 30 kilometers or less.

Table 16.1. World-Wide Distribution of Earthquakes

Location of Focus	% of W/W E/Qs
$D^a \geq 50$	33
$D \geq 50$ & $W^b(S^c \geq 25)$	83
$D \geq 50$ & W (S $\geq$ 15)	86
$D \geq 50$ & W (S $\geq$ 0)	89
$D < 50$ & L^d (S $\geq$ 0)	11
$D \geq 30$ & W (S $\geq$ 25)	90

[a]D = Depth (in kilometers).
[b]W = Water.
[c]S = Distance from Shore (in kilometers).
[d]L = Land.

waves whereas m_b values are based upon 1-second P waves. All m_b values have been normalized for regional bias. A few earthquakes having low 20-second Rayleigh waves were evaluated based upon their 40-second Rayleigh waves.[7] We will discuss later the problem of spectral holes induced by depth of focus and how to handle this discrimination problem. The aspects of the data on the figure requiring explanation are:

1. Base of the earthquake population has a 1:1 slope below m_b 5.75.
2. This limiting line steepens sharply to the right so that there is a maximum m_b value of 6.5 for the data plotted. More extensive data place this limit at about 6.75.
3. The limiting curve of the earthquake population on the left is also steep.
4. The M_S:m_b slope for explosions is 1:1 below m_b or so.
5. There is an 0.5 to 0.75 M_S separation of the base of the earthquake population and the mean of the explosion population in the region of 1:1 M_S:m_b slope for both event types.

Figure 16.3 documents that the 1:1 slope continues to m_b 2.75 for earthquakes and to m_b 3.75 for explosions with the separation of the two sets of M_S:m_b values remaining as on the previous figure.[10] Figure 16.4 indicates that the same long period versus short period relationship persists for earthquakes to at least magnitude 0.[11]

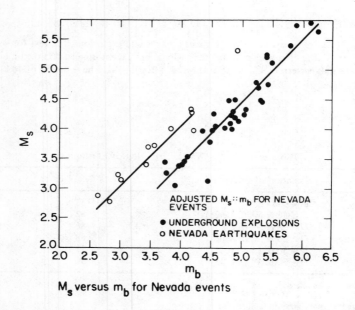

M_s versus m_b for Nevada events

FIGURE 16.3. M_S versus m_b values for Nevada earthquakes and explosions.

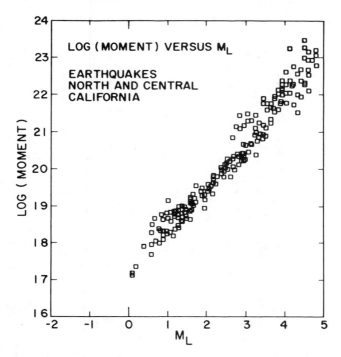

FIGURE 16.4. Log (Seismic moment) versus M_L for earthquakes of north and central California.

Figure 16.5 illustrates that the slope of a line comparing earthquake surface wave magnitudes based on 20 and 100 second Rayleigh waves is 1:1, implying a 1:1 slope for m_b versus $M_S(100)$ to and below m_b 5.75,[12,13] indicating a flat source spectrum at wavelengths many times the length of rupture. Any source theory must explain the physical basis of strong generation of long periods relative to short periods for an earthquake with very small length of break.

Table 16.2 illustrates in three different orders of application the utility of depth, location, and $M_S:m_b$ in identifying the 948 earthquakes of m_b 4.5 or greater that occurred in the first 162 days of 1972.[7] All are seen to be identified by the conservative criteria of (B) (decision line of $M_S:m_b$ as drawn on Figure 16.2). Most of the earthquakes can be identified by location far at sea (A) but such location was required for identification of only 2 of the smallest events (C), illustrating the great overlap in the applicability of these criteria.

Another spectral criterion requiring explanation is the contrast in spectrum of the short period P waves of explosions and earthquakes. Table

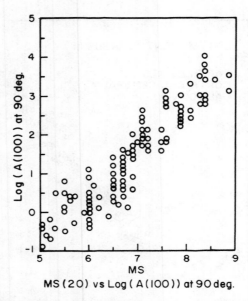

FIGURE 16.5. $M_S(20)$ versus log(Amplitude at 100 second period) normalized to a distance of 90°.

16.3 (A), based upon analysis of data of 225 Eurasian earthquakes and 108 Soviet explosions as recorded at LASA, illustrates this constrast via a discriminant "D".[14,15] This discriminant compares the sum of spectral amplitudes in the (0.4–1.0) Hertz and (1.0–4.5) Hertz spectral windows, D

Table 16.2. Discrimination Test

Discriminant	No. Identified
A	
Depth ≥ 50 km	375
+Location > 25 km at Sea	801
+Depth ≥ 30 km	856
+M_S:m_b	948
B	
Depth ≥ 50 km	375
+M_S:m_b	944
+Location > 25 km at Sea	948
C	
Depth ≥ 30 km	565
+M_S:m_b	946
+Location > 25 km at Sea	948

Table 16.3. P Wave Spectra, Eurasian Earthquakes and Soviet Explosions

A. Discrimination Based on D and/or Depth ≥ 50 km

(*D* Values Normalized for Magnitude)

D Value	Explosions (High *D*)		Earthquakes (*D+* ≥ 50) (Low *D*)	
	Pass	Fail	Pass	Fail
0	91	17	221	4
−1	98	10	215	10
−2	104	4	205	20

B. Mean D Value Versus Magnitude

Magnitude (m_b)	Explosions	Earthquakes
6.0	1.0	−3.7
5.0	3.3	−3.6
4.0	5.6	−4.8

D values (0.4–1.0 Hertz versus 1–4.5 Hertz)
Data of LASA Subarray
108 Explosions and 225 Earthquakes.

increasing in value as the relative content of the higher frequency window increases in value ($D_{explosions} > D_{earthquakes}$). A very significant but less than perfect separation by a discriminant based upon (D + depth ≥ 50 kilometers) is achieved. All explosions at the Soviet test sites (Novaya Zemlya and Semipalatinsk) are successfully separated from all earthquakes, those explosions not separated being numerous of the off-test-site explosions. Table 16.3 (*B*) illustrates that the discrimination capability of the *D* discriminant increases with decreasing m_b value, at least to m_b 4.0.[15]

Figure 16.6 illustrates a different criterion exploiting the same spectral characteristic, the data coming from the WWSSN station at Kabul, Afghanistan. The plotted explosions occurred at two Soviet explosion sites (Figure 16.7), the earthquakes in nearby areas, and the discriminant is based on m_b-type measurements based on narrow band filters centered at 0.6 and 3.25 Hertz. Note again that the data suggest an improvement in discrimination with decreasing m_b value.

It has been suggested that the contrast in P spectra shown in Table 16.3 and Figure 16.6 is not related to the source spectrum but only to increased high frequency loss from the radiated earthquake P waves because of their location above crust/mantle regions of low *Q* or high attenuation. This suggestion is certainly false. Note on Figure 16.7 the essentially common propagation path for earthquakes and explosions near the Caspian Sea to Kabul (KAAO) as well as the proximity of several of the eastern earth-

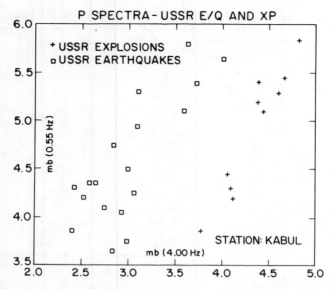

FIGURE 16.6. Spectral discriminant [m_b(0.55 Hz) versus m_b(4.00 Hz)] for U.S.S.R. earthquakes and explosions, as recorded at Kabul, Afghanistan.

quakes to the Semipalatinsk explosions. No credible model of Q variation over such short distances could explain the observed spectral differences particularly as the phases being analyzed are short period crustal phases. Figure 16.8 illustrates the Q-corrected spectral contrast of the P waves of four central Aleutian earthquakes and MILROW, a nuclear explosion on Amchitka Island in the Aleutians.[16] All data were recorded at the same U.S. station. The higher rate of fall-off of the earthquake spectra at high frequencies is obvious. The exceptional rate of fall-off of the explosion spectrum at lower frequencies, a relationship that provides a very powerful discriminant between larger explosions and earthquakes, also requires explanation.

Other facts denying the suggestion that observed P spectral differences between earthquakes and explosions are simply products of propagation are: (a) nearly all deep focus earthquakes, earthquakes certainly below any region of excessive attenuation, are discriminated from explosions by both of the previously described P spectral criteria; (b) nearly all earthquakes are in Benioff or subduction zones overlying high Q oceanic crust and mantle, thus being above regions with even higher Q than that underlying the Soviet test sites; (c) seismic stations in island arcs often have abnormally fast P times and high m_b values, confirming their location above high Q mantles; and (d) the observed fact reported in 1977[15] that earthquake spectra

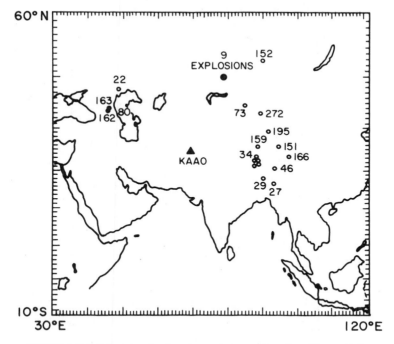

FIGURE 16.7. Map showing locations of events plotted on Figure 16.6.

tend to have a common high frequency asymptote whereas explosions do
not is unexplainable by relative path attenuation differences, while being
demanded by source theory as described below.

Table 16.4 lists some questions relative to earthquake spectra that require
answers. Table 16.5 indicates the scaling law predictions of relaxation theory that are relevant to answering the questions of Table 16.4.[5] Note the
assumption of rupture velocity (U_R) approaching shear-wave velocity
(V_S), this condition giving earthquake $M_S:m_b$ values most closely similar
to those of explosions. The effects induced by lower rupture velocities will
be used later to explain some particular details of the $M_S: m_b$ distribution
of smaller earthquakes. For $U_R \cong V_S$, both P and S spectra are predicted to
be flat below a corner frequency, both corner frequencies being functions
of fault length but not of stress drop. The predicted flat spectrum at low
frequencies, independent of earthquake size, derives from the large volume
character of the earthquake source. Effectively, the entire world relaxes a
bit for each earthquake of any magnitude. Source amplitudes of S waves
are about 5 times those of P waves and all source amplitudes are proportional to stress drop. The predicted rate of fall-off of amplitude at high fre-

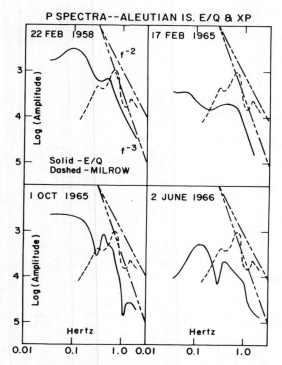

FIGURE 16.8. P spectra for central Aleutian Islands earthquakes and MILROW, a nuclear explosion on Amchitka Island in the Aleutians.

quencies for P waves is proportional to frequency^{-3}, whereas that for S waves is frequency^{-2}.

Another important aspect of the predicted behavior of P wave spectra is the prediction of a common high frequency P wave asymptote for all earthquakes of common stress drop independent of M_S or m_b value. Figure 16.9

Table 16.4. Questions about Earthquakes

1. Why is M_S:m_b slope 1:1 at small magnitude?

2. Why do m_b values attain a maximum value of ~6.75?

3. Why do earthquake M_S:m_b values cover such a large domain on an M_S:m_b plot?

4. Why don't the M_S:m_b values of strike-slip earthquakes lie well below those of thrust earthquakes?

5. Why are M_S:m_b values less a function of depth than suggested by M_S versus depth calculations?

Table 16.5. Scaling Laws — Earthquakes

ASSUMPTION: Rupture velocity $(U_R) \cong$ Shear wave velocity (V_S)
ASSUMPTION: Relaxation volume great ($\cong$ world). Independent of magnitude

P and S spectra flat for frequencies < corner frequency

P corner frequency $\propto (U_R / \text{Length of Break})$
High frequency fall-off for P waves $\propto \text{frequency}^{-3}$
(Conditions may lead to decade-width segment with slope from f^0 to f^{-2})

S corner frequency $\cong 0.7$ of P corner frequency
High frequency fall-off for S waves $\propto \text{frequency}^{-2}$

(Amplitudes of S)/(Amplitudes of P) $\propto (V_P / V_S)^3 \sim 5$
All amplitudes $\propto$ stress-drop

Common high frequency asymptote for P waves of all earthquakes.

---

illustrates in an approximate way the predicted behavior of P wave spectra of earthquakes. The reason for the observed maximum value of m_b is obvious as is the reason for the 1:1 slope of the $M_S : m_b$ curve at small magnitude, that is, the fixed ratio (1:1) of source spectra at 1 and 20 seconds (0.05 Hertz) at all small magnitudes. It may be of interest to note that this figure was originally published to provide the simplest possible explanation of the observed shape of the $M_S : m_b$ curve.[17]

The next figures explain the reasons for the wide distribution of the earthquake $M_S : m_b$ values of Figure 16.2. Consider Figure 16.10. For a given stress-drop and a given rupture velocity, an $M_S : m_b$ curve like that shown is predicted, that is, 1:1 slope at small magnitude, the line curving steeply upwards at some m_b value and reaching a limiting m_b while M_S continues to increase. Because all amplitudes scale linearly with stress-drop, curves for different stress-drops are obtained by moving the original curve along a 45° line, a 10-fold change in stress-drop being correlated with a one unit change in M_S and m_b. Full modeling with specified crust/mantle type, earthquake and depth leads to a quantitative plot such as Figure 16.11. If observed $M_S : m_b$ values for Aleutian thrust earthquakes are plotted on an appropriately calculated figure, one obtains Figure 16.12. The figure includes some explosion data for comparison, the three Amchitka explosions being indicated by special symbol. Nearly all of the larger earthquakes fall between the 10 and 100 bar curves, while the points with low M_S for a given m_b are coincident with the base of the predicted distribution.

At low m_b, numerous of the earthquake points move into the 1 to 10 bar domain. Remember that the figures used above were drawn under the assumption of rupture velocity approaching the shear wave velocity. The predicted effect of low rupture velocity on the P wave spectrum is to drastically lower amplitudes near to and above the corner frequency before

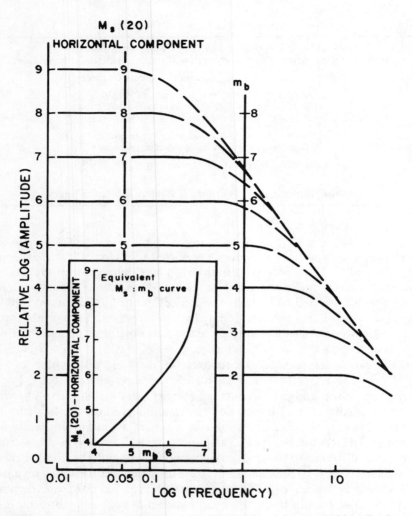

FIGURE 16.9. Predicted P wave spectra of earthquakes in conformance with scaling laws of Table 16.5.

affecting amplitudes at low frequencies such as .05 Hertz. Thus, a second possible explanation for the smaller earthquakes with abnormally high $(M_S - m_b)$ values is that the pertinent small earthquakes were associated with low rupture velocities. Other P wave spectral data discussed by Blandford and von Segern[18] imply clearly that a major factor controlling the data of the small earthquakes of Figure 16.2 is indeed low rupture velocity. Details on this matter are given in Evernden et al., 1986.[19]

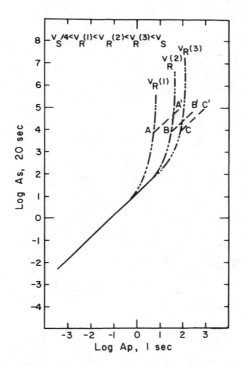

FIGURE 16.10. Influence of rupture velocity and stress drop on spectral composition of earthquake signals [log(amplitude of 1 Hz. P waves) versus log(amplitude of .05 Hz. S waves)].

Figures 16.13 and 16.14 illustrate the predicted contrast in Rayleigh waves for strike-slip and 45°-thrust earthquakes of identical moment and occurring in a continental crust. We mentioned earlier the presence of spectral holes in earthquake Rayleigh wave spectra. Such zero-amplitude holes occur at all azimuths at the same period for strike-slip earthquakes, at all azimuths but different periods for 45°-thrust earthquakes, but at only one azimuth and period for most other earthquakes (the failure of the amplitude curves on Figure 16.13 to reach zero is a result of the mode of calculating the amplitude versus period curve). However, when the 20-second amplitudes are low, amplitudes of 40-second waves are high, much higher than predicted for explosions of the same m_b value. Thus, for any shallow-focus seismic event for which comparison between m_b and $M_S(20)$ suggests an explosion, investigation of $M_S(40)$ will establish whether it is an earthquake or an explosion.

Comparison of Figures 16.13 and 16.14 indicates that predicted Rayleigh wave amplitudes for the 45°-thrust earthquake are several times greater

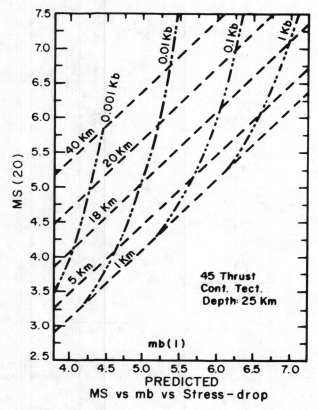

FIGURE 16.11. Prediction of $M_S(20)$ versus $m_b(1)$ for 45° thrust earthquakes of 25-kilometer depth in tectonic continental region. M_S versus m_b versus stress-drop versus length of rupture.

than those predicted for a strike-slip earthquake of the same moment and depth. Unless some other factor plays an important countervailing role, the $M_S:m_b$ values of strike-slip earthquakes would be predicted to lie amongst the explosion values of Figure 16.2. The evidence is clear that no such thing happens, and there is indeed another factor. It is the effect on the amplitude of far-field P waves and thus on m_b of the different radiation patterns of P waves for the two earthquakes. The radiation pattern being spoken of is the amplitude of the P wave as a function of azimuth from the strike of the fault and of angle from the downward vertical. Due to the pronouncedly asymmetric pattern of the earthquake source and the linking of that pattern to the plane of the fault and the direction of fault movement in the fault plane, the rotation of the fault plane and movement direction

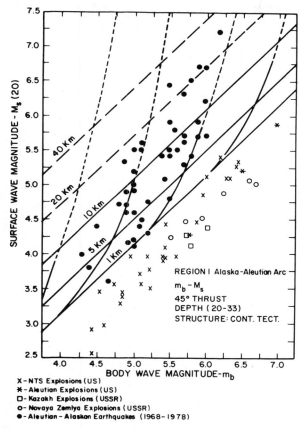

FIGURE 16.12. Comparison of prediction and observation for central Aleutian earthquakes (M_S versus m_b). Data of Aleutian explosions (asterisk) and other explosions included (normalized m_b values).

relative to the vertical leads to drastically different amplitudes of P waves being radiated to distance. The effect of this factor is illustrated in Table 16.6, where relative m_b, M_S, and $(M_S - m_b)$ values for earthquakes of both types and several depths are shown. The m_b values of this table are the average m_b over all rays that pass through the solid angle including all rays reaching the surface at teleseismic distances as P waves. Depth affects these values because P velocity is a function of depth and the set of rays radiated to teleseismic distance is a function of the P velocity at the source. The M_S values are the average over all azimuths of 20-second Rayleigh waves. Because Rayleigh waves are a surface wave experiencing a complicated exponential decrease in amplitude with depth, the M_S values in the

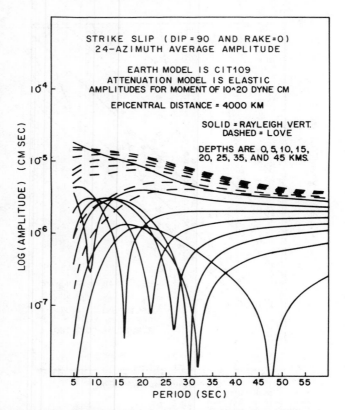

FIGURE 16.13. Predicted mean amplitude (as a function of azimuth) versus period for Rayleigh and Love waves of strike-slip earthquakes of various depths. Epicentral distance = 4,000 kilometers. The mode of calculating the curves kept the spectral nulls from attaining their actual zero values. Earth model is CIT 109C. Attenuation model is elastic.

table are also a function of depth. Relative M_S and m_b values vary greatly as a function of depth and event type. However, relative $(M_S - m_b)$ values are nearly identical except for the effects of spectral holes and for very shallow strike-slip earthquakes, these latter earthquakes actually being the easiest to distinguish by $M_S{:}m_b$ because of their very low m_b values. Thus, $M_S{:}m_b$ values of most strike-slip earthquakes of the same depth, dimensions, and stress-drop as 45°-thrust earthquakes will plot to the left of and lower than the thrust earthquakes along a line of nearly 1:1 slope, thus remaining within the earthquake population. Note, also, that the relative $(M_S - m_b)$ values are not a function of depth, though the relative M_S values are. This relationship explains why there is no observed sensitivity of $M_S{:}m_b$ values to depth of focus for depths of 10 to 50 kilometers.

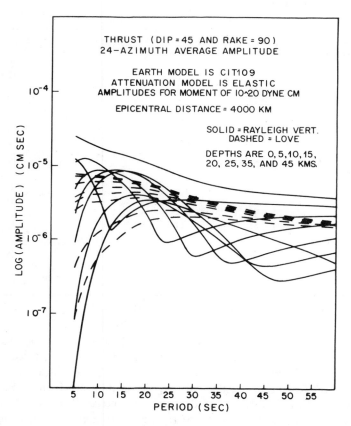

FIGURE 16.14. Predicted mean amplitude (as a function of azimuth) versus period for Rayleigh and Love waves of 45° thrust earthquakes of various depths. Epicentral distance is 4,000 kilometers. Earth model is CIT 109C. Attenuation model is elastic.

If one plots the approximate stress-drop curves for strike-slip and 45°-thrust earthquakes ($U_R \cong V_S$) on the 1972 data of Figure 16.2, we obtain Figure 16.15. Most larger earthquakes fall between the 100 bar thrust and the 10 bar strike-slip lines. Numerous small earthquakes still fall outside the 10 bar curves, suggesting a role for even lower stress drop and/or low rupture velocity.

Data for explosions illustrating questions requiring answers is now presented. These data are used in preference to many others in the literature because of the rigidly controlled procedures and data source used in estimating the magnitudes and the careful normalization of each observation to that expected in eastern United States for an explosion at the Nevada

Table 16.6. Relative $M_S(20)$ versus Relative m_b

Strike-slip	Depth	Relative M_S	Relative m_b	Difference
$V_p = 6$ km/sec	0	.9	.0	.9
	5	.6	.0	.6
	10	.1	.0	.1
	15	−.4*	.0	−.4*
7 km/sec	20	.2	.15	.05
	25	.3	.15	.15
	35	.1	.15	−.05
8 km/sec	45	.2	.25	−.05
Thrust (45°)				
$V_p = 6$ km/sec	0	1.0	.8	.2
	5	.5*	.8	−.3*
	10	.4*	.8	−.4*
	15	.7	.8	−.1
7 km/sec	20	.8	.7	.1
	25	.85	.7	.15
	35	.6	.7	−.1
8 km/sec	45	.5	.6	−.1

*Low values because of spectral holes near 20 sec. at these depths.

Test Site. Figure 16.16 presents M_S versus $\log(W)$ (W = yield) for some U.S. explosions as recorded in eastern United States or as recorded in western United States after careful calibration by use of data from eastern United States for larger events. All magnitude data are from U.S. LRSM stations, a set of carefully operated and closely intercalibrated stations. The fact of relevance is that the slope of the best-fitting curve is a straight line with a slope of about 1.25 (amplitude rises faster than yield). As illustrated in Figure 16.17, the behavior of m_b versus $\log(W)$ is markedly different. The best-fitting line has essentially the identical slope at low yields as does M_S versus $\log(W)$, it being important to note that this linear relationship extends to very small yields (fraction of a kiloton). However, there is a marked flattening of the curve at about 75 kilotons or m_b 5.6. Calculations show that, whatever source spectral shape explains the lower part of the m_b versus $\log(W)$ curve, the indicated flattening is exactly equivalent to a change in source spectral shape by a factor of frequency^{-2}. Note on Figure 16.17 that in contrast to earthquake data, there is no evidence of a maximum m_b value for explosions. It was pointed out in 1977 that data recorded at LASA (Montana) from Soviet explosions indicated the same relationship.[14]

The questions about these observations requiring answers are as in Table 16.7, whereas Table 16.8 is a listing of the theoretical scaling laws pertinent to explanation of explosion spectra. The predictions are based upon com-

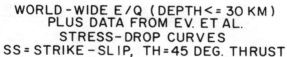

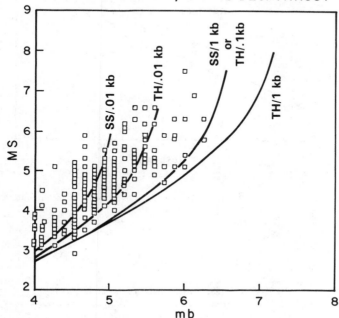

FIGURE 16.15. Predicted M_S versus m_b values for strike-slip and 45° thrust earthquakes (stress-drops of 1 kilobar and .01 kilobar) superimposed on earthquake data of Figure 16.2.

plex theoretical predictions for explosions in a medium stressed only by load.[20] The effects of the pre-stress supplying the energy for earthquakes and the relaxation associated with creation of the explosion-induced fractured volume[1,2,21,22] lead to second order effects which though important in some contexts are not germane to the theme of this paper and will be ignored.

Table 16.7 Questions—Explosions

1. Why do explosion m_b values increase indefinitely?

2. Why does the M_S versus m_b relationship for explosions have a uniform 1:1 slope at all yields while the m_b versus $\log(W)$ curve flattens by frequency^{-2} factor at about 75 kilotons?

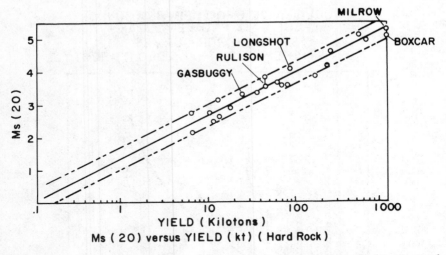

FIGURE 16.16. M_S versus log(Yield) for U.S. explosions in other than alluvium at several sites.

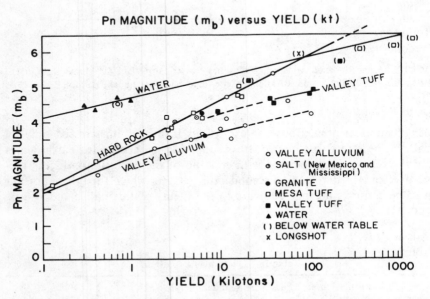

FIGURE 16.17. m_b versus log(Yield) for explosions in a variety of media. Most explosions were at Nevada Test Site. For others, m_b values were normalized to western U.S. crust/mantle conditions.

Table 16.8. Scaling Laws — Explosions

ASSUMPTION: C(Velocity of shock wave) $\cong$ P wave velocity (V_P)
ASSUMPTION: R_0 (Radius of fracture) $\propto$ yield$^{1/3}$

P spectrum flat for frequencies < corner frequency
Corner frequency $\propto C/R_0 \propto$ yield$^{-1/3}$
Amplitudes of high frequency P $\propto$ frequency^{-2}

$m_b \propto \log$(yield) if corner frequency > 1 Hertz
$m_b \propto \log[$(yield)/(1 − corner frequency)$^2]$ if corner frequency $\geq$ 1 Hertz
m_b values increase without limit as yield increases

$M_S \propto \log$(yield) for all yields of less than 100s of megatons

No direct S or Love waves from symmetric explosion in stress-free medium

---

Note that the critical controlling velocity is now the shock wave or P velocity. The predicted spectral characteristics of an explosion are a flat P spectrum at long periods, a corner frequency which is markedly higher than for an earthquake of equivalent low frequency source amplitude, a corner frequency which scales with $W^{1/3}$, and thus with frequency^{-3}, and a high frequency fall-off proportional to frequency^{-2}. These predictions lead to the relationships of Figure 16.18. There is predicted to be no limiting value for m_b, there not being a high frequency asymptote approached by spectra of all explosions. A marked flattening of the m_b versus $\log(W)$ curve around m_b 6 is predicted, as the spectral value associated with a period of 1 second moves from the flat portion of the spectrum to the portion having a slope of frequency^{-2}. The exact positioning of the flattening as a function of m_b is somewhat arbitrary due to the marked regional bias that effects m_b.[1,2,23,24,25] Note that the change in slope shown on the plot of m_b versus $\log(W)$ (Figure 16.17) is exactly that predicted by source theory.

A fact causing much perplexity over many years has been the 1:1 slope of the explosion M_S:m_b curve at small yield and the linear shape of the m_b versus $\log(W)$ curve from a W of 75 kilotons to a W of 0.1 kiloton (see Figure 16.17). This observation is in drastic disagreement with the predictions of simple linear elastic theory. The United States sets off explosions at scale depths so that 1 kiloton is exploded at about 450 feet while a megaton is exploded at about 4,500 feet. The very shallow depth of very small explosions is predicted by linear theory to lead to marked lowering of the m_b value below that predicted by source theory as the result of strong cancellation of P by the reflected pP phase (the reflected upgoing P wave reflected at the free surface with complete phase reversal). The predictions of this theory are shown on Figure 16.19 by lines labeled "linear," these lines being predictions by linear theory of m_b and ($m_b - M_S$) values for 150 kiloton explosions at depths ranging from 1000 to 150 meters (~450 feet) in hard

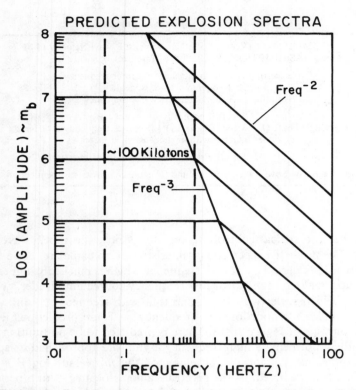

FIGURE 16.18. Predicted P spectra of explosions in accordance with the scaling laws of Table 16.8.

rocks of uniform characteristics. Note the incorrect prediction of a marked decrease in $(m_b - M_S)$ as depth decreases. The predicted effect is seen to be strong even for depths equivalent in normal scaling to 1-kiloton explosions. The predicted effect would be even more drastic for explosions at shallower depths. What then is the explanation of observations? The data points connected by solid lines and labeled "non-linear" on Figure 16.19 result from modeling the entire explosion process with all of its non-linear aspects via very complex finite element calculations.[26,27] The prediction of such theory is that both m_b and M_S are independent of depth of the explosion, as are $(m_b - M_S)$ and $M_S:m_b$. Thus, the proper theory for near-surface explosions predicts that linear calculations are in error and predicts m_b and M_S values to be unaffected by depth of the explosion, in agreement with observations. The many efforts in the seismological literature to incorporate the effects of pP into estimations of m_b are mistaken.

Something that we cannot explain at this time is the 1.25 slope of the M_S

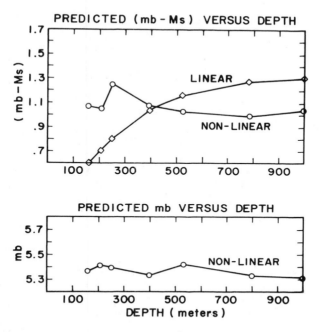

FIGURE 16.19. Predicted m_b versus depth and $(m_b - M_S)$ versus depth for 150 kiloton explosions, predictions being based upon both simple linear calculations ("linear") and finite element non-linear codes ("non-linear"). See references 23 and 24.

versus yield curve at all yields and the equivalent slope at small yields for the m_b versus $\log(W)$ curve. As noted above, this effect really influences the entire m_b versus $\log(W)$ relationship. The m_b value, or logarithm of ground motion amplitude, rises faster than linear scaling with logarithm of the radiometrically calculated yield, while source theory predicts that m_b should scale linearly with $\log(W)$. We are getting higher amplitude ground motion than expected, this increased ground motion being a uniform function over more than 4 orders of magnitude of yield and at both 1 and 20 seconds. These data may suggest a systematic error in calibration rather than an unaccounted-for physical process. One can only suggest that radiometrically determined yields may systematically fail to provide the supposed $W^{1/3}$ scaling for estimating amplitudes of ground motion.

An explanation for the scatter of M_S versus $\log(W)$ values for NTS explosions shown on an earlier figure is suggested by Figure 16.20, which gives theoretical predictions of source spectra (RVP) for explosions in different hard-rock materials at NTS.[28] The 3-fold difference (0.5 spread in m_b values) in low frequency source levels is obvious.

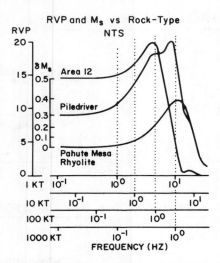

FIGURE 16.20. Reduced velocity potential (RVP) and M_S versus rock-type at Nevada Test Site. Scaling relationships at the bottom of figure are simple yield$^{1/3}$ scaling.

We now can answer the critical questions of why the $M_S{:}m_b$ discriminant of Figure 16.2 is so successful, and why a discriminant based on spectra of short period P waves is of great utility. Table 16.9, in conjunction with previous tables and figures, provides the answer to the first question. Figure 16.14 illustrates the relative generation of Rayleigh waves for thrust earthquakes of various depths and explosions of zero depth, the zero-depth thrust and zero-depth explosion having nearly the identical mean amplitudes of Rayleigh waves for events of the same moment. A zero-depth or very shallow explosion of a given moment will generate higher amplitude Rayleigh waves than any several kilometer or deeper earthquake of equivalent moment. However, the m_b values of these two

Table 16.9 Relative $M_S(20)$ Values (Earthquake–Explosion)

Component	Strike-Slip		45° Thrust	
	D = 10 km	D = 45 km	D = 10 km	D = 45 km
Equal Moments	−0.7	−0.9	−0.6 (−0.3)*	−0.5
Source P	+0.7	+0.7	+0.7	+0.7
Rad. Pattern	+0.9	+0.7	+0.2	+0.4
SUM	+0.9	+0.5	+0.3 (+0.6)*	+0.6

*Low values of $M_S(20)$ for thrust at 10 km depth result from spectral hole around 20 second period. Values in parentheses are $M_S(40)$ values.

events will be markedly different because the P source spectrum of the explosion is about 5 times that of the earthquake of equivalent moment, and because the P rays used for m_b measurements are a higher fraction of the maximum amplitude for explosions than for earthquakes. Table 16.9 shows the relative combined effects of these three factors for zero-depth explosions, strike-slip earthquakes and 45°-thrust earthquakes of 10- and 45-kilometer depths. The bottom row of the table indicates the predicted level of $M_S:m_b$ discrimination. It is seen, by comparison with Figure 16.2, to agree with observations.

Secondly, why is there a useful discriminant based on the spectral content of short period P waves? Figure 16.21, based on scaling of the predicted PILEDRIVER spectrum of Figure 16.19 and the scaling of predicted earthquake spectra assuming a 75-bar stress drop and a rupture velocity approaching the shear wave velocity in the rocks surrounding the fault-break, provides the explanation. Predicted spectra are given for explosions and earthquakes of m_b 4.0 and 6.0. Even if m_b 4.0 earthquakes are characterized by 75-bar stress drops and high rupture velocities, discrimination is predicted to be possible between earthquakes and explosions in hard rock using the bandpasses of the D discriminant described earlier. Because $M_S:m_b$ values presented earlier suggest that the typical small earthquake is characterized by lower rupture velocity and/or lower stress drop than the average larger earthquake, we have included on Figure 16.21 predicted spectra for the cases of high and low rupture velocity associated with a 15-bar stress drop for m_b 4.0 earthquakes, again in agreement with observations. These curves lead to a higher predicted discrimination capability by a D-type discriminant for m_b 4 earthquakes than for larger earthquakes, the observed relationship. A significant point to be noted on this figure is that discrimination is predicted to increase as the high frequency spectral window increases in frequency. There is little doubt that observations of Eurasian earthquakes and explosions at distance of 5 to 20 degrees will permit detection of frequencies of at least 10 to 20 Hertz, providing increased discrimination capability against explosions in hard rock.

We suggest that the demonstrated failure in Table 16.3, A,[15] of the short period P spectral discriminant to separate some Soviet PNEs from earthquakes results from these explosions having been in water-saturated sediments. The highest curve on the left-hand side of Figure 16.17 indicates the observed m_b versus $\log(W)$ relationship for explosions in water and water-saturated sediments, this behavior implying a frequency^{-2} spectral slope to low frequencies for such explosions. This observed behavior was predicted by theoretical discussions of many years ago.[29] Such a spectral shape for an explosion will lead to a higher ratio of low frequency amplitudes to high frequency amplitudes in passbands where the spectrum for explosions in rock flattens (see Figure 16.21).

Table 16.10 lists several spectral criteria that have been investigated over

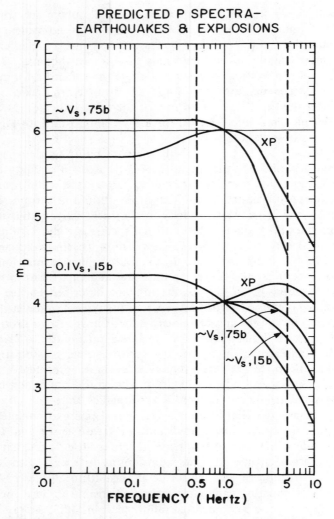

FIGURE 16.21. Predicted P wave spectra of earthquakes and explosions for various rupture velocities and stress drops. Curves for explosions are labeled "XP" whereas those for earthquakes are characterized by rupture velocity and stress-drop.

the years. All of these can be as well explained by the developed relaxation theory as can the two we choose to discuss in some detail. It may be interesting to note that the anelastic effects causing no cancellation of 1-second P wave amplitudes by the reflected pP wave are predicted to have little effect on the strong P − pP cancellation at periods of 20 seconds or so

Table 16.10. Several Useful Spectral Discriminants

1. $m_b(1)$ versus $M_S(20)$ and/or $M_S(40)$
2. $m_b(.5$ to 2 Hz.$)$ versus $m_b(2$ to 10 Hz.$)$ or some variation
3. $m_b(1)$ versus $m_b(10$–20 seconds$)$
4. $m_b(1)$ versus long period S
5. $m_b(1)$ versus Love wave amplitudes
6. $m_b(1)$ versus L_g (short period surface wave)
7. Details of spectral shape of surface waves

predicted by linear theory. The anelastic effects seem to be nearly equivalent to a time shift of pP relative to P, a time shift that achieves adequate phase shift around 1 Hertz to prevent cancellation, but such small phase shift at a period of 20 seconds that strong cancellation takes place. This $P - pP$ cancellation at long periods is the explanation of the rapidly falling amplitudes of the P waves of MILROW as a function of lengthening period on Figure 16.8. The reason for emphasis on Rayleigh waves in discrimination research rather than long period P and S, phases giving far better discrimination at the magnitudes for which they are useful, is the greater amplitude and thus greater detectability of Rayleigh waves. A criterion based on Rayleigh waves is useful at much lower magnitude than is one based on long period P and S. The limited use of Love waves to date is simply a result of the mode of siting of long period seismometers followed until recently. Though not the perfect qualitative discriminant originally supposed, Love waves constitute a very powerful quantitative discriminant down to their threshold of detection.

We conclude that our physical and theoretical understanding of seismological observations relative to discrimination of the seismic waves of explosions and earthquakes is essentially complete.

MONITORING OF A CTBT OR LOW TTBT BY SEISMOLOGICAL MEANS

The recent discussions[1,2,28] of monitoring of the U.S.S.R. by means of networks both within and without the U.S.S.R. are up-to-date discussions within their terms of reference. We will not duplicate the discussions of those papers, but we will discuss a couple of the controlling parameters of those analyses, parameters whose previously used values will be shown to be non-binding and inappropriate. Those earlier discussions are based upon the concept of detecting P and Pn signals of both earthquakes and explosions in the passband historically used by seismologists, that is, around 1 Hertz. Very serious problems arise from use of that bandpass. For one thing, noise levels in that bandpass can change drastically, thus creating the possibility of deliberate exploitation of such high noise levels when attempting to hide the signals of clandestine small explosions. The credibility of such a scenario depends upon the planned signal amplitudes and the details of the distributions of high noise amplitudes and seismometers. There certainly would be a situation at some magnitude where the problem would occur when the evasion scheme included large cavity decoupling. Whether this situation would have real significance depends upon a host of parameters, but it would create an aura of doubt and uncertainty about the utility of seismological monitoring. Another problem elaborately investigated years ago[29] is based upon deliberate use of the P codas of large distant earthquakes as a noise field in which to hide the P waves of an explosion. It was shown in the cited study that, in principle, this evasion procedure of hiding-in-an-earthquake when combined with decoupling in large cavities would allow successful evasion at the several kiloton level even in the face of a multi-station network within the U.S.S.R. Therefore, no really satisfactory totally seismological solution to the surveillance of the U.S.S.R. for a CTBT or a Low TTBT exists based upon such monitoring procedures as used in the cited papers. In earlier work by one of us,[29] it was implicitly assumed that other national technical means (NTM) would play an important role in monitoring such treaties, several characteristics of the U.S.S.R. that would make use of other NTM of great importance having been discussed. Recent analysis indicates that all of these earlier seismological analyses, including that published recently by Hannon[28], have failed to exploit two truly crucial facts. In fact, seismologists have only very recently become generally cognizant of these facts and are only now appreciating their importance in monitoring test ban treaties.

These points are (a) the difference in spectral shape of earthquakes and explosions, and (b) the observed amplitudes of high frequency noise. Figure 16.22 illustrates data relevant to both of these points. The set of solid lines indicate the source spectral displacement amplitudes for tamped and "fully" decoupled explosions of 5, 1, and 0.1 kilotons and for a tamped 100-pound explosion. Conditions similar to those of SALMON (5.3-kt tamped explosion in salt in Mississippi) are assumed for this figure. The figure is probably about correct for most hard rock sites because regionally normalized m_b values for explosions in salt and a variety of hard rocks lie on the same m_b versus $\log(W)$ curve.

All spectra are flat at low frequencies with a factor of ~200 difference in amplitude for tamped and decoupled signals. All spectra have a sharp corner frequency with the corner frequency for the decoupled explosion being far higher than for the tamped explosion of the same yield ($CF_{decoupled} = CF_{tamped} \times 200^{1/3}$), resulting in a drastic reduction of the decoupling factor at high frequencies. The curve labeled "16.5 m" on Figure 16.23 illustrates the same data as Figure 16.22 expressed in terms of decoupling factor

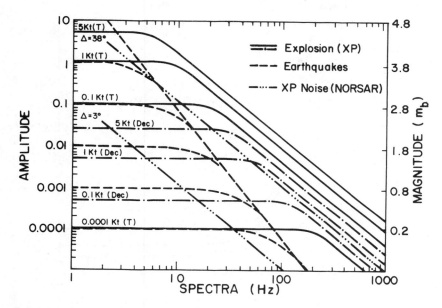

FIGURE 16.22. Source P wave amplitude spectra for earthquakes (dashed lines) and explosions, both tamped ("T," solid lines) and fully decoupled ("Dec," dash-dot lines), plus scaled noise amplitudes allowing estimation of signal-to-noise ratios at 38° and 3° (dash-dot-dot-dot lines). Left-hand scale in arbitrary relative amplitude units, right-hand scale in equivalent m_b values (eastern U.S., central U.S.S.R. type terrains). Stress drop for earthquakes approximately 75 bars. Amplitudes scale as stress drop.

versus frequency. The term "fully decoupled" means use of a cavity just large enough to cause elastic deformation of the cavity walls. In the case of Figures 16.22 and 16.23, this dimension is a 16.5-meter radius for a spherical cavity. Further increase in cavity size ("over-decoupled") does not increase low frequency decoupling and only slowly increases high frequency decoupling.

Earthquake spectra are indicated by the set of dashed lines in Figure 16.22. These spectra also display flat low frequency spectra and sharp corner frequencies. However, the corner frequency for an earthquake of given low frequency amplitude level is much lower than for an explosion of equivalent low frequency level. Also, as noted previously, the fall-off of amplitudes of earthquakes at high frequencies is steeper than for explosions (frequency^{-3} versus frequency^{-2}). Thus, the situation should develop when monitoring at frequencies of around 30 Hertz that only explosions will be detected at some stations. A truly remarkable feature of the earthquake spectra is the common high frequency asymptote for all earthquakes of the same stress drop. Thus, all such earthquakes of m_b 1 or larger mag-

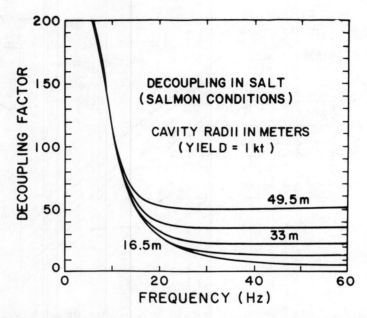

FIGURE 16.23. Predicted decoupling ratio versus cavity size versus frequency for explosions in salt (SALMON salt conditions, elastic behavior of salt at 440 bars). The smallest radius (16.5 meters) is for a fully decoupled 1 kiloton explosion. See text for scaling of this figure to different yields.

nitude have the identical source amplitude at 30 Hertz! This is to be compared with a difference of amplitude of 3×10^5 at 1 Hertz between m_b 6.5 and m_b 1 earthquakes. This spectral behavior of earthquakes at high frequencies means that the hiding-in-an-earthquake scenario is impossible of exploitation against a network equipped to record to frequencies of 20 Hertz or greater. A simple illustration of this point is provided by Figure 16.24, a mixing at NORSAR of microseismic noise and the signal of a distant explosion. By the criteria used in all previous studies, this event would have been treated as undetectable since noise amplitudes are as great or greater than explosion amplitudes. However, simple high pass filtering rejects the microseismic noise and provides a signal/noise ratio of ten or more. Since the average period of the P coda of large earthquakes is greater than that of NORSAR noise, the effect of highpass filtering would be even more dramatic when striving to detect signals of explosions mixed in high amplitude P wave codas.

An m_b 2.8 explosion has higher source amplitudes at 10 Hertz than does any earthquake. The monitoring situation where the explosion is much nearer the detecting seismometer than is the earthquake will lead to an

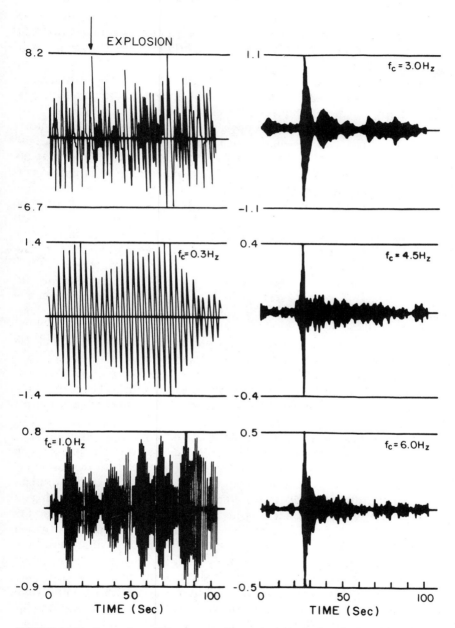

FIGURE 16.24. Comparison of the spectra of normal microseismic noise at NORSAR (Norway) and of an explosion. The figure in upper left shows the mixed signals, while the other five figures illustrate the contrasting spectra of the two signals, showing clearly the greater high frequency content of the explosion signal.

increased ratio of explosion and earthquake signal. Therefore, the factor which was the basis for pronounced confounding of the internal network in the study by one of us in 1976[29] plays absolutely no role when detecting at high frequencies.

The cited work by Evernden focused on use of distant large earthquakes because of the statistical improbability of being able to use an adequately large nearby smaller earthquake in a meaningful testing program. However, the seismological group at Lawrence Livermore National Laboratory has proposed just such a scenario when considering detection in the neighborhood of 1 Hertz. Figure 16.22 makes it clear that detection at 10 to 30 Hertz or higher renders this idea totally irrelevant because no earthquake of any size generates as high 20 Hertz amplitudes as does an m_b 1.8 explosion or as high 30 Hertz amplitudes as does an m_b 1 explosion (equivalent to a tamped 2-ton explosion). Even a few tens of seconds separation in times of origin of the earthquake and explosion will lead to marked increase in detectability of the explosion high frequencies relative to those of the earthquake (see Evernden[28] for the necessary critical parameters to support this statement, the primary one being the typical rate of decrease of amplitude of the P codas of earthquakes). Therefore, all scenarios for hiding-in-an-earthquake lose credibility if the surveillance network detects at high frequencies.

The other confounding factor in previous studies was the occasional rise of 1-second microseisms due to local or somewhat distant atmospheric storms, such storms developing uncommonly high 1-second microseisms. However, this factor becomes irrelevant when recording at high frequencies. It has been widely observed that high amplitude 1-second microseisms do not imply high amplitude high frequency microseisms (see Figure 16.24), this fact being exploited by all seismological networks located near ocean boundaries (the source of the highest amplitude 1-second microseisms). In central California, stations within a few tens of kilometers of the coast may be affected at high frequencies when the 1-second microseisms are high. However, at distances of 50 to 200 kilometers from the shore, depending on the region, wave-induced microseisms never influence detection capability at frequencies of a few Hertz or higher. For the network modeled within the U.S.S.R., most stations are at least several hundred kilometers from shorelines. At inland stations, the causes of high frequency noise are either cultural or wind. The former is eliminated by careful site selection, the latter by siting and/or burial. Even if a station is affected by a local windstorm, amplitudes of noise will decrease by a factor of more than 100 within a few tens to a hundred kilometers. Thus, the widely dispersed network modeled within the U.S.S.R. will not be significantly impacted by high-frequency noise. The suggested scenario of waiting for a time of high noise levels will be useless.

A point not addressed as yet but one requiring emphasis is the behavior of microseismic noise as a function of frequency. All of the discussion so far has no real significance unless ambient noise levels are so low that the small amplitude high frequency signals of explosions are indeed detectable. Fortunately, such is the case. Recent results at three different sites in Norway and two sites in the United States (by the only investigators who have yet searched carefully for such sites)[30,31,32] indicate that noise levels are indeed low enough. The dash-dot-dot-dot lines of Figure 16.22 are not noise levels directly but do allow estimation of the relative amplitudes of the indicated signals and ambient noise at reasonably quiet sites at ranges of 3 and 38 degrees if the structure of the far-field noise and signal are as observed at NORSAR. It has been observed at NORSAR that the rate of fall-off of noise and of the high frequency spectrum of explosion signals from Semipalatinsk are the same and follow a frequency$^{-2.5}$ relationship, that is a half-power of frequency greater than source amplitudes of explosions. This implies a low rate of anelastic attenuation for ray paths that have twice transmitted through the upper crust and mantle of northern Eurasia. Both earthquake and explosion data, obtained in the United States, indicate that ray paths in the eastern United States, which do not transit the upper mantle but refract along the crust/mantle boundary, display small relative attenuation of frequencies in the range 1 to 100 Hertz. For such ray paths, there would be an even greater detectability at 3° than shown on Figure 16.22 (noise amplitudes falling as freq$^{-2.5}$ with signal amplitudes falling only as freq^{-2}). Figure 16.22 indicates that a fully decoupled 5-kiloton explosion is predicted to have a signal-to-noise ratio of 2 at greater than 30 Hertz at an epicentral distance of 38° and a signal-to-noise ratio of 100 at 30 Hertz and greater at an epicentral distance of 3°. A fully decoupled 0.1-kiloton explosion is predicted by Figure 16.22 to display a signal-to-noise ratio of 4 or so at 30 Hertz at 3°. This ratio would increase if we modeled according to Pn observations in eastern United States, a region with Pn velocities similar to those in most of the U.S.S.R. All of the above predictions are based upon ray paths like Semipalatinsk to NORSAR or crust/mantle structures like eastern United States and most of the U.S.S.R. Limited areas in the southern mountains of the U.S.S.R. would be expected to show greater attenuation, possibly requiring increased monitoring emphasis by one means or another. For most of the U.S.S.R., there seems no doubt that signal and noise amplitudes will be such as to allow detection of even small decoupled explosions at long ranges.

The resultant predicted detection capabilities by a seismological network composed of 15 stations external to the U.S.S.R. and 25 stations internal to the U.S.S.R. for explosions within the U.S.S.R. are now discussed. For the sake of being conservative, noise levels are assumed to be twice those reported in the cited NORSAR documents, even though both the investiga-

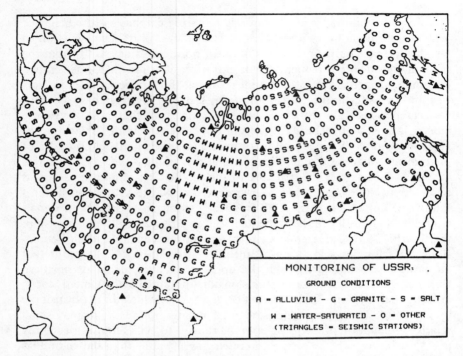

FIGURE 16.25. Digitized ground conditions for the U.S.S.R. A = dry alluvium possibly of adequate thickness to allow execution of a 1- to 2-kiloton explosion without cratering. G = granite. W = water-saturated sediments, Kamchatka/Kuriles, and Sakhalin Island. O = other rocks. Triangles indicate approximate locations of the hypothesized seismic stations internal and external to the U.S.S.R.

tors at NORSAR and Herrin in the United States have found sites with significantly lower noise level. Figure 16.25 indicates the pattern of geological ground condition used. "A" indicates dry alluvium possibly thick enough to simulate conditions at Yucca Flat,[1,29] Nevada, up to yields of 1 or 2 kilotons. "W" indicates water-saturated sediments in north central U.S.S.R. and the water-saturated volcanic rocks of Kamchatka/Kuriles and the island of Sakhalin. All of these "W" sites are considered as inappropriate for execution of decoupled explosions. There is a small area of granitic rocks on Kamchatka and the station placed on the peninsula sits atop this granite mass, thus making it useless as a decoupling site. Another station is placed on northern Sakhalin Island in order to eliminate use of this island for decoupling. "G", "S", and "O" indicate granitic rocks, salt deposits, and other rocks.

In Figure 16.26, it is presumed that full decoupling could be executed in

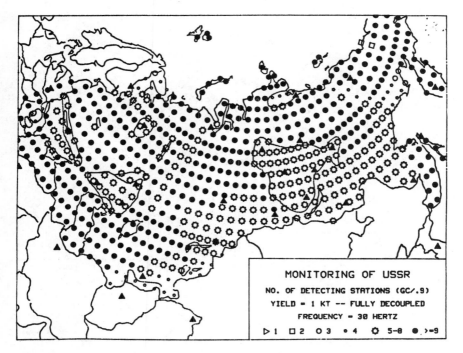

FIGURE 16.26. Predicted number of detecting stations at 0.9 probability for 1-kiloton explosions. Full decoupling is assumed possible in all salt and granite areas, tamped explosions elsewhere. Frequency of detection is around 30 Hertz. Areas of salt are outlined.

all salt and granite deposits (except Kamchatka) but not in "other" rocks. The figure gives predictions for number of stations detecting a fully decoupled 1-kiloton explosion at 0.9 probability when detecting at 30 Hertz (signal spectra as at NORSAR). All salt and granite sites are predicted to have 0.9 probability of 5 to 8 station detection, whereas "O" sites are predicted to have detections by 9 or more stations. If one wishes to consider these sites as potential sites of decoupling, then the proper number of detecting stations is 5 to 8.

Figure 16.27 assumes decoupling to be possible in salt, granite, and other formations. Figure 16.27 is again for a 1-kiloton explosion but for one placed in a cavity large enough to fully decouple an 8-kiloton explosion, that is, the 1-kiloton explosion is strongly over-decoupled. The detection probability used for this figure is .3 rather than .9, the assumption being that no one who had gone to the effort to clandestinely build such a large cavity would give a monitoring network even a 30% chance of detecting each and every explosion in the hole at a level surely adequate to detect,

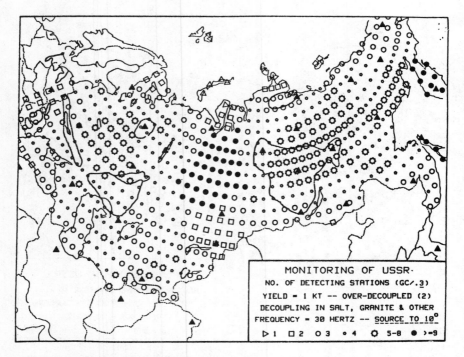

FIGURE 16.27. Predicted number of detecting stations at 0.3 probability for 1-kiloton explosions. Strong over-decoupling (8-kiloton holes) is assumed possible in all salt, granite, and other sites, tamped explosions at other sites. Frequency of detection is around 30 Hertz. Areas of salt outlined.

locate, and identify it. Out to an epicentral distance of 10°, the source spectrum without relative frequency attenuation is used. Nearly all decoupling sites yield 4 station detection. There are areas with 5 to 8 and areas with 2 and 3. Redesign of the 25 internal network could give a more uniform capability. The addition of one or two more stations might be required to bring all areas to 4 station detection (except the extreme northern edge of the mainland and the islands of the Arctic Ocean). A figure for 0.5 kiloton in a 1-kiloton hole would be identical to the last figure. If sites as quiet as or quieter than the cited NORSAR value are used in analysis, the capability on Figure 16.27 can be achieved easily at 0.9 probability.

It is useful to note that detection at 30 Hertz for a fully decoupled or even a strongly over-decoupled 1-kiloton explosion constitutes detection on the flat portion of the explosion spectrum. No direct use of the shape of the spectrum beyond the corner frequency is used.

If, in the network analyses, we had used a noise level equivalent to that implied on Figure 16.22 rather than 6 db higher, the capabilities predicted on Figures 16.26 and 16.27 would have been obtained for yields one-half of that indicated on the figures, that is, 4- to 8-station detection at 0.3 probability for 0.5 kt over-decoupled in a 4 kt hole, etc.

Given that detection is successful via resort to high frequencies, the residual problem is identification of the detected event as an explosion. A variety of means of identification are available on theoretical grounds. Because virtually everything we now know about the spectra of explosions and earthquakes agrees quantitatively with theory, it seems reasonable to assume that the theoretical predictions for this problem will be fulfilled by observations. The first and most remarkable identification criterion available is a quantitative estimate of source amplitude at 30 Hertz or, in other words, a magnitude value based on high frequency data. As can be seen on Figure 16.23, mere detection of 30 Hertz amplitudes at or above those expected from a fully decoupled 1-kiloton explosion (5-ton tamped) constitutes identification of the causative event as an explosion. The higher the maximum frequency of detection, the lower the threshold of utility of such a criterion.

As can be seen on Figure 16.22, the spectral shape predicted for fully decoupled 1- and 5-kiloton explosions is flat or nearly flat up to 40 Hertz while the spectra of earthquakes with equivalent amplitudes at 10 Hertz are falling rapidly at 30 to 40 Hertz. The predicted explosion spectra are thus nearly flat rather than having a slope of $freq^{-2}$ while the earthquake spectra are falling at a $freq^{-3}$ rate at 30 to 40 Hertz. Extremely simple and clear discrimination via spectral shape is possible in this range. Thus, in the critical range of decoupled (either fully or over-decoupled) 1- to 5-kiloton explosions, spectral level at around 30 Hertz and spectral shape in the 10 to 30 Hertz bandpass will provide overlapping discrimination capabilities. For higher amplitude high frequency signals, their mere detection proves the causative event to be an explosion. For explosion signals smaller than those expected of fully decoupled 0.5 kiloton explosions, spectral shape and spectral levels in the 10 to 30 Hertz band become less useful to useless as discrimination criteria since the spectra of both event types are flat in that frequency range. Use of equivalent criteria at higher frequencies would be effective if such frequencies are detectable at adequate range. Only further research will resolve this point.

The other class of criteria available for exploitation are those based on the contrast in source symmetries and source depths. The former relate to the usual high symmetry of explosion sources compared with the highly asymmetric source of earthquakes. The explosive source primarily generates radially symmetric compressional waves while the earthquake source primarily generates shear waves with both P and S waves showing highly radially asymmetric amplitude patterns. The differences in typical depths for explosions and earthquakes means that in nearly all cases each event type should be distinguishable by aspects of their seismic waves which are strongly influenced by depth of focus. Details on the type of phenomena to be expected are beyond the scope of this paper.

Our conclusions are that detection of 30 Hertz signals of fully decoupled 0.5- to 1-kiloton explosions is possible on a 5- to 8-station basis at 0.9 probability throughout the U.S.S.R. when using a network such as shown on previous figures and that strongly over-decoupled explosions of the same yields are detectable at nearly the same number of stations at 0.3 probability. We also conclude that identification of all high frequency signals as large or larger than those expected of fully decoupled 1-kiloton explosions are easily identified as deriving from explosion sources. For smaller signals, detection at frequencies higher than 30 Hertz is required for use of spectral criteria. Criteria based on phase structure and relative generation of P and S waves are still available for exploitation subsequent to careful modeling of critical regions in the U.S.S.R., such modeling to follow upon installation of the internal network.

REFERENCES

1. Sykes, L. R., and J. F. Evernden. The Verification of a Comprehensive Nuclear Test Ban. *Scientific American* 247 (1982): 47–55.
2. Sykes, L. R., J. F. Evernden, and I. Cifuentes. Seismic Methods for Verifying Nuclear Test Bans. *A. Inst. Physics Conf. Proc.* 104, Chapter 5, 1983.
3. Aki, K., and P. G. Richards. *Quantitative Seismology, Vol. 1*, San Francisco: W. H. Freeman & Co., 1980, 557 p.
4. Archambeau, C. B. General Theory of Elastodynamic Source Fields. *Rev. Geophysics* 6 (1968): 241–288.
5. Minster, J. B. Elastodynamics of Failure in a Continuum. Ph. D. Thesis, California Institute of Technology, Pasadena, CA, 1973.
6. Archambeau, C. B., and J. B. Minster. Dynamics in Prestressed Media with Moving Phase Boundaries: A Continuum Theory of Failure in Solids. *Geophy. J. R. A. S.* 52 (1978): 65–96.
7. Evernden, J. F. Adequacy of Routinely Available Data for Identifying Earthquakes of $m_b \cong 4.5$. *B. S. S. A.* 67 (1977): 1099–1151.
8. Marshall, P. D., D. L. Springer, and H. C. Rodean. Magnitude Corrections for Attenuation in the Upper Mantle. *Geophy. J. R. A. S.* 57 (1979): 609–638.
9. Evernden, J. F., W. J. Best, P. W. Pomeroy, T. V. McEvilly, J. M. Savino, and L. R. Sykes. Discrimination Between Small-Magnitude Earthquakes and Explosions. *J. G. R.* 76 (1971): 8042–8055.
10. Blandford, R., unpublished data.
11. Hanks, T. C., and D. Boore. Moment-Magnitude Relations in Theory and Practise. *J. G. R.*, in press.
12. Brune, J. N., and C. Y. King. Excitation of Mantle Rayleigh Waves of 100 Seconds Period as a Function of Magnitude. *B. S. S. A.* 57 (1967): 1355–1365.
13. Brune, J. N. Seismic Moment, Seismicity, and Rate of Slip Along Major Fault Zones. *J. G. R.* 73 (1968): 777–784.

14. Evernden, J. F. Spectral Characteristics of the P Codas of Eurasian Earthquakes and Explosions. *B. S. S. A.* 67 (1977): 1153–1171.
15. Evernden, J. F., and W. M. Kohler. Further Study of Spectral Composition of P Codas of Earthquakes and Explosions. *B. S. S. A.* 69 (1979): 483–511.

16. Wyss, M., T. C. Hanks, and R. C. Liebermann. Comparison of P-wave Spectra of Underground Explosions and Earthquakes. *J. G. R.* 76 (1971): 2716–2729.
17. Evernden, J. F. Further Studies on Seismic Discrimination. *B. S. S. A.* 65 (1975): 359–391.
18. Blandford, R., and D. H. von Segern, unpublished data.
19. Evernden, J. F., C. B. Archambeau, and E. Cranswick. An Evaluation of Seismic Nuclear Test Monitoring Using High Frequency Seismic Data. *Reviews of Geophysics*, in press.
20. Bache, T. C., T. G. Barker, N. Riner, and J. T. Cherry. The Contribution of Two-Dimensional Source Effects to the Far-Field Seismic Signatures of Underground Explosions. Science, Systems, and Software Rept. SSS-R-80-4569, VSC Rept. VSC-TR-80-2, 1980.
21. Archambeau, C. B. The Theory of Stress Wave Radiation from Explosions in Prestressed Media. *Geophy. J. R. A. S.* 29 (1972): 329–366.
22. Archambeau, C. B., and C. Sammis. Seismic Radiation from Explosions in Prestressed Media and the Measurement of Tectonic Stress in the Earth. *Rev. Geophy. & Space Phys.* 8 (1970): 473–499.
23. Evernden, J. F., and D. M. Clark. Study of Teleseismic P, Parts I and II. *Phy. Earth & Planet. Int.* 4 (1970): 1–31.
24. Perl, N., F. J. Thomas, J. Trulio, and W. L. Woodie. Effect of Burial Depth on Seismic Signals, Volume 1. Pacific Sierra Research Technical Report submitted to DNA/DARPA, PSR Report 815, 1979.
25. Perl, N., and J. Trulio. Effect of Burial Depth on Seismic Signals, Volume II. Pacific Sierra Research Technical Report submitted to DNA/DARPA, PSR Report 815, 1979.
26. Cherry, J. T., C. B. Archambeau, G. A. Frazier, A. J. Good, K. G. Hamilton, and D. J. Harkrider. The Teleseismic Radiation Field from Explosions: Dependence of Seismic Amplitudes upon Properties of Materials in the Source Region. Science, Systems, and Software Final Report, DNA 3113Z, 1973.
27. Weston, D. E. *Explosive Sources*, edited by V. M. Albers, Inst. on Underwater Acoustics. New York: Plenum Press, 1961.
28. Hannon, W. J. Seismic Verification of a Comprehensive Test Ban Treaty. *Energy & Tech. Rev.*, Law. Liver. Nat. Lab., Doc. UCRL-52000-83-5, 1983.
29. Evernden, J. F. Study of Seismological Evasion, Parts 1, 2, and 3. *B. S. S. A.* 66 (1976): 245–280, 281–324, and 549–592.
30. Bungum, H. Special NORSAR Study of High Frequency Noise, comm. by L. R. Sykes, 1983.
31. Trourod, L. Semiannual Technical Summary 1 April–30 September 1982. Scientific Rept. No. 1-82/83. Kjeller, Norway: NORSAR, 1983.
32. Herrin, E. Resolution of Seismic Instruments Used in Treaty Verification Research. *B. S. S. A.* 72 (1982): S61–S68.

17.

Unattended In-Country Stations for Seismic Verification

Paul A. Stokes

Introductory Note by Kosta Tsipis

The capabilities and requirements of unmanned seismic stations placed by one signer of a treaty banning underground testing within the boundaries of another for purposes of verification become newly significant in light of the discovery reported in the previous chapter by Evernden and Archambeau. If it is now possible to detect underground nuclear explosions down to the level of a kiloton or so, the only remaining technical questions on the way to a Complete Test Ban Treaty concern the seismic stations, which are described in the following chapter.

The National Seismic Station was developed to implement a concept that originated in the late 1950s and early 1960s for verification of compliance with the terms of a Comprehensive Nuclear Weapon Test Ban Treaty. During that period, intensive treaty negotiations were in process and seismic experts concluded that owing to the size of the U.S.S.R., adequate treaty verification could only be accomplished by placing seismic stations within its borders. The Soviet Union has traditionally objected to arms control verification activities for which a foreign presence in their country was required; consequently, the usual seismic station operation by an inspection organization posed a problem. In 1962, a statement was issued at the Pugwash Conference, jointly signed by U.S. and Soviet scientists, proposing automatic seismic stations "sealed in such a way that they cannot be tampered with" as a means to provide the necessary seismic monitoring without requiring the presence of foreigners. This concept of unattended seismic stations for Comprehensive Test Ban Treaty verification was endorsed, in principle, by the Soviet Union at the Geneva Disarmament Conference.

The Defense Advanced Research Projects Agency undertook an investigation to determine the characteristics of unattended seismic stations required to accomplish the verification task. It became clear that in addition to high-quality seismic instrumentation, special features were needed to protect against tampering that could interfere with the collection of valid seismic data. Prototype equipment, called the Unattended Seismic Observatory, was built with the necessary features; it stored seismic data on magnetic tapes that needed to be periodically retrieved by an authorized (i.e., foreign) entity.

In the late 1960s a new technology was being developed for the transmission of data via satellite; it was clear that the transmission of seismic data in real time by this means would be a substantial improvement for the purpose of verification. A concept was developed in which seismic stations would use satellites for the worldwide transmission of authenticated seismic data. The National Seismic Station was developed to implement the new concept.

In October 1977, development of the National Seismic Station was begun. In the fall of 1978, an engineering model of the NSS was emplaced at a site near McMinnville, Tennessee; data have been transmitted since that time to the System Control and Receiving Station (SCARS) located at Albuquerque, New Mexico.

In February 1980, a second NSS was installed near Fairbanks, Alaska, to evaluate operation in a northerly environment. That station transmitted data to SCARS in Albuquerque through July 1980.

A Regional Seismic Test Network (RSTN) was installed in 1981 and 1982 to evaluate long-term operation of the equipment and to acquire regional seismic data for research of seismic monitoring and analysis techniques. The RSTN consists of five stations located in the United States and Canada. Data from these stations are transmitted to SCARS in Albuquerque, to the Lawrence Livermore National Laboratory in Livermore, California, and to Department of Defense facilities in the Washington, D.C., area.

NATIONAL SEISMIC STATION DESIGN PHILOSOPHY

The fundamental goal of the NSS is to provide seismic data from within countries party to a Comprehensive Test Ban Treaty for verification of compliance with the treaty. In order to meet this goal, specific design features and an integrated design concept were developed. In summary, the NSS was designed to

- Provide high-quality seismic data suitable for regional seismic analysis and teleseismic analysis;
- Provide evidence of tampering that could hide incriminating data;

- Be reliable enough so that it would be impractical to induce failures or use natural failures to hide incriminating data;
- Minimize maintenance activities; and
- Minimize intrusiveness into the host country.

These system characteristics will be discussed more fully.

Seismic Data Quality

The seismic data system is able to acquire relevant data from regional events without sacrificing its ability to acquire teleseismic data (this latter ability is in recognition of the size of the U.S.S.R.). This is accomplished with a design in which earth motion is sensed in three orthogonal axes over a frequency band ranging from 0.02 to 10 Hz with no gaps in band coverage. Sensitivity is below earth noise at quiet sites. The dynamic range is 120 dB. Practical considerations dictate that this dynamic range is covered by automatically reducing gain for large signals. The data are digital, and the largest available low-power analog-to-digital converters (14 bits) were selected to maximize the range covered before automatic-gain reduction occurred. A capability to calibrate the data channels is included. A source of universal time is used in the seismic data system.

System characteristics contributing to seismic data quality include installation of the seismometer in a 100-m-deep borehole to avoid surface noise, and minimum power dissipation near the seismometer that could generate convection currents and induce noise.

System Security

The system was designed to prevent tampering that could hide incriminating data. It was recognized that the host country could not be prevented from cutting off the flow of data from the seismic station (e.g., by interrupting communications or by damaging the equipment). Therefore, the goal of tamper protection is for the system to provide evidence to the monitor that tampering has taken place.

Tamper protection is woven into the overall system design. The authenticator prevents undetected substitution of false data into the data stream transmitted from the station. Authenticator keys are located near the bottom of the borehole to inhibit unauthorized physical access. Slow, careful access attempts would be detected by the seismometers and the data would be available to the monitoring party, assuming near real-time data are transmitted. Rapid access attempts during a simulated or real communications outage (whereby the borehole equipment is raised to the surface for purposes of tampering) would be detected by a device that senses motion of the borehole equipment and destroys the authenticator codes.

Universal time for the seismic data system is transmitted to the station and included with internally generated time in the authenticated data to prevent the substitution of false timing information.

High reliability (discussed more fully below) is part of the tamper protection inasmuch as equipment failures and data-link outages could be exploited to hide clandestine tests.

The seismic station requires no interaction of host-country personnel during normal operation. Although it is recognized that host-country personnel cannot be denied the right of access to the equipment, the fact that there is no technical justification for access should limit opportunities for tampering.

The seismic station is also designed to be as independent as possible of host-country facilities; it provides its own power, shelter, and environmental control. This was intended to minimize contrived but credible failures of host-country equipment that would cause the system to fail. The alternative seemed to be to place ironclad specifications for reliable operation on the applicable host-country equipment as part of the treaty, but the development of such specifications does not seem possible.

Reliability

Because the stations would be unattended by our own personnel, a design approach similar to that applied to satellite equipment was used — for example, the equipment should operate reliably without routine or frequent maintenance. Our initial goal was to be able to operate for several years without failure. During the development program the reliability goals were stated as a Mean Time Between Failures (MTBF) of at least one year for the complete system, and at least three years for the borehole equipment.

An additional reason for high reliability is to minimize intrusive activities associated with maintenance. Specific measures taken to achieve high reliability are:

- Whenever possible, the use of technology that has proven to be highly reliable (examples are CMOS electronics and thermoelectric generators).
- The use of high-quality parts and fabrication techniques developed for satellite applications.
- Extensive testing during all levels of equipment fabrication and sufficient integrated operating time to precipitate the failure of faulty components before system deployment.
- The incorporation of redundancy for critical system elements (e.g., seismometers, prime power, both real-time and delayed data, tape recorder backup, ability to switch to a back-up satellite).
- The use of satellite communication links that minimize link outages and have a low enough bit-error rate to permit authentication of the data.

- The incorporation of an extensive set of equipment status monitors (state-of-health and calibration) from which trends in equipment operation that may affect reliability could be observed, and decisions to initiate the operation of redundant components or to call for the replacement of failed components could be made.
- The seismic station is designed to operate with no human interaction at the site. Experience shows that human factors are a source of failures and should be eliminated when possible.

The foregoing approach to reliability was carried through the satellite communications (e.g., ability to move to a back-up satellite without losing data). Reliability was considered less critical for equipment outside the U.S.S.R. at satellite earth stations and in SCARS, because it was believed that failures at these locations were not predictable or could not be induced for the purpose of hiding incriminating data.

Maintenance

In order to minimize adverse effects on reliability when failed components must be replaced, the seismic station was designed for replacement of major subassemblies in the field. Diagnostics to determine which subassembly required replacement would usually be derived from state-of-health readings in SCARS. Failed subassemblies would be repaired in the laboratory.

Scheduled maintenance would be limited to fueling the thermoelectric generators and cleaning filters and burners once a year, and replacing the authenticator package to renew the codes. The code supply is not exhausted for several years, but it may be desirable to replace the unit more often for other reasons.

Intrusiveness

The system was designed to minimize intrusiveness because of the sensitivity of the U.S.S.R. to foreign incursion into their country. The principal relevant design feature is its ability to operate unattended by monitoring personnel; other features that were thought to contribute were the complete openness of the equipment to host-country inspection, the transmission of plain-text data, infrequent maintenance, simple maintenance procedures when required (i.e., replacement of major subassemblies), simple installation, and a surface installation that was as small as possible. It was even thought that satellite communication, inasmuch as it is widely used in the U.S.S.R. and places no operational burden on the host country, might be relatively unintrusive when compared to the operational burdens of tape delivery or land-lines. (The ability to inspect the data prior to its transmission did not seem to be an important issue because it was assumed that the treaty would not permit deletion of data segments by the host.)

NATIONAL SEISMIC STATION DESCRIPTION

The National Seismic Station consists of instrumentation installed at the bottom of a cased borehole 19 cm in diameter and approximately 100 m deep, and a surface installation as shown in Figure 17.1. The borehole equipment includes three primary seismometers, three back-up seismometers, and electronics to filter, amplify, digitize, format, and authenticate the data.

The data are transmitted through a cable to the surface installation where it is processed for transmission in real-time via satellite to central processing facilities (Figures 17.2 and 17.3). Commands may be received via satellite to initiate calibration, switch to back-up components, or perform other functions necessary for proper operation of the station. The station provides its own electrical power with propane or liquid-fueled thermoelectric generators.

Broadband seismometers (Teledyne-Geotech Model KS-36000-04) provide seismic signals in the frequency band from 0.02 to 10 Hz, in three orthogonal axes (Figures 17.4 and 17.5). These seismometers are force-balanced instruments in which the internally generated noise is less than earth noise in the frequency band of interest, and the dynamic range exceeds the 120-dB range used in the seismic signal-processing electronics.

Short-period seismometers (Teledyne-Geotech Model S750) are also included to provide seismic data in the event of failure of the KS-36000 seismometers. These instruments are compact and are relatively simple and reliable; however, they cannot adequately cover the frequency range below 1 Hz because of excessive noise in this band.

Calibration of the seismometers is commanded as appropriate. Calibration of a complete seismic channel can be selected by electromagnetically driving the seismometer mass for the axis selected. Calibration of the signal-processing electronics independent of the seismometers can also be selected. Calibration signals are sinusoidal at one-half octave frequency spacings and amplitudes varying in seven binary steps throughout the dynamic range. Positive and negative step signals are also provided.

Calibration signals can be introduced to one axis at a time, and the calibration signals are added to the seismic signals being detected by the seismometer. Consequently, data for detected seismic events are not lost during calibration.

Control of the borehole instrumentation is achieved by transmitting commands to the station through the satellite communications link. These com-

FIGURE 17.1. The National Seismic Station.

mands are relayed to a command decoder in the borehole package if the command decoder in the surface installation determines that the command includes the station identification. If it is a valid command for the station, it is inserted into the data stream. The sender checks the command in the data stream and, if the intended command was received, an execute command is sent. The command decoder then distributes the command to

FIGURE 17.2. National Seismic Station satellite communications.

accomplish the intended function. Commands include initiating a variety of calibration signals and selecting back-up seismometers.

Communications with the seismic station can be provided by existing satellites in the INTELSTAT system or various other communications satellites. Data from each of several stations would be frequency-division-multiplexed; that is, each station would transmit data on its own carrier fre-

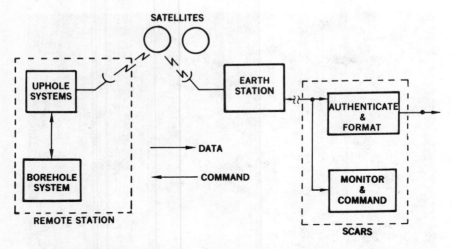

FIGURE 17.3. Block diagram of National Seismic Station satellite communications.

quency. Commands to seismic stations would be received at all stations on a single carrier frequency. Commands include a station identifier; only the station with the matching identifier would respond to these commands. An identifier common to all stations could be used if it is desirable for all stations to simultaneously recognize some commands.

The power used by the station varies between 135 and 175 W, depending upon whether or not the tape recorder is operating. The power is generated by thermoelectric generators that may be fueled by either propane or liquid fuel such as kerosene. Three 4,000-liter tanks provide sufficient fuel to last about one year.

Three thermoelectric generators are connected in parallel and have enough capacity so that two of the three generators can supply adequate power for the system in the event that one fails.

Lead-acid batteries are placed in parallel with the thermoelectric generators; these can provide power for at least 24 hours in case of complete failure of the thermoelectric generators. This time period is intended to permit the repair of a catastrophic thermoelectric generator failure without loss of seismic data from the station.

The 100-m borehole for the seismometer is cased with a casing 19 cm in diameter and grouted in place. This provides for seismometer installation in a dry environment at a depth sufficient to avoid locally generated surface seismic noise. A holelock (Figure 17.4) is fixed to the borehole casing to provide a solid base for the seismometer.

NSS
Downhole Seismometer Package

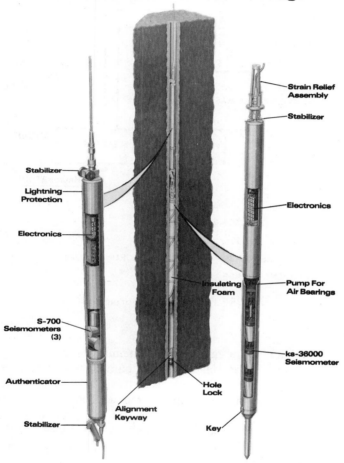

FIGURE 17.4. Borehole equipment.

After the borehole equipment has been emplaced, the top of the borehole is sealed to prevent moisture and barometric changes from generating seismic noise.

The antenna mount was specifically designed to permit repositioning the antenna to a secondary geosynchronous satellite in case the primary satellite fails. Thus, the antenna can be originally pointed to any elevation and

KS-36000 SEISMOMETER

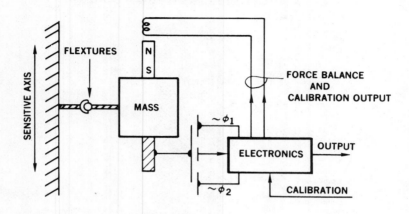

MASS $\approx$ 365 GRAMS

T_0 $\approx$ 5.5 SECONDS

RESPONSE $\approx$ 0.015 VOLTS/MICRON/SECOND

FREQUENCY RANGE $\approx$ 0 $\longrightarrow$ 10.0 Hz

FIGURE 17.5. KS-36000 seismometer.

then rotated so that a motor can drive the antenna axis along the equatorial arc. (In general, the equatorial arc is not parallel to the surface of the earth.)

Because the antenna must remain pointed with an accuracy of a few tenths of a degree, the antenna mount must not be subject to settling. Settling is prevented, even in marginal permafrost conditions, by fixing the mount to pilings that extend down into stable material (e.g., permanently frozen material in regions of marginal permafrost). Pilings are made from the same casing used in the borehole.

18.

Seismic Arrays

Eystein Husebye and Shane Ingate

Introductory Note by Kosta Tsipis

This chapter reviews the concept of seismic arrays as it has evolved over the years, beginning with the early discussions in Geneva in 1958 on technical means for monitoring compliance with a potential comprehensive nuclear test ban treaty. These efforts culminated with the deployment of the two large aperture arrays LASA (Montana, 1965) and NORSAR (Norway, 1970), the design principles and operations of which are described here in considerable detail. The chapter also examines bold and promising initiatives within the seismological community per se — namely, the deployment and operation of a global network of some 100 digital broad-band stations with options for satellite telemetry of data to centers around the world. International test ban discussions under U.N. auspices in Geneva have generated considerable interest in advanced research in regional seismology and design of sophisticated small arrays reflecting recent advances in microprocessor and communication technologies. These developments, which are portents of the generation of a much enlarged high-quality seismic data base, are likely to have a significant impact on future seismological monitoring capabilities and therefore on the confidence of verifying very small underground nuclear tests.

The seismological experience that has been accumulated over the years, in particular resulting from the large array program, has provided important insight into the practical value of arrays and array processing techniques for comprehensive test-ban treaty verification. In this context, the emphasis will always be on low-magnitude events, and the superiority of arrays compared to single stations in detecting such events has been established beyond discussion.

In addition, we are now able to recognize additional scientific objectives of very broad scope that can be brought to bear by seismic array research. In brief, some scientific objectives are:

- static and dynamic properties of the earth as a planet;

- global mapping of the lithosphere and deeper lateral heterogeneities;
- resolution of the anisotropy in the lithosphere and deeper parts of the mantle; mapping of mantle flow;
- understanding of the dynamics of earthquakes; and
- nearly real-time analysis of large events that are available immediately to the scientific community.

The term "seismic array" can be applied to any grouping of stations satisfying the criteria for an array used to study a seismological problem, and, as such, arrays are conveniently classified according to spatial scale. Local and regional arrays distributed over areas with characteristic horizontal dimensions ranging from ten to several thousand kilometers are essential for studying the details of seismic activity in tectonic zones and the structure of the crust and uppermost mantle. Small arrays with apertures of only a few kilometers are ideal for surveillance of events at local and regional distances.[1] Indeed, global deployment of many small arrays is envisaged for monitoring compliance with a potential comprehensive test ban treaty.[2] Larger regional arrays will be most useful for three-dimensional mapping of the crust and upper lithosphere. However, many problems critical to seismology and other earth sciences can only be approached using global arrays — that is, distributions of seismic stations of truly worldwide coverage. These problems range from studies of very large earthquakes and earthquakes far removed from regional arrays to the structure of the deep interior. Moreover, the data collected by a global array of fixed, high-performance, continuously operated stations can provide the spatial and temporal baselines needed to calibrate and tie together the information collected by local and regional arrays.

THE SEISMIC ARRAY CONCEPT

Exploration geophysicists appear to have been the first ones within earth sciences to take practical advantage of the array concept by combining clusters of geophones as early as in the 1920s. The seismological concept of arrays emerged from the nuclear test ban negotiations in Geneva in 1958, when the need for improved capability to study weak seismic events was clearly recognized. On the basis of past experience, a seismic array is generally taken to fulfill the following requirements:

1. three or more sites at which seismometers (of uniform instrumentation) are located;
2. spatial extent (aperture) ranging from a few hundred meters to a few hundred kilometers; and
3. a common time basis, and a central control point to which all or selected time intervals are communicated for integrated on-line and/or off-line processing.

Array design reflects the desire to achieve phase identification, to suppress noise and interfering signals, and to reduce waveform distortion caused by source/receiver scattering effects through two-dimensional sampling of the seismic wave field. The common denominator for these objectives is that the two-dimensional wave-field sampling permits, via Fourier transform operations, mapping of incoming signals into their appropriate location in the frequency-wavenumber space. This knowledge gives an immediate clue to the ray path of the signal through the earth and also the approximate geographical location of the source. The time-domain processing scheme equivalent to the frequency-wavenumber mapping is that of "steering" the array to a prespecified area — that is, inserting time shifts prior to summing the individual sensor traces to ensure that potential signals would be in phase. Signals originating in that area would be "seen" by the array without non-linear distortion, while a time-coincident signal from another area would be suppressed. This results in the improvement of the signal-to-noise ratio by a factor equal to the square root of the number of sensors.

The array performance, or its response to incoming signals, would naturally reflect the geometry of the seismometers installed in the field. Specifically, the array response is the magnitude of the gain of the array in frequency-wavenumber space when a straight sum processing of the number of sensors is used (i.e., phased to a vertically incident signal).

Naturally, prior to the field installation the array response would be simulated to ensure proper design of the array, notwithstanding minor repositionings of instruments due to logistics and actual field conditions. The ensuing array response should have a maximum gain at the origin in wavenumber space, surrounded by regions of uniformly low gain. In practical terms, the central main lobe has an apparent width that is roughly inversely proportional to the aperture of the array, and prominent sidelobes can exist through which considerable energy can leak in the beamforming process, resulting in an increased false alarm rate. Thus, the array aperture reflects a compromise between detection (small aperture) and precision in locating the source of the seismic energy (large aperture). The array response of the NORSAR array in Norway is shown in Figure 18.1.

ARRAY OPERATION — REAL-TIME SURVEILLANCE OF SEISMIC EVENTS

Array operation as seen today is principally aimed at real-time monitoring of seismic activity on local, regional or global levels, and this comprises five major tasks, namely:

1. Data transmission from seismometer to computer;
2. Real-time event detection processing;

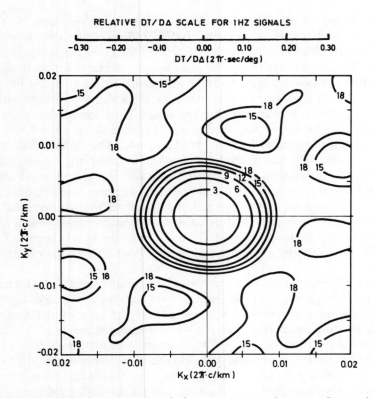

FIGURE 18.1. NORSAR array response in frequency-wavenumber space. Contour levels are in decibels down from maximum.

3. Event analysis; signal parameter extraction and event log (bulletin) creation;
4. External hardware testing and operational software modifications; and
5. Communication, data storage and exchange.

Of these five, the two tasks with the most relevance to the monitoring of nuclear explosions are items 2 and 3.

Real-Time Signal Detection

This process is aimed at detecting weak signals in ambient noise and is as such the most critical part of the array's monitoring function of explosions and earthquake activities. It is a three-step process which comprises noise suppression, detector design per se and the determination of an acceptable false alarm rate. The following comments apply:

Noise Suppression. To take the NORSAR arrays again as example, noise suppression is achieved in two independent ways, namely, through simple bandpass filtering (receiving only the frequencies of interest and filtering out the rest), and through beamforming. In beamforming, the signal received by each detector in the array is appropriately delayed in its arrival time at other detectors. The result of this "organizing" of signal receptions is that only signals that come from a small, distant locus are constructively summed by the array at any moment. Summing received signals arriving from all other points would interfere destructively, and these others are therefore suppressed. In the case of beamforming, the approximately valid assumptions are that signals are identical and in-phase and the noise uncorrelated, so an improvement in the signal-to-noise ratio by the square root of the number of sensors is achieved. The in-phase requirement reflects the fact that the beamforming process literally is that of focusing an array on various points on the earth, as illustrated in Figure 18.2. Notice that beamforming is a computer-costly operation, as very many beams must be formed in real-time to ensure an adequate and timely coverage of seismic and other zones of interest. In practice, the many array beams are formed on the basis of relatively few subarray beams, as the latter have substantially larger beam widths. Further economy may be obtained by the so-called envelope beamforming, by which envelopes of the subarray beams are formed via a Hilbert-transform operation prior to the array beamforming process. The envelope operation transforms nonlinearly the relatively high-frequency subarray beams into relatively low-frequency ones, which in turn results in a substantial increase of the array beam width or areal coverage. This in turn gives computational efficiency, but at the expense of signal-to-noise ratio gain; envelope beamforming suppresses the noise variance while conventional beamforming suppresses the noise level. In the case of NORSAR, practical experience shows that envelope beamforming detects about 85% of the events reported by conventional beamforming.[3]

Detector Design. The purpose here is simply to detect potential signals in ambient noise, and such a search is usually performed almost continuously in real time on the beam trace of individual sensor traces. The type of detector most commonly used in seismology is tied to comparing average signal power (or rectified amplitudes) over a short time average (STA) with a similar one estimated over a long time window (LTA). Whenever the STA/LTA ratio exceeds a preset threshold one or more times, a detection is declared as illustrated in Figure 18.3. Over the years many types of detectors have been suggested in the seismological literature,[4] but few if any seem to perform significantly better than the STA/LTA detectors. In addition, STA/LTA remains attractive due to its simplicity of real-time implementation. More recently, considerable attention has been given to the so-

NORSAR beam deployment

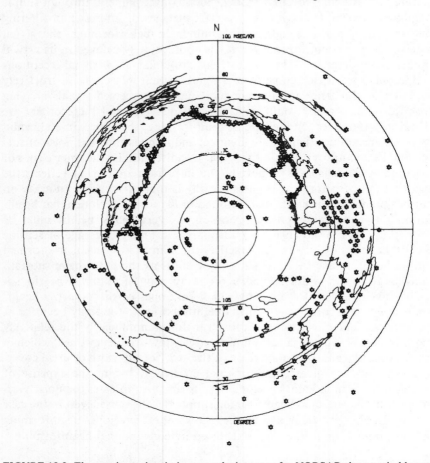

FIGURE 18.2. The steering points in inverse velocity space for NORSAR short-period beams as formed by the real-time detection processor. The highest density of beams corresponds to the most active seismic regions.

called Walsh detector, whose performance is said to be considerably better than that of the STA/LTA. However, as the Walsh transform is akin to the Fourier transform, the performance differences are limited mostly to reflecting experimental conditions like sampling local and regional seismicity (detector run on individual sensor traces) versus global seismicity (detector run on array beams).

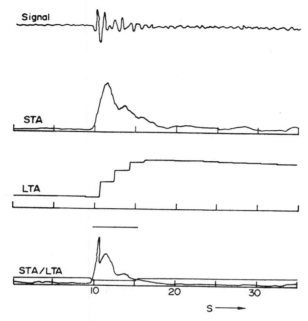

FIGURE 18.3. Beam, STA, LTA, and STA/LTA traces for earthquake from Tsinghai, China; arrival time January 27, 1970, 10 h 59 m 40.1 s filtered 1–3 Hz. STA integration time is 1.85 and LTA computation rate is 5/9 Hz. The short line above the STA/LTA curve indicates detection state, and the line crossing the curve is the threshold.

False Alarm Rate. As mentioned above, when STA/LTA exceeds a threshold, a detection is declared, which might be either a noise wavelet or a seismic signal generated by an earthquake or underground explosion. If the threshold is lowered, the number of false alarms (noise wavelets) per unit time increases much faster than the likely occurrence of seismic signals, as illustrated in Figure 18.4. In order to avoid overloading the array processing system, the threshold may be arbitrarily set so that the average false alarm rate amounts to one to two per hour. It should be added that the false alarm rate is dependent not only on the number of tests performed, but also on the noise frequency spectrum. In the case of a uniform background noise field, the observed increase in false alarms during night time has been credited to a decrease in relatively high-frequency cultural noise.[5]

Comments. Over the last decades large concentrated research efforts have been undertaken with the explicit aim of optimizing array configurations, maximizing signal-to-noise enhancement by adaptive filtering of the Wie-

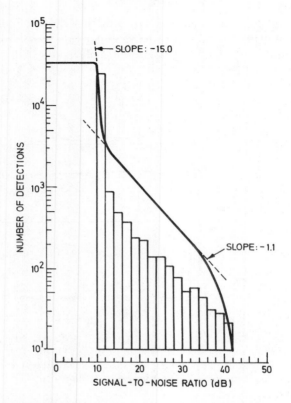

FIGURE 18.4. Number of detections by the automatic NORSAR real-time detection processor as a function of STA/LTA (signal-to-noise) ratio. The number of detections increases sharply below an SNR of 12 dB, where fake alarms generated by noise fluctuation dominate the detections triggered by real events.

ner type, and improving event detector designs. Parallel but far more extensive research efforts have taken place in related fields like electrical engineering, radar, acoustical oceanography, radio astronomy, and other sciences. By comparison, the simple bandpass filtering/delay-and-sum processing schemes adapted for the event detection systems of NORSAR and LASA (the Long Arm Seismic Array, in Montana) appear simplistic. The basic problem seems to be that the more sophisticated methods are not very robust—that is, their performance is not optimal when assumptions of stationarity and distribution functions of band-limited noise are not strictly valid.

Computer-intensive adaptive filtering may result in an average gain of 1–2 dB at the subarray level. This has recently been demonstrated by Ingate and his colleagues,[6] experimenting with a class of Wiener filters tested on a prototype (NORESS) regional array. A similar gain may be easily achieved by just adding a few additional seismometers in the field. Likewise, the approximately log-normal amplitude distribution across NORSAR implies that the "best" subarray has a signal-to-noise ratio up to about 10 dB greater than those for the "least sensitive" subarrays. The array site amplitude response pattern is rather strongly dependent on the earthquake source region; some subarrays are consistently better than others. Finally, it is rather obvious that it would be relatively easy to detect nearby disturbances as compared to those occurring at teleseismic distances due to geometrical spreading and intrinsic attenuation effects. Detectability differences here should be of the order of 10 dB on the signal amplitude level.

Event Analysis

On the basis of declared detections and associated original sensor recordings, event analysis is aimed at extracting signal parameters like phase arrival times, amplitude, and period (Level 1 data), creating an event log or seismic bulletin, and finally storing relevant parts of the signal wave train (Level 2 data). In the NORSAR system this process is automated, but analyst intervention is needed in about 70% of events identified as real signals. Practical problems often arise from sidelobe detections, for example, secondary phases may be detected on other beams and classed as a P wave from a separate event. Most of these intricacies are easily handled by an experienced analyst.

As an array provides a two-dimensional sampling of the wavefield, direction (azimuth), and velocity of the incoming signals are easy to determine. A first approximation to the velocity vector is immediately derived from the location of that beam on which detection shows the event most clearly. In other words, the observed velocity vector can be easily converted via standard tables into a location vector—that is, it can provide the latitude and longitude of the epicenter. For the full-size NORSAR (aperture about 100 km), the epicenter locations were generally within 100 km of the ISC locations. However, focal depth and the associated origin time estimates of these parameters are difficult to quantify on the basis of array recordings only unless clear-cut recordings of secondary phases of multiply reflected signals like pP or sP are available. An experienced analyst, however, can avoid large errors in focal depth estimation on the basis of P waveform shape and general knowledge of the zones where deep earthquakes occur— primarily in circum-Pacific subduction zones.

During the many technical discussions in Geneva on the design of a global seismological monitoring system for test ban verification, the problems of focal depth estimation and more extensive parameterized source descriptions have implicitly become major issues. Because explosions occur near the surface of the earth and earthquake activity occurs much deeper, these parameters also are important discrimination criteria for seismic source identification. The four focal parameters of a seismic event can be estimated on the basis of P wave arrival times only (Level 1 data), which constitutes the observational basis for record-keeping at national and international data centers. On the other hand, more refined and extensive estimates of source parameters (and implicitly source type) are feasible given access to wave form (Level 2) data.[7] The global monitoring system as currently envisaged by Geneva experts should confine the analysis work to Level 1 data, while Level 2 data would only be passively routed via the international data centers upon request from national authorities. This sharp distinction between Level 1 and Level 2 data, not seismologically or technically justified, reflects political considerations in the apparent desire to have "source identification by national means." In practice this implies that national authorities should be responsible for explicit statements on source type, for example, natural earthquakes or underground nuclear explosions. To do so, these national authorities must have access to all original recordings from all stations in the global network.

Comments. The event analysis functions of seismic arrays are important in surveillance of global earthquake activity as such systems provide an almost instant estimate of focal parameters for any detected event. Although these parameter estimates are not very precise and are somewhat dependent on array aperture and relative epicenter distances, they still are very helpful for keeping track of seismic events at international centers. The reason is that arrays provide a rough epicenter estimate, while individual stations only give phase arrival times and associated amplitudes. On a global scale, it is quite a problem to associate a large number of phase recordings with the proper number of confirmable events.[8] An illustrative example here is that the NORSAR and LASA reported event populations had only about a 40% overlap.

It should be rather obvious that while the tasks of recording and detecting seismic events are highly efficient and automated, event analysis is still predominantly a manual process.

EXAMPLES OF SEISMIC ARRAY RESEARCH

Seismic arrays, in particular the large arrays like NORSAR and LASA, have over the years provided a very valuable data base for seismological research, and the most striking results obtained are a direct consequence of the relatively unique features of the arrays, namely, excellent data quality, generally high signal-to-noise ratios, and fine spatial resolution. The number of important contributions is far too great to permit a detailed review, so we will confine this discussion to a few areas only.

Noise Field Decomposition

Array data analysis has provided an improved understanding of the seismic noise field, both with respect to noise propagation and directionality, spatial coherence of noise, frequency characteristics, and spatial temporal fluctuations in the noise level. In the high frequency range, the noise decomposition study of Ingate and his colleagues[6] is instructive. For example, cultural noise and steady-state noise produced by hydroelectric turbines were used to detect time-dependent load effects on seismic velocity fluctuations.[9]

Spatial Characteristics of Seismic Signals — Lithosphere Heterogeneities

Short-period P waves sampled by a large-aperture array exhibit waveform distortions and travel time and amplitude anomalies that had no physical counterpart in the early, rather simplistic seismological concept of homogeneous lithospheric structures. One of the first approaches to explain such anomalies in terms of local receiver structures was made by modelling the lithosphere in the array siting area as a random Chernov medium.[10] The random medium approaches could not explain these anomalies fully, so deterministic modelling was clearly required. A breakthrough here was made by Aki and his colleagues,[11] whose inversion technique of three-dimensional lithosphere/asthenosphere seismic velocity perturbations (now termed seismic tomography) has found wide-spread usage.[12] An extension of this inversion concept has been to include hypocenter parameter estimation, as described by Aki and Lee, and by Spencer and Gubbins.[13]

Unexpected large amplitude variations have proved very difficult to model accurately, but promising results have been reported.[14] The ultimate approach here would be to invert the amplitude anomalies directly via the wave equation, since the observed anomalies are clearly frequency-dependent — the holographic approach of Troitskiy et al.[14] accounts primarily for diffraction effects.

Observed waveform distortions can sometimes be efficiently modelled by synthetic seismogram analysis, but this very seldom applies to the signal coda. At present, a quantitative scattering approach including frequency-dependent Q appears most efficient.[15]

Seismic Source Identification

This avenue of array research has been pursued rather vigorously, although in this respect an array must be considered a high-quality single station. Among various essential one-dimensional source discrimination criteria developed, the robust m_b/M_s is the most widely used (m_b = short-period P wave magnitude; M_s = long-period [20 sec] Rayleigh-wave magnitude). This discriminate breaks down at m_b values around 4.5–4.0 and below, because surface waves are not observable for small events at large distances. Tjostheim has introduced elegant multivariate feature extraction techniques that, in combination with pattern recognition schemes, have resulted in relatively refined source discrimination methods.[16]

The major problem in seismic source identification studies today is to develop discriminants on the basis of short-period recordings only, as P and Lg waves occasionally are clearly observable at m_b magnitude down to 2.5 m_b units. In such cases, however, a prerequisite appears to be a reasonable azimuth sampling in order to achieve source modelling.[17]

Comments. The actual deployment of an array (its location) relative to the stationary global seismicity pattern may be seen as a permanent seismological experiment. For example, NORSAR provides excellent recordings of PKP (or core) wave complexities for sources in the Tonga-Kermadec region; underground nuclear explosions in certain parts of the U.S.S.R. are well recorded by the array together with sharp structural details of the so-called "400-km" and "670-km" upper mantle discontinuities. On a larger time scale, it is obvious that experiments of similar kinds must be conducted for other source/receiver combinations, and such undertakings may be realized by temporary deployments of mobile arrays and establishing of a digital, global network. Such ideas are not particularly novel, but the exciting thing is that at this time academic consortia are being established to implement these longstanding instrumentational and earthquake observational goals.

Recent and expected future advances in digital seismometry, computer technology, and digital data transmission will significantly influence future developments in seismology and, not least, cut operational costs. Microprocessors are becoming available that can easily and inexpensively perform the functions of local digital seismic data recording, processing, and exchange. The establishment of small, low-cost, portable digital array stations might thus in the future become a very attractive alternative to present analog-recording seismograph stations.

Modern technology has also made feasible the interconnection of existing seismological observatories on a global scale through digital communications links.[18] Any homogeneous network of seismic arrays – across a continent or globally distributed – can in principle be considered as a single, very extended seismic array. Clearly, signal coherence across such a network will not be adequate for application of conventional array processing methods, although techniques such as envelope beamforming hold some promise in this regard.[19] An alternative approach to such "global array processing" would be a maximum-likelihood formulation of the detection and location problem by determining the most probable event hypocenter given a suite of signal arrival and amplitude reportings from single stations and arrays tied together in a global network.

CONCLUDING REMARKS

Initiatives arising from international discussions about seismic data exchange and global seismic monitoring have stimulated the recent concommitant advances in seismic instrumentation, and use of microprocessor and telecommunication technologies. These developments will permit participation by the entire seismological community in deployment and operation of different classes of seismic arrays. Advanced research requires ready access to high-quality data as well as software infrastructure for analyzing the data in a thoroughly scientific manner. In the past, the latter factor seems to have prevented more widespread use of large array data and digital recordings from the current Global Deployment Seismic Network (GDSN). Yet another problem has been the excessive formalism in internationally cooperative seismological efforts. This has clearly been the case with the technical discussions held in Geneva concerning monitoring compliance with a potential Comprehensive Test Ban Treaty. The present drive for the future deployment of an unprecedented number of digital array stations is strongly motivated, and we feel that it is likely to succeed; present advances in theoretical seismology cannot be maintained without a fresh injection of a high-quality data base for testing of hypotheses. Also for the individual small research organizations the benefit would be large; actually with an "investment" of, for example, one broad-band station and/or one regional array, data access will be granted to many similar systems elsewhere even having a global coverage, plus the excitement of international research cooperation.

REFERENCES

1. Mykkeltveit, S., K. Åstebol, D. J. Doornbos and E. S. Husebye. Seismic Array Configuration Optimization. *Bull. Seism. Soc. Am.* 73 (1983).
2. Sykes, L. R., J. F. Evernden and I. Cifuentes. Seismic Methods for Verifying Nuclear Test Bans. In *Am. Inst. Physics Volume on Arms Race*, Ch. 5 (1983).

3. Ringdal, F., E. S. Husebye and A. Dahle. P-wave Envelope Representation in Event Detection Using Array Data. In *Exploitation of Seismograph Networks*, edited by K. G. Beauchamp. Holland: Noordhoof-Leiden, 1975.

4. Ringdal, F. and E. S. Husebye. Application of Arrays in the Detection, Location and Identification of Seismic Events. *Bull. Seism. Soc. Am.* 72 (1982).

5. Steinert, O., E. S. Husebye and H. Gjøystdal. Noise Variance Fluctuations and Earthquake Detectability. *J. Geophys.* 41 (1975).

6. Ingate, S. F., E. S. Husebye and A. Christoffersson. Regional Arrays and Optimum Data Processing Schemes. *Bull. Seism. Soc. Am.*, in press.

7. Jackson, J. and T. Fitch. Basement Faulting and the Focal Depths of the Larger Earthquakes in the Zagross Mountains (Iran). *Bull. Seism. Soc. Am.* 64 (1981).

8. Nordstrand, I. and R. Slunga. Preparation of a Computer Algorithm for Automatic Association of Arrivals. Stockholm, Sweden: FOA Report, 1983.

9. Bungum, H., T. Risbo and E. Hjortenberg. Precise Continuous Monitoring of Seismic Velocity Variations and their Possible Connection to Solid Earth Tides. *J. Geophys. Res.* 82 (1977).

10. See Aki, K. Scattering of P-waves under the Montana LASA. *J. Geophys. Res.* 78 (1973); Capon, J. Characterization of Crust and Upper Mantle Structure under LASA as a Random Medium. *Bull. Seism. Soc. Am.* 64 (1974); Bertueussen, K.-A., A. Christoffersson, E. S. Husebye and A. Dahle. Wave Scattering Theory in Analysis of P-wave Anomalies at NORSAR and LASA. *Geophys. J. Res.* 82 (1975); King, D. W., E. S. Husebye and R. A. W. Haddon. Processing of Seismic Precursor Data. *Phys. Earth Planet. Inter.* 12 (1977).

11. Aki, K. Three-dimensional Structure of the Lithosphere under Montana LASA. *Bull. Seism. Soc. Am.* 66 (1976); Aki, K., A. Christoffersson and E. S. Husebye. Determination of the Three-dimensional Seismic Structure of the Lithosphere. *J. Geophys. Res.* 82 (1977).

12. Aki, K. 3-D Seismic Inhomogeneities in Lithosphere and Asthenosphere: Evidence for Decoupling in Lithosphere and Flow in Asthenosphere. *Rev. Geophys. Space Phys.* 20 (1982).

13. Aki, K. and W. H. K. Lee. Determination of Three-dimensional Velocity Anomalies under a Seismic Array using First P Arrival Times from Local Earthquakes. 1. A Homogeneous Initial Model, *J. Geophys. Res.* 81 (1976); Spencer, C., and D. Gubbins. Travel-time Inversion for Simultaneous Earthquake Location and Velocity Structure Determination in Laterally Varying Media. *Geophys. J.* 63 (1980).

14. Thomson, C. J. Use of Ray Theory in Determining the Velocity Structure of the Lithosphere. Ph.D. diss., Cambridge University, U.K., 1981; Troitskiy, P., E. S. Husebye and A. Nikolaev. Lithospheric Studies Based on Holographic Principles. *Nature* 294 (1981).

15. As demonstrated by Aki, K. Attenuation and Scattering of Short-period Seismic Waves in the Lithosphere. In *Identification of Seismic Sources—Earthquake or Underground Explosions.* edited by E. S. Husebye and S. Mykkeltveit. Dordrecht, Holland: D. Reidel Publishing Co., 1981; Malin, P. E. A First-order Scattering Solution for Modeling Elastic Wave Codas—I. The Acoustic Case. *Geophys. J.* 63 (1980).

16. Tjostheim, D. Improved Seismic Discrimination using Pattern Recognition. *Phys. Earth Planet. Inter.* 16 (1978).

17. Key references to the comprehensive references on seismic source discrimina-

tion problems are: Dahlman, O. and H. Israelson. *Monitoring Underground Nuclear Explosions.* Amsterdam: Elsevier, 1977; Blandford, R. R. Seismic Event Discrimination. *Bull. Seism. Soc. Am.* 72 (1982); Husebye and Mykkeltveit, eds. op. cit. (1981); and Sykes et al. op. cit. (1983).

18. Husebye, E. S. and E. Thoresen. Personal Seismometry Now! *EOS* (August, 1984).

19. See Ringdal, Husebye and Dahle, op. cit. (1975); Roy, F. Common Data Base Experiment; Depth Estimation Using Multi-Station Data. Stockholm, Sweden: FOA Report, 1982.

19.

Satellite Verification of Arms Control Agreements

Harold V. Argo

Introductory Note by Kosta Tsipis

The way in which verification requirements generated by diplomatic activity in the arena of arms control agreements can stimulate the development and deployment of adequate technical means to meet these requirements is vividly demonstrated in this chapter by Harold Argo.

In support of U.S. and Soviet efforts to ban the testing of nuclear weapons above ground, scientists and engineers devised detectors of nuclear radiation to be placed in high earth orbits from which any nuclear tests in the atmosphere or in outer space could assuredly be detected. With these instruments in place, the task of detection became relatively straightforward. An exoatmospheric nuclear detonation releases enough elementary particles that travel huge distances in the void of outer space to be unconcealable; nuclear explosions within the atmosphere generate uniquely characteristic phenomena. No other natural or man-made event can cause the simultaneous appearance of all these interrelated phenomena, in a precisely predictable time sequence and with foreseeable energy distributions. Thus, the detectors flown into space to look for clandestine above-ground nuclear tests have a very high probability not only of spotting them, but also, almost equally important, of not misidentifying other events as nuclear explosions.

This chapter describes the characteristics of the physical phenomena on which detection of nuclear detonation is based, as well as the instruments designed to implement such detections. The evolution over the years of past instruments into present systems and towards future systems is described and evaluated. The chapter leaves little doubt that our ability to detect nuclear tests above ground has always been adequate and that it is constantly being improved and refined nevertheless.

EARLY HISTORY OF THE VELA SATELLITE

During the summer of 1958, the United States began serious discussions with the U.S.S.R. and U.K. that were eventually to lead in 1963 to the Limited Test Ban Treaty prohibiting any signatory from testing nuclear weapons in either the atmosphere or space. The U.S. government needed answers to many questions about test verification techniques before committing itself to a treaty, so the President's Science Advisory Committee made several hurried, but in general reasonably thorough and accurate, studies of the problems associated with detecting and verifying a nuclear test anywhere in the atmosphere or space. In March 1959 and again in May, the Panel on High Altitude Detection, headed by Wolfgang K. H. Panofsky, issued reports on the results of their studies. The Panofsky Report concluded that "the concealment of such tests appears extremely difficult," and it made many constructive suggestions for detection systems, with a clear preference for some satellite-based instrumentation.

By June of 1959, a study group of Los Alamos physicists and Sandia Laboratory engineers was studying the Panofsky Report and comparing the merits of various satellite configurations together with the most appropriate instrumentation for detecting and characterizing the nuclear burst radiations. Within a period of several months, the Air Force's Advanced Research Projects Agency (ARPA) was working with the Atomic Energy Commission (AEC) group on the design and procurement of what became the Vela Hotel Nuclear Test Detection Satellite System. The first pair of Vela Satellites, built by TRW, was launched into circular orbits with a radius of 115,000 km on the 17th of October, 1963. The two spacecraft were positioned approximately 180° apart in their common orbit, so that almost the whole earth was under observation at all times, as well as space out to very substantial distances.

Two more Vela launches followed in rapid succession, the second on July 17, 1964, and the third on July 20, 1964. The launches were phenomenally successful for those early space age days, and the instrumentation worked gratifyingly well. Each successive launch carried improved instrumentation, partly because of lessons learned on earlier launches, but mostly due to rapid improvements in space technology then taking place. The spacecraft in the first 3 launches were spin-stabilized at 6 rpm, with fixed axes in space.

By the time of the 4th Vela launch in April 1967, the objectives for the test and verification program had become more ambitious. Encouraged by the early successes both in launches and in equipment performance and longevity on orbit (original estimates had predicted nine-month lifetimes), the Program Office introduced a new family of spacecraft with its spin axis pointing to the earth's center at all times. This permitted the expansion of the Vela system from a purely space-oriented detection system to one encompassing both space and the earth's atmosphere down to ground level. Three more pairs of this improved version of Vela satellites were successfully launched into far earth orbits, each successive pair having the latest in improvements in electronics and sensor technology. The final launch in the

Vela series was in April 1970. Several of these satellites are still functioning fourteen years after launch, providing test and verification information.

With the end of the Vela satellite series, the follow-on Vela functions were transferred to a new generation of large, multipurpose Air Force satellites in geosynchronous orbit. As with the Vela series, there has been a steady improvement in test and verification performance as the technology grows. But from its earliest deployment, the Vela-type instrumentation has detected every nuclear event set off above ground that it has been in a position to see.

Monitoring the 1963 Limited Test Ban Treaty has been the joint responsibility of the Department of Energy (originally the Atomic Energy Commission) and the Department of Defense. The DOE sister laboratories at Los Alamos and Albuquerque, the Los Alamos National Laboratory and the Sandia National Laboratory, from the beginning have assumed the responsibility for the conceptual design, construction, testing, and delivery to the Air Force spacecraft contractors of the many nuclear-test detection

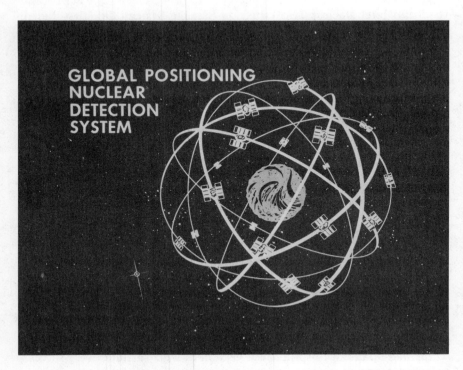

FIGURE 19.1. Artist's conception of the full 18-satellite constellation of the Global Positioning System.

instruments now in orbit in support of the treaty. The Air Force Space Division at Los Angeles has selected the spacecraft contractors and launch vehicles and has provided support for interfacing, launching, and data retrieval.

The newest addition to the satellite-based nuclear test detection system is the Navstar Global Positioning System (GPS) of satellites, originally intended to provide very precise navigational data to the military with eventual extension to the civilian sector. GPS has now been modified to include a simplified nuclear detection system of the Vela type and renamed GPS/NDS. The first such instrumentation was launched into orbit on July 14, 1983.

When fully operational, probably by 1988, the GPS/NDS will have eighteen satellites deployed in six circular orbits of 26,600 km radius inclined at 60° to the equator, and equally spaced in azimuth. Any spot on the earth's surface will be visible from four to eight of these satellites at all times. Figure 19.1 is an artist's conception of the full GPS/NDS constellation in orbit.

The primary component of the Navstar GPS satellites is a very accurate clock capable of 10 ns absolute timing. The spacecraft transmit their identification and time signals continuously, so that an appropriate receiver within view of four of the spacecraft can be used to locate the position of the receiver to about 10 meters, as well as its velocity. Conversely, the same clock system can be used to locate with great accuracy a nuclear burst seen by four satellites.

NUCLEAR DETONATION CHARACTERISTICS

Before discussing the specific nuclear detection instrumentation on the Vela and GPS/NDS satellites, we should review briefly the observable characteristics of a nuclear detonation. The nuclear chain reaction that is the nuclear detonation takes place in the core of the bomb in a time span of a few tens of nanoseconds, releasing energy ranging from 10^{12} to 10^{15} joules or more. Most of the energy initially released is in the form of kinetic energy of the resultant fission and fusion products. The temperature of the core rises in this same time interval to several tens of millions of degrees Kelvin. At these temperatures the core is a superheated plasma of photons, electrons and nuclei in thermal equilibrium, with most of the energy residing in the radiation field of the photons. This thermal energy works its way to the surface of the bomb case by a complicated mixture of shock wave and radiation diffusion, heating the intervening material to comparable temperatures. In a time comparable to the burning time, the case temperature rises to an equivalent black body temperature of a few keV and the photons, still in equilibrium with their surrounding plasma, are free to radiate into ambient space with a characteristic black-body photon distribution representative of the case temperature.

As a point of reference, a 1-meter-radius sphere at a temperature of 1 keV will radiate a "megaton" of energy, 4×10^{22} ergs, in about 0.3 μsec, with a most probable photon energy of 2.85 keV. The rate of energy radiation will increase as temperature to the fourth power. Typical weapons can release up to 70% of their energy in this black body x-ray burst, with most of the remaining energy residing in the kinetic energy of the expanding debris.

The very first radiation leaving the scene of the nuclear detonation will be a burst of energetic neutrons which escape with little or no delay in time. Associated with these neutrons will be a burst of "prompt" gamma rays, generated by those neutrons suffering inelastic collisions in the last mean-free-path of the bomb case. The neutrons carry away 1% or less of the energy of the bomb, and the prompt gamma rays perhaps one tenth of that.

If the weapon is a staged device with a small primary driving a secondary, there will be two prompt gamma ray and neutron bursts, separated by the interstage time.

Signals from weapons as small as 1 kiloton are surprisingly large and difficult to conceal, as pointed out by the Panofsky committee. I will borrow a table from an article by Sidney Singer in the December 1965 *Proceedings of the IEEE*[1] to illustrate the nominal characteristics of a nuclear burst in space (see Table 19.1).

Table 19.1. Nominal Characteristics of Some of the Radiations Emitted by a Nuclear Detonation

	X-Rays 0.1–100 keV	Gamma-Rays 0.3–3 MeV	Neutrons ~Few keV–16 MeV
Fraction of Bomb Yield	0.5	0.003	~0.01
Duration of Signal at Detector (sec)	5×10^{-7}	10^{-7}	Depends on Time of Flight
Dependence of Signal on Yield and Distance (MeV/cm^2)	1×10^{14} Y/R^2	6×10^{11} Y/R^2	10^{12} Y/R^2 neut/cm^2
Example	10^3 kt at 3×10^8 km: 1.1 MeV/cm^2	10^3 kt at 3×10^6 km: 67 MeV/cm^2	1 MT at 10^5 km get 10^4 neut/cm^2-sec for ~6 sec

Note: Y measured in kilotons (kt) and R in kilometers (km).
(From: "The Vela Satellite Program for Detection of High-Altitude Nuclear Detonations," by Singer, Sidney, *Proceedings of the IEEE*, 1982, 53, No. 12, December 1965. Copyright 1965 by The Institute of Electrical and Electronics Engineers, Inc. Used with permission.)

NUCLEAR BURSTS IN SPACE

When discussing the characteristic radiations from a nuclear burst as seen by an observer, one needs to distinguish between detonations in space and those in the atmosphere. In space the picture is essentially that described above. Most of the energy will be in the form of an x-ray burst occurring in the time of a μsec or so, and reasonably well described spectrally as the sum of one or more black-body sources with temperatures from 1 to 10 keV. The much smaller but earlier prompt gamma ray burst will have photons with energies from 0.5 to 10 MeV occurring in less than a μsec. The gamma ray spectrum will be strongly dependent upon the amount of fusion energy released in the bomb; i.e., the number of 14 MeV neutrons released in the thermonuclear reaction.

The neutron signature from a space detonation is very characteristic and contains technical information about the bomb design. The source can be considered as a delta function in time, and the time of flight to the observer will separate the energy spectrum beautifully. A pure fission device will have an easily recognized neutron energy spectrum peaking at about 1 MeV, while a fission/fusion device will have a peak due to the 14 MeV neutrons from the thermonuclear reaction, which of course will arrive first at the observer, followed by the fission neutron peak. Figure 19.2 is a neutron time-of-flight signature obtained by Sam Bame[2] during the 1962 high altitude nuclear test series. The nuclear burst occurred near Johnston Island above the atmosphere, and the neutron detector was carried above the atmosphere by an appropriately timed sounding rocket launched from Kauai, Hawaii, approximately 1,300 km away. The 14 MeV peak of $T(d, n)$ neutrons is clearly delineated, beginning several tens of milliseconds after the burst, followed by the fission neutron peak spreading from about 50 to 100 ms. The very interesting third bump or peak, much lower on this log–log scale, is made by those neutrons that became semi-thermalized in the bomb plasma before escaping.

The fission debris, which together with other bomb components carries away perhaps 25% of the explosive energy in the form of kinetic energy of the spatially expanding particles, will release both delayed fission gamma rays and electrons that can be very useful for detecting and verifying a nuclear detonation high in the atmosphere or in the magnetosphere. The debris will generate a population of trapped energetic electrons with characteristic energies from 1 to 8 MeV superimposed on the normal geomagnetically trapped population, which has very few electrons above 2 MeV in energy.

The delayed fission gamma rays, with energies from a few hundred keV to several MeV, have a characteristic time-decay curve that is distinctive. Figure 19.3 is a generic fission gamma ray decay curve for a fission debris

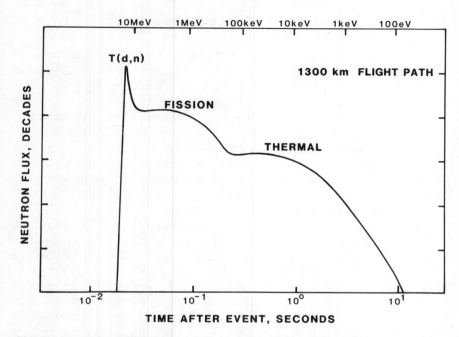

FIGURE 19.2. Time-of-flight spectrum of neutrons emitted by a nuclear burst above the atmosphere near Johnston Island and observed by rocket instrumentation above Kauai, Hawaii, 1,300 km away. The 14 MeV $T(d,n)$ neutrons arrived first and are clearly distinguished from the lower energy fission neutrons. A signature of this type gives useful confirmatory information on the nature of the event.

cloud released in space or the upper atmosphere. The most notable feature is the very rapid drop in intensity in the interval from the first few microseconds to about 1 millisecond when a flat plateau in energy release with time is maintained for about 1 second. After 1 second, the energy release again drops off at a rate $\sim t^{-1.2}$, continuing for weeks and months. These delayed fission gamma rays are readily observed from a space platform, even from a nuclear burst deep in the atmosphere if it is large enough. The fission debris cloud from a burst of a megaton or larger near the surface of the earth will rise thermally into the upper atmosphere where the delayed gamma rays will be able to penetrate into space and be observed. The motion of the cloud laterally with upper air currents can thus be tracked by satellite and aircraft.

ATMOSPHERIC BURSTS

The escaping gamma rays, neutrons and x-rays followed later by the expanding bomb debris will interact with the atmosphere and geomagnetic

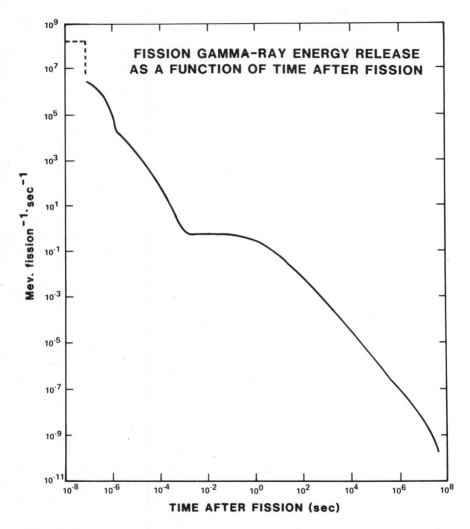

FIGURE 19.3. Generic fission gamma-ray decay curve, showing the characteristic plateau from about one millisecond to one second after the nuclear burst. After one second the gamma-ray energy release follows a time decay curve of $t^{-1.2}$.

field producing an interrelated complex of effects that have been a subject for study for almost 40 years. I will not attempt to cover these effects in detail but will single out major effects which have been useful for satellite observations.

The initial burst of x-radiation, lasting for a μsec or less and containing from 50% to 75% of the total weapon energy yield, will be absorbed in the first few meters of air surrounding the case, heating it to temperatures near 10^6K. Very shortly thereafter, the expanding ionized bomb debris carrying most of the remaining energy will join this initial fireball. The violent expansion of this completely ionized plasma is governed by complex hydrodynamical and radiation transport processes. However, at the rapidly expanding outer surface a very strong shock wave is generated, moving into the cooler surrounding air. The intensely shocked gas will be highly luminous, producing the visible fireball. The shocked gas will be opaque to the higher temperature plasma contained behind it. The intensity of the shock will drop as the fireball expands until the apparent luminosity of the fireball, which is the product of the surface brightness and the area, reaches a maximum and begins to drop off. As the shock weakens and the shocked air at the surface cools, its opacity to the higher temperature plasma behind it drops and the radiation begins to escape, driving the apparent luminosity back up to a second maximum. In a matter of seconds the energy loss by radiation and the mixing of the shocked gas with ambient cool air will drop the fireball luminosity back to a low level. A time history of the luminosity of the expanding fireball will have two peaks generated by the interfering phenomena just described and thus will be highly characteristic of any nuclear detonation in the atmosphere.

The general shape of the light-signature pulse is independent of yield and weapon design and depends only on having a large amount of energy dumped into a small volume of air in a very short time. The times to maxima and minimum are functions of yield alone and give multiple confirmation that an observed optical signal is the result of a massive release of energy in the atmosphere in a very short time.

The time to minimum is a relatively sensitive function of the total energy released and probably gives the best estimate of yield available. The time to second maximum also gives a measure of the yield and provides confirmatory information. The optical photometer developed to record the optical time signature of a nuclear burst in the atmosphere was long ago named a "bhangmeter" and has been well calibrated over the years. Figure 19.4 is a bhangmeter recording of a 19 kiloton atmospheric test.[3] The time to maximum is ~0.3 msec, to minimum ~12 msec, and second maximum ~130 msec. Simple algorithms for detonations in the lower atmosphere are:

$$\text{time to minimum} = 2.5 \text{ ms } \sqrt{Y_{kt}}$$

$$\text{time to second maximum} = 32 \text{ ms } \sqrt{Y_{kt}}$$

where Y_{kt} is the numerical yield in kilotons.

Optical bhangmeters on a satellite platform have an inherent handicap not experienced by ground-based instruments. The earth is a very bright object when viewed from space, with a luminosity perhaps several thousand

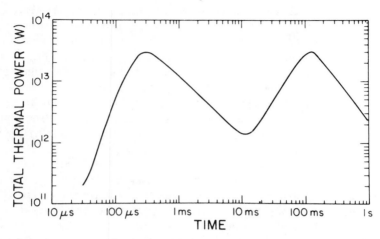

FIGURE 19.4. Bhangmeter recording of the 19-kiloton atmospheric nuclear test. The optical photometer records the luminosity of the fireball as a function of time.

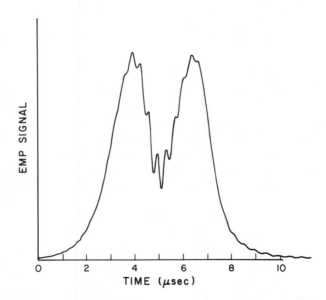

FIGURE 19.5. Simulated EMP signal as seen by a satellite receiver tuned to 50 MHz with a 2 MHz bandwidth. The ionosphere disperses the signal time as the function of frequency, complicating the interpretation of the received signal. In this example the second peak is a ground reflection.

times greater than that of a fireball from a small weapon. However, the optical signal from the earth as seen by a satellite instrument is slowly varying, and a signal from a nuclear burst will be a fast-rising short-duration optical pulse superimposed on, essentially, a d.c. signal. Appropriate filtration separates the desired pulse signal from the many-times-larger background and makes a satellite-based bhangmeter feasible.

Lightning strokes also have time constants in the millisecond range but do not normally have the duration or the characteristic maximum–minimum–maximum double pulse that has to meet yield criteria. They will trigger sensitive systems but simple logics criteria can reject them.

Another important observable effect from a nuclear burst in the atmosphere is the so-called electromagnetic pulse, or EMP.[4] The prompt-gamma-ray burst striking the air molecules will ionize them, giving the ejected electrons a component of velocity in the outward direction. This current of electrons will be deflected by the geomagnetic field, producing in some cases very large EMP signals. Figure 19.5 is an example of a simulated EMP signature recorded in a 50 MHz channel. The EMP is in general very sensitive to the weapon design and to the physical circumstances of the burst location, for example, proximity to a ground plane. The ground reflection is clearly shown in Figure 19.5. However, when an EMP signal is recorded, it can be used to give confirmatory evidence for the detonation.

SATELLITE NUCLEAR DETECTION INSTRUMENTATION

Evolution of Vela Instrumentation

The nuclear burst instrumentation on the first three pairs of Vela satellites was space-oriented only, that is, it looked for bursts above the atmosphere, and then only for x-ray, gamma ray, and neutron signatures. The third pair of spacecraft had optical instruments in the development stage with which to test the feasibility of a bhangmeter system on a satellite and, by the fourth launch, optical bhangmeters looking at the earth had been incorporated into the payload. The fifth and sixth Vela launches also contained EMP detectors.

The basic Vela x-ray, gamma-ray, and neutron detection systems have been described in some detail by Singer,[1] so I will give only brief descriptions here. Originally there were 10 x-ray detectors, each located on an apex of the icosahedron-shaped spacecraft, clearly visible in Figures 19.6 and 19.7. CsI(T1) fluors with photomultiplier tube technology were used for detection, with thin beryllium-foil light shields to exclude sunlight. A credible x-ray burst would have to trigger all the sensors on one side of the satellite.

The gamma-ray detectors also employed scintillation detector technology, with photomultiplier tubes imbedded in large plastic fluors about 10

FIGURE 19.6. Photograph of the first two Vela satellites mounted in tandem, and ready to be mounted on their booster rocket. Each satellite had an internal injection motor used to position it in final circular orbit of 115,000 km radius, approximately 180° apart. These satellites had an icosohedron configuration, with cubic shaped x-ray detectors at each apex. The gamma-ray and neutron detectors were inside.

cm in size. Six of these detectors can be seen in Figure 19.7, separated as widely as possible in the satellite to provide multifold coincident signals to distinguish a true gamma ray burst from cosmic-ray showers generated within the spacecraft. The solar panels and spacecraft skin were sufficiently

FIGURE 19.7. Early Vela satellite skeletal frame with solar panels removed. The injection motor, gamma-ray detector, and neutron detector are visible in the interior.

thin to permit the penetration of the gamma rays to the detectors. By the fourth launch, with the advent of gamma ray detectors with high resolution "time history" capability, the now famous gamma ray bursts of cosmological interest were discovered. It took multiple satellite observations of the same event with identical time structure and crude time-of-arrival identification of source direction to convince the world they were real.

The neutron detectors made use of large (approximately 5 kilograms) polyethylene moderators to thermalize the incident neutrons, which were then detected in He³-filled proportional counters buried within the moderator. One of these detectors is visible inside the satellite frame in Figure 19.7. When the neutron background count rate exceeded some adjustable level, a time-history recording was made and stored for later transmission to ground terminals.

The Vela instrumentation evolved with state-of-the-art detector technology. Photomultiplier tubes gave way to lighter and perhaps more reliable solid state detectors. Complexity increased as multiple energy channels and higher time resolution were introduced in order to better characterize a candidate signal and separate it from natural background signals. In Figure 19.8 we see one of the later series earth-oriented Vela satellites, in this case a Vela V/VI spacecraft. Three of these are still functioning more than fourteen years after launch.

FIGURE 19.8. Later model Vela spacecraft with earth-oriented bhangmeters, EMP sensors, and charged-particle analyzers, as well as more modern versions of the x-ray, gamma-ray, and neutron detectors.

The GPS/NDS Satellites

One of the primary detection systems of the future will be the Global Positioning System/Nuclear Detection System (GPS/NDS). These satellites are unique in the nuclear detection community in that they started out as an unclassified system, which makes it possible for me to describe the system, its purpose, and its general performance in some detail. Figure 19.9 is a photograph of an early instrument package for a GPS/NDS phase I satellite. The GPS/NDS system when fully deployed will contain:

1. optical bhangmeters for atmospheric bursts;
2. x-ray burst detectors for bursts from the top of the atmosphere to outer space, the range determined by the yield;
3. energetic charged-particle analyzers and dosimeters for assessing radiation damage and satellite longevity, and identifying any man-made trapped particle populations;
4. EMP detectors for location of the burst point, if in the atmosphere, and for providing confirmatory information on the nuclear burst itself; and
5. data processing units that monitor the health of each of the above instruments, provide timing signals, and process and store all data for later transmission to the ground terminals.

The x-ray and dosimeter instruments are interchangeable on a spacecraft and will be flown one to a satellite, the ratio being five x-ray detectors to

GLOBAL BURST DETECTORS

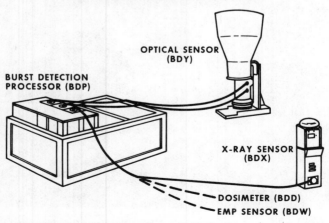

FIGURE 19.9. Schematic diagram of the simple but very effective nuclear test detection payload now being placed on the GPS satellites.

one dosimeter. The orbits for the three dosimeters will be selected to optimize the sampling of the geomagnetically trapped charged particles. The GPS/NDS complement of instruments does not contain all possible types of sensors. Neutron detectors, along with prompt and delayed fission gamma-ray detectors, are missing. But these are well represented on other systems, including the geostationary orbit satellites that have succeeded the old Vela system.

The GPS/NDS Bhangmeters

Bhangmeters can be as sophisticated as weight allowance and power permit. Spectral and spatial discrimination can be employed to improve credibility of an observation and, in the case of single satellite systems, one always wants mechanical redundancy to improve reliability. Among the advantages of the GPS/NDS constellation of satellites as platforms for bhangmeters are the high order redundancy provided by the eighteen satellites, relatively close-in orbits, and burst location capability provided by the accurate on-board clocks. These advantages allow the employment of a relatively simple and reliable bhangmeter. In Figure 19.9, the instrument with the large sunshade is the bhangmeter. The sunshade keeps direct sunlight out of the lens used to focus an image of the earth upon the light-sensitive detectors.

The time history of the optical signal is digitized and stored in memory. The trigger, or threshold, level of the sensor is commandable from the ground. When triggered the instrument provides two types of data sets usually referred to as "slow channel" data and "fast channel" data. The slow channel data provided a full-time history of the event consisting of light intensity data points vs. time starting at 200 μsec before the slow channel trigger conditions are satisfied and extending over a 6.86 second period after the trigger. The data are taken at 12.5 μsec intervals and, using an averaging technique, the post-trigger data are condensed into 128 samples, pseudo-logarithmically spaced in time and resolving both the first maximum and the following minimum and maximum. The fast channel data do not contain the 200 μsec precursor data but extend over only the first 6.3 ms after the fast trigger conditions are satisfied. The data consist of 48 samples averaged in the same manner as the slow channel data. The fast channel data provide a more accurate timing of the initial light pulse and hence a more accurate determination of the event's location.

The GPS/NDS X-Ray Burst Detectors

As shown in Table 19.1, characteristic signals from even a small weapon at GPS/NDS orbit distance are impressively large and easily identified. A

1-kiloton weapon with 50% x-ray yield would give an integrated x-ray fluence of $2.4(10)^5$ MeV/cm^2 at the satellite, a very robust signal with which to work. A credible verification of this signal as an x-ray burst from a nuclear detonation will have to identify it as of short duration, for example, a μsec or less, having an energy distribution of photons more or less well described by a black-body source with an identifiable temperature and yield. Multiple satellite observations with high time resolution will locate the source and provide redundant yield and spectral characteristics.

The basic sensor is a thin silicon foil with filter in front. The four spectral channels measure four spectral intervals of the photon energy spectrum. The spectral selectivity of each channel is achieved by tailoring the thickness and material of the filter together with the thickness of the silicon sensor. With the a priori knowledge that the spectrum has to be reasonably close to that of a black body or even the sum of two black body sources, four points on the spectral curve give sufficient information to reconstruct the source temperatures and together with the range, provide a yield. In addition, the four channels give redundancy for a single satellite.

The x-ray instruments are located on the forward bulkhead of the satellites, facing toward the earth and viewing all space between the satellite and earth plus that space beyond the earth and not in its shadow out to ranges determined only by the size of the burst. The very large x-ray signal from even a one kiloton burst combined with the highly redundant fields of view of the 18-satellite constellation provide very positive verification capability for any tests in the vicinity of the earth.

The GPS/NDS Dosimeter

The Block II dosimeters are relatively sophisticated charged-particle analyzers using the latest technology to distinguish between electrons and ions and perform pulse-height analysis on the signal from each particle. Two nested hemispherical scintillators are optically coupled to a single microchannel plate photomultiplier tube that has a split anode capable of supplying separate signals from the thin outer scintillator shell and the hemispherical core. The signal from the thin hemispherical outer shell serves to identify an incident particle as either an electron or ion, according to the different rates of energy loss, dE/dx; and the signal from the hemispherical core is used to measure its total energy. The electron energy spectra are recorded with eight-channel resolution covering the energy range 0.25 MeV $\leq$ E $\sim$10 MeV. Ion spectra have four-channel resolution covering the range 8 MeV $\leq$ E $\leq$ 85 MeV. The wide range of fluxes encountered along the GPS orbits at 20,000 km altitude is accommodated by having two complete assemblies with suitable geometric factors.

The normal geomagnetically trapped energetic electrons at 20,000 km altitude typically have energy spectra that are well represented by an exponential of the form e^{-E/E_o} where E is the energy and E_o is a spectral index in the range 0.2 MeV $\leq E_o \leq$ 0.6 MeV. There are very few electrons above 2 MeV. A population of fission decay electrons injected into the trapping regions will show up clearly in the 2 to 8 MeV portion of the spectrum, as witnessed during the high altitude test series of 1962. The GPS orbit, inclined at 60° to the equator, samples most of the geomagnetic trapping "shells" four times during each orbital pass, providing a good indication of the total environment.

The GPS/NDS EMP Detector

An electromagnetic pulse detector in principle need be only an antenna to intercept the signal and an amplifier with analog to digital converter. In fact, because of the frequency distribution and time structure of the signal at its source, which is distorted by the frequency dispersion and path straggling introduced by the ionosphere, the EMP detector system is very complex. The lower frequency cut-off for transmission through the ionosphere is a function of the integrated electron content along the ray path and is normally below 40 MHz. Therefore, the useful frequency band for EMP reception extends from the 40 MHz cut-off upwards until one runs out of signal. A reasonable compromise for the upper end of the band is 150 MHz.

The geomagnetic field provides a birefringent medium for the EMP signals and the circularly polarized ordinary and extraordinary waves will arrive at the satellite receivers with enough time separation induced by the ionosphere to further complicate interpretation. By paying careful attention to the antenna design and selecting narrow frequency bands suitably separated at both the low and high frequency ends of the useful spectrum and by very careful timing of the signals, one gets sufficient information to characterize the ionosphere and untangle the multiplicity of signals arriving from the source.

Lightning strokes generate a troublesome background of natural EMP signals. Worldwide, these occur at a rate of approximately 1,000 times a second.

From the above discussion it is clear that an EMP detector by itself is not a very useful nuclear test detector. However, by combining it with an optical bhangmeter and requiring coincidences within a reasonable time window, one has an important supportive piece of information. The GPS/NDS timing accuracies will provide close co-location information about the sources of the two independent signals.

REFERENCES

1. Singer, Sidney. The Vela Satellite Program for Detection of High-Altitude Nuclear Detonations. *Proceedings of the IEEE* 53, 12 (December 1965).
2. Bame, Sam. Time of Flight Measurements Made with Neutrons from Nuclear Explosions in Space. Paper given at American Physical Society meeting in New York, January 22-25, 1964.
3. Barasch, Guy E. Light Flash Produced by an Atmospheric Nuclear Explosion. *LASL Mini-Review*, LASL-79-84, November 1979.
4. Longmire, Conrad L. On the Electromagnetic Pulse Produced by Nuclear Explosions. *IEEE Transactions on Antennas and Propagation* AP-26, 1 (January 1978).

20.

Verifying a Fissile-Material Production Freeze in Declared Facilities, with Special Emphasis on Remote Monitoring

E. V. Weinstock and A. Fainberg

Introductory Note for Chapters 20 and 21 by Kosta Tsipis

In the two chapters that follow, the reader will find full descriptions of the technology and methodology of monitoring nuclear materials in civilian installations such as reprocessing plants, reactors, and reactor fuel manufacturers. The Weinstock and Fainberg chapter describes the methods and equipment available for monitoring a production cutoff of fissile materials as well.

The adequacy of these methods depends on the amount of the material necessary to construct a nuclear weapon compared with the annual throughput of such materials in reprocessing plants, fuel-rod fabrication plants, plutonium and highly-enriched uranium production plants, and in isotopic enrichment facilities. The fundamental approach of such monitoring is based on the principle of the conservation of mass—things do not simply vanish—and on a detailed accounting approach that endeavors to keep track of fissile material in facilities like the ones named above.

The two chapters give a quantitative description of the instruments and methods used to meet the requirements for monitoring generated by various types of possible arms control agreements aimed at stopping the production of weapons-grade fissile materials. Each reprocessing or manufacturing facility presents a special set of quantitative problems. Their technical solutions and the attendant level of confidence each offers are examined by Weinstock and Fainberg, while Keepin describes the performance characteristics of the instruments used to implement the processes described.

Together with the von Hippel–Levi chapter that follows them in this volume, these chapters constitute a more-or-less complete discussion of the problems and the available solutions for any effort to restrict or terminate the production of nuclear materials by an international agreement.

INTRODUCTION

The argument has been made in favor of a freeze on the production of fissile materials for nuclear weapons as an arms-control measure in its own right.[1] In a chapter in this book, von Hippel and Levi discuss a production cutoff as a backup to a weapons freeze.[2] It is assumed here that such a cutoff, involving only plutonium and highly enriched uranium, is both desirable and negotiable between the United States and the Soviet Union. An important question, then, is how would a production freeze be verified — that is, what activities would have to be monitored, how would they be monitored, what sensitivity would be required, and who would do the monitoring? Von Hippel and Levi[2] suggest some possible answers to these questions. The present discussion will be based on some of those suggestions, particularly in regard to the required sensitivity, but will concentrate on the technical means of verifying a cutoff in the production of fissile material for weapons in declared facilities, by means analogous to those now used by the International Atomic Energy Agency to verify peaceful nuclear activities.

The necessary sensitivity is determined by the minimum amount of cheating — that is, diversion of fissile material — that could affect the strategic balance between the United States and the U.S.S.R. On the basis of somewhat arbitrary but reasonable assumptions von Hippel and Levi suggest as a minimum the capability to detect a diversion of at least 1,000 kg of plutonium or 6,500 kg of highly enriched uranium over a one-year period. These quantities represent approximately one percent of the stockpiles assumed to be available for weapons in both countries.

Facilities that would have to be monitored would include some or all of the following:

1. Production and power reactors;
2. Spent-fuel reprocessing plants;
3. Plutonium and highly enriched uranium fuel fabrication plants;
4. Isotopic enrichment plants; and
5. Plutonium and highly enriched uranium stores.

It might also be desirable to monitor the activity of uranium mines and mills for gross indications of the expanded production of uranium required to support correspondingly large increases in the production of plutonium and highly enriched uranium; however, this would be only a tertiary measure (a back-up to a back-up, so to speak) and might best be carried out by means other than those considered here.

In addition to verifying the operation of declared facilities, there would have to be some means of detecting clandestine facilities. Since it is unlikely that either party — or even a third party — would be given a license to roam at will over the territory of the other, monitoring for clandestine facilities would have to be carried out by intelligence gathering, for example by satellite surveillance. Von Hippel and Levi discuss this possibility, which will not be considered further here.

Epstein[1] favors giving the responsibility for verifying the production freeze in declared facilities to the International Atomic Energy Agency. Because the IAEA system depends on more-or-less frequent (and, in some cases, continuous) on-site inspection and on periodic reporting by the inspected state, it may be regarded, particularly by the Soviet Union, as excessively intrusive. To avoid this objection, the approach suggested here emphasizes the use of remote monitoring.

Before discussing the problem of verifying a production cutoff, it may be useful to review briefly the main features of the IAEA Safeguards System.

THE IAEA SAFEGUARDS SYSTEM

This description of the IAEA Safeguards System[3] will be confined to the safeguards applied to non-weapon states adhering to the Treaty on Non-Proliferation of Nuclear Weapons (NPT), and will therefore apply to most countries. Although the formal arrangements for those safeguarded under other types of agreements are somewhat different, the actual safeguards system is essentially the same.

NPT safeguards are based on the fundamental principle of accounting for all declared nuclear material in peaceful use. This is called "material accountancy," and is carried out essentially by measuring the material inputs to and outputs (including discards) from each facility under safeguards and, periodically, the inventory of material within it. The operator of the facility performs these measurements and reports the results to the IAEA, which, by making independent measurements, usually only on a randomly selected sample of the material flows and inventories (to conserve inspection resources), verifies the operator's measurements. By comparing material receipts during an interval (e.g., three months or a year, depending on the importance of the material) and the amount on hand at the beginning of the interval with shipments (and discards) and the inventory at the end of the interval, the IAEA can determine if all the material for which the operator is responsible is accounted for, to within the inherent measurement uncertainties. This process is called "verifying a material balance."

Certain other measures lumped under the term "containment and surveillance" are also applied. "Containment" refers to the use of physical barriers to restrict the movement of or access to nuclear material. The pressure vessel of a light-water reactor is one example. "Surveillance" refers to observation, by inspectors or devices, to detect undeclared movements of material, tampering with equipment, falsification of data, and so forth.

Examples are cameras used to monitor the spent fuel at a reactor and tamper-indicating seals placed on the missile shield or dry-well head of a light-water reactor to ensure that it is not opened without the knowledge of the IAEA. The IAEA regards material accountancy as "a safeguards measure of fundamental importance" and containment and surveillance as "important complementary measures."[4] In effect, this means that the latter must always be backed up by material accountancy, and that it is unlikely that the IAEA would ever draw a conclusion of a safeguards violation purely on the basis of surveillance evidence. In IAEA language, surveillance can only detect anomalies — that is, apparently abnormal conditions that require further investigation for their resolution.

The safeguards system just described is both manpower-intensive and, in the opinion of some countries, unduly intrusive. To illustrate, fuel-fabrication plants handling substantial amounts of plutonium or highly-enriched uranium are inspected every two weeks. Plants reprocessing spent fuel from power reactors are inspected on a continuous basis, requiring an expenditure of several man-years of inspection effort per year. Because the agency has limited resources (its safeguards budget for 1984 was approximately $40 million), and because some countries have complained strongly about the burden of safeguards on their nuclear industry, there is considerable incentive to develop improved inspection methods not so heavily dependent on manpower. This was the motivation behind the development of remote monitoring.

RECOVER AND REMOTE MONITORING

The U.S. Arms Control and Disarmament Agency, concerned about the increasing burden of safeguards on the Agency's resources and also aware of the concerns of operators over the intrusiveness of inspections, began in 1976 to develop a remote-monitoring system that, it was hoped, would reduce the frequency of inspections of safeguarded facilities without impairing, and indeed even enhancing, safeguards effectiveness. The system was given the acronym RECOVER, for Remote Continual Verification.[5]

RECOVER was essentially a system for monitoring the performance of certain safeguards sensors, storing the information, and, upon command, transmitting the information in encrypted form over the international telephone system to some central receiving station. That station could be at the IAEA's headquarters in Vienna or at some regional or local office of the IAEA.

Although in principle any kind of sensor could be monitored, for various political and technical reasons it was decided to limit the application to surveillance devices like cameras (for example, those observing the spent-fuel pools of power reactors) and seals. Further, because of the sensitivity of nations to the transmission of encrypted data of unknown content across their borders, it was agreed to monitor only the working status of the sensors, not the actual information they were collecting. Thus, in the case of a TV camera information on electrical power, light levels, tape advance, remaining tape capacity, and so forth, would be transmitted, but not the pictures themselves. This restriction, which limited the design of the system to a relatively narrow range of capabilities, was peculiar to the political situation of the IAEA and would not necessarily apply to the present case. Indeed, it is entirely possible that, as experience with remote monitoring accumulates, the initial restrictions on its use will be relaxed, even with the IAEA.

The system consisted of a microprocessor-based control unit located at the central station and sensors, monitoring units, and a multiplexer at the site. The control unit and the multiplexer were both equipped with modems for communication via the telephone system. The monitor units attached to each sensor would monitor its working status, storing the information and updating it frequently. Similarly, the multiplexer would query each monitor unit at some programmed frequency and store the information until interrogated in turn by the central station. Transmissions between the monitor units and the multiplexer and between the multiplexer and the central station were encrypted. The equipment at the site was designed to detect any attempts at tampering and would store and transmit such information along with the information on working status.

The control unit had a wide range of capabilities. It could automatically dial each facility on the network at some programmed average frequency with a certain degree of randomness, could store and display information in a variety of forms, and could analyze the information for significant anomalies (e.g., failure of equipment or tampering) that would cause an alert. Repeated failure to reach a facility would cause an alert.

The encryption feature served two purposes: authentication of the transmission and security. It is possible that in the present situation only authentication would be important. In that case, both parties could have the encryption key and monitor the transmissions but would not be able to alter them in any way without detection.

An evaluation of the RECOVER system was performed by Brookhaven National Laboratory and completed in 1983.[6] It concluded that, subject to the existing constraints of IAEA operation, the system would be cost-effective in certain situations.

A prototypical system having been developed and tested, further work on remote monitoring for safeguards is proceeding at Sandia National Laboratories and at BNL.

For the purpose of verifying a fissile-material production freeze, certain improvements and changes would have to be made in the RECOVER equipment. It would have to be adapted to new kinds of sensors. A capability for picture-taking and transmission might be desirable. Its memory and information-processing capabilities would have to be expanded, its transmission speed increased, and its reliability improved. The limitations of the international telephone system could be avoided by transmitting the information over dedicated lines or by satellite.

VERIFYING A PRODUCTION CUTOFF

Verifying a freeze on the production of fissile material for weapons in the United States and U.S.S.R. is both similar to and, in important ways, different from verifying the peaceful uses of nuclear energy in non-weapons states. The main similarity is that in both cases the disposition of fissile material must be verified; this suggests a form of material accounting, supplemented by surveillance techniques. Important differences are the acknowledged existence of nuclear-weapon programs and plants for the manufacture of the weapons, the atmosphere of hostility and suspicion between the two countries, the antipathy of the Soviet Union to inspections on its territory, and the amount of cheating that would have to occur to upset the strategic balance.

The problem is further complicated by the need in both countries for weapons-usable fissile material for non-explosive uses such as the fueling of shipboard and submarine reactors, research reactors, breeders, thermal reactors recycling plutonium, high-temperature gas-cooled reactors using highly enriched uranium, and miscellaneous research activities. Any agreement on freezing the production of fissile material for weapons would have to allow for these activities. Furthermore, if strategic nuclear weapons can be made with reactor-grade plutonium, the spent fuel of power reactors fueled with natural or low-enriched uranium would have to be monitored. Logically, a freeze on fissile-material production for weapons would require safeguards over all the peaceful U.S. and Soviet nuclear activities using or capable of producing weapons-usable material in substantial — that is, strategically significant — quantities. Research reactors and facilities handling only natural or low-enriched uranium or small quantities of plutonium and highly enriched uranium could be exempted. Uranium mines and mills would be monitored, if at all, only in order to detect gross increases in production of the feedstock for enrichment plants and production reactors (the IAEA does not now safeguard mines or mills.).

We now consider in briefest outline how the major facilities could be safeguarded. Obviously, before an actual system could be designed a much more detailed and quantitative analysis would have to be performed, taking into account the actual design of U.S. and Soviet facilities. Except for power reactors, very little about the latter is available in the open literature.

Production and Power Reactors

Because plutonium production reactors would be shut down, unless they were dual purpose, monitoring them is particularly simple and could be done primarily by remote means, with occasional visits by inspectors as a check. Radiation detectors located in or around a reactor would be an extremely sensitive means of detecting clandestine operation. Cooling systems could also be monitored. The thousands of megawatts of thermal power at which large production reactors operate would also make it easy to detect their infrared emissions from suitably equipped satellites, although this would not be part of the system we are describing.

Under a production ban power reactors and dual-purpose production-and-power reactors would continue to operate. It would be necessary to monitor only the spent fuel of uranium-fueled reactors. A spent-fuel assembly from a standard pressurized-water reactor (PWR) contains only 4 kg of plutonium at full burnup. Over 250 assemblies, corresponding to approximately four years of operation of a large PWR, would have to be diverted to get 1,000 kg of plutonium. In the near future there will be on the order of 100 power reactors in the United States. If the diversion were spread over all reactors, 2–3 fuel assemblies would have to be diverted from each reactor every year. Because current IAEA safeguards over power reactors are designed to detect the diversion of a single spent-fuel assembly, a diversion of such a magnitude would be obvious (even if the probability of detecting the diversion of the 2–3 assemblies in a single reactor were only 5%, the probability of detecting such a diversion in at least one of the 100 reactors would be better than 99%). Annual inspections of a day or two, together with accounting for spent-fuel shipments, should suffice. Monitoring the reactor power, which could be done remotely and which would verify fuel consumption, might also be desirable. If, as in the United States at present, spent fuel is stored indefinitely in the reactor pool, remote monitoring of that area might even eliminate the need for regular annual inspections. Instead, inspections might be triggered only by some anomaly in the transmitted surveillance record.

All power reactors in the United States are refueled during shutdown at intervals of roughly a year to eighteen months. Such reactors are relatively easy to safeguard, because the core fuel is accessible only during a shutdown and because fuel discharge occurs at relatively predictable and infrequent intervals. Approximately half the Soviet power reactors are of the graphite-moderated, on-line refueled type. Because fuel is being charged and discharged more or less continuously, safeguarding them is somewhat more complicated. The Canadian CANDU reactors, for example, which are also refueled on-line, have a rather elaborate safeguards system. However, the target quantities of plutonium are so much greater in the present case that this additional complication might not be necessary.

In addition to the spent fuel, the fresh fuel of thermal reactors using recycled plutonium and of breeder reactors, as well as of HTGRs fueled with highly enriched uranium, would need safeguarding. The annual fissile requirements of such reactors range from a few hundred kilograms to one or two metric tons. At present, there is little or no recycle in either country, and breeders, non-existent in the United States, are only at the demonstration stage in the Soviet Union. There is only one relatively small HTGR in the United States. The IAEA is developing safeguards approaches for these types of reactors. Since they are designed to detect the diversion of as little as 8 kg of plutonium or 25 kg of highly enriched uranium, they should be more than adequate for the present case. The IAEA approach is also designed to detect a diversion of fresh fuel at such reactors within two or three weeks of its occurrence, and consequently requires relatively frequent visits by inspectors. With the much higher target detection values for a production cutoff, it should be possible greatly to reduce this frequency. Power monitoring, for example, should provide an independent measure of fuel consumption with more than sufficient accuracy to detect operation at greatly reduced power to compensate for a massive diversion of fresh fuel.

Shipments of spent fuel from all reactors would have to be tracked to provide assurance that the shipped fuel had arrived either at a storage repository or at a reprocessing plant, both of which would have to be safeguarded also. The safeguarding of spent-fuel repositories is similar to that for the spent-fuel pool of reactors.

Reprocessing Plants

It would be necessary to monitor the throughput of spent-fuel reprocessing plants to ensure that plutonium is not being diverted from them.

The IAEA has a well-defined approach for safeguarding reprocessing plants. It is based on material accountancy and requires the essentially continuous presence of inspectors to sample and analyze all inputs and outputs. The inherent measurement uncertainties are such that a diversion of more than 1–2 percent of the annual throughput (extended, say, over a year) would be detected.[7] For a commercial reprocessing plant like the unfinished one at Barnwell, South Carolina (capacity 1,500 tonnes of heavy metal per year), one percent of the annual plutonium throughput would be, at most, 150 kg. The sensitivity of the IAEA's detection capability at such a plant would therefore be on the order of a few hundred kilograms of plutonium or better. If the plutonium throughput of the Soviet reprocessing plants is no larger than that of the Barnwell plant, a diversion of 1,000 kg per year would amount to at least 7% of the annual throughput, or about five times the IAEA's verification capability. In actuality, the concentration of plutonium in spent fuel from production reactors is at least an order of magnitude lower than that in spent power-reactor fuel. The plutonium throughput of military reprocessing plants is therefore likely to be correspondingly lower (although the uranium throughput may be similar) and, other things being equal, the absolute uncertainty in the material balance correspondingly smaller. A diversion of 1,000 kg of plutonium in one year should therefore be easily detected. Current IAEA inspection frequencies could probably be much reduced by following only the feed of fuel elements to the plant, which has to follow a well-defined path, and the withdrawal of the plutonium product by means of automatic sensors located at the head-end and product end of the plant. For example, cameras could monitor the receiving pool and the fuel-assembly shear, and electromanometers the liquid levels in the plutonium nitrate storage tanks. These, also, could be monitored remotely.

There is an important reservation in this analysis. It assumes that the reprocessing plants are designed for accurate measurement of the flows of fissile material through them. Current U.S. accountability regulations for commercial reprocessing plants (of which none are operating in the United States at present) call for even better performance than that assumed above, and the Japanese reprocessing plant at Tokai-Mura, which has a capacity of 210 tonnes of spent fuel per year, can also meet those standards. However, older military plants may not be designed for good accountability measurements, and we have no knowledge at all about this aspect of the design of Soviet plants. Still, one would expect that if only for reasons of good management and operational safety, the measurement system would be good enough for the purposes discussed here.

Plutonium and Highly Fabricated Uranium-Fuel Fabrication Plants

Plutonium-fuel fabrication plants will have capacities sized, in the aggregate, to accommodate all or most of the output of the reprocessing plants. These activities do not lend themselves so well to remote monitoring, but because their feedstock comes from the reprocessing plant whose withdrawals should be verified, it should be necessary only to verify their total annual production of fuel assemblies and inventories of in-process material. Verification of the fuel assemblies would probably require only a few visits per year. At one of these the inventory of in-process materials could also be verified. As before, the necessary accuracies are easily achievable.

Similar considerations apply to fabrication plants for highly enriched uranium fuel, except that their feed will come from enrichment plants. At present the total non-military use of highly enriched uranium probably amounts to less than a ton a year in the United States, and Soviet usage is probably even smaller. Plants fabricating fuel for propulsion (e.g., submarine) reactors would most likely not be safeguarded, since the manufacturing process, the design of the fuel, and the production capacities are all classified. It would therefore be necessary to verify at the enrichment plant that the output of highly enriched uranium intended for use in propulsion reactors does not exceed some mutually agreed-upon level. It is estimated that U.S. production for this purpose is approximately four tonnes per year,[2] or two-thirds the target quantity.

Enrichment Plants

The safeguarding of enrichment plants is complicated by classification problems and their sheer size and complexity, as well as by the accessibility to the operation of all parts of the process, made possible by the relatively low radiation levels (as compared with a reprocessing plant).[8] This latter feature permits changes in configuration and operation to be made relatively easily, changes which might not be detected unless inspectors are granted adequate access. Also, the IAEA has very little experience with safeguarding enrichment plants, especially very large ones, and is only now developing an approach for centrifuge enrichment plants.

Little, if anything, has been published in the open literature about Soviet enrichment plants; presumably they are all of the gaseous-diffusion type. The discussion will therefore be based on the characteristics of American plants.

At present all enriched uranium produced in the United States comes from diffusion plants. These are designed to produce either low- or high-enriched uranium (LEU and HEU, respectively), or both.

A diffusion plant designed to produce only LEU will have approximately 1,200 enrichment stages. Such a plant could, in principle, be "stretched" to produce, at maximum, a 60%-enriched product, which would then have to be recycled for enrichment to 90% or more. Operation in this fashion would reduce the plant's output to nearly zero. Multiple-batch recycle of product to the feed point would also be extremely time-consuming. In addition, the presence of HEU in the upper stages could be detected by appropriate radiation detectors. Although these could be monitored remotely, frequent (and possibly unannounced) visits by inspectors might be necessary to ensure that they were not being shielded from the radiation they were supposed to detect. Given such access, the safeguarding of such plants against surreptitious conversion to HEU production should be straightforward.

The U.S. diffusion plant at Portsmouth, Ohio, produces both LEU and HEU. It has a separative capacity of 7,300 metric tons of separative work units per year (as of 1976). The maximum possible HEU output of such a plant would be 30,000 kg per year. The strategically significant quantity of HEU we are concerned about is therefore 20% of this, or probably much larger compared to the present actual HEU production.

A relatively intrusive regime of inspection by the IAEA employing isotopic tracers (U-236) could verify the annual material balance of a Portsmouth-size plant with an uncertainty on the order of 1,000 kg of U-235. Such a regime would involve measurement of the gas-phase inventory, which is currently classified. It would also involve frequent visits by inspectors. If this were acceptable to both parties, there is no question that the production and diversion of 6,000 kg of HEU could be detected. However, this technique could not be used if there is substantial recycle of uranium from reactors, since such uranium would already have large amounts of U-236.

Assurance might also be obtained by a combination of tamper-proofed on-line instrumentation and remote monitoring. For example, the gas pressures in the upper portion of the cascade could be monitored, since increased HEU production would require greater flows and therefore higher pressures. However, these pressures are also classified.

Increasing the HEU production rate of a cascade would also alter the relationship between feed and tails (for full HEU production feed and tails are very nearly equal). Remotely monitored on-line instruments might measure both the flow and assay of these two streams with more than adequate precision, provided measures were taken to preclude undeclared feed. Such an alternative might be preferable on classification grounds to those suggested above.

The design of centrifuge enrichment plants, currently under construction in the United States, Western Europe, and Japan, is quite different, of course, but similar safeguards techniques can be employed. The LEU cascades would be separate from the HEU cascades, unlike the situation in diffusion plants, where there is only a single large cascade. The HEU cascades would have three times as many stages as the LEU cascades, but would use the same feed points. It would be difficult to use the LEU part of the plant to produce HEU, because that would require multiple recycle. As in the gaseous-diffusion case, the operation of the LEU cascade to produce HEU could be detected by monitoring the feed and tails or by the use of HEU radiation detectors (in the latter case, with the same caveat concerning inspector access to guard against shielding of the detectors).

One scenario that might be of concern is the surreptitious use of excess capacity in a centrifuge plant to produce HEU. This could be detected either by sensing the operation of supposedly idle machines or the positions of supposedly closed valves. Either of these would lend itself to remote monitoring.

Not considered here is the monitoring of advanced isotopic enrichment techniques, such as those employing laser excitation. Preliminary approaches to safeguarding these have been developed in the United States. They are designed with present IAEA inspection goals in mind, so that one may be optimistic about their application in the case under consideration here.

Plutonium and Highly Enriched Uranium Stores

Verification of a production freeze would be incomplete if it did not also include plutonium and HEU in stockpiles outside actual weapons. If for no other reason than the inevitable mismatch between production and use, these are bound to occur. The two parties would have to declare the size of these stockpiles and be confident that the initial declaration could be verified, presumably through intelligence estimates. The verification of these declarations is a crucial point, but obviously outside the scope of the present discussion.

Once declared, the stockpiles would have to be subjected to periodic inspection. One possibility would be to place them under an international storage regime similar to the International Plutonium Storage concept (IPS), which has been under discussion at the IAEA for the past several years.[9] Under this concept, the purpose of which is to prevent stockpiling of excess plutonium in the peaceful nuclear program of member states, custody of the material would be the joint responsibility of the IAEA and the host state, and release of material for use would be subject to certain ground rules to ensure that it would be for peaceful purposes.

Under storage conditions, the safeguarding of the material would be particularly simple. If the stores were relatively inactive, a combination of remote monitoring and occasional visits by inspectors would probably be adequate. For large active stores, more frequent, possibly even continuous, inspector presence might be necessary.

No agreement has been reached on IPS among the member states of the IAEA. However, impetus might be given to the establishment of the concept if it were deemed to be useful in the present context. As with the other measures discussed here, such a development would also strengthen the nonproliferation regime.

CONCLUSIONS

From the foregoing discussion and with certain reservations it seems clear that a freeze on the production of fissile materials for weapons could readily be verified to within an acceptable uncertainty by techniques and approaches already developed or under development for international safeguards. Those reservations have to do with how much confidence could be placed in declarations of the size of stockpiles of plutonium and highly enriched uranium not in actual warheads, the design of Soviet reprocessing and enrichment plants (of which little is known), and the extent to which classification policies might impair the effectiveness of safeguards at enrichment plants. Resolution of the last question is particularly important for the verification of the amount of HEU going to submarine propulsion reactors.

A considerable part of the instrumentation needed for safeguarding plutonium-processing plants and enrichment plants has been developed by the various safeguards research and development groups at Los Alamos National Laboratory[10] and other laboratories throughout the world. The combination of on-line measurement or surveillance instruments and remote monitoring along the lines of the RECOVER concept could probably greatly reduce the need for frequent inspector presence, an important advantage when safeguarding installations like enrichment and reprocessing plants having national security significance.

Considerable development would still have to be undertaken to adapt the remote-monitoring equipment and the sensors to the somewhat different conditions being envisaged here. In particular, to avoid frequent false alarms, equipment would have to be designed to operate reliably for long periods of time, unattended, and tamper-proofing would have to be highly developed. These improvements would probably only call for a relatively straightforward extrapolation of the present development.

New methods for producing weapons-usable fissile material and expansion of old ones may complicate the picture. Examples are laser enrichment, the plutonium breeder, and high-temperature gas-cooled reactors fueled with highly enriched uranium. However, there is no a priori reason to believe that these, and others, could not be safeguarded at the necessary levels of assurance.

The conclusion seems inescapable that a complete verification scheme would require the application of safeguards to almost the entire peaceful nuclear programs of both parties. On this basis alone the IAEA would seem to be the logical choice for the role of verification. Such a choice would go a long way towards reducing the resentment over the present unequal treatment accorded weapons and non-weapons states under the NPT.[1]

Before a freeze could be implemented, a number of basic questions would have to be resolved. Among these are what sensitivity to cheating the verification system should have (Von Hippel and Levi[2] merely suggest some possibilities), how certain and timely detection should be, what balance should be struck between on-site inspection and other means of verification, and how to respond to suspicious or anomalous indications. Controversy over these questions, essentially having to do with the degree of assurance one expects from the system, has marked the development of the international safeguards system and continues to this day. As in that enterprise, critics may hypothesize conceivable but barely credible worst-case scenarios in order to discredit the system, or, for perceived reasons of security or to gain an advantage, may try to emasculate it. However, it should be kept in mind that a production cutoff of fissile material for weapons would only be a part, and a redundant part at that, of a freeze on the production and development of the weapons themselves. Verification of both kinds of activities, although employing very different approaches, would be mutually supportive.

REFERENCES

1. Epstein, William. A Ban on the Production of Fissionable Material for Weapons. *Scientific American*, 243, no. 1 (July, 1980).
2. von Hippel, F. and B. Levi. *Verification of Cutoff in the Production of Plutonium and Highly-Enriched Uranium for Nuclear Weapons*, Chapter 22 in this volume.
3. IAEA/SG/INF 3. *IAEA Safeguards, An Introduction.* Vienna: International Atomic Energy Agency, 1981; see also INFCE/SEC/11. *The Present Status of IAEA Safeguards on Nuclear Fuel Cycle Facilities*, IAEA, 1979.
4. INFCIRC/153 (Corrected). *The Structure and Content of Agreements between the Agency and States Required in Connection with the Treaty on the Non-Proliferation of Nuclear Weapons*, paragraphs 29 and 30. Vienna: IAEA, 1972.
5. Prokoski, F. J. Global Monitoring of International Nuclear Safeguards. In *Proceedings of the Fifth International Conference on Computer Communication*, Atlanta, GA, October 27–30, 1980.
6. Weinstock, E. V. and J. B. Sunborn. ISPO-198. *An Evaluation of a Remote, Continual Verification System RECOVER, for International Safeguards.* Prepared for the Office Safeguards and Security of the U.S. Department of Energy, Washington, DC, May, 1983.
7. Higinbotham, W. A. and L. G. Fishbone. *Case Study: Application of the Safeguards Assessment Methodology to a Medium Sized Reprocessing Plant.* Forthcoming Brookhaven National Laboratory report, Brookhaven, NY.
8. U.S. contribution to Working Group 2 of the International Nuclear Fuel Cycle Evaluation. *Safeguards Considerations for Uranium Enrichment Facilities, As Applied to Gas Centrifuge and Gaseous Diffusion Facilities*, March 1, 1979.
9. IAEA-IPS/SG/61. *Draft Final Report of Working Group on IPS and Safeguards of the Expert Group on International Plutonium Storage.* Vienna, December 18, 1981.
10. Keepin, G. Robert. *State-of-the-Art Technology for Measurement and Verification of Nuclear Materials.* Chapter 21 in this volume.

21.

State-of-the-Art Technology for Measurement and Verification of Nuclear Materials

G. Robert Keepin

INTRODUCTION

Modern technology plays an increasingly important role in the ability of regulatory bodies such as the IAEA to account for the growing quantities of nuclear material under safeguards, including the more complicated forms and composition of nuclear materials used in the expanding fuel cycle activities of many different nations. A broad range of techniques and methods is now available for the detection, identification, assay, and verification of special nuclear materials (notably ^{239}Pu and ^{235}U) in various configurations and in a variety of physical and chemical forms. In this discussion, we shall focus on a selected group of state-of-the-art instruments and techniques that are used by the International Atomic Energy Agency (IAEA) in carrying out its worldwide safeguards inspection and verification responsibilities. With regard to the topic of the verification of arms control treaties, it appears reasonable that much of this new technology and experience could ultimately find application to a broad range of problems that may arise — in whatever context — in the future involving the inspection, verification and control of nuclear materials. For the present purpose this new technology will be examined in the context of nuclear materials safeguards measurement and accounting, as it is this professional discipline that has provided the major impetus and ongoing support for the development and implementation of modern safeguards methods and techniques, including the so-called "near-real-time" monitoring and materials accounting and control systems.[1,2]

Nuclear materials measurement and accounting is unique among safeguards and security measures in that it alone enables a direct and independent determination of the amount and location of the nuclear material in a plant at any given time. Such a capability for determining the nuclear material inventory with adequate sensitivity and timeliness thus can provide an overall quantitative check on the combined effectiveness of all other safeguards, security, and control measures at a facility. This unique role of measurement and accounting has led over the years to increasingly stringent requirements being placed on measurement capabilities (i.e., with respect to timeliness, accuracy, and detection sensitivity) for all types of nuclear materials; this in turn has led to the development and implementation of a new measurement technology—now commonly known as nondestructive assay, or simply "NDA."

NDA MEASUREMENT TECHNOLOGY AND INSTRUMENTATION

NDA techniques are especially well-suited for nuclear materials measurement and verification applications under the following frequently encountered conditions: (a) when there are problems in obtaining representative samples for chemical analysis (e.g., in heterogeneous solids, material in sealed containers, spatially distributed material, or valuable finished products); (b) when many repetitive measurements are needed (e.g., incoming material at receiving stations, material in process lines, waste streams, etc.); (c) when timely material accounting is needed (e.g., material balance must be closed in hours rather than days or weeks); and, in general, (d) when it is necessary to reduce inspection manpower and effort while maintaining (or even increasing) overall verification effectiveness.

NDA instruments, methods, and techniques complement and in some cases supplant the traditional destructive assay methods of analytical chemistry. NDA techniques fall into two major categories, active and passive. Active assay involves irradiation with neutrons or photons to induce fissions in the sample. The resulting neutron or gamma-ray "signatures" are interpreted to determine quantitatively the amount of fissionable material present. Passive assay uses naturally occurring gamma-ray and/or neutron radiations as direct signatures of fissionable materials.

NDA methods are being developed and applied to various aspects of inspection, assay, and accountability of fissionable materials found throughout the nuclear fuel cycle. NDA instruments range in size and complexity from small portable units (e.g., as small as a carry-on suitcase) for use by safeguards inspectors in on-site verification of nuclear materials, to large in-site NDA systems designed for routine in-plant use, for example, by plant operators, subject to independent authentication by IAEA and State System inspectors.[3,4] When and as appropriate, measurement results can be formatted for direct input to a computerized "near-real-time" materials accounting and control system, for instance, the so-called DYMAC (for Dynamic Materials Control) system, or other advanced nuclear material control systems. Such systems can serve not only the needs of safeguards and materials management, but also of plant process and quality control, criticality safety, and radiological protection.

A classification of NDA techniques into passive and active gamma ray and neutron methods and calorimetry is shown in block diagram form[4] in Figure 21.1. In the following section, some of the more important NDA techniques are described briefly and illustrated by specific instruments presently in use or in advanced stages of development, test, and in-field evaluation.

PASSIVE GAMMA-RAY METHODS

All isotopes of uranium and plutonium are radioactive and decay by alpha emission, beta emission, or spontaneous fission. Following either alpha or beta emission, each isotope decays by emission of characteristic gamma rays according to a unique decay scheme. Table 21.1 lists some of the gamma-ray energies and emission rates for uranium, plutonium, and americium isotopes that are commonly used for the NDA of these nuclear materials.

There are two main kinds of gamma-ray detectors: scintillation counters (usually activated sodium iodide crystals—NaI) and semiconductor detectors (e.g., lithium drifted germanium Ge(Li) or high purity germanium

Table 21.1. Uranium, Plutonium, and Americium Gamma-Ray Characteristics

Isotope	Half-life (years)	Activity Level (Ci/g)	Principal Gamma Rays (keV)	Emission Rate (gamma rays/s/g)
^{235}U	7.04×10^8		185.7	4.5×10^4
^{238}U	4.47×10^9		766.4	39
			1000.1	103
^{238}Pu	87.79	17.1	152.8	6.4×10^6
			766.4	1.5×10^5
			1000.1	8.2×10^3
^{239}Pu	24,082	0.0621	129.3	1.4×10^5
			375.0	3.6×10^4
			413.7	3.5×10^4
^{240}Pu	6,537	0.228	160.4	3.5×10^4
			642.3	1.2×10^3
^{241}Pu	14.35	103.4	148.6	7.3×10^6
^{242}Pu	3.79×10^5	0.0039	none	
^{241}Am	434.1	3.42	368.6	2.6×10^5
			662.4	4.4×10^5

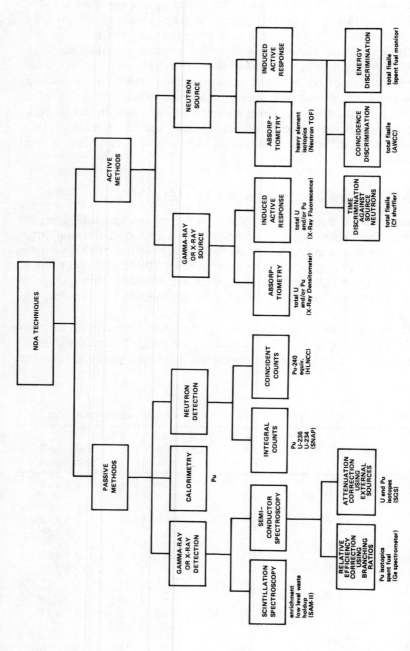

FIGURE 21.1. Classification of nondestructive assay (NDA) techniques for measurement and verification of nuclear materials. (Source: U.S. Department of Energy, *Proceedings, International Training Course on Implementation of State Systems of Accounting for and Control of Nuclear Materials*, Report LA-9609-C, December 1982.)

crystals — Ge). The NaI detectors have low energy resolution, but have much higher detection efficiency than Ge detectors.

Gamma-ray measurements using the so-called "enrichment meter" principle are based on the fact that for fixed detector-sample geometry and for samples that are thick relative to the penetration depth of the 186 KeV ^{235}U gamma rays, the count rate due to 186 KeV gamma rays is proportional to enrichment. One such in-line instrument has been in service for many years measuring UF_6 product enrichment at the Portsmouth Gaseous Diffusion Plant in the United States.

A more recent example of NDA instrumentation for UF_6 enrichment measurement, for example, in gas centrifuge enrichment plants, is the gas phase enrichment monitor (GPEM). This instrument is designed to make measurements on UF_6 samples taken from the usual plant sampling points in feed, product, and tails lines. A UF_6 sample cylinder is connected to the monitor and the UF_6 is allowed to evaporate into the previously evacuated measurement chamber of the GPEM. The total uranium content of the UF_6 gas within the measurement chamber is determined by measuring the attenuation of the 59.5 KeV gamma rays from an ^{241}Am source placed beneath the chamber; the gamma rays traverse the chamber to reach a $5'' \times 1''$ NaI detector placed directly above it. Measurement of the principal gamma ray from the decay of ^{235}U at 185.7 KeV provides an accurate estimate of the total ^{235}U content of the sample. Thus, from a comparison of the two count rates in the same NaI detector, the enrichment of the UF_6 sample can be determined. The system must be calibrated with standards previously measured by mass spectrometric methods; measurement accuracies are in the range $\pm 1\%$ using a minimum sample size of 3 g and a counting time of 1,000 seconds. The entire process of sample handling and measurement is under the control of a portable computer (HP-85), with interactive software that guides the user through every stage of the operating sequence and calculates both sample enrichment and its uncertainty.

High resolution gamma-ray spectrometry (using intrinsic Ge and Ge(Li) detectors) can be used for the accurate measurement of isotopic ratios, for example, in Pu samples and in spent-fuel fission products. In recent years, portable high resolution spectrometers have become available through the advent of intrinsic Ge detectors (which can be transported at room temperature) and the development of compact battery-powered multichannel analyzers. Such a unit, the "portable mini-MCA" (PMCA), uses an intrinsic Ge detector; the PMCA can also be used with a NaI detector. Communication between the operator and the instrument is via a keyboard and LCD (liquid crystal diode) display, with interactive software that prompts the operator at all necessary steps in setting up and running the instrument. The relevant computer programs can be written on interchangeable read-only memories (ROMs). With appropriate standards and calibration procedures, the PMCA is used to measure U enrichment as well as ^{235}U content in various physical and chemical forms of nuclear materials. For well-characterized feed and product materials, an enrichment measurement together with weighing can be used to verify total ^{235}U content of materials to within 1 or 2%. Used in conjunction with small intrinsic Germanium detectors (e.g., < 1 cc), the PMCA can also provide rapid, positive identification for various uranium and plutonium samples, coupons, foils, pellets, etc. In general, the PMCA provides an extremely valuable tool for in-field verification of both U and Pu content in many different types of feed, product, scrap, and waste materials.

Another high resolution gamma spectroscopy system is based on the plutonium isotopic analysis unit (PIAU), which is used with a multichannel analyzer. This system provides an independent field capability for determining plutonium isotopic composition from high-resolution gamma spectra (accumulated at counting rates up to ~ 30,000 c/s). The PIAU guides the operator through the measurement procedure by requesting appropriate actions to be taken and indicating when erroneous entries are made by the user or poor gamma-ray spectra are obtained. Once a suitable gamma-ray spectrum has been accumulated and the user has identified the approximate channel position of two easily identified gamma-ray peaks (148 KeV ^{241}Pu and 208 KeV ^{241}Pu [via α decay to ^{237}U]), the complete plutonium isotopic analysis is generated automatically together with estimated uncertainties. Resulting accuracies in Pu isotopic ratios (weight fractions) are typically the order of 1% for ^{239}Pu and ^{241}Pu. Gamma-ray spectra can also be stored on magnetic tape cassettes for later analysis.

An important application of high-resolution gamma (or x-ray) spectrometry that is proving useful in the assay of plutonium in solutions is the K-edge densitometer (KEDG). This technique is used to determine the (elemental) plutonium concentration in a sample by measuring the transmission of the sample at x-ray energies just above and below the K-absorption edge for Pu. Measurements are made with a high-resolution gamma-ray detector, external radiation sources, and suitable collimators for viewing the sample. For a K-edge assay of Pu concentration, the sample transmission is measured at 121.1 KeV (^{75}Se isotopic source) and 122.1 KeV (^{57}Co isotopic source), which closely bracket the 121.76 KeV absorption edge for plutonium. Measurement precisions on the order of 0.5% can be obtained in a 30-minute assay. K-edge (or L-edge) densitometers are presently in routine use for measuring product solutions at some reprocessing facilities, for example, in Japan at PNC, Tokai, and in the United States at the Savannah River plant.

Very recently a new "compact K-edge densitometer" (CKED) has been developed that permits concentration measurements on Pu samples in glove boxes without breaching or affecting in any way the glove box containment. The CKED unit is introduced into the glove box via the glove envelope, which is kept fully intact while at the same time permitting a fixed sample-source-detector geometry. A simple hand-operated lever permits the operator to remotely turn "on" and "off" the ^{57}Co and ^{75}Se isotopic sources required for the densitometer transmission measurements. All necessary calculations for calibration (e.g., with a standard Pu foil) and for determination of Pu concentration directly in grams/liters are readily carried out using the Portable Mini-MCA Unit (PMCA) with interactive software written specifically for the compact K-edge densitometer.

A method that holds promise for future safeguards applications is x-ray fluorescence. For many years, x-ray fluorescence has been used as a laboratory tool for chemical (elemental) analysis based on the fact that characteristic x-ray energies depend on atomic number. Most previous applications used electron bombardment to produce the characteristic K or L x-rays; hence, careful sample preparation was required, much as is the case for alpha particle counting. More recently, low-energy gamma-rays (or x-rays) from isotopic sources or alternatively from x-ray generators have been used as the excitation source, allowing measurement of plutonium and uranium in their existing containers. X-ray fluorescence has been shown to have high precision over a wide dynamic range of U and Pu concentrations. In mixed U-Pu solutions, the method is capable of giving an accurate determination of the Pu/U ratio. This, combined with a K-edge concentration measurement on Pu, can provide accurate assays of the individual concentrations of both U and Pu; such a "hybrid" NDA technique is currently being evaluated (at the Transuranium Institute, Karlsruhe in the Federal Republic of Germany) for the in-situ assay of both U and Pu content in the spent fuel dissolver tank at the head end of a reprocessing plant.

PASSIVE NEUTRON METHODS

Neutrons originating in nuclear materials are primarily due to (a) spontaneous fission (largely in Pu-238, 240, and 242) and (b) α, n reactions in light elements (e.g., in oxides and fluorides or in B, Be or Li impurities). Passive neutron measurements can be influenced by neutron multiplication in the sample and by the presence of neutron moderators, reflectors, and absorbers in or near the sample. Unlike gamma rays, neutrons readily penetrate high-Z materials; this makes neutron techniques invaluable for assaying large heterogeneous samples or other dense configurations containing plutonium. Neutron detection involves straightforward counting of neutron-induced events rather than comparatively sophisticated gamma-ray spectroscopy, so passive-neutron-based NDA equipment is generally simpler and easier to use in the field than high-resolution gamma-ray equipment. The most frequently used neutron detector for NDA instrumentation is the He^3 or $^{10}BF_3$ filled gas proportional counter, chosen for relatively high neutron detection efficiency, insensitivity to gamma rays, reliability, and long-term stability. Although passive neutrons can be detected either as single counts ("gross neutron counting") or as coincident neutron counts ("coincidence neutron counting"), the latter is generally preferred because coincidence methods are less sensitive to variations in low-Z matrix materials and to changes in neutron background.

The high level neutron coincidence counter (HLNC) is widely used for the assay of bulk plutonium samples ranging from a few grams to ~ 5 kg, and ^{240}Pu content from a few percent to ~ 30%. The HLNC consists of a detector chamber with 18 ^3He counters in a hexagonal polyethylene shield, an electronics unit (using so-called "shift register" coincidence counting to accommodate the high counting rates from very large Pu samples), and a programmable calculator or portable computer. Coincidence counting detects the neutrons from spontaneous fission of ^{240}Pu and other even-mass Pu isotopes, while discriminating against α,n neutrons in the sample. The quantity actually measured by the HLNC is "^{240}Pu effective," defined as $2.49\ ^{238}Pu + 1.0\ ^{240}Pu + 1.57\ ^{242}Pu$. Total plutonium is then calculated from plutonium isotopic composition, for example, as determined from high-resolution gamma-ray spectroscopy. When standards are available with similar characteristics to the unknown, measurement accuracies using the HLNC are the order of 1%–5%.

The utility of the basic HLNC coincidence system has been further extended by the development of a number of specialized detector heads. Thus, detectors have been designed for NDA of plutonium in critically safe "birdcage" containers (BCNC counter), for fast critical assembly fuel assemblies in the "channel counter" (CNCC), for FBR fuel pins stored in trays (FPTC counter), and for NDA of small inventory samples (INVS). The inventory sample counter (INVS) is used to verify the plutonium content in small inventory samples such as PuO_2 powder, MOX pellets, and Pu nitrate solutions.

ACTIVE NEUTRON METHODS

The successful application of neutron coincidence counting techniques using the shift register principle developed for the high level neutron coincidence counter led to other major applications of neutron coincidence counting, including the active well coincidence counter (AWCC), for assay of ^{235}U content in enriched uranium materials. Two neutron sources (AmLi, each ~ 5×10^4 n/s) located above and below the sample well are used to interrogate the sample, and the induced fission reactions are counted with standard HLNC coincidence electronics. Coincidence counting effectively discriminates against single neutrons from the AmLi sources while detecting coincident neutrons from neutron-induced fissions in the ^{235}U present in the sample. The AWCC is used to measure bulk UO_2 samples, high-enrichment uranium metals, LWR fuel pellets, and ^{233}U-Th fuel materials having high gamma-ray backgrounds. The AWCC can also be applied to the assay of MTR (high-enriched ^{235}U) fuel assemblies. Use of AWCC to verify total ^{235}U content can provide an important advantage over gamma-ray techniques for some applications — for example, for large and/or dense heterogeneous samples, the high penetrability of the neutrons makes the assay results dependent on the entire ^{235}U content of the samples rather than just the surface layer. Typically, highly enriched uranium samples can be assayed with overall accuracies of 3%–5% in amounts up to several kg of ^{235}U.

It has long been recognized that a suitable NDA instrument for determining the plutonium content of fast breeder reactor (FBR) fuel assemblies would be of tremendous value to nuclear safeguards and materials control. It now appears that this need is met by the newly developed universal FBR assembly counter (UFBC), which is yet another outgrowth of the HLNC family of neutron coincidence counters. The unique feature of the UFBC instrument is that in addition to the usual passive measurement of ^{240}Pu-effective, the fissile Pu content (and thereby total plutonium) in an FBR fuel assembly can also be obtained through an active "self-interrogation" technique, as follows. When the UFBC is operated in the active mode, spontaneous fission neutrons from the Pu in the assembly are moderated and reflected back into the assembly to induce fission reactions in the fissile component of the fuel. The emitted fission neutrons then provide a signal that is proportional to the amount of fissile material (odd-numbered Pu isotopes) present in the assembly. To determine the fraction of neutrons resulting from the reflection process, the albedo, or reflection characteristics, of the boundary surrounding the assembly is changed by inserting or removing a cadmium liner. In effect, with the Cd in place the system operates like the HLNC to measure even-numbered Pu isotopes; with the Cd removed, thermalized neutrons are reflected back into the assembly and produce additional fissions, thus giving a measure of the fissile (odd-numbered) isotopes of plutonium. In particular, it has been shown that the difference in the coincidence rates with and without Cd divided by the total neutron emission rate is a linear function of the fissile content of the assembly, essentially independent of the location of the fissile material within the assembly (i.e., the self-multiplication of FBR reactor fuel assemblies is sufficiently high to propagate surface fission reactions into the interior of the assembly and provide essentially uniform response from fissile material throughout the interior of the assembly).

In general, the neutron "self-interrogation" technique described above can be applied to high-mass samples or configurations of pure Pu and/or

Pu compounds such as Pu nitrate or Pu oxide, including all types of mixed-oxide fuel assemblies. The major requirements are that the sample must have: (a) a reasonably strong self-source of neutrons (e.g., $10^5 - 10^6$ n/s); (b) a well-defined geometry; and (c) good geometrical coupling of the reflected neutrons back into the sample, thereby providing sufficient flux of interrogating neutrons for the active mode assay of fissile material (odd isotopes). In summary, the neutron self-interrogation method, using appropriately optimized detector efficiency and neutron "die-away" characteristics together with coincidence counting to enhance both sample penetrability and uniform fissile response, provides a significant new NDA capability for monitoring and verification of plutonium in various chemical and physical forms and configurations.

Before leaving the general subject of neutron coincidence counting, it should be noted that neutron coincidence and associated "neutron multiplicity" data, properly analyzed, can also provide information on the so-called "neutron multiplication" (i.e., state of "reactivity") of a given unknown. For the present purposes, suffice it to say that appropriate combinations of neutron coincidence counting and unique gamma-ray "signatures" can provide incisive means for analyzing and characterizing the general nature of an unknown or obscure configuration, object, enclosure, and so forth, that has been found or is suspected to contain special nuclear material (whether ^{239}Pu, ^{235}U, ^{233}U, or a combination thereof).

OTHER NDA TECHNIQUES

Cerenkov Glow Observation

Observation of the Cerenkov radiation from irradiated reactor fuel elements provides a valuable tool for qualitative verification of spent fuel in storage pools. Electro-optical night vision devices incorporate an image intensifier tube that requires ambient lighting to be reduced to suitably low levels. The Cerenkov radiation (produced by the interaction of the intense radiation from the spent fuel with the water of the storage pool) varies in intensity and for highly active fuel can be seen in darkness with the naked eye. For fuel with low burnup and/or long cooling time, the glow is of very low intensity, but is readily seen using the light-amplifying capability of the night vision device. Qualitative verification (attribute test) of the fuel stored in a pool can be quickly and easily accomplished by scanning rows of assemblies from the pool bridge. Characteristic patterns formed by the arrangements of rods and holes in fuel assemblies can readily be seen. Current development work is aimed at an improved version of the night vision device (e.g., using appropriate light filters) that can be used under normal lighting conditions.

Gross Gamma-Ray and Neutron Measurements on Spent Fuel

There is at present no practical technique available for direct measurement of plutonium content in spent fuel at a reactor site. High-resolution gamma-ray spectrometry can be combined with ionization chamber measurements of gross gamma rays from spent fuel to infer burnup and cooling time for comparison against operator calculations (when these are made available to a safeguards inspector); however, in actual practice this technique is seldom if ever used because of the operational procedures and measurement time required. An alternative NDA technique involving considerably simpler equipment and procedures is the ION-1 gamma/neutron detector that uses fission chambers to measure gross neutron emission and ion chambers to measure gross gamma emission from a spent fuel assembly. These hybrid gamma/neutron measurements can be correlated with the operator's declared burnup and time-since-discharge ("cooling time") of the spent fuel assembly to provide, in effect, an independent verification of the operator's declared values. The water-tight detector "fork" incorporating the gamma-ray and neutron detectors is positioned along the side of the fuel assembly, and the measurement takes place underwater (e.g., in a spent fuel storage pool) with only minimal movement of the fuel from the storage position. The primary application of ION-1 is the measurement and verification of spent reactor fuels stored at a reactor site or in away-from-reactor storage pools.

Weight Verification

The weight of items containing nuclear materials is an important quantity to be independently verified for safeguards and materials-control purposes. In many cases this can be accomplished by verifying the calibration of a facility operator's weighing system using standard weights, but in the case of very large items such as uranium hexafluoride (UF_6) cylinders, this is not feasible. This problem has been resolved by the development of a transportable load-cell-based system (LCBS) for weighing large, heavy objects such as uranium hexafluoride (UF_6) product cylinders. The load cell senses the weight of the suspended product cylinder, and the results are displayed by an electronic readout unit. After assembly and set-up (requiring ~20-30 minutes), weighing time is typically 3 to 5 minutes per cylinder with an accuracy of better than ±1 kg.

CONTAINMENT AND SURVEILLANCE

Although the emphasis in this paper is on NDA measurement techniques as applied to material accountancy and control, nevertheless containment and surveillance clearly do provide important complementary measures for nuclear safeguards, so we note briefly here some selected recent developments in the area of containment and surveillance techniques.

Optical surveillance systems are in widespread use for monitoring the movements of nuclear materials and for maintaining continuous observation of stored materials, mainly in the spent fuel areas of nuclear reactors. Of the two optical surveillance techniques, photographic surveillance and television surveillance, the latter is preferred in cases where light levels are low, radiation levels are sufficient to fog film, a high picture capacity is required, or there is an immediate playback requirement — for instance, to provide quick detection of any anomalies. TV surveillance units have been greatly improved since their first introduction and are now equipped with new cassette video recorders. Each control unit is capable of running two TV cameras, and the images can be combined, if desired, on a split-screen monitor, with recording at selected intervals. Date and time annotation are provided, and the cameras can be located up to 500 meters from the control console. At present TV systems are roughly an order of magnitude more expensive than film cameras, but the rapid advances currently being made in TV technology can soon be expected to make TV surveillance fully competitive with film systems.

An advanced TV surveillance system (STAR) is currently being introduced into field use for IAEA safeguards. The STAR system is a microprocessor-controlled system using solid state TV cameras with provision for backup and slave cassette video recorders. Recording can be initiated by a motion detector, as well as at timed intervals. Time and date information is recorded on each frame. Images are stored temporarily on video discs before being copied to a cassette video recorder. In addition to the STAR system, a compact TV surveillance unit (CTVS) is currently being evaluated for IAEA safeguards use as a successor to the present photo-surveillance units and for a wide variety of monitoring applications (both short term and long term). The new CTVS unit includes a scene counter, event counter, time and date indicator, and provision for connection of a second video tape recorder.

With regard to safeguards seals and sealing systems, three basic components are involved: (a) the containment enclosing the nuclear material to be safeguarded, (b) the means of applying the seal (e.g., a metal wire), and (c) the seal itself. All three components must be examined in order to verify that the sealing system has fulfilled its function of assuring continuity of knowledge about the identity and quantity of the nuclear material concerned. The IAEA presently uses conventional metallic cap seals (Type "E" and "X") and adhesive label seals (for short-term applications); current developments are aimed at producing a seal that is uniquely identifiable and verifiable in the field. One advanced prototype is the fibre optic seal (FBOS), which employs a multi-strand plastic fibre-optic loop whose ends are enclosed in the seal. The seal unit is configured so that a unique random pattern of fibres is formed. This unique pattern can then be verified by comparing the observed pattern of fibres with the original pattern established at the time of applying the seal.

Also under development for safeguards applications are more elaborate electronic seals (such as VACOSS III), which employ electronic encoding techniques for identification and to generate and store coded information about the application of the seal and its status. Both the VACOSS III and the FBOS seals are designed to permit immediate identification and verification on the spot.

SOME GENERAL COMMENTS, PERSPECTIVES, AND PROSPECTS

Many of the instruments described in this paper exemplify an important trend in nondestructive assay (NDA) instrumentation development, namely computerization and standardization of measurement equipment and procedures for safeguards inspection and verification. Insofar as possible the new, so-called "intelligent" NDA instruments are equipped with their own built-in diagnostics, calibration procedures, and so forth. They feature software programs designed to prompt the user through the basic instrument functions, to provide automation, as far as possible, of specific inspection measurement procedures, and to perform all necessary calculations internally. The resulting intelligent and mutually compatible instruments offer many important advantages in inspection performance in the field, in new equipment acceptance and inspector training, as well as in significantly reduced equipment maintenance and field-logistics problems. Major emphasis in the years just ahead will be on the practical field implementation of these and other instruments that, together with containment and surveillance techniques, provide the technical basis for increasingly effective and efficient IAEA safeguards of nuclear materials in all types of fuel cycle facilities.

In this brief survey, we have confined our attention to a purely technical discussion of state-of-the-art safeguards technology, purposely avoiding any discussion of specific applications of this new technology in the sensitive area of arms control verification. As regards that topic, suffice it to say the new technology described herein is available for adaptation, as appropriate, to a broad range of nuclear materials control and verification problems as they may arise — in whatever context — in the future. Also, the IAEA's safeguards experience could provide useful guidelines for future consideration of various possible verification systems. The extent of any new technology application or adaptation would clearly depend, *inter alia*, on the type of verification envisaged. It would seem plausible, for example, that if there were to be some form of limited cutoff or cutback agreement (e.g., one that might call for a halt or cutback at certain designated facilities in the production of plutonium and highly enriched uranium suitable for use in weapons), under such circumstances the IAEA's safeguards and on-site verification experience could be quite relevant. (IAEA safeguards clearly have an important restriction in that they are applied only at installations that have been identified and designated by the country accepting safeguards inspection.)

Viewed from the broad perspective, it is fair to say that the IAEA has considerable experience in applying safeguards to power and research reactors, critical assemblies, (including sizeable stores of ^{239}Pu and highly-enriched-U), and low-enriched-uranium fuel fabrication plants. The agency also has some experience with safeguarding mixed oxide ($PuO_2 + UO_2$) fuel fabrication and spent fuel reprocessing plants. Regarding safeguards at the "front end" of the fuel cycle, the recently concluded Hexapartite enrichment project has resulted in a consensus approach to safeguards at ultra-centrifuge type (low-enriched-uranium-producing) enrichment facilities in Japan, the United States, and three member states of the European Economic Community (Federal Republic of Germany, Netherlands, and U.K.). It thus appears that the IAEA experience in this important area can be expected to increase rapidly in the years just ahead.

As would be the case with any conceivable arms control verification system of the future, an indispensable attribute of IAEA international safeguards is credibility—both real and perceived—and this clearly requires a real (not merely perceived), technically sound capability for effective performance of IAEA safeguards in various types of nuclear facilities around the world. As the IAEA Director General has pointed out, the success of this first bold experiment in institutionalized international verification could serve as an inspiration and useful guideline for developing needed control measures in the context of nuclear disarmament—or conversely, should international safeguards be perceived to falter, this could be a significant setback in the prospects for nuclear arms control.

Finally, with regard to the role of inspection and verification technology—which has been the specific focus of this paper—it seems abundantly clear that modern NDA technology, suitably adapted when and as necessary, will play a key role in the achievement of credible and effective verification of nuclear arms control agreements, of whatever type, that may be forthcoming in the future.

REFERENCES

1. Shipley, J. P. and E. A. Hakkila. State-of-the-Art of Near-Real Time Materials Accounting. *Proceedings, International Conference on Nuclear Power Experience.* Vienna: IAEA, September 13-17, 1982. Paper IAEA CN-42/282.

2. Chapter 20 in this volume, by Weinstock and Fainberg.
3. See for example IAEA/SG/INF/3. *IAEA Safeguards, An Introduction*. Vienna: IAEA, October 1981; see also IAEA/SG/INF/2. *Guidelines for States' Systems of Accounting for and Control of Nuclear Materials*. Vienna: IAEA, December 1980.
4. U.S. Department of Energy. *Proceedings, International Training Course on Implementation of State Systems of Accounting for and Control of Nuclear Materials*. Report LA-9609-C, Los Alamos, NM: Los Alamos National Laboratory, December 1982.

22.

Controlling Nuclear Weapons at the Source: Verification of a Cutoff in the Production of Plutonium and Highly Enriched Uranium for Nuclear Weapons

Frank von Hippel and Barbara G. Levi

INTRODUCTION

All nuclear weapons contain at least a few kilograms of chain-reacting fissionable ("fissile") material—uranium-235 and/or plutonium-239. The bomb that killed 100,000 people in Hiroshima got its explosive energy from the fission of about 1 kilogram out of 60 kilograms of U-235 in the device,[1] and the bomb that destroyed Nagasaki released the fission energy from one kilogram out of 6 kilograms of plutonium in the weapon.[2] The development of thermonuclear, or "hydrogen," weapons by both the United States and the Soviet Union in the early 1950s did not obviate the need for such "fissile" materials: a fission explosion is required in such weapons to ignite the hydrogen fusion reaction.

Because fissile materials are an essential ingredient in all nuclear weapons, a cutoff in the production of such materials for weapons would limit the number of nuclear warheads that could be produced. It would furthermore be a necessary prerequisite to stockpile reductions, for the superpowers must stop producing before they can begin reducing.

Proposals for a production cutoff have been on the international arms control agenda virtually since the invention of nuclear weapons.[3] Between 1956 and 1969, a fissile production cutoff was repeatedly put forward by the United States as a separate arms control proposal.[4] The Soviet responses were not encouraging—perhaps because at the time the U.S.S.R.

had many fewer nuclear warheads than the United States.[5] By the 1980s, however, the two stockpiles were comparable and, in 1982, Soviet Foreign Minister Gromyko announced that the U.S.S.R. believed that the "cessation of production of fissionable materials for manufacturing of nuclear weapons" could be usefully made one of the "initial stages" of a "nuclear disarmament program."[6] The time may therefore be at hand when the production of fissile materials for nuclear weapons can at last be brought to an end.

The recent resurgence of public concern about the nuclear arms race makes a fissile production cutoff especially timely; it could be part of a larger package of mutually reinforcing nuclear arms control and disarmament proposals. For example, because a "freeze" on the superpower nuclear weapons stockpiles would mean the end of requirements for new nuclear weapons materials, a cutoff on the production of fissile materials for nuclear weapons would be an ingredient of such a freeze and would increase its verifiability. Similarly, a fissile cutoff would be an essential part of any comprehensive agreement to reduce the superpower nuclear warhead stockpiles, since such an agreement, to be meaningful, would require assurances that new warheads were not being produced.

A fissile material production cutoff would put a ceiling on the superpower nuclear arsenals at a time when it is becoming increasingly difficult to verify limits on nuclear weapons delivery vehicles. The development of more precise guidance systems has increased the vulnerability of land-based missiles and has stimulated proposals for small, mobile and *less detectable* land-based intercontinental nuclear missiles such as the proposed U.S. "Midgetman." Furthermore, the era of precision guidance is motivating proposals to produce large numbers of small, long-range cruise and ballistic missiles equipped with conventional explosive as well as nuclear warheads. Indeed, the new systems are being designed from the beginning as "dual-capable" systems so that nuclear and conventionally-armed delivery systems will be virtually indistinguishable.

Such ambiguous and concealable systems may soon make it exceedingly difficult to arrive at comprehensive nuclear arms control agreements based, like SALT II, on verifiable counts of delivery vehicles. Agreements limiting and reducing the amounts of nuclear weapons materials available to the two sides may therefore become an increasingly important tool for limiting new nuclear weapons systems as well as reducing the sizes of the nuclear arsenals.

Finally, continued production of fissile materials for nuclear weapons by the superpowers is seriously undermining their efforts to discourage similar activities in other nations. During the 1950s and 1960s, when the United States was putting forward proposals for a superpower fissile cutoff, these proposals were often linked to U.S. efforts to persuade nonnuclear weapon states to support the Treaty on the Non-Proliferation of Nuclear Weapons. That treaty came into force in 1970 and has since that time been signed by more than one hundred nonnuclear weapon states. The fact that the United States and the Soviet Union, the nations that devised the Non-Proliferation Treaty, have not brought their own arms race under control has produced increasingly strong expressions of dissatisfaction with the treaty on the part of the nonnuclear weapon states signatories at the treaty review conferences of 1975, 1980 and 1985. In this context, a superpower agreement to cut off the production of fissile materials for nuclear weapons would be in the interests of nonproliferation as well as superpower arms control.

The purpose of this chapter is to provide some of the technical background required for a constructive public discussion of the feasibility of a fissile material production cutoff. We start by describing what can be deduced from publicly available information about the magnitudes of the stockpiles of fissile materials in the superpower nuclear arsenals as well as their current sources, production rates, and non-weapons uses. Then we consider how a production cutoff might be verified. Finally, we discuss briefly how the fissile material stockpiles could be reduced.

THE SOURCES OF FISSILE MATERIALS

The only fissile isotope that occurs in nature in significant quantities is uranium-235 (U-235 for short). Fortunately, U-235 does not occur naturally in a form that is readily usable for nuclear weapons manufacture. It is found mixed with approximately 140 times as much of the heavier uranium isotope, U-238, which cannot sustain a chain reaction. In order to make possible in a practical mass of uranium the "fast neutron" chain reaction that releases the fission energy in a nuclear explosion, the percentage of U-235 in this mixture must be increased; for example, the uranium must be enriched, to a concentration above about 20%.[7] The amount of material required to make an explosive is much reduced by going to higher enrichments, however. The enrichment level of U.S. weapon-grade uranium is 93.5%.[8]

The development of uranium-235 enrichment techniques on an industrial scale was one of the major technological challenges faced in the U.S. nuclear weapons program. The technology adopted involves the diffusion of a gaseous compound, uranium hexafluoride, through a succession of thousands of barriers.* The resulting plants were so huge that only three

---

*Because molecules carrying the isotope U-235 move slightly faster on average than molecules with the heavier isotope, U-238, the portion of the gas that diffuses through a barrier will be slightly enriched in U-235.

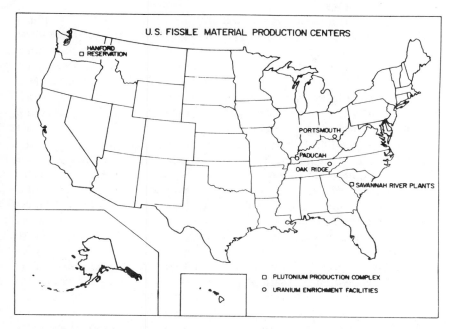

FIGURE 22.1. U.S. uranium-enrichment and plutonium-production facilities.

were built. They are at Oak Ridge, Tennessee; Paducah, Kentucky; and Portsmouth, Ohio (see Figure 22.1). U.S. government production of highly enriched uranium for nuclear weapons ended in 1964.[9] Although these enrichment plants have produced highly enriched uranium for naval and research reactors, the United States has added no highly enriched uranium to its nuclear weapons stockpile since 1964, and all weapon-grade uranium used in new U.S. nuclear warheads has come from the material stockpiled before 1964 or has been recycled from weapons being retired. Since 1964, the U.S. uranium-enrichment complex has been used principally to produce low-enriched uranium containing only a few percent U-235 to fuel commercial nuclear power reactors. Recently, however, because of the increased demands associated with its nuclear weapons buildup, the Reagan administration has proposed the resumption of production of highly enriched uranium for weapons.

The other fissile material used in the manufacture of nuclear weapons, Pu-239, is produced by neutron bombardment of U-238 in nuclear reactors. After absorbing a neutron, the U-238 atom is transmuted into an unstable isotope, which then undergoes two radioactive decays to become Pu-239. The neutrons are supplied by the fissioning of U-235, which typically produces two to three neutrons for each atom that fissions. Since, in ordinary production reactors, it requires on average the fission of approximately one atom of uranium-235 to supply the neutron required to transmute one atom of U-238 into an atom of Pu-239, approximately one kilogram of U-235 must be fissioned to produce one kilogram of Pu-239. Plutonium production does not therefore increase the total amount of fissile material. However, nuclear weapons designers prefer Pu-239 to U-235 for modern, compact nuclear warheads because a much smaller amount — only a few kilograms — is required to produce a fission explosion.

During most of the period from 1955 to 1964, the United States had in operation 13 plutonium production reactors — eight at the Hanford site on the Columbia River near Richland, Washington, and five at the Savannah River site near Aiken, South Carolina (see Figure 22.1).[10,11] These reactors together produced about 5 tonnes of plutonium each year — enough for roughly one thousand warheads. Figure 22.2 shows the total number of U.S. plutonium production reactors operating in each year from 1944 to 1983. In the eight years following President Johnson's 1964 decision to cut back U.S. production of fissile materials for nuclear weapons, all of the original eight Hanford reactors were shut down and two of the five newer Savannah River production reactors were mothballed. The remaining three Savannah River reactors and one "dual-purpose" (electric power plus plutonium production) reactor, which was completed at Hanford in 1964, have remained in operation.

Although the first reactors were built to produce plutonium for nuclear weapons, since about 1960 the United States and U.S.S.R. have built, respectively, about 80 and 30 large nuclear *power* reactors, which produce plutonium as a byproduct. As of the end of 1982, U.S. nuclear power reactors had produced about 40 tonnes of Pu-239.[12] Almost all of this plutonium is still where it was originally created, in "spent" reactor fuel mixed with highly radioactive fission products. Plutonium can be separated from this mixture only in a special nuclear fuel "reprocessing" plant in which the chemical separations are done by remote control behind heavy shielding.

Only fragmentary information is available about the Soviet complex for producing nuclear weapons material. The locations and outputs of Soviet nuclear power plants are known, however. We estimate that Soviet nuclear power reactors had, by the end of 1982, produced 15–45 tonnes of Pu-239. The larger number would apply if all Soviet graphite-moderated reactors have been operated in a mode to maximize their production of plutonium as well as electric power.[13]

Most of the plutonium that has been produced in U.S. power reactors is not considered "weapon-grade" by U.S. nuclear weapon designers, who prefer plutonium that contains less than 6% of the plutonium isotope Pu-240.[14] The percentage of Pu-240 increases with the residence time of

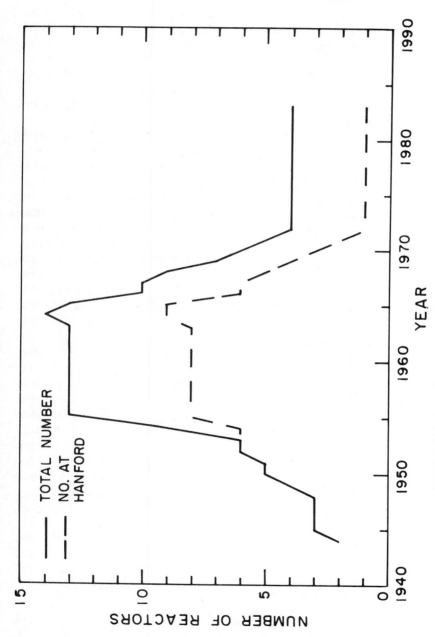

FIGURE 22.2. Operating history of U.S. plutonium production reactors.

the fuel in the reactor as a result of neutron captures by the Pu-239. The plutonium produced by U.S. nuclear power reactors typically contains about 20% Pu-240.[15] Operation of these reactors to produce weapon-grade plutonium would require uneconomically frequent shutdowns for refueling.

In the Soviet Union, the use of power reactors to produce weapon-grade plutonium is not as improbable because over one-half of Soviet nuclear power is supplied by graphite-moderated reactors containing channels in which the fuel can be exchanged while the reactor is in operation. It appears that the first of these reactors were operated primarily to produce plutonium.[16] This set of reactors is probably located at Troitsk (see Figure 22.3). A statement by Assistant Secretary of Defense for Atomic Energy Richard L. Wagner expresses concern about the "surge" production capability of Soviet channel power reactors—not their current use.[17] The locations of the Soviet channel reactors are shown in Figure 22.3.[18,19] This map also shows the location of the Soviet nuclear fuel reprocessing plant at Kyshtym, made famous in 1976 by the revelation that sometime during the winter of 1957–1958 an accident there contaminated a large area with radioactivity.[20]

Even plutonium that is not "weapon-grade" must be considered potential weapon material. The United States has designed and tested a nuclear explosive made with "reactor-grade" plutonium.[21] In the future, the distinction between civilian and military plutonium may become further blurred: The U.S. Department of Energy is currently designing a laser isotope separation facility that it hopes can be used to separate plutonium-239 from any mixture of plutonium isotopes.[22] Indeed, concern about this possibility led the Congress in 1982 to pass legislation* specifically barring the Department of Energy from using U.S. civilian power reactor plutonium for "nuclear explosive purposes."

THE STOCKPILES OF WEAPONS MATERIALS**

Enough information about the U.S. nuclear weapons material production complex is publicly available to allow reasonably accurate estimates of

---

*The Hart-Simpson Amendment to the Atomic Energy Act states: "Special nuclear material [such as plutonium] produced in facilities licensed under Section 103 or 104 may not be transferred, reprocessed, used or otherwise made available by any instrumentality of the United States or any other person for nuclear explosive purposes."[23]

**This section is a summary of the preliminary results of an analysis that will be documented in greater detail in a forthcoming report.[13] Similar estimates of the sizes of the U.S. stockpiles of weapon-grade uranium and plutonium have been made by Cochran and Hoenig.[11]

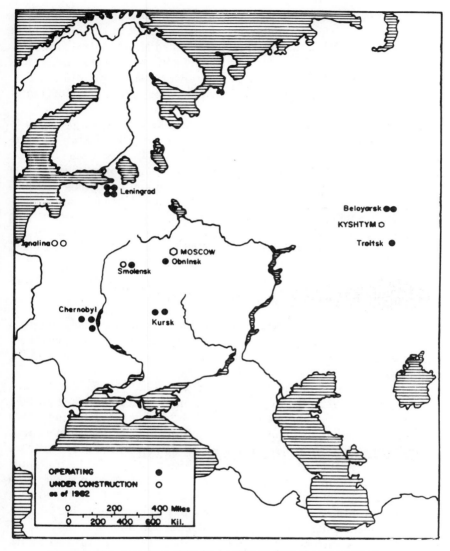

FIGURE 22.3. Locations of Soviet graphite-moderated power reactors.

the amounts of fissile materials in the U.S. weapons stockpile. The much more sparse *public* information available about the Soviet weapons production complex allows only a rough estimate of the size of their plutonium stockpile, however, and yields no clues as to the size of the Soviet stockpile of weapon-grade uranium. U.S. intelligence agencies have, of course, made estimates of the Soviet stockpiles of fissile materials ever since the beginning of the Soviet nuclear weapons program. It is presumably based upon their familiarity with past intelligence estimates that Rathjens and Scoville stated in a letter to Senator Ernest Hollings, dated March 4, 1983, that "we believe that Soviet stocks of strategic [fissile] material are substantially less than on hand in the United States."[24] Below, however, we estimate that U.S. and Soviet stockpiles of weapons plutonium are currently comparable.

Our estimates of the sizes of the U.S. stockpiles of weapon-grade fissile materials begin with the public records of the amount of uranium purchased by the U.S. government (see Figure 22.4). According to these records, since 1944 the government has bought approximately 250,000 tonnes (1 tonne equals 1,000 kg) of natural uranium containing approximately 1,780 tonnes (0.711%) of U-235.[25-28] No additional natural uranium has been purchased since 1970. Indeed, earlier purchases so far exceeded the needs of the period that approximately one-quarter of the U-235 originally bought still remains stockpiled in natural and low-enriched uranium.

U.S. Highly Enriched Uranium

As noted above, the United States stopped producing highly enriched uranium for nuclear weapons in 1964. The annual amounts of "separative work" done by the U.S. government's uranium enrichment plants and the percentage of U-235 remaining in the depleted uranium "tails" produced by them are matters of public record (see Figure 22.5).[29-31] The amount of enrichment work required to produce a given amount of enriched product depends upon the amount of U-235 left in the "depleted uranium tails." We therefore also show in Figure 22.5 the history of the "enrichment tails assay." For a tails assay of 0.2%, 237 tonne-SWUs are required to produce one tonne of weapon-grade uranium.[32] These numbers can be translated into equivalent amounts of weapon-grade uranium.[32] We find that, if all uranium enrichment work prior to Fiscal Year 1965 (July 1, 1964) had gone to the production of weapon-grade uranium, the amount of U-235 in this weapon-grade uranium would have been about 750 tonnes.

Some of the enrichment work prior to July 1, 1964, was required, however, to provide the fuel for various types of reactors (plutonium production, naval propulsion, electric power, and research) — both in the United States and abroad — and some of the weapon-grade uranium was consumed in nuclear weapons tests. Our estimates of all of these uses reduce our estimate of the amount of U-235 in the U.S. nuclear weapon stockpiles by only 50–200 tonnes, however — to the equivalent of 500–700 tonnes of weapon-grade uranium (see Table 22.1).[13]

Table 22.1. U.S. Stockpile of Weapon-Grade Uranium

	Metric Tonnes
Weapon-Grade Uranium Equivalent of all U.S. Enrichment Work Prior to Jan. 1 or July 1, 1964	714–775
Enrichment Work Used to Produce Slightly Enriched Fuel for the Hanford and Savannah River Production Reactors Through 1964	−(5–10)*
Enrichment Work Used to Produce Low-Enriched Fuel for Civilian Reactors Through 1964	−(10–15)*
Estimated Production of Highly Enriched Uranium Prior to 1965	689–760
Consumption by the Savannah River Production Reactors -pre-1964 -1965–89	−(0–15) −(10–25)
HEU Equivalent to U-235 in Fuel Delivered to U.S. Naval Propulsion Reactors (through 1964)	−(4–13)
Delivered to Domestic and Foreign Research Reactors	−(15–35)
Exported to the U.K. and France for Military Use	−(3–10)
Remaining After Uses for Reactor Fuel	591–728
Consumption in U.S. Nuclear Weapons Tests	−(10–30)
Miscellaneous Losses and Non-Weapons Stockpiles	−(0–50)
Estimated HEU Remaining in U.S. Weapons Stockpile	511–728

Source: Draft of report by F. von Hippel, B. Levi and D. Albright, *Quantities of Fissile Materials in U.S. and Soviet Nuclear Weapons Stockpiles*. Princeton University: Center for Energy and Environmental Studies Report #168, in press. Final estimates may differ slightly.
*Note that these numbers represent the amount of *weapon-grade uranium* that *could* have been produced with the enrichment work used to produce this low-enriched uranium. The tonnage of low-enriched uranium produced with this enrichment work and the tonnage of U-235 that this uranium contained were both much larger.

U.S. Plutonium

We have also been able to use public information to estimate how much plutonium was produced at government production reactors. By knowing the quantities of the long-lived (30-year half-life) fission products, Strontium-90 and Cesium-137, stored in the high-level radioactive waste at the Hanford and Savannah River sites, one may deduce the approximate amount of U-235 that was originally fissioned and hence the amount of plutonium produced. In this way, we estimate that somewhat less than 10% of the U-235 purchased by the government (about 130 tonnes) was consumed in producing about 100 tonnes of weapon-grade plutonium.[13] In addition, a much smaller quantity of tritium was produced.[11]

The estimate made here of the magnitude of the U.S. stockpile of

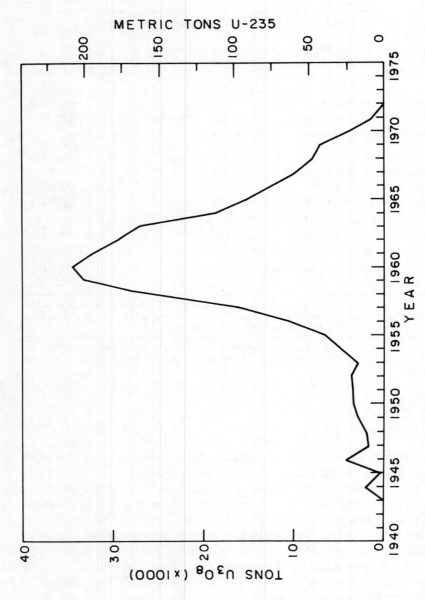

FIGURE 22.4. History of U.S. government purchases of natural uranium. (Source: Atomic Energy Commission, *Statistical Data of the Uranium Industry*, Report No. GJO-0100(74) 1974); and Robert Pitman, Department of Energy, private communication.)

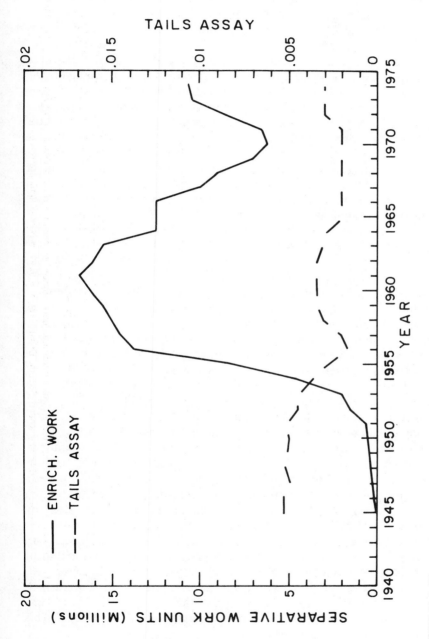

FIGURE 22.5. History of U.S. uranium enrichment activity. (Source: Enrichment work from ERDA conference 750924-7, 1975. Tails assay from Cochran et al.)[11]

weapon-grade fissile material provides some insight as to the relative contribution of the fissile materials to the explosive power of the current weapons arsenal. If the total fissile stockpile of about 700 tonnes were in warheads and if about one third of the atoms fissioned, the yield would be about 4,000 TNT equivalent. That is about half of the total estimated yield of the U.S. nuclear weapons in 1980.[33] As another comparison, if we divide the 700 tonnes by an estimated 26,000 warheads in the U.S. stockpile,[33] we obtain an average of about 27 kilograms of fissile material per warhead — 23 kilograms of U-235 and 4 kilograms plutonium. This average is considerably higher than the minimum required to make a nuclear weapon. An end to further acquisition of fissile material by U.S. nuclear weapons manufacturers would therefore not by itself prevent the number or the yields of U.S. nuclear warheads from growing considerably. Such growth would, however, require compromises of such qualitative features as high yield per unit weight and volume.

An example of such a tradeoff appears in 1982 testimony before the Senate Armed Services Committee. In discussing the design of the Mk-21 warhead for the MX, Deputy Under Secretary of Defense James P. Wade, Jr., confirmed that the yield could be increased without any penalty in weight by "trading orolloy [weapon-grade uranium] for depleted uranium." According to Wade, the government had made a decision not to implement this option fully in order to conserve weapon-grade uranium and thereby "protect the option of deploying an ABM system" to defend the MX.[34]

The fact that only about one-sixth as much plutonium as weapon-grade uranium is in the government's weapon stockpile does not accurately reflect the relative importance of these two fissile materials. As has already been noted, much smaller amounts of plutonium are required to make a nuclear explosive. Furthermore, a small admixture of plutonium can reduce dramatically the amount of U-235 required to make a nuclear weapon.[35]

About one-half of the U-235 originally bought by the U.S. government either ended up in weapon-grade uranium or was consumed in plutonium-production reactors. Most of the other half remains in the government's hands — principally in a stockpile of natural and slightly enriched uranium and a stockpile of uranium whose U-235 content has been "depleted" by the removal of U-235 in enrichment plants or by fission in production reactors. A small percentage of the government's U-235 has been mixed with electric utility-owned uranium at the government's uranium enrichment plants and shipped out to power reactors in slightly enriched nuclear fuel, and another few percent is government-owned reactor fuel. Our independent estimates of the various dispositions of the U.S. government's U-235 add up to within 5% of the amount purchased (see Table 22.2).[13] This serves as one check on our estimates.

Table 22.2. Disposition of the U.S. Government's Stockpile of U-235
(as of the end of 1980)

	Tonnes
In highly enriched uranium produced prior to 1965	671–716
In low-enriched uranium shipped to power reactors prior to 1965	13
In low-enriched uranium shipped to power reactors because of "split" diffusion plant "tails" 1972–77	42
Consumed in the original eight Hanford production reactors	58
Consumed by the N-reactor or contained in its unreprocessed spent fuel	30
In naval reactor fuel shipped between 1964 and 1981	40
In depleted uranium* from uranium enrichment associated with: highly enriched uranium fuel for original eight Hanford reactors N-reactor fuel low-enriched pre-1965 power reactor uranium low-enriched 1972–77 power reactor uranium	284–302 7 6 4 24
In burned-out uranium from original eight Hanford production reactors	46
Associated with government stockpiles of natural and low-enriched uranium at the end of 1980	481
Total	1696–1769

Source: Draft of report by F. von Hippel, B. Levi, and D. Albright, *Quantities of Fissile Materials in U.S. and Soviet Nuclear Weapons Stockpiles.* Princeton University: Center for Energy and Environmental Studies Report #168, in press. Final estimates may differ slightly.
*We assume that all uranium enrichment "tails" originally containing more than 0.2% U-235 will have subsequently been "stripped" down to that level.

Soviet Plutonium

An upper-bound estimate of Soviet plutonium production can be obtained even more indirectly—from the history of the concentration of Krypton-85 (Kr-85) in the earth's atmosphere. Kr-85 is a fission product which accumulates in nuclear reactor fuel and is ordinarily released into the atmosphere when such fuel is chemically "reprocessed." Because it is chemically inert, Kr-85 accumulates in the atmosphere. Its radioactive half-life (10.76 years) is sufficiently long for it to become relatively uniformly distributed—a fact which facilitates estimates of its global inventory.

Measurements of the atmospheric concentration of Kr-85 have been made since approximately 1954. Most of these measurements have been made in the Northern Hemisphere—particularly in Europe. We estimate, from the few measurements in the Southern Hemisphere (see Figure 22.6)[36] and in the stratosphere (see Figure 22.7),[37] that the average concentration of Kr-85 in the global atmosphere is about 85% of that near ground

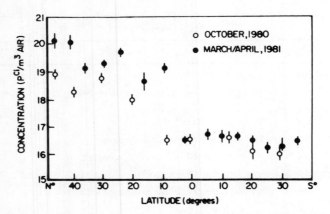

FIGURE 22.6. Ground level concentration of Kr-85 as a function of latitude, 1980–1981. (From: "Large-Scale Atmospheric Mixing Derived from Meridional Profiles of Krypton-85" by W. Weiss, A. Sittkus, H. Stockburger, and H. Sartorius, 1983, *Journal of Geophysical Research*, *88*, p. 8575. Copyright 1983 by the American Geophysical Union. Used with permission.)

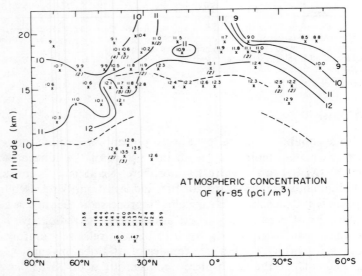

FIGURE 22.7. Distribution of Kr-85 (in picoCuries per standard cubic meter of air) as a function of altitude and of latitude for the period April through November 1973. Solid lines are contours of nearly constant concentration. Dashed lines represent the mean altitude of the tropopause. (From: "Atmosphere Concentration and Inventory of Krypton-85" by K. Telegadas and G. Ferber, 1975, *Science*, *190*, p. 882. Copyright 1975 by the American Association for the Advancement of Science. Used with permission.)

level in the Northern Hemisphere. We have used this assumption to derive an estimate of the buildup of Kr-85 in the global atmosphere.[13] (The 5% increase in Figure 22.6 of the Northern Hemisphere Kr-85 concentration between October 1980 and March/April 1981 occurred principally because the vertical atmospheric mixing conditions were different during these two periods[36] and because the Kr-85 is released in the Northern Hemisphere at the ground level where the measurements were being made.)

Figure 22.8 shows our estimate of what the cumulative inventory of Kr-85 in the atmosphere would have been *in the absence of radioactive decay*.[13] The error bars indicate our estimate of the uncertainty in these estimates due to uncertainties in the Kr-85 concentration measurements and in our simple extrapolation from these measurements to a global inventory. Also shown in Figure 22.8 are estimates of the cumulative amounts of Kr-85 that have been released into the atmosphere from nuclear weapons tests in the atmosphere[38,39] and from civilian and military nuclear fuel reprocessing in Western Europe,[40,41] and the United States.[13] The curve in Figure 22.8 denoted by square data points shows the cumulative amount of Kr-85 released from sources other than nuclear fuel reprocessing in the U.S.S.R. The difference between this curve and the top one represents the Soviet contribution to the global inventory.

Taking into account the various uncertainties, we estimate that a residual of 40–66 MegaCuries of Kr-85 could have been released from Soviet plutonium-production operations. Because the release of one MegaCurie of Kr-85 from such an operation would be accompanied by the production of about 2.3 tonnes of weapon-grade plutonium,[13] the Soviet Union could have produced as much as 95–150 tonnes of weapon-grade plutonium — that is, an amount comparable to that which has been produced by the United States. This estimate should be reduced somewhat to reflect the amount of Kr-85 released from the reprocessing of nuclear fuel from Soviet reactors other than plutonium production reactors. For the United States, the corresponding reduction would be about 20%.[13] The correction for the Soviet Union could be considerably larger if that nation has, like Britain and France, engaged in the large-scale reprocessing of nuclear power reactor fuel for other than military purposes.

Our estimate of the amount of fissile material in the superpower nuclear weapon stockpiles establishes a scale by which the significance of the verification problems for a production cutoff agreement can be measured. If the superpowers already have hundreds of tonnes of fissile material in their nuclear weapons arsenals, then it would take the production of at least several tonnes per year over more than a decade to make a noticeable difference in the arsenals. As will be seen below, the detection of the clandestine production or diversion of nuclear weapon material on this scale is a

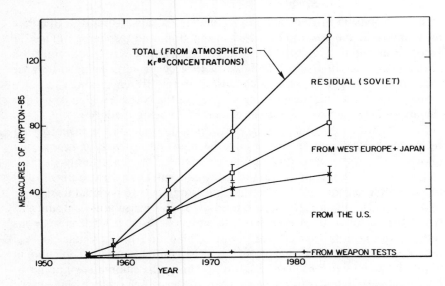

FIGURE 22.8. Cumulative release of Kr-85 to the atmosphere (undecayed).

much different challenge from the detection of the few kilograms that could change the status of a nonnuclear weapon state.

PRODUCTION ACTIVITIES AND PLANS

As we have seen, beginning in the mid-1960s, the rate of production of fissile material for nuclear weapons in the United States declined to relatively low levels. This decline reflects a decision in 1964 by President Johnson that the U.S. nuclear stockpile had grown large enough. In his State of the Union address that year, Johnson announced:

Even in the absence of agreement we must not stockpile arms beyond our needs or seek an excess of military power that could be provocative as well as wasteful. And it is in this spirit that in this fiscal year we are cutting back our production of enriched uranium by 25%. We are shutting down four plutonium piles [reactors]. . .[42]

Three months later Johnson announced:

. . . a further substantial reduction in our production of enriched uranium, to be carried out over a four-year period.[43]

Johnson remarked that:

We must not operate a WPA nuclear project, just to provide employment, when our needs have been met.[43]

Soviet Premier Khrushchev made a simultaneous announcement of a cutback in his government's plans for the production of plutonium and highly enriched uranium, as did British Prime Minister Douglas-Home.[44]

The Johnson administration then went ahead — apparently without further public announcement — to end altogether U.S. production of highly enriched uranium for nuclear weapons and to shut down another three plutonium production reactors. The Nixon administration continued this program of unilateral cutbacks by shutting down three more production reactors (see Figure 22.2). The actions by the British government were also dramatic: It appears that British production of both weapon-grade plutonium and uranium had been stopped completely by 1965. Since that time Britain has obtained from the United States the highly enriched uranium required to fuel its submarine reactors — in part at least in exchange for British non-weapon-grade plutonium.[45]

All these cutbacks reduced the rate of U.S. production of fissile material for nuclear weapons during the 1970s to 1–2 tonnes of weapon-grade plutonium per year from three Savannah River reactors.[13] The size of the U.S. nuclear weapons stockpile declined during this period — measured both in numbers of weapons and in their average yield.[46] According to U.S. officials, during this period

> . . . most of the nuclear materials required for building new [U.S.] warheads [were] obtained by reclaiming and recycling existing materials from retired weapons.[47]

In 1983, however, the number of nuclear weapons in the U.S. nuclear weapons stockpile began to increase again,[17] and the stockpile mix continues to shift toward compact weapons, such as cruise missile and MIRV warheads, which require plutonium. The U.S. Department of Energy (DOE), which operates the U.S. weapon-production complex, has therefore undertaken a number of new initiatives to increase the rate of U.S. production of weapon-grade plutonium. These initiatives include increasing the refueling frequency of the one remaining production reactor at the Hanford site (the "N-reactor") so that it will produce weapon-grade plutonium;[47] restarting the Savannah River "L-Reactor," which has been shut down since 1968; and initiating design work on a new production reactor, which would probably be sited at the Department of Energy's Idaho Nuclear Energy Laboratory.[48] The restart of the L-reactor has been delayed by local concern about environmental and safety questions, however, and the need for a costly new production reactor has been seriously questioned within Congress. The principal justification given for the new production reactor in Idaho is "to assure the production of tritium that is so vital to maintaining our nuclear weapon stockpile." It is argued that, due to their age, "there is an increasing probability over time that we will not be able to continue to confidently rely on the Savannah River production reactors to produce [this] tritium."[47]

The DOE is also planning to use for weapons purposes some of its stockpile of about 17 tonnes of non-weapon-grade plutonium[49] that had previously been reserved for its research program on the plutonium breeder reactor. This will be done by diluting some of the "fuel-grade" (about 12% Pu-240) plutonium with "super-grade" plutonium, in which the concentration of Pu-240 is well below the weapon-grade limit of 6%. This approach is, of course, limited by the availability of super-grade plutonium for blending. For this reason among others, the DOE has proposed the construction of a "demonstration" plutonium isotope separation plant, which would allow it to extract relatively pure Pu-239 from any grade of plutonium.[47]

Of course, none of these initiatives — with the possible exception of those relating to tritium production — would be necessary if the United States and U.S.S.R. were to agree to a bilateral cutoff in the production of fissile material for nuclear weapons.

We have no information on the current rate of production of weapon-grade uranium in the Soviet Union. Soviet plutonium production, however, seems to be of greater concern to the U.S. weapons establishment.[17] Our analysis of Soviet Kr-85 releases suggests that although the U.S.S.R. appears to have lagged behind the United States by five to ten years in embarking on large-scale production of plutonium, it had caught up by about 1980. There also is no clear evidence of a production cutback such as that which occurred in the United States in the late 1960s.

"ADEQUATE" VERIFICATION OF A PRODUCTION CUTOFF

We have assumed for the purpose of this analysis that a fissile production cutoff agreement would be adequately verifiable if it were possible to detect with a reasonable probability the clandestine production or diversion of an amount of fissile material greater than 10% of the current U.S. stockpile over a period of ten years. At the current stockpile level, therefore, the threshold for a significant violation of a cutoff would be the average production each year for a period of ten years of:

- 6.0 tonnes/year of weapon-grade uranium, or
- 1.0 tonne/year of plutonium.

Undetected violations of a fissile cutoff at a level less than this could still provide the wherewithal for the production of hundreds of warheads per year — and therefore would hardly be regarded as insignificant in isolation. Measured against the existing stockpiles, however, such increments could not be considered as significant. In fact, the strategic significance of such small violations would be so minor that it is doubtful that either super-power would consider the potential gains from successful evasion at this scale worth the risks of detection.

Opponents to a fissile cutoff might still emphasize the absolute magnitude of possible undetected violations. As Harold Brown has noted:

> For an American president, the political problem is the real one. One metric ton of Pu and five of HEU [Highly Enriched Uranium] per year is likely to be equated to up to a thousand bombs per year. . . . For President Carter (or even President Reagan) to be accused of . . . taking a position . . . allowing the U.S.S.R. that many bombs a year in violation of an agreed ban . . . would quite likely make the front page of the *New York Times*.[50]

Our criteria for "significant" violations of a superpower fissile cutoff are much less stringent than those established by the Non-Proliferation Treaty (NPT) for more than 100 non-nuclear weapon states that have signed it. The IAEA has specified that the diversion of 25 kg of U-235 in highly enriched uranium or 8 kg of plutonium—the approximate quantities required for the manufacture of a single nuclear weapon—would be a "significant" violation of the Non-Proliferation Treaty.[51] These values are more than one hundred times smaller than the amounts which we have taken as our threshold values for significance in the context of a super-power fissile production cutoff agreement. Similarly, the IAEA has defined "timely detection" of a significant diversion as detection within the length of time which it would take to convert the diverted material into a weapon—days to months, depending upon whether or not the material is in separated form or irradiated spent fuel.[51] This period of time is also on the order of 100 times smaller than the ten years that we have allowed for the detection of a threshold violation of a superpower fissile production cutoff agreement.

The reason for the differences is that the International Atomic Energy Agency (IAEA), which administers the NPT safeguards, is responsible for detecting the diversion by a non-nuclear weapon state of enough material to make a *single* weapon, whereas a fissile cutoff would aim to prevent the strategically significant growth of already enormous stockpiles. On the basis of these comparisons, therefore, it would appear that the problem of adequately verifying compliance with a superpower fissile production cutoff agreement should be much easier than that of adequately verifying compliance with the NPT. Other considerations—notably the large background "noise" level of activity from which the "signal" of a violation in a superpower nuclear establishment would have to be detected—will be seen below to offset this conclusion only partially.

In the next two sections, we discuss: (a) the problem of verifying that no significant quantity of fissile material is diverted to weapons production from an acknowledged or "declared" nuclear facility, and (b) the problem of verifying that there are no clandestine or "undeclared" production facilities producing significant amounts of weapon-usable fissile materials.

SAFEGUARDS AT DECLARED NUCLEAR FACILITIES

The United States has always assumed that under a fissile material production cutoff agreement there would be a system of on-site inspections of nonweapons facilities processing fissile materials to assure that no significant amounts of fissile material were being diverted to weapon use. Since about 1965, official U.S. statements have suggested that the inspection job could be assigned to the International Atomic Energy Agency, which would use similar techniques to those it has developed to safeguard fissile materials in nonnuclear weapon states.[52]

Indeed, as part of its campaign for the Non-Proliferation Treaty, the United States offered to put *all* of its own nuclear facilities under such IAEA safeguards, except those "with direct national security significance." A U.S.-IAEA agreement making possible the implementation of this offer entered into force in 1980. Similar agreements with the IAEA were finalized in 1976 by U.K. and in 1981 by France.[53] Due to its limited resources, however, the IAEA has actually implemented safeguards arrangements at only a very few of the nuclear facilities in these nuclear-weapon states.

As has already been noted, in 1982, Foreign Minister Andrei Gromyko expressed Soviet interest for the first time in a superpower fissile production cutoff agreement as a separate arms control measure. In the same statement, Gromyko also indicated that the Soviet Union would be willing to allow the IAEA to conduct onsite inspections in the U.S.S.R. He announced:

> The Soviet Union is agreeable to placing under the control of the International Atomic Energy Agency a part of its peaceful nuclear installations — atomic power plants and research reactors.[6]

Negotiations between the IAEA and the U.S.S.R. on the implementation of such an arrangement began in early 1983 and were signed in March, 1985.

Figure 22.9 shows schematically the types of nuclear facilities present in a nuclear weapons state and the flows of fissile material between them. Under a fissile cutoff, all of these nuclear facilities, except for the weapon-material stockpiles and weapons production facilities, would have to come under safeguards. In the following section, we discuss first the safeguards that would be required at shutdown facilities. Then we will turn to the more difficult problem of assuring that significant amounts of fissile material are not diverted from operating facilities.

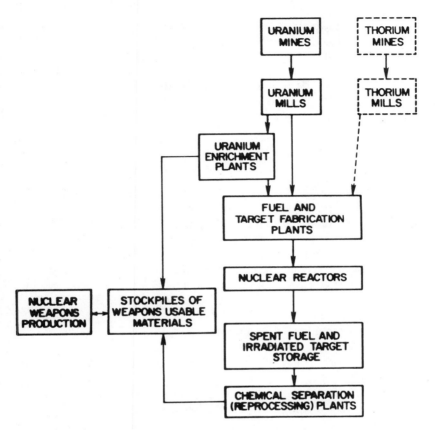

FIGURE 22.9. Flows of fissile material in a nuclear weapons state.

Shutdown Production Facilities

In the United States, the production of highly enriched uranium for nuclear weapons has already been stopped and, except for the N-reactor at Hanford, a clear line separates plutonium production from civilian power programs. The fissile cutoff agreement would therefore dictate the closing of the nuclear fuel reprocessing plants at Hanford and Savannah River and all but perhaps one of the currently operating dedicated production reactors at Savannah River. (The remaining production reactor might be kept in use to maintain the tritium stockpile—see below.) The corresponding facilities would also have to be shut down in the U.S.S.R.

The least intrusive safeguards would be required if the facilities were disassembled in a manner that was observable by satellite. If the plants were merely mothballed, satellites could be used to look for indicators of activity such as infrared heat emissions. Some on-site inspections would probably also be desirable, however. If the facilities were adequately sealed, these inspections could be nonintrusive. Periodic on-site checks could ascertain that the seals had not been tampered with. Radiation measurements could also be made in the environments of production reactors and reprocessing plants to detect indications of recent operation.[54]

Operating Facilities

As indicated in Figure 22.9, the safeguarding task at operating facilities involves keeping track of the U-235 and plutonium in the fuel cycles of various types of nuclear reactors. Thorium mines and mills are shown dotted in Figure 22.9 as a reminder that if in the future the fertile material thorium was introduced into nuclear reactors on a large scale, it would be necessary also to extend safeguards to the artificial fissile uranium isotope, U-233. It would be necessary to confirm, to within a specified accuracy, that any fissile material delivered to or produced at each plant was still there, had been fissioned, or had been delivered to another safeguarded location. These tasks can be accomplished with IAEA-type safeguards.

After nuclear reactor fuel is manufactured and as long as its physical form is unchanged, the nuclear safeguards problem is quite similar to a currency safeguards problem confronting a bank inspector. Visiting inspectors can periodically check the consistency between the actual and reported inventory. Radiation and other non-destructive measurements can be used on randomly selected samples to check that there has been no large-scale diversion involving the substitution of "counterfeit" fuel.[55] In cases where fissile material is in inactive storage, the IAEA simplifies its task by applying tamper-proof seals to the containers and storage vaults involved so that their contents need not be checked on each visit. Storage areas that cannot be sealed are monitored for suspicious activities by tamper-proof cameras that automatically take pictures at short intervals for later review. Systems have been developed that would make possible the remote real-time monitoring of the functioning of such systems.[55]

It is also necessary to ensure that significant quantities of extra fertile material are not secretly introduced into the reactor to produce plutonium—in much the same way as extra paper might be secretly run through the printing presses at a mint. (In contrast to the situation at the mint, however, the limited availability of extra neutrons from a nuclear reactor core strictly limits the amount of fissile material that could be clandestinely produced in this way.) In the case of the most common type of power reactor, the light-water reactor, which ordinarily needs to be opened up only approximately once a year for refueling, the IAEA seals the pressure vessel to ensure that it has not been opened in the absence of an inspector. In the case of continually fueled reactors, such as the Canadian heavy-water reactor or the graphite-moderated channel reactors, which make up approximately one half of Soviet nuclear generating capacity,[56] other arrangements must be made. Here the IAEA has devised a system in which seals, radiation monitors, and surveillance cameras are used to ensure that no spent fuel can be removed undetected from a "containment" area which includes the reactor and its spent fuel storage facility.[51]

At facilities such as uranium enrichment, fuel fabrication and reprocessing plants, the nuclear materials are in powdered or fluid form, for at least some stages of the processing, rather than in discrete countable fuel rods. Such facilities pose the additional complication of measurement error and process losses with loose materials. In the U.S. nuclear weapons program, such losses and errors have resulted in fissile material accounting uncertainties on the order of 1%.[57,58]

The analogous problem in this case is that of detecting the diversion of precious metals at a mint. The IAEA has concluded that it would be necessary to have inspectors continually present at major facilities handling fissile materials in bulk.[51] With inspectors present, measurement and accounting techniques have improved enough so that diversions on the order of a percent should be detectable.[54,59] Below we consider how these capabilities compare with the requirements of adequate verification of a superpower fissile cutoff agreement. The discussion is organized according to reactor types.

Power Production Reactors and Their Fuel Cycles

By far the largest flows of fissile material in the superpower nuclear economies occur in their civilian nuclear power systems. Each year, about 0.75 tonnes of U-235 are loaded into and approximately 0.14 tonnes of Pu-239 are discharged from a typical U.S.[15] or Soviet[60] light-water reactor (LWR) with an electric generating capacity of one million kilowatts. (We assume a heat-to-electric-energy conversion efficiency of one third, an average capacity factor of 65% and fuel "burnup" of 30 thermal megawatt-days per kilogram of uranium in the fissile fuel.) The numbers for Soviet graphite-moderated channel reactors are not greatly different—if these reactors are operated to produce electric power most economically (i.e., are not used as dual-purpose electricity and weapon-grade plutonium production reactors).[61]

Table 22.3 shows our estimates of the number of nuclear plants operating and under construction at the end of 1982 in the United States and U.S.S.R. (i.e., those expected to be operating in the early 1990s).[56] These plants will require the flow through their fuel cycles of tens of tonnes of fis-

Table 22.3. Fissile Material Flows in Nuclear Power Systems
Operating [plus those under construction] as of 1982

	Generating Capacity GW(e)	Fissile Material Flows (tonnes)	
		U-235 IN	PU-239 OUT
U.S.	62 [130]	47 [98]	9 [18]
U.S.S.R.	17 [47]	13 [35]	2 [7]

sile material—mostly mixed with much larger quantities of U-238. Even when the two nations complete the reactors now being built, a significant violation of a fissile cutoff agreement would require the diversion of the equivalent of more than 5% of the U-235 or Pu-239 flow through the U.S. nuclear power fuel cycle—more than 15% in the case of the Soviet Union.

Reprocessing. Previously, we have stated that an IAEA-type safeguards system should be able to detect diversions on the order of 1% of the flow of fissile materials through all types of nuclear fuel cycle facilities. We have also seen that, given the current scales of the superpower nuclear power establishments, diversions at this level would be much less than the threshold levels that we have defined as significant in the context of a superpower cutoff agreement. It would not be necessary, therefore, to restrict the types of nuclear power systems which could be deployed out of concern that they might make impossible the verifiability of a fissile production cutoff.

However, the low-enriched uranium, once-through fuel cycle, which is currently the dominant nuclear power fuel cycle throughout the world, contains intrinsic and significant barriers to the diversion of fissile material that are not fully shared by any other fuel cycle:

- The fissile material in the fresh fuel is U-235 diluted by so much U-238 that it is not usable for nuclear weapon purposes without isotopic enrichment; and
- The plutonium remaining in the spent fuel is mixed with highly radioactive fission products from which it cannot be separated except in a specialized nuclear fuel reprocessing facility in which chemical processing must be conducted remotely in a heavily shielded enclosure.

It now appears that nuclear power could be sustained with this fuel cycle for many decades.

During the 1960s and 1970s, the energy research and development establishments of the major industrialized countries were anticipating the widespread introduction before the end of the century of plutonium breeder reactors and their associated fuel cycle, which involves the recovery and recycle of plutonium in fresh reactor fuel. This "plutonium economy" would have involved the recycle of enormous quantities of weapons-usable plutonium through fuel fabrication and reprocessing plants. Undetectable diversions of this plutonium could have resulted in major nuclear weapons proliferation and terrorism problems. During the past five to ten years, however, it has become clear that the plutonium fuel cycle will not for the foreseeable future be economically competitive with the current once-through fuel cycle.

Projections of worldwide nuclear capacity in the year 2000 have fallen several-fold,[62] while the cost of nuclear fuel reprocessing and the cost differential between conventional and plutonium breeder reactors have *increased* several-fold. As a result, it now appears likely that nuclear reactors fueled with low-enriched-uranium will continue for many decades to be the most economical way to exploit fission energy.[63]

There are still a number of major plutonium breeder reactor research, development, and demonstration programs in the world, however, and these programs still have significant governmental and industrial support. Furthermore, a number of nations have found reprocessing a convenient — if temporary — solution to their indigenous debates over radioactive waste disposal; they send their spent nuclear reactor fuel to Britain and/or France for reprocessing. The negotiation of a fissile cutoff agreement would provide an opportunity for high-level political officials to consider the dangers associated with a continuation of these programs.

Enrichment Plants. There are only a few prototype gas-cooled reactors that use highly enriched uranium in their fresh fuel. It currently appears unlikely that these reactors — or for that matter any other new type of reactor — will be commercialized in the foreseeable future. But if they are, it has been shown that they too could be operated economically on the more proliferation-resistant low-enriched-uranium, once-through fuel cycle.[64]

If all nuclear power plants were fueled by low-enriched fuel, only relatively small amounts of highly enriched uranium would be required for naval reactors and a few research reactors (see below). These needs could be supplied from stockpiles or by small dedicated enrichment plants.

The objective of the safeguards applied to the large enrichment plants producing low-enriched uranium would then be primarily to detect any alterations that might result in the production of highly enriched uranium. These alterations might be either in the operating mode of the plant (i.e., the batch recycle of already enriched uranium to reach higher enrichments), or in its plumbing (the rearrangement of parallel enrichment stages in series). The difficulty in implementing these methods of producing highly enriched uranium depends very much upon the enrichment technology involved.

The three operating U.S. enrichment facilities are diffusion plants. The Soviet Union also has at least one large diffusion plant located "somewhere in Siberia."[65] Both the design and operation of these plants are very inflexible and it would require a major effort to produce weapon-grade uranium at a plant that was designed to produce only low-enriched uranium. Such an effort would be nearly impossible to conceal from on-site inspectors if they had the ability to monitor the operation of the plant and even limited access to its interior. The equilibrium time and inventory of these plants are both so large that batch recycling is utterly impractical.

A second uranium enrichment technology that is just coming into commercial use involves the use of ultra-high-speed centrifuges. In these machines, a gaseous uranium compound is spun at high speeds so that the gas molecules containing the heavier U-238 atoms tend to be driven further away from the axis of the rotor—leaving gas closer to the axis slightly depleted in U-238 and hence enriched in U-235. Higher enrichments are achieved by extracting this slightly enriched gas and introducing it into another centrifuge.

Small demonstration centrifuge plants are operating in Europe and Japan, and larger plants are under construction in Europe. The United States cancelled construction of its Portsmouth Gas Centrifuge Plant in 1985 to concentrate its efforts on laser isotope enrichment. Because the isotope separation that can be attained with a single centrifuge is much larger than for diffusion elements, these facilities can be smaller and built in more modular fashion. In European plants, the modules consist of thousands of identical centrifuges (see Figure 22.10). In principle, it would not be difficult to reconnect these centrifuges to produce highly enriched uranium. Batch recycling is also more feasible in plants of this type than in diffusion plants.

All diffusion enrichment plants are in nuclear weapons states and currently not subject to safeguards. Indeed, the only enrichment plant of any kind to which the IAEA has applied safeguards is a small R&D centrifuge plant in Japan. Safeguard agreements have been delayed at the relatively small centrifuge plants built at Almelo, the Netherlands, by the "Urenco" consortium (the Federal Republic of Germany, the Netherlands, and the U.K.), because of concerns on the part of the Urenco partners about the loss of proprietary and classified information if international inspectors were allowed inside the centrifuge "cascade" halls. However, recently a study sponsored jointly by the IAEA, Euratom, Australia, Japan, the United States, and Urenco may have resolved this issue. This "Hexapartite Safeguards Project" concluded by recommending "limited-frequency unannounced access" to the interior of centrifuge enrichment facilities during which inspectors could check that the arrangement of interconnections between the centrifuges had not been altered and could also check with sensitive radiation detectors that none of the piping was carrying highly

FIGURE 22.10. Centrifuge "cascade" in the Urenco enrichment plant at Almelo, the Netherlands. (Source: Urenco, the Netherlands.)

enriched uranium. The inspectors would be escorted and their activities limited so as to minimize the possibility of their obtaining sensitive design information.[66]

Such inspections would serve as a supplement to the "materials balance accounting" approach whose purpose is to make impossible undetected diversions of large quantities of fissile material. Recently the detection sensitivity of this accounting approach was analyzed for U.S. Portsmouth Gas Centrifuge Enrichment Plant, a facility that if completed[67] would have been to produce annually low-enriched uranium containing approximately 60 tonnes of U-235. According to the safeguards system design for this facility, inspectors would monitor all measurements of the weight and enrichment of the uranium entering and leaving the enrichment plant, and would make their own random checks of these measurements. The analysts conclude that it should be possible with this approach for the inspectors to detect diversions of more than about 0.3% of the U-235.[68]

Currently both the United States and U.S.S.R. have high-priority research programs in another area of enrichment technology: laser isotope separation.[65] Methods for safeguarding laser isotope separation plants are also under development in the United States. As with safeguards for diffusion and centrifuge plants, if methods can be developed that meet the requirements of the IAEA for verifying the Non-Proliferation Treaty, they should be more than adequate to verify a fissile cutoff agreement.

The demand for U-235 by reactor types other than nuclear power reactors is relatively small but many of these reactors are fueled with weapon-grade uranium. Below, we discuss in turn the special safeguards problems at: research reactors, naval power reactors, and tritium production reactors.

Research Reactors

For the purposes of this article, we will define as "research reactors" all reactors other than: plutonium production reactors (which would be shut down under a fissile cutoff agreement), power plants (we have already discussed these), naval propulsion reactors, and tritium production reactors. There are more than 100 research reactors operating in the United States and presumably a comparable number in the U.S.S.R.[69] As of September 1982, 46 U.S. research reactors were being fueled by uranium enriched to greater than 70% in U-235. However, their total demand for U-235 was relatively small on the scale of concern to a superpower fissile cutoff — only about 0.5 tonnes per year — and 85% of this demand was due to three reactors operated by the U.S. Department of Energy.[70]

IAEA-type safeguards have been thoroughly worked out to detect diversions from research reactors. However, due to the short time that would be required to turn diverted highly enriched uranium into nuclear weapons, there has been a considerable interest in converting those research reactors that are fueled by highly enriched uranium to uranium which is enriched to less than 20% in U-235. Programs are under way in the United States and elsewhere to develop fuel elements in which the uranium density is increased sufficiently to accommodate the extra amount of U-238 required to dilute the U-235 to such levels. The developers believe that this program could make low-enriched replacement fuel available for all research reactors by 1989.[71] There are two U.S. university research reactors, that if converted to low-enriched uranium (LEU) without any change in their fuel geometries would require fuels with uranium densities higher than those currently under development (up to 7 grams of uranium/cc).[72] The same thing is true of the U.S. Department of Energy's Advanced Test Reactor, which by itself consumes as much U-235 as all other U.S. research reactors combined.[70] Nevertheless, at 7 grams U/cc, the enrichment in the fuels of all these reactors could be reduced to 25% or below. Implementation of such a conversion program would further reduce the difficulty of safeguarding research reactors.

Naval Propulsion Reactors

The United States and the Soviet Union each have over 100 ships propelled by nuclear reactors.[73] U.S. naval reactors are fueled by uranium enriched to the level of 97.3% in U-235. During the three fiscal years 1983–1985, the U.S. Navy's purchases of enrichment services have corresponded to a demand of approximately 5 tonnes of U-235 per year.[11] In addition, the United States contracted in 1981 to supply the U.K. for its naval propulsion reactors an amount of enrichment work equivalent to that required to produce up to about 0.4 tonnes of highly enriched uranium per year for the following five years.[74] Since the total estimated shaft horsepower of the Soviet nuclear navy is about the same as that of the United States,[73] and Soviet ships are at sea a much smaller percentage of the time,[75] it is unlikely that the Soviet consumption of highly enriched uranium for naval reactor fuel would be greater.

How would this flow of highly enriched uranium be safeguarded from diversion to nuclear weapons under a fissile production agreement? One possibility would be for the two superpowers to agree on an amount of highly enriched uranium that each would be allowed to produce for naval reactors at safeguarded uranium enrichment plants. If it were also specified that an equivalent amount of irradiated reactor fuel would have to be turned in at a safeguarded facility within a specified number of years, the cumulative amount of U-235 in the naval fuel cycle and therefore the amount that could be diverted would be kept from growing to the scale of a potentially significant violation. The fuel could be mechanically and chemically processed before being turned in to destroy any sensitive fuel design information.

An alternative possibility would be to fuel naval power reactors with highly enriched uranium from the weapons stockpiles. A comparison of our estimate of the size of the U.S. stockpile of highly enriched uranium with the size of U.S. naval demand for U-235 indicates that less than 1% of the stockpile would be consumed in this way each year. This corresponds to a *very* modest rate of disarmament!

Finally, it would be highly worthwhile to determine whether it might not be possible to convert naval propulsion reactors to 20%-enriched uranium using advanced fuel technology similar to that which is being developed for research reactors.

Tritium Production Reactors

If a superpower fissile cutoff were not accompanied by an agreement to reduce the nuclear arsenals as well, it would have to allow the nuclear weapon states to maintain their stockpiles of tritium. The fusion of this isotope with the lighter hydrogen isotope deuterium is used in nuclear weapons as a convenient source of neutrons. The tritium-deuterium fusion reaction is used to provide the neutrons that initiate the chain reaction in fission explosives. It is also used in many fission explosives to increase the fraction of the material which is fissioned and thereby to "boost" the yield of the explosion by providing a burst of extra neutrons just as the chain reaction is reaching its final stages. Finally, the tritium-deuterium reaction is the source of most of the lethal neutrons that are radiated by a "neutron bomb." Because tritium has a twelve-year radioactive half-life, it must be replenished if the characteristics of the nuclear weapons stockpile are not to change. In 1982, Herman Roser, Assistant Secretary of Energy for Defense Programs, stated in testimony before the Senate Armed Service Committee:[14]

> As you can see here, in the event we were to quit producing tritium this year, the yield of the stockpile would drop. . . .

The magnitude of the drop was deleted in the sanitized transcript. Tritium is produced by neutron absorption in lithium-6. A given production reactor can yield either plutonium or tritium depending upon the "fertile" material used as a target.

Cochran, Arkin, and Hoenig[11] have estimated that as of the end of 1980 there were 54–85 kilograms of tritium in the U.S. nuclear arsenal. Due to radioactive decay, this quantity was only about half of the total that had been produced. To maintain a tritium inventory of nearly 100 kilograms would require the production of 6 kilograms of tritium each year. Because it takes the absorption of one neutron in an appropriate "fertile" atom to produce one atom of either tritium or plutonium-239, and because the plutonium atom is 80 times heavier, the production of 6 kilograms of tritium would require an amount of production reactor capacity equivalent to that required to produce about 0.5 tonnes of weapon-grade plutonium. This is approximately the average production rate of one of the Savannah River reactors.[13]

Although a superpower fissile production cutoff agreement would not necessarily include a limit on their stockpiles of tritium, such a limit would be consistent with the basic idea of constraining the further development of the superpower nuclear arsenals. This could be accomplished by an agreement between the two nations limiting their tritium production to below a common ceiling. If the estimate by Cochran et al. of the U.S. tritium stockpile is correct, the United States could maintain its stockpile with a single production reactor. Because the warheads with the largest tritium requirements are neutron bombs and, since the public record at least indicates that the United States has given such weapons a higher priority than does the U.S.S.R., the Soviet stockpile could probably be maintained within the same ceiling. Once an agreed production rate had been established, the observance of this agreement could be verified by international inspectors and the tritium production reactor could be safeguarded against diversion of fissile materials just like any other reactor. As a result of a common production rate and radioactive decay the two tritium stockpiles would, in the absence of changes in the production rates, asymptotically approach a common plateau.

Although there are also civilian uses of tritium, their scale is currently not significant relative to military uses.

DETECTION OF CLANDESTINE PRODUCTION FACILITIES

In contrast to the situation for declared facilities, the U.S. approach to the problem of potential undeclared or clandestine facilities for the production of fissile materials for weapons evolved considerably between 1962, when verification of a fissile cutoff was first discussed, and 1969, when the government made its last major public statement on the matter. In 1962, U.S. proposals envisioned each superpower deploying roving inspection teams in the territory of the other to search out any clandestine facilities.[76] In 1969, however, the United States completely dropped this demand and announced that it deemed that IAEA inspections of declared facilities would be adequate.[77] Implicit in this position was confidence that the United States could detect large-scale clandestine production by "national technical means." What had happened to bring about this dramatic change?

An important part of the answer is surveillance satellites. Routine surveillance of the Soviet Union with satellites began in 1961 and, by 1969, the technology involved had progressed quite far. In the case of optical surveillance, it appears that the current capabilities of U.S. "close-look" satellites — resolutions on the order of 0.3 meters — had already been achieved.[78-80] It is obvious that, with such capabilities, every structure of significant size on the surface of the earth can, in principle at least, be subjected to detailed satellite inspection — during both construction and operation. It is such capabilities that gave the United States confidence that it could adequately verify Soviet compliance with the SALT II Treaty, which, among other things, limits changes in the dimensions of the missile silos on each side and bars the Soviet Union from deploying its SS-16 mobile intercontinental ballistic missile.

Surveillance from space with telescopes operating at visible wavelengths is only one of the technologies with which the superpowers have rendered each other's societies relatively transparent. Orbiting telescopes operating in the thermal infrared wavelength region can detect temperature differences on the order of tenths of a degree Centigrade and thereby reveal hidden sources of heat. And ground-based, ship-borne, airborne, and satellite receivers are used by the superpowers to monitor each other's internal radio and microwave communications.[81] Finally, the two superpowers read each other's publications and reports and collect information through interviews with emigrés and from insiders—some of whom have been quite highly placed.[82]

The integrated product of all these many intelligence activities is stunning—as has recently been revealed in the U.S. Defense Department publication, *Soviet Military Power*.[83]

In view of these capabilities, it appears unlikely that either superpower could conceal from the other the existence of a major program—such as that required to produce clandestinely the one tonne of plutonium or 6.0 tonnes of highly enriched uranium per year which we have defined as the minimum significant violation of a fissile cutoff agreement. Below, we consider some of the ways in which such a program might be detected: first through the detection of the construction of the production facilities, then through their uranium demand, and finally through some other distinctive emissions of the operating facilities.

Detection of Construction Activities

The production of weapon-usable fissile material entirely outside of a safeguarded civilian system would require either:

- one or more clandestine uranium enrichment plants; or
- one or more clandestine plutonium (or U-233) production reactors and associated nuclear fuel reprocessing plants.

The construction and operation of clandestine uranium enrichment plants, plutonium production reactors, or reprocessing plants with capacities on the scales being considered here would be billion to multibillion dollar (or dollar-equivalent) enterprises:

- The production of 6.0 tonnes of weapon-grade uranium would require 1.5 million separative work units, the equivalent of 12% of the annual capacity of the Portsmouth Gas Centrifuge Enrichment Plant—as proposed in 1983, when the ultimate cost of this facility was estimated at $9 billion.[67,84]
- A plutonium production rate of 1 tonne a year would be about equal to the combined average production rate of two of the Savannah River production reactors.[13] The new production reactor proposed by the Department of Energy was estimated in 1983 to cost $3–6 billion.[48]
- At the low neutron exposures required for the production of weapon-grade plutonium, only about one kilogram of plutonium would be produced per tonne of natural uranium in the fuel.[15] To recover one tonne

of plutonium, about 1,000 tonnes of irradiated uranium would therefore have to be reprocessed. This is comparable to the design capacity of the partially-built commercial reprocessing plant at Barnwell, South Carolina. Approximately $500 million was spent on that plant and in 1983 it was estimated that $700 million would be required to complete it.[85]

Assuming a construction time of five years, and the equivalent of $50,000 per job-year, about 4,000 workers would be involved in a billion-dollar construction job. It would be extremely difficult to successfully conceal all the manifestations of an effort on this scale.

Detection Through Uranium Demand

The production of 6.0 tonnes of highly enriched uranium would require the equivalent of 1,200 tonnes of natural uranium feed at the associated enrichment plant(s) (assuming 0.2% U-235 in the depleted uranium "tails"[32]), and the production of 1 tonne of plutonium would require about 1,000 tonnes of natural uranium feed for the production reactor, assuming no uranium recycle. Uranium has been recycled at U.S. production reactors but this has required the use of enriched fuel. With highly enriched fuel and recycling, about 250 tonnes of natural uranium are required at the enrichment plant per tonne of weapon-grade plutonium produced by the Savannah River reactors. About 500 tonnes were required at the original Hanford production reactors.[13] The use of enriched uranium as fuel would provide another means for detecting a clandestine production reactor.

Although these are not physically massive amounts of material, they do correspond to significant fractions of the current uranium flows in the superpower nuclear power systems. Twelve to fourteen hundred tonnes of natural uranium per year would be enough to fuel ten large million-kilowatt nuclear power reactors[64] — the equivalent of about 10% of the nuclear capacity that the United States (20% in the U.S.S.R.) had in operation or under construction as of the end of 1982 (see Table 22.3).[56] To make more difficult the channeling of this much uranium to clandestine production facilities, safeguards could be extended to cover the source of uranium. Specifically, it might be practical to put under safeguards uranium "mills" where the uranium is separated out from much larger quantities of uranium ore. Such uranium mills are traditionally divided into two categories: "conventional" and "other."

Conventional Mills. At conventional uranium mills, ore transported from local mines is crushed and the uranium leached out of the ore — usually with a strong acid solution. As of the beginning of 1980, the United States had in operation 21 conventional uranium mills with an average processing capacity of 2,300 tonnes of ore per day.[86] For typical uranium ore containing 0.1% uranium, an average mill operating at full capacity could recover 840 tonnes of natural uranium containing 6 tonnes of U-235 each year. Almost a million tonnes of leached ore "tailings" would also be produced. (The tailings piles associated with conventional uranium mills are usually their most visible feature.*)

Safeguarding a conventional uranium mill would involve arrangements to ensure that significant quantities of uranium-oxide product were not removed from it until the containers were logged out and sealed by an inspector. In view of the massive amount of materials that pass in and out of these facilities, it might be difficult to devise a practical containment system. An accounting system may be more feasible, however, since it may be possible to monitor the quantities of uranium being recovered by measurements of the amounts in solution. A more detailed study of this problem would be useful.

In addition to conventional mills, in 1980, eighteen small-scale, "unconventional" uranium recovery operations accounted for about 15% of U.S. uranium production.[86,87] The two most important types of unconventional uranium recovery operations are solution mining and the recovery of uranium as a byproduct. Typically, these operations are relatively small in scale (about 200 tonnes of natural uranium recovered per year).

Solution Mining. In a solution-mining operation, a strong acid or alkaline solution is pumped down into a uranium-bearing formation through "injection" wells and is then pumped out again through "collector" wells into a chemical plant where the dissolved uranium is then "stripped" out of the recovered solution which is then recycled (see Figure 22.11). Although solution mining does not generate conspicuous large piles of tailings at the surface, the development of a solution mine producing hundreds of tonnes of uranium a year would require the drilling of hundreds of wells.[88] Such an operation might be distinctive enough to identify by satellite.

Byproduct Uranium. Another type of operation involves the recovery of uranium as a byproduct of other mineral-extraction processes involving acid solutions—notably at phosphate plants which produce phosphoric acid as an intermediate product. Because the uranium is typically found in phosphate ore at concentrations on the order of 100 ppm,[89] significant

---

*Assuming a specific density of 2, 1 million tonnes of mill tailings would make a pile 500 meters long, 100 meters wide and 10 meters thick.

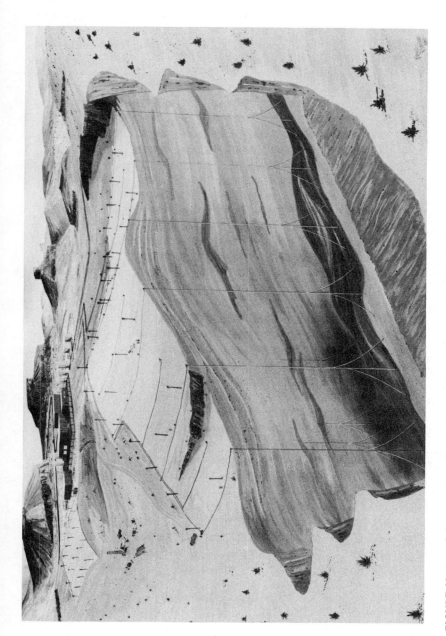

FIGURE 22.11. Artist's conception of a uranium solution mining operation. (Source: U.S. Department of Interior, Bureau of Mines.)

quantities of uranium can only be recovered at huge mining operations. Such operations would be easy to identify by satellite. On-site inspections could then determine whether uranium was being recovered.

Although the mining stage is quite different for conventional and unconventional mills, similar solution and precipitation steps are involved and a material accounting system developed for conventional mills might be applicable to unconventional recovery operations as well.

An indication of the difficulty of concealing uranium-mining operations is the fact that although the Soviet Union has gone to great lengths to keep its uranium mining operations secret it has been possible to determine many of their locations from public sources. Often it was the very effort to conceal the existence of a town or the presence of administrative arrangements that were appropriate to a much larger town that provided a key clue to the presence of uranium-mining activities.[18]

The Problem of Secret Stockpiles. Even if safeguards on uranium milling activities were completely effective, however, it would still be necessary to have reasonable confidence that clandestine enrichment plants and plutonium production facilities could be detected. This is because of the possible existence of secret stockpiles of already-separated uranium. As will be seen from Table 22.2, the United States has built up stockpiles of depleted, natural and low-enriched uranium containing a total of hundreds of tonnes of U-235. Similar stockpiles probably exist in the U.S.S.R. Although such stockpiles could be put under safeguards during the implementation of a fissile production cutoff, it is all too easy to imagine that natural or low-enriched uranium—containing perhaps as much as one hundred tonnes of U-235—might have been previously hidden. Such stockpiles might only become detectable if the original records of the materials production complexes were to become available. It would be extremely useful to have a detailed study of what information would be required for such a reconstruction and how the authenticity of such information could be verified.

To the extent that major stockpiles of uranium of any enrichment are declared, it would be desirable to put them under safeguards. Fortunately, there is every reason for such major stockpiles to be co-located with major fuel cycle facilities—especially uranium enrichment plants. The arrangements for safeguarding the uranium stockpiles might therefore be integrated with the safeguard arrangements for the associated facilities.

Direct Detection of Clandestine Production Facilities

In addition to the generic indicators associated with their construction and uranium demands, each of the major fissile material production facilities has certain emissions characteristic of its operation that might make it more detectable. Below, we discuss some of these characteristic emissions by facility type.

Uranium Enrichment Plants. The ease of detection of an enrichment facility varies with the technology involved. Gaseous diffusion plants are reasonably conspicuous because of their large size and heavy power demand. Both characteristics stem from the fact that each passage of the UF_6 gas through a diffusion barrier increases its enrichment by only a very small percent. As a result, several thousand enrichment stages are required to produce weapon-grade uranium. This same feature makes it relatively expensive to make small-capacity diffusion enrichment plants.[90]

The long building labeled (1) towards the rear of the complex shown in Figure 22.12 is Britain's gaseous diffusion enrichment plant that was shut down in 1982. Its separative work capacity was 400,000 separative work units (SWUs) per year[65] — enough to produce 1.7 tonnes of weapon-grade uranium per year. This is only one quarter the production level of 6.0 tonnes per year which we have defined as our threshold level for a significant violation, yet the building is massive (about 0.5 kilometers long) and — as is evidenced by the cooling towers — its energy demand was quite large. A diffusion plant producing 6.0 tonnes of weapon-grade uranium annually and using the same technology as is currently employed in the recently modernized U.S. diffusion plant complex[29] would consume an average of 400,000 kilowatts of electric power — about as much as the electricity demand of an average U.S. city of 400,000.

Gas centrifuges have a much larger separation gain per stage and therefore require only tens instead of thousands of enrichment stages to produce weapon-grade uranium.[65] As a result, these plants are smaller, consume an order of magnitude less energy per SWU, and are much less conspicuous than diffusion enrichment plants. Furthermore, because of the small unit sizes of the centrifuges, centrifuge enrichment plants can be built at quite small size.

The white square building (2) in Figure 22.12 is a demonstration gas centrifuge enrichment plant with an enrichment capacity of 200,000 SWUs per year — one-half the capacity of the adjacent diffusion plant. The longer building (3) adjacent to the demonstration plant and opposite the diffusion plant is another centrifuge enrichment plant, which is programmed to contain upon completion an additional 1 million SWUs/yr of enrichment capacity.[91] Note that no cooling towers appear to be associated with either centrifuge plant — reflecting their relatively low energy consumption. When the second plant is completed, the two centrifuge enrichment facilities could together produce at full capacity about 5 tonnes of weapon-grade uranium per year — almost the amount that we have defined as a threshold level for a significant violation of a fissile cutoff agreement. For such rela-

FIGURE 22.12. An aerial view of the Capenhurst works of BNFL near Chester. One of the world's first production plants for the enrichment of uranium by the gas centrifuge process is operating at Capenhurst (labeled 2). A second plant is being commissioned (3). The long facility labeled (1) is the original gaseous diffusion enrichment plant — now shut down. (Source: British Nuclear Fuel Ltd.)

tively undistinctive plants, it is likely that satellite observation would be a supplementary rather than sufficient method for their identification. The larger intelligence effort would probably be able to identify them, however, by picking up distinctive indications of the enormous effort associated with the manufacture and installation of the very large numbers of unique ultracentrifuges.

Although the technology is still under development, laser isotope enrichment is expected to require no more energy and have still larger enrichment gain per stage than gas centrifuge enrichment.[65] These facts give no encouragement that laser enrichment plants would be any more visible to satellites than centrifuge plants. An intriguing suggestion has been made, however, that:

> Detection of operation could be accomplished by reliance on the distinctive electromagnetic signature of a [laser enrichment] plant resulting from the pulsed operation of the lasers, flash lamps, and other items.[92]

Plutonium Production Reactors. The most conspicuous emission of a production reactor is its heat output, which must be discharged to the environment. A set of clandestine production reactors capable of producing 1 tonne of plutonium a year would produce waste heat at an average rate of about 3 million kilowatts. This is equal to the *total* energy consumption of an average U.S. city of 300,000 people.

The outflows of hot water from the Savannah River production reactors (1.6 million kilowatts average output in fiscal year 1983)[93] are startlingly visible in thermal infrared photographs taken from an altitude of 1.2 km.[94] They are so broad that there would be no difficulty in detecting them from satellite altitudes as well. Unfortunately, the photographs are in false color and therefore cannot be reproduced here. In the photographs, the hot water shows up as red and orange against the blue background of the surrounding area for a distance of more than 2 kilometers from the reactor. The streams are about 100 meters wide until they flow into a swamp, where one spreads out into a delta 1.5 km wide before it cools below a "red" heat. (See *Scientific American*, September 1985, p. 41.)

Of course, a nation wishing to produce plutonium clandestinely might build, say, ten less-detectable, small production reactors instead of one large one. The advantage of this approach is reduced somewhat, however, by the fact that detection of any one of the production reactors would reveal the existence of the entire program. Attempts could also be made to hide the thermal output of the production reactors. The hot water from a production reactor with a 3-million-kilowatt thermal output would, for example, raise the average temperature of the Columbia River by only 0.1°C — the approximate limit of detectability — *if it were possible to mix the hot water into the river uniformly.*[95] It would require quite an elaborate arrangement to accomplish such mixing, however.

Figure 22.13 illustrates the visibility in the thermal infrared of the heated cooling water discharged into coastal waters from a steam-electric power plant in Jakarta, Indonesia.[96] The intensity of the thermal infrared radiation increases as the shading of the image phases from black to white. The dark area covering the bottom half of the picture is land — the Jakarta harbor-front. The grey area covering the top half is the ocean, which appears to have been warmer than the land at the time the image was made. The white area at the left is water that has been heated by passing through the steam-condenser of the power plant.

Fuel Reprocessing Plants. The releases of Kr-85 from current nuclear fuel reprocessing plants are sufficiently large that they can be detected out to large distances. Figure 22.14 shows the time-averaged excess concentrations of Kr-85 in the atmosphere around the Savannah River reprocessing plant

FIGURE 22.13. Infrared image of the thermal plume made by the cooling water discharged into the ocean by a steam–electric power plant. Spots are mostly the hot tops of smoke stacks. (Source: Indonesian National Institute of Aeronautics and Space.)

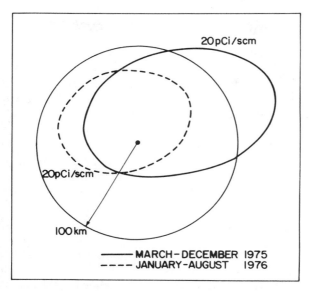

FIGURE 22.14. Excess concentrations of Kr-85 (in picoCuries per standard cubic meter of air) around the Savannah River Reprocessing plant. Background level = 15 pCi/scm. (Source: Pendergast et al.[97])

for two periods during 1975–1976 when the three production reactors there were producing 1–2 tonnes of plutonium per year. The average concentration was more than twice the background level of about 15 pCi/m^3 out to distances on the order of 100 kilometers, with weekly averages frequently exceeding 100 pCi/m^3 at distances of 50 kilometers.[97]

A clandestine reprocessing plant could, of course, include arrangements for trapping the Kr-85. This has been done using cryogenic techniques at the Idaho Chemical Processing Plant where U.S. naval reactor fuel is reprocessed.[98] The experience with that facility suggests, however, that it would be very difficult to maintain an average collection efficiency greater than 90% and that malfunctions could be expected to result in major episodes of leakage.[99] As a result, it seems likely that, even with Kr-85 trapping, reprocessing plants would be detectable through their Kr-85 emissions at distances on the order of 50 kilometers. Of course, the vastness of the territories of the superpowers would mean that clandestine reprocessing plants could be located at much greater distances than this from any likely air-sampling station. However, further study of the possibility of detecting reprocessing plants through their emissions of Kr-85 and other effluents might prove useful.

Distinctive features of clandestine fuel reprocessing plants might also be recognizable by satellite during construction or operation. For example, the high-level waste tanks might reveal the nature of the plant to thermal infrared radiation detectors because their radioactive contents would be generating considerable amounts of heat. The accumulated wastes would generate about 1,000 kilowatts of heat after three years of recovering plutonium at the rate of one tonne per year. (We base this calculation on the fact that light-water reactor fuel containing one tonne of uranium, in which 33,000 megawatt-days of fission energy has been released over three years, generates about 10 kilowatts of heat one year after discharge.[100] The production of 1 tonne of weapon-grade plutonium in a production reactor would involve the release of about 1.2 million megawatt-days of fission heat.[13] We further assume that the fuel cools one year before reprocessing.)

Detection Synergisms

Although in theory each of the means of detection discussed above could be evaded, the clandestine production of either weapon-grade uranium or plutonium would require the successful concealment of the construction of *all* the major facilities and activities involved from *all* efforts at detection for *many* years. Assuming adequate safeguards on civilian facilities:

- The clandestine production of a significant amount of weapon-grade uranium would require that the secret construction of the equivalent of a major enrichment plant *and* its undetected operation *for a period of ten years*.
- The clandestine production of a significant amount of weapon-grade plutonium would require the secret construction of the equivalent of *both* a major production reactor and a major reprocessing plant *and* the operation of these facilities undetected *for a period of ten years*.

Ambiguous evidence of clandestine production activities could be brought to a body such as the Standing Consultative Commission which was originally set up to handle questions concerning compliance with the 1972 U.S.-U.S.S.R. Treaty on the Limitation of Anti-Ballistic Missile Systems. In the absence of satisfactory explanations, on-site inspections might be requested. The United States, U.S.S.R. and U.K. agreed to similar "challenge inspections" prior to the suspension of their negotiations of a Comprehensive Nuclear Weapons Test Ban Treaty in 1980. Systematic obstruction of efforts to obtain answers to legitimate questions would, of course, threaten the continuation of the cutoff agreement.

Of course, the reward for the successful concealment of a threshold-size clandestine production program would hardly be spectacular: an increase by 10% in fissile material stockpiles that are already absurdly large.

REDUCTION OF THE STOCKPILES

A cutoff in the production of fissile materials for nuclear weapons would facilitate verifiable reductions in the quantities of these materials in the superpower nuclear arsenals. The fissile materials being eliminated could be burned as fuel in existing nuclear power reactors.

Some of the highly enriched uranium could be used to fuel naval and research reactors. The remainder could be diluted with depleted or natural uranium down to the few percent enrichment level used in power reactor fuel. The U.S. stockpile of weapon-grade uranium could fuel the current U.S. nuclear power system for about a decade (see Table 22.3).

The stockpiles of weapon-grade plutonium would have to be disposed of with greater care, because, unlike the weapon-grade uranium, the material could not be easily rendered unusable for weapons by mixing with a natural nonfissile isotope of the same element. One possibility would be to use the plutonium as fuel in a relatively few heavily safeguarded reactors operated in a once-through mode (i.e., without fuel reprocessing). Because plutonium-239 could be substituted on approximately a one-for-one basis for the U-235 in the fuel of these reactors, the reactor capacity required to consume the plutonium in a given period of time would be smaller than that required to consume the highly enriched uranium by a factor approximately equal to the ratio of the stockpiles — approximately one sixth in the United States.

Between the times when they were released from the weapons stockpiles and when they were consumed in reactors, weapon-grade fissile materials would be kept under international safeguards. Suitable arrangements are apparently already under development by the IAEA — in large part because of its concerns about the security of the large amounts of plutonium currently being separated at civilian reprocessing plants.[54]

The negotiation of *drastic* reductions (e.g., ten-fold or more) in the fissile stockpiles of the superpowers might require them to make available more information concerning the magnitudes of these stockpiles. Since the two superpowers can probably estimate each other's stockpiles of weapons fissile materials reasonably well, there is no obvious reason why they could not, on the basis of these estimates, negotiate reductions in their stockpiles of weapons materials by 50% or so. In the absence of better information, however, deeper reductions might be difficult to negotiate, for each would tend to exaggerate the size of the other's remaining stockpile and put forward unacceptable reduction proposals. Also, when the stockpiles have been much reduced, smaller violations than we have considered here might assume more importance. For these reasons, more information exchange and more refined analyses would be desirable.

CONCLUSIONS

The results of this survey encourage us to believe that—at the current levels of the superpower nuclear arsenals at least—adequate verification of an agreement to cut off the production of fissile material for nuclear weapons could be achieved. Of course, if and when nuclear disarmament proceeds to the point where the stockpiles have been greatly reduced, the task of adequate verification may become more difficult. In this "first cut" analysis, we cannot estimate how far such reductions might proceed before considerations of verifiability become a serious impediment. Such considerations should not, however, delay the quite dramatic actions that could be taken immediately. Indeed, successful conclusion of a superpower fissile cutoff could create a more conducive atmosphere for the negotiations of drastic reductions.

Acknowledgments—David Albright obtained for us a number of the references used in this study. Thomas Cochran and Milton Hoenig have been generous in sharing with us before its publication[11] the information that they have been gathering on the U.S. nuclear weapons complex. Anthony Fainberg collaborated on an early draft before other commitments made it impossible for him to see the project through. Harold Feiveson collaborated with one of the authors on a previous short article in which some of the ideas presented here were first outlined.[101] The analysis was developed further for presentation at a set of hearings held in March 1983 on the technical basis for a nuclear weapons freeze. The hearings were held under the auspices of the Federation of American Scientists (FAS) and organized by FAS Director Jeremy Stone.

REFERENCES

1. McPhee, John. *The Curve of Binding Energy*. New York: Ballantine, 1973, p. 9.
2. Groves, L. R. The Test. Memorandum for the Secretary of War, 18 July 1945. (Reprinted in Sherwin, M. J. *A World Destroyed: The Atomic Bomb and the Grand Alliance*. New York: Alfred A. Knopf, 1975, Appendix P.)
3. U.S. Department of State. Statement by the United States Representative (Baruch) to the United Nations Atomic Energy Commission, June 14, 1946. In *Documents on Disarmament, 1945-1956*. Washington, DC: U.S. Department of State, 1960, p. 7. See also, *First Report of the United Nations Atomic Energy Commission to the Security Council*, December 31, 1946, *ibid.*, p. 50.
4. U.S. Department of State. *Documents on Disarmament*. Washington, DC: U.S. State Department [starting in 1961 taken over by the U.S. Arms Control and Disarmament Agency]: *1945-1959*, pp. 593–595, 953–967; *1960*, pp. 222–223; *1961*, p. 469; *1962*, pp. 146–147, 285–286, 567; *1963*, p. 333; *1964*, p. 4, 35–36, 162, 165–166, 335–338, 399–403; *1965*, p. 117; *1966*, p. 7, 222–226, 538–546, 554–560; *1967*, pp. 452–454; *1969*, pp. 109–110; 158–161.
5. *Ibid. 1961*, pp. 432–433; *1962*, pp. 423–446; *1964*, 339–340; *1965*, p. 191; *1966*, p. 604; *1969*, pp. 171–172.
6. "Statement by Andrei A. Gromyko, Member of the Politburo of the Central

Committee of the CPSU, Minister of Foreign Affairs of the U.S.S.R., at Plenary Meeting of the Second Special Session of the United Nations General Assembly Devoted to Disarmament, June 15, 1982." (unofficial translation distributed June 15, 1982, by the Soviet mission to the U.N.).

7. Taylor, Theodore B. Nuclear Safeguards. *Annual Reviews of Nuclear Science* (1975):407.

8. United States. Senate. Armed Services Committee. Roser, Herman E., Assistant Secretary of Energy for Defense Programs. In *Department of Defense Authorization for Appropriations for Fiscal Year 1983, Part 7: Strategic and Theater Nuclear Forces.* Hearings, 17 March 1982, p. 4979.

9. United States. House of Representatives. Committee on Appropriations. Subcommittee on Energy and Water Development. Morgan, Robert L., Deputy Assistant Secretary for Defense Programs, Department of Energy. In *Energy and Water Development Appropriations for 1985.* Hearings, 13 March 1984, pp. 346–347.

10. U.S. Atomic Energy Commission. *Draft Environmental Statement, Waste Management Operations, Hanford Reservation, Richland, Wash.* (WASH-1538), 1974, p. II.1–7.

11. Cochran, T. B., W. M. Arkin and M. M. Hoenig. *Nuclear Weapons Databook, Volume II: The Production Complex.* Cambridge, MA: Ballinger, in press.

12. Albright, D. *World Inventories of Civilian Plutonium and the Spread of Nuclear Weapons.* Washington, D.C.: Nuclear Control Institute, 1983.

13. von Hippel, Frank, Barbara G. Levi and David H. Albright. *Quantities of Fissile Materials in U.S. and Soviet Nuclear Weapons Stockpiles.* Princeton, NJ: Princeton University: Center for Energy and Environmental Studies Report No. 168, in press.

14. United States. Senate. Committee on Armed Services. Subcommittee on Strategic and Theater Nuclear Forces. Roser, Herman E., Assistant Secretary for Defense Programs, Department of Energy. In *Department of Energy Fiscal Year 1983 National Defense Programs Authorization.* Hearing, 26 April 1982, pp. 30, 47.

15. *Heavy-Element Concentrations in Power Reactors.* Clearwater, FL: NUS Corporation, 1977, Report SND-120-2.

16. Petrosy'ants, A. M. *Problems of Nuclear Science and Technology: The Soviet Union as a World Nuclear Power, 4th Edition.* Oxford, England: Pergamon Press, 1981, p. 104.

17. United States. House of Representatives. Committee on Armed Services. Procurement and Military Nuclear Systems Subcommittee. Wagner, Richard L., Assistant Secretary of Defense for Atomic Energy. In *Department of Energy National Security and Military Applications of the Nuclear Energy Authorization Act of 1984.* Hearing, March 1983, pp. 19, 23.

18. Dienes, Leslie and Theodore Shabad. *The Soviet Energy System: Resource Use and Policies.* New York: V. H. Winston & Sons, 1979, pp. 156, 160, 170–182.

19. Semenov, B. A. Nuclear Power in the Soviet Union. *IAEA Bulletin* 25 (June 1983):47.

20. Medvedev, Z. Two Decades of Dissidence. *New Scientist,* 4 (1976).

21. Wohlstetter, Albert. Proof of Evidence on Behalf of Friends of the Earth, Ltd. Submitted to the Public Local Inquiry into an Application by British Nuclear Fuels Limited for Planning Permission to Establish a Plant for Reprocessing Irradiated Oxide Fuels and Support Site Services at Windscale and Calder

Works, Cumbria, September 5-6, 1977. California Seminar on Arms Control and Foreign Policy, 1977.

22. Palmer, George and Dan I. Bolef. Laser Isotope Separation: The Plutonium Connection. *Bulletin of the Atomic Scientists* (March 1984):26.

23. The Hart-Simpson ammendment (subsection 57(e) to the Atomic Energy Act), *Congressional Record*. March 30, 1982, p. S2959.

24. Letter from George Rathjens and Herbert Scoville to Senator Ernest Hollings, March 4, 1983.

25. U.S. Atomic Energy Commission. *Statistical Data of the Uranium Industry.* U.S. Atomic Energy Commission, GJO-100(74), 1974, pp. 9, 11.

26. Hewlett, Richard G. and Oscar E. Anderson. *A History of the United States Atomic Energy Commission I: The New World (1939-1946).* Washington, D.C.: U.S. AEC, Report No. WASH-1214, 1972, pp. 291–292.

27. Hewlett, Richard G. and Francis Duncan. *A History of the United States Atomic Energy Commission II: Atomic Shield (1947-1952).* Washington, D.C.: U.S. AEC, Report No. WASH-1215, 1972, p. 674.

28. U.S. uranium import numbers for the periods 1945–1947 and 1953–1956 have been taken from an unpublished report by Robert Pitman (DOE), quoted in 1977 to Kirk Smith (now at the East-West Institute, University of Hawaii).

29. Hill, James H. and Joe W. Parks. Uranium Enrichment in the United States. Energy Research and Development Administration, Report No. CONF 750324-7, 1975, Fig. 1.

30. U.S. Department of Energy. *Uranium Enrichment, 1980 Annual Report.* Oak Ridge Operations Office, Report No. ORO-822, 1980, pp. 32, 33.

31. U.S. Department of Energy. *1982 Uranium Enrichment Annual Report.* p. 28.

32. U.S. Atomic Energy Commission. *Gaseous Diffusion Plant Operations.* Oak Ridge Operations Office, Report No. ORO-684, 1972.

33. Arkin, W. M., T. B. Cochran and M. M. Hoenig. Resource Paper on the U.S. Nuclear Arsenal. *Bulletin of the Atomic Scientists*, Aug./Sept. 1984.

34. United States. Senate. Armed Services Committee. Wade, James P., Deputy Under Secretary of Defense for Research and Engineering. In *Department of Defense Authorization for Appropriations for Fiscal Year 1983, Part 7—Strategic and Theater Nuclear Forces.* Hearings, February–March 1982, pp. 4963, 4966.

35. Paxton, H. C. *Los Alamos Critical-Mass Data.* Los Alamos, NM: Los Alamos National Laboratory, Report No. LA-3067-MS, Revised, 1975.

36. Weiss, W., A. Sittkus, H. Stockburger and H. Sartorius. Large-Scale Atmospheric Mixing Derived From Meridional Profiles of Krypton-85. *Journal of Geophysical Research* 88, No. C13, (1983):8574–8578.

37. Telegadas, K. and G. J. Ferber. Atmospheric Concentrations and Inventory of Krypton-85 in 1973. *Science* 190 (1975): 882; and *Health and Safety Laboratory Environmental Quarterly* (New York, NY: Health and Safety Laboratory, U.S. Energy Research and Development Administration [now Department of Energy], Report No. HASL-294, 1975).

38. *Report of the United Nations Scientific Committee on the Effects of Atomic Radiation.* New York: United Nations, 1964, Table III.

39. *Sources and Effects of Ionizing Radiation, 1977.* New York: United Nations, 1977, p. 121.

40. *Radioactive Effluents from Nuclear Power Stations and Nuclear Fuel Reprocessing Plants in the European Community: Discharge Data, Radiological Aspects.* Data for 1972-1976 in the 1978 edition and for 1974-1978 in the 1980

edition. Luxembourg: Commission of the European Communities, 1978 and 1980.

41. U.K. data for 1971–1981 from a letter from R. S. Edmonds, Senior U.K. Atomic Energy Authority Liaison Officer, British Embassy, Washington, D.C., to David Albright, 21 March 1984.

42. State of the Union Address by President Johnson to the Congress [Extract], January 8, 1964. In *Documents on Disarmament, 1964.* Washington, DC: U.S. Arms Control and Disarmament Agency, p. 4.

43. Address by President Johnson Before the Associated Press. Reduction of Fissionable Materials Production [Extract]. April 20, 1964, *ibid.* 165.

44. Statement by Premier Khrushchev on Reduction of Fissionable Materials Production, April 10, 1964, *ibid.*, p. 166; Statement by Prime Minister Douglas-Home to the House of Commons. Reduction of Fissionable Materials Production. April 21, 1964, *ibid.*, p. 171.

45. Simpson, John. *The Independent Nuclear State: The United States, Britain, and the Military Atom.* London: Macmillan, 1983.

46. United States. Senate. Committee on Armed Services. Wagner, Richard L., Assistant Secretary of Defense for Atomic Energy. In *Department of Defense Authorization for Appropriations for Fiscal Year 1984, Part 5: Strategic and Theater Nuclear Forces.* Hearings, March-May 1983, p. 2438.

47. United States. House of Representatives. Committee on Armed Services. Subcommittee on Procurement and Military Nuclear Systems. Gilbert, F. Charles, Deputy Assistant Secretary of Energy for Nuclear Materials. In *Department of Energy National Security and Military Applications of Nuclear Energy Authorization Act of 1984.* Hearings, March 1 and 2, 1983, pp. 144, 147, 151; 149–150.

48. Norman, Colin. DOE Chooses Idaho for New Weapons Plant. *Science* 26 (August 1983):839.

49. Enclosures to letters from Secretary of Energy Donald Paul Hodel to U.S. Representative Richard L. Ottinger, August 30, 1983 and March 5, 1984.

50. Brown, Harold. Letter to Frank von Hippel, March 2, 1984.

51. The Present Status of IAEA Safeguards on Nuclear Fuel Cycle Facilities. *International Atomic Energy Agency Bulletin* 22 (Special Issue for the Second NPT Review Conference, August 1980):4, 6.

52. United States Memorandum Submitted to the Disarmament Commission. Measures to Stop the Spread of Nuclear Weapons, Halt and Turn Down the Arms Race, and Reduce International Tension, April 29, 1965. *Documents on Disarmament, 1965.* Washington, D.C.: U.S. Arms Control and Disarmament Agency, pp. 104, 107.

53. *Arms Control and Disarmament Agreements, 1982 Edition.* Washington, D.C.: U.S. Arms Control and Disarmament Agency, pp. 86, 254–255.

54. Weinstock, E. V. and A. Fainberg. Verifying a Fissile-Material Production Freeze in Declared Facilities with Special Emphasis on Remote Monitoring. Chapter 20 in this volume.

55. Keepin, Robert. State-of-the-Art Technology for Measurement and Verification of Nuclear Materials. Chapter 21 in this volume.

56. Power Reactors 1983. *Nuclear Engineering International*, August 1983 Supplement.

57. "ERDA Issues Report on Inventory Differences for Strategic Nuclear Materials." U.S. Energy Research and Development Administration [now Department of Energy] Press Release 77-130, 1977.

58. NRC Issues Report on Nuclear Material Inventory Differences (MUF) at Licensed Commercial Nuclear Facilities. U.S. Nuclear Regulatory Commission, Press Release 77-151, 1977.
59. Lovett, J., K. Ikawa, M. Tsutsumi and T. Sawahata. *An Advanced Safeguards Approach for a Model 200 t/a [tonne uranium/annum] Reprocessing Facility*. Vienna: IAEA, IAEA Report No. STR-140, 1983.
60. Zaritskaya, T. S., A. K. Kruglov and A.P. Rudik. The Formation of Transuranium Nuclides in Connection with the Combined Use of VVER and RBMK Power Reactors. Translated from *Atomnaya Energiya* 46, 3 (1979):183–185 (Plenum Publishing Corp.).
61. Emel'yanov, I. Ya., A. D. Zhirnov, V. I. Pushkarev and A. P. Sirotkin. Increasing the Efficiency of Uranium Utilization in the RBMK-1000 Reactor. Translated from *Atomnaya Energiya* 46, 3 (1979):139–141 (Plenum Publishing Corp.).
62. *Uranium: Resources, Production and Demand*. Nuclear Energy Agency of the Organization for Economic Co-operation and Development [Paris] and the International Atomic Energy Agency [Vienna], annuals, 1972–1982.
63. Feiveson, Harold A., Frank von Hippel and Robert H. Williams. Fission Power: An Evolutionary Strategy. *Science*, 26 (January 1979):330.
64. International Nuclear Fuel Cycle Evaluation, Working Group 8. *Advanced Fuel Cycle and Reactor Concepts*. Vienna: International Atomic Energy Agency, Report INFCE/PC/2/8, 1980, Tables VIII and II.
65. Krass, Allan S., Peter Boskma, Boelie Elzen and Wim A. Smit. *Uranium Enrichment and Nuclear Weapon Proliferation*. Stockholm: International Peace Research Institute, 1983, pp. 214, 23–24, 160.
66. Hexapartite Safeguards Project. Safeguards Approach for Gas Centrifuge Type Enrichment Plants. *Nuclear Materials Management* (Winter 1983):30.
67. Norman, Colin. Hard Times in Uranium Enrichment. *Science* 9 (March 1984):1041.
68. Gordon, D. M., J. B. Sanborn, J. M. Younkin and V. J. DeVito. An Approach to IAEA Material-Balance Verification at the Portsmouth Gas Centrifuge Enrichment Plant. *Proceedings of the Fifth Annual Symposium on Safeguards and Nuclear Material Management*. Commission of the European Communities, Joint Research Center, 1983, p. 39.
69. *Research Reactors in Member States*. Vienna: International Atomic Energy Agency, microfiche No. IAEA-mf-1, 1980.
70. Matos, J. E. *RERTR [Reduced Enrichment Research and Test Reactor] Program Summary—September 1982*. Argonne, IL: Argonne National Laboratory, 1982.
71. Travelli, A. RERTR [Reduced Enrichment Research and Test Reactor] Program Activities Related to the Development and Application of New LEU [Low-Enriched Uranium] Fuels. Paper presented at the International Symposium on the Use and Development of Low and Medium Flux Reactor Fuels, MIT, October 17-19, 1983. Argonne, IL: Argonne National Laboratory, 1983.
72. LEU Study Group. *Assessment of the Implications of Conversion of University Research and Training Reactors to Low Enrichment Uranium Fuel*. Nuclear Regulatory Commission, 1983.
73. *Jane's Fighting Ships, 1982-83*. London: Jane's Publishing Company, Ltd.
74. Ref. 45, p. 201.
75. U.S. Joint Chiefs of Staff. *U.S. Military Posture, Fiscal Year 1979*. p. 28.
76. Statement by the United States Representative (Dean) to the Eighteen Nation Disarmament Committee. Replies to the United Arab Republic, May 30, 1962.

In *Documents on Disarmament, 1962*. Washington, D.C.: U.S. Arms Control and Disarmament Agency, p. 567.
77. Statement by ACDA Director Fisher to the Eighteen Nation Disarmament Committee, April 8, 1969. In *Documents on Disarmament, 1969*. Washington, D.C.: U.S. Arms Control and Disarmament Agency, p. 160.
78. Greenwood, Ted. Reconnaissance and Arms Control. *Scientific American*, (February 1973):14. See also the backup report, *Reconnaissance, Surveillance and Arms Control*. London: International Institute for Strategic Studies, Adelpha Paper No. 88, 1972.
79. See the satellite photographs reproduced in *Aviation Week and Space Technology (AWST)* (13 August 1984):26, 27. (Identified as satellite photographs in *AWST* (8 October 1984):27.
80. *The Implications of Establishing an International Satellite Monitoring Agency*. New York, NY: United Nations, 1983, p. 8.
81. Bamford, James. *The Puzzle Palace: A Report on NSA, America's Most Secret Agency*. Boston, MA: Houghton Mifflin, 1982.
82. Penkovskiy, O. *The Penkovskiy Papers*. (Garden City, NY: Doubleday & Co., 1965.
83. *Soviet Military Power*. Washington, D.C.: U.S. Department of Defense, 1984.
84. Norman, Colin. Uranium Enrichment: Heading for the Abyss. *Science* (19 August 1983):730.
85. Walsh, John. End of the Road for Barnwell. *Science* (26 August 1983):835.
86. *Statistical Data of the Uranium Industry*. Washington, D.C.: U.S. Department of Energy, Report No. GJO-100(80), 1980, pp. 88, 94.
87. *An Assessment Report on Uranium in the United States of America*. Washington, D.C.: U.S. Department of Energy, Report No. GJO-111 [80], 1980, p. 135.
88. Toth, George W. and Clement K. Chase. *Uranium Solution Mining Cost Model*. Palo Alto, CA: Electric Power Research Institute, Report No. EPRI EA-731, 1978, pp. 2–9, 2–15.
89. Cathcart, J. B. *Uranium in Phosphate Rock*. Washington, D.C.: U.S. Geological Survey, Open File Report No. 75-32, 1975.
90. *Data on New Gaseous Diffusion Plants*. Washington, D.C.: U.S. Atomic Energy Agency [now the Department of Energy] Report No. ORO-586, 1972, p. 37.
91. R. S. Edmonds, Senior Liaison Officer, United Kingdom Atomic Energy Authority, British Embassy, Washington, D.C., private communication to FvH, 17 July 1984.
92. Jersey Nuclear-Avco Isotopes. *Laser Isotope Separation: Proliferation Risks and Benefits*. Bellevue, WA: 1979, Volume I, p. 33.
93. United States. House of Representatives. Committee on Armed Services. Procurement and Military Nuclear Systems Subcommittee. Denise, Richard P., Deputy Manager, Savannah River Operations Office. In *Department of Energy National Security and Military Applications of Nuclear Energy Authorization Act of 1984*. Hearing, March 1 and 2, 1983, p. 272.
94. *A Study of Thermal Plumes at the Savannah River Plant, Aiken, South Carolina*. Aiken, South Carolina: Savannah River Laboratory, Report No. EGG-1183-1827, 1982.
95. *World Almanac and Book of Facts, 1981*. New York: Newspaper Enterprise Association, p. 445 (for average flow of Columbia River).
96. Thermal infrared image courtesy of the Indonesian National Institute of Aeronautics and Space (LAPAN, June 1976).

97. Pendergast, M. M., A. L. Boni, G. L. Ferber and K. Telegadas. *Measured Weekly ^{85}Kr Concentrations Within 150 km of the Savannah River Plant (March 1975 Through August 1976)*. Aiken, SC: Savannah River Laboratory, Report No. DP-1486, 1979.

98. Benixsen, C. K. and G. F. Offutt. *Rare Gas Recovery Facility at the Idaho Chemical Processing Plant*. Idaho National Energy Laboratory, Idaho Nuclear Corp., Report No. 1221, 1971.

99. See, for example, Benixsen, C. K. and F. O. German. *Operation of the ICPP Rare Gas Recovery Facility During Fiscal Year 1970*. Idaho National Energy Laboratory, Allied Chemical Corp., Report No. ICP-1001, 1971.

100. *The Safety of Nuclear Power Reactors and Related Facilities*. Washington, D.C.: U.S. Atomic Energy Commission [now the Department of Energy], Report No. WASH-1250, 1973, Table 4-23.

101. Feiveson, Harold A. and Frank von Hippel. Cutting Off the Production of Fissile Material for Nuclear Weapons. *FAS Public Interest Report* (June 1982): pp. 10–11.

23.

Afterword

Philip Morrison

This was a series of compact and elaborating reviews of all kinds of questions — questions as broad as the political aspects and as narrow as the properties of emulsions. What I want to do is give a personal reaction to the development and flow of ideas over the three days here. It is not meant to be a definitive statement nor indeed a careful abstracting, but rather a series of reflective reactions on the part of one participant who has long been a student of these matters.

Our topic was put into a much wider context by the varied experiences of the distinguished people who spoke. The purpose of the report from the conference is to put salient the problem of understanding what verification is all about and how technology assists it; to inform a wider, reflective public about the matter and, possibly, to provide some guidance to those unknown persons who will someday be carrying out negotiations for agreements that will require compliance and will need technical verification.

I have to begin by saying that it was already clear on the very first morning from the personnel here that between our topic of verification and the problem of military intelligence in the modern world there is a very close interaction. It is, in fact, intelligence that we are talking about, though of a specific quality, through somewhat specified means, to serve a particular end. I felt a little bit at home in this because I come from a time of amateur and cruel intelligence organizations, namely World War II, when from 1942 through 1945 we did all manner of things on rather flimsy justification, because we could and because the urgency seemed high. People were willing to do all manner of things in those days. And it turns out, just a little to my surprise, that there is a profound continuity in the whole operation, because the nuclear phenomena are in the background of almost all that we have talked about here. And, of course, they were already visible in 1942; that's why we did what we did. The things we have discussed here, the imaging of mining districts and pit heads, the inventories and fuel cycle calculations, activities-sniffing by remote sensing and by more intrusive meth-

ods—all those things were tried in the derring-do style of the OSS agents
and the ALSOS Project at the end of the war. There is a long history. Intelligence was not very successful then, and led us to the gloomiest possible
conclusions on the basis of the worst-case analysis, which, as far as I can
see, is not absent even in these days of better resources and much better-
trained people to do the same things.

It is important to realize the effect of the irony of the conflict that Mr.
Colby noted, between the desperate need for public understanding of what
it all means and an equally desperate need for secrecy and avoidance of
public discussion. In this ironic twist it is hard to define sensible policy. It
also seems clear that intelligence is not enough, that even military intelligence in the strict sense always becomes at most the tool—I should say the
weapon—of those who seek and hold political power and the benefits of
political power, both domestically and in the grand international context
with respect to the other superpower. The diversity of talks and points of
views that we heard is just the sign of that.

On the other hand I would agree with something that Noel Gayler said:
that we make a great mistake if we forget that, complex as these problems
are and tied up as they are to a very long history of what states do and how
they behave towards each other, something quite new has entered. The
inordinate energy release of a nuclear explosion has given a new dimension
to the problem. It is likely that what we are talking about here is the most
important single security issue that people have ever faced. I myself think
the survival of the species depends upon coming to grips one way or
another with these problems. It seems to me that the perpetual standoff
that we have been into, metastable and dangerous as it is (and I have
devoted thirty-five to forty years to saying how dangerous it is), still
remains an inhibition to statesmen, even the most convinced of hawks.
There is an inhibition about losing even one city, like Tucson or Dallas,
even if you thought it was a fair price to pay to save New York or
Washington.

Whenever you talk about verification, you may talk about its risks and
its confidence, but in the end what you're asking is: Does the agreement or
the absence of the agreement better U.S. security? This is an objective way
of putting it, so that it allows a possible answer, not an easy answer. There
are quite a few people who see the agreement not in terms of the measure
the language of the agreement gives to security, but in terms of a future that
may bring a still greater confrontation, and they ask themselves, possibly
with sincerity: If I oppose the deepening confrontation now, do I not make
myself less ready for a more important and larger-scale confrontation
tomorrow? I think this is a curious political stance towards agreements, but
I expect it's a very real one. I think that it's the one that dominated the discussion of the Partial Test Ban Treaty, which destroyed that treaty as a

contribution to arms control and left it as only a wonderful example of solving ecological and public health problems on a world scale. I don't think that anybody really felt that the danger to the security of the United States of Soviet illicit testing was, in fact, real. Rather the use of that fear to convince people that an agreement should not go all the way, should leave our hands free for large-scale developments of our own through many, many generations of weapons, was the principal motivation of people like Edward Teller and many others who in those days—and still today—support this point of view.

I couldn't fail to mention what I thought was a telling anecdote in the late George Kistiakowsky's wonderful and rudely candid account of his years in the White House. Around election day of 1960, when he was about to turn over the helm as Eisenhower's Science Adviser to others, he was having a meeting involving the British on problems of international weaponry. Harold Brown, who was part of the group advising Kennedy, came early to the meeting, and Kistiakowsky's question to him—he was apparently in some doubt about it—was whether his aim was destruction of the Soviet Union or preservation of the peace. And Brown said, of course, the latter. George said, 'Ahh . . . I hoped so.''

In so many cases verification becomes an aim in itself. It is not so much the objective part of the intelligence art that matters, the part that distinguishes between intentions and capabilities, adds confidence to judgments, protects the forces at their level, knows what the other guy is doing—none of these is as important as the political goal you are after. Which one is it? Destruction of the enemy, or preservation of the peace? One should not lose sight of that question.

I think that Romm's paper (Chapter 5 of this volume) made quite clear, by explicit example, what for me is a necessary condition for discussing an agreement, namely, that neither breakout nor slow leakage nor incremental deficiencies in the noise of every verification system can shake our secure deterrent under present circumstances. This is a necessary condition for the rationality of pushing agreements in the presence of noise—for all agreements will have some noise. Therefore it seems to me that it's very valuable to have this well established, and the analysis made over and over again for every state of the existing forces. It's something we should keep forward in all discussions.

How important the present hyperbolic level of destructive capability is was shown by Frank von Hippel's account, in which everything about the fuel cycle that is noisy and difficult is lost in the fact that there is so much stuff out there now that it hardly makes any difference what you overlook in the next years! Thirty years of full-tilt, uninhibited accumulation has created stores of fissionable material everywhere; you only have to turn your hand to it to make something out of it. Now this is most important; it

will become less important and make the verification situation more difficult once we have any success in rolling back this extraordinary overpower.
On the other hand, we can probably face it. It's an encouraging fact that
this verification situation is at its best because the position is so bad overall,
and that when verification gets harder, it will be because the overall position has improved — not the least paradox to deal with. These stocks are
extraordinary. I was much impressed simply on the technical side by the
possibility of good estimates which are fairly consistent and, again, rest
upon multiple foundations. There's not very much you can say is wrong
with those estimates. And I am sure that similarly good ones exist, as Pete
Scoville assured us, for the Soviet side as much as for ours, although he did
not try to work that out in public.

Now I come to what was for me the best news of the last three days, but
I want to lead up to it by talking a little about the Partial Test Ban Treaty
again. The PTBT was a huge success if you look at the radio-strontium surface deposit or any radioactive substance in fallout you wish. You will see
an incredible rapidly rising curve, then a cutoff and a slow decay. The
treaty really worked. The presence of an occasional French or Chinese or
Rajastan leak is only to emphasize how well it works and how little these
people do compared to what the big boys did in the free decade of making
tests bigger and better and more frequent. So it showed that you could *do*
something. I emphasize that it could be done. The Partial Test Ban Treaty
came about not only because of the statesmanlike behavior of people and
the succession of historical crises that intervened, but also because of very
widespread public opinion that for a while shook the whole world. It had
the explicit intervention of the government of India and a host of other
quite remote powers, accompanied by housewives from St. Louis and the
rest of the phenomena of the rallying of public opinion. It is fair to say that
not since those years of the late fifties and early sixties have we seen a similar resounding concern in the world public, until the 1980s. That can give
some sense of potential to the people who are talking about improving the
situation in verification.

There were those who were naive enough to believe that given the
predilection of practical military leadership, operational testing is a vital
part of the preparation of weapons systems. We thought that banning tests
might mean stopping improvement, and then the gradual plateauing and
cooling of the arms race. Of course, it was not to happen. As everyone
knows, the number of tests is somewhat greater since than before the Test
Ban Treaty. They are underground tests; this is an inhibition on the collection of data, but by no means a cessation of it. It requires more money in
the test labs, more ingenuity, probably yields less information per test, but
it doesn't make any real difference. Information is not the true aim of most
tests anyhow. It was a lesson to me, a naive partisan, that it's difficult to

avoid the race; the animus which is here is deeper than any particular mani-festation of it. And of course, the invention of decoupling and all the shenanigans that went on with trying to argue that it was worthwhile to spend a hundred million dollars to conceal the next 2-kiloton test when you'd already made 300 of them somewhere in Siberia can only be regarded as hyperbolic but very successful behavior.

When President Kennedy was asked at some point after the decision to sign the treaty why it was that Edward Teller didn't agree, he said it would be very difficult to find *any* agreement with which Edward Teller would go along. That's a legitimate statement and puts the cart in the right position — after the horse: it's rather cause than effect; it has nothing to do with the quality of the agreement, it has more to do with the view towards the future of the superpower relationship than with anything else.

But of course nothing has a one-sided effect. We heard quite a lot about Vela Hotel, Sierra and Uniform afterwards, and even here at this confer-ence. Some of the most interesting things occurred out of this operation, which I think was simply set up to pay off the opposition for having gone that far. They wanted to protect against tests behind the moon and in solar orbit and heaven knows where else. So you made equipment for doing that and when you make new equipment, something good often comes out of it. And something good has come out of it. And this is the good news that I referred to.

It is now possible to distinguish nuclear explosions from earthquakes, reliably, cheaply and in real time. This excellent news was brought first by Jack Evernden, who explained to us how much information is contained in high-frequency seismology, above 30 Hertz, where seismologists are not wont to look. Not so long ago seismologists used equipment reminiscent of old physiology techniques, with smoked paper and frogs' legs to knock on the drum. Nowadays you can buy these capabilities in a digital processor and life is much better. Life is better, of course, for a very clear reason, not a reason that is accidental, but a reason that is intrinsic to the issue. Let me put it this way. I can't really derive the rolloff function for the frequency tail of earthquakes. You can't do that easily, but you can see that the cor-ner frequency, where it turns over, is important and you can see something about the effect in the following way, I think.

The key question here is energy density. Here earthquakes and nuclear explosions differ. In order to make an earthquake you must store energy in elastic deformation of rock, and you can't store very much energy in deformed rock. The amount of energy contained in nuclear explosive per gram is a million times greater than that, or even ten million times, so the volume of the region, if you match energy for energy, goes down by some-thing like ten-million-fold. Therefore the calculations of the dimension of the region go down by at least a factor of a hundred, or something like that. So you have a much smaller region in which the energy release occurs. Since the speed of the shock, of the sound, is much the same for both once you get a little distance away, then you have a much shorter time of explosion. That's clear; I mean everyone knows that an explosion is different from an earthquake. If you look in high frequencies, that's where you'll see the biggest effect. A really high frequency can't be generated at all by a great rock volume ten miles across because it takes seconds for the wave to propagate. This is a fundamental reason why high frequencies are like gold if they can be observed and if they can propagate through the earth without serious attenuation. We now have evidence that they do, in a very beautiful fashion.

That was about the most encouraging thing from the technical side that I've heard for a very long time. The releasing fact is that now it seems highly possible to make a modest multiple-headed network — a seismic array — that would report with high reliability, distinguishing even a small or a strongly-decoupled modest explosion from a minor earthquake. Almost better was the fact that a marvelously ingenious, simple and relatively inexpensive system, the National Seismic System, has been worked out at Sandia, reported to us by Paul Stokes. It is a beautiful example of what you can do in terms of a tamperproof, self-authenticating, self-maintaining system, requiring a visit once a year with a tank of propane, hardly an intrusive activity. Yet it reports reliably, in real time, seismic information about the region in which it sits. This is a *tour de force*. The fact that it is working at five or six stations in the United States at the present time for seismic research purposes is a wonderful earnest for what could happen if we could make this treaty work. In terms of public information, as we were exhorted quite correctly to keep in mind, the whole thing is marvelous. I would like to see such a system made public, even initially just a single public U.S. station, but certainly later if we ever manage to make it into a two-power-based system. To have such a station working at the Smithsonian, so that people could go down and visit it and watch it record the effect of somebody walking into a door or of the ground shaking in the Soviet Union, in real time, any day, would be a very interesting thing. It could be a confidence-building measure of greater importance than those that refer to more esoteric elements. I was very encouraged by that, and I think everybody will go away with that as a key memory. I am surprised by it. I have read up on the situation, and I had no idea how well this system worked, how cheap it was, or that stations of this kind were actually installed and operating all the way from Fairbanks, Alaska, to Arkansas. It is quite impressive to me.

What is the course of technical change? This is the next thing we will ask, and it is clear that we heard a number of very technical reports filled with information about changing technologies. Experts tried to spill some of it out to us, which we caught in more or less loose palms as the juices dripped down. I think the general conclusion is pretty clear, that just as in 1942 one saw what one could try to do, and very crudely could do them, so today in 1984 we see — and in 1990 we will have — improved sensors, improved detectors, improved resolution, improved gathering means of every kind. It seems unlikely that a limit of a technical kind will be set to these things. Certainly not everything can be done, but many things can be done, and limitations by line pairs per millimeter or any such simple parameter of present-day systems will surely not remain forever as limitations. Only physical limitations that are set by the nature of the phenomenon and, above all, social and political limitations set by interpretation, by ambiguity, by the complexity and the effect of concealment — these things will always exist. But generally we can speak of improved technical means of verification. This is plain. You can name a few cases where it is occurring, particularly imaging in the optical, radar and infrared bands of the spectrum. The limits are not set at any level, but in time, or by interpretation, or by antagonistic activity.

Then we come to the problem of treaties themselves. Here again there are two things I think are encouraging and several things that I think are relatively discouraging. Between these two you have to form some sort of a judgment; we are struggling with a problem, a heavy problem. First of all, in spite of the efforts of eloquent participants to minimize the importance of the institution they were talking about, I still think the Standing Consultative Commission is a remarkable institution, a very good invention. In spite of the absence of plenipotentiary powers, it represents a forum in which substantive, technical, weapons-related matters can be discussed in a reasonable way, between persons who know what they are talking about and are not doing it mainly for political opinion, however guided they are by their superiors to take a stance. This is what we very much need. The improvement of the rational at any level can only do good. It seems to me this is an extremely important point, and a very valuable institution.

I don't know that I would urge its modification, though of course it could grow, as institutions can. I was taken by the discussion of the possibility of a post-hoc public report, three years or so after the event, so that with minimal compromise of national positions there would be a record that could be relied upon in future. That would be a valuable thing, if it could be coaxed out of our opposite numbers. If it couldn't be, that would not lessen my enthusiasm for the continuation, extension, praise and effort to rewrite into other relations the existence of such standing consultative committees. I am not sure what relationship this has to the proposals on crisis management by various members of the Senate not usually supportive of arms control, but I find them somewhat parallel. This is a rather good sign, because we don't have many actions that unite us to what I would say broadly is the opposition to rational verification of sensible agreements. Maybe this is a place where something could be done to extend mutual interest.

Second, we come to the presence of cooperative measures written explicitly into treaties that have been successfully carried out. We heard of several. We heard also about one such measure that is now the basis of genuine dispute, as far as I can see a legitimate dispute, in which two sides with their different perceptions fall on two sides of an objectively valid legal argument. The argument is over the ability to gather information about testing by the other side, as agreed upon in SALT II. One side says that telemetry is encrypted, yet that encryption does not block all information but only some information. The other side's view is that the encryption impedes the gathering of information, because every loss of information impedes the gathering of information. The two sides have different views. I find the whole thing very curious. It's nice that such cooperation goes on, but it would not have occurred to a physicist—maybe too naive—to imagine the telemetry made freely available as a gift from the other side could be relied upon, because of its obvious unverifiable referent.

It seems to me that a more unambiguous and physically well-defined and, therefore, unarguable piece of cooperation could have been added. I don't know if it's technically feasible. I'm not expert enough to say that. But to give the flavor of what I think would make good verifiability, what I think is meant when we talk about needing physically unambiguous results, what about tying a continuous wave (CW) beacon by agreement to every such test bus, and just listening to it and measuring its frequency with the best Doppler means. You can get every acceleration out of that, and it gives you the full kinematics of the situation with two stations. It seems to me there is no fooling around with it. Telemetry gives you a lot more, it's true—if you trust it. But if you trust it so much, why don't you trust them to abide by the specifications? I find that a little hard to figure.

My final remark is to say that I do think that the biological warfare ban, without verifiability implied in any way that I can see, is nevertheless by sheer historical accident the most successful of all arms control agreements. Let me put it the other way around: The reason I think that is that since 1972 the revolutionary exploitation of recombinant DNA techniques has given a world of power to biologists that I observe, from quite a lot of looking around, is not reflected in military technology in the United States and therefore probably not anywhere. It is missing in the Soviet Union. In Western Europe and in Japan it does not occur. The momentum is simply not there. It's not that there are no six people hidden somewhere trying to do it, but the variety of biological ingenuity that has gone into the problem of recombinant DNA and genetic modification at a grand level simply has not been put into a structure of military or private, corporation or university laboratories to produce new weapons. I guarantee that had this not been prevented by treaty, there would be a lot of money being made out of it, and a lot of terrible things would be proposed today. They would be covert, but they would be real. I think they would probably be specific means of selectively destroying crops. I think it's quite easy to do in such a way that you could protect the principal varieties in your country and yet destroy those in another country. I think you could reduce the crop yield by a factor of three with no trouble at all, with even modest means of propagation, a weapon not perhaps quite like nuclear war, but a terrible weapon in the hands of the great powers. The fact that this has not been developed substantially — in fact the antidotes are probably at hand — is a great tribute to a fortunate juncture in arms control.

So, I think arms control is most important. A physicist may feel that if an agreement isn't verifiable, it isn't doing anything, but I think it has been made clear that this is not strictly true. By reducing motivation, reducing legality and interest, an agreement can do something in many states, even quite differently organized states. The biological warfare ban did that at the very juncture when a revolution of technology occurred. I don't think they intended it that way. I fear that if somebody had to do it over again and knew what we know now, it wouldn't have been adopted as American policy. But they didn't know, and they couldn't say this was going to happen. That's a general phenomenon, because we are in a time, struggling to a future, when the capability of our species for self-destruction is intense and getting greater all the time. It is an urgent moment for working on it.

Let me end with a brief story. When Robert Fulton was a bright young portrait painter, he went to London. He became seized with technology, he became a friend of James Watt and people like that. In the course of time he applied himself to military matters and he presented to the Admiralty Board in 1796, so the story goes, a proposal for submarine warfare, a complete device which, indeed, he later made. Because the British were the masters of the sea, he tried to sell it to the Admiralty Board. They explained to him, simply and clearly I imagine, that that was the last thing in the world they would sponsor. While it was possible that he could destroy all surface fleets with this means, why should they encourage that, because what they had was the chief surface fleet in the world? This is a sense of self-knowledge that is rare among boards of admiralty.

The fact is that 175 years later, the surface sea has probably been lost to submarine warfare, but it took a long time, during which the British Empire played out quite a major role. By turning down Fulton they did not save themselves forever; obviously they didn't. But they resisted the opposite opportunity — to get into the game and do the best they could with the most to get there first, and so on. They played it cool. That was the right thing to do. They bought time. Not all American advisers have had that self-understanding.

MIRV was mentioned. I would concur it is a very curious invention. A dozen years after its introduction, a commission sanctioned by this administration turned up to say it was probably not such a good idea in the end, and maybe it would go away if we closed our eyes enough. I think the people who said that twelve or fifteen years ago were regarded as very heretical indeed.

That the cruise missile is another example of this sort of thing was pointed out, at least in an arms control context, by Mr. McCrory. He said, "This is MIRV revisited, squared, and in spades." This wonderfully mixed metaphor expresses exactly the right opinion, I think, about the cruise missile and arms control. On the other hand, I'm not so sure that the missiles are themselves so worrisome. I suspect the growth of military countermeasures will be rapid. Still, the presence of a thousand of them with a one-hour flight trajectory from a dozen attack submarines off shore, coming towards our coasts, does not encourage great confidence in the future, even with elaborate searching, homing and killer missiles against the air-breathers. It's a can of worms, and no one is optimistic about the matter.

If you look at the history of this country since its foundation, the clear implication, already secure by the middle of the last century, was that it would grow to be a great world power, as de Tocqueville saw, and many others too. It was unique among powers and among large sovereign states in that it has no substantial border with any equivalent state, and likely never will have. Mexico and Canada, however they grow, will not grow up to be anything like the power the United States is. Cuba, the Bahamas, and even Grenada will not make it either. We therefore have a unique strategic geopolitical advantage: namely, we have no borders from which to fear attack. We never had any substantial internal attack since the burning of Washington by our friends in 1814, and two shells against the California coast, I think, by the Japanese, and five or ten hot air balloons from the Japanese. That's about it. I don't suppose we'll see much else, except for the danger of strategic intercontinental warfare. But I submit that the leader, step by step, in the development of strategic intercontinental warfare, from 1916 until 1984 and not yet stopped, was the United States, and chiefly the United States Air Force, which developed successfully the idea of long-range bombardment, the intercontinental bomber, the nuclear weapon, the thermonuclear weapon, the ballistic missile, and so on. Not that they didn't have help and competition; they did. But certainly the leadership was intense throughout this entire period. You may ask what is the nature of a strategy that does that — that has now turned us into a country fearful for our survival, along with our adversaries to be sure, but nevertheless genuinely fearful. Was that strategic wisdom?

In this sense arms control seems, by differentiation, probably the only path for national security and species survival, in a world that was characterized by von Neumann in the early fifties. He said very clearly that the world has a single, fixed area and a single fixed atmospheric volume, and more people to inhabit it all the time. Our weapons to render parts of it unfit grow all the time, or nearly all the time. This is an asymptotic situation from which there is essentially no escape. That's what von Neumann saw as the problem of our day. I think we all concur in seeing that problem. No single topic is more important than doing something about this. How to do it—I don't know, but we have many ways to try.

24.
Bibliography

Dietrich Schroeer and David Hafemeister

INTRODUCTION

Verification is of great concern in the establishment of any arms control agreements, as well as being very important in its other incarnation as surveillance and reconnaissance to keep track of the opponent's military capabilities. One would therefore expect to find a voluminous, comprehensive, critical, and readily accessible literature focussing on verification. This is not the case; the resources available on this topic are relatively scarce, uneven in emphasis, and often not of first-rate quality.

Trying to establish a technically oriented bibliography for verification presents major problems. In spite of the fact that as much as 90% of U.S. expenditures for verification go toward data gathering, particularly by national technical means such as reconnaissance satellites, little has been written about the technical aspects of verification. The readily accessible writings tend to be by journalists, rarely by active experts. Most of the existing information is scattered in the proceedings of congressional hearings, comes as leaked tidbits from the Department of Defense through trade journals such as *Aviation Week and Space Technology*, and is hidden in political commentary; or it is buried in the technical literature for experts working in some technical subfield, as in proceedings of meetings of the Society of Photo-Optical Instrumentation Engineers. Few critical and comprehensively detailed technical reviews exist. Political reviews of verification are more plentiful, but they tend to focus on a specific issue, for example, the details of one treaty, and tend to bypass the technical side of verification. No journals in fact exist that might readily accept technical articles on verification issues. In turn, there are no professional rewards for studies of these issues, such studies are unlikely to pay off in the "publish or perish" atmosphere of the academic community.

Another reason for the lack of discussion of technical aspects of verification may be that such discussions are not in the interest of the intelligence community. Any revelations of actual capabilities might be of use to the intelligence services of other nations. In that sense the craft of intelligence cannot have a community of scholars as is the case in the sciences and technology: the norm of internationalism cannot be satisfied if one wants to keep information from other nations.

Because there is a dearth of good technical literature about verification, this resource bibliography includes references that are not directly concerned with verification but deal with technologies that are relevant to verification. Thus the literature on photogrammetry for remote sensing of earth resources can be used to understand the working of space-based verification reconnaissance technologies.

A few specific verification issues, such as the monitoring of nuclear test ban treaties, have been talked about in more technical details than others, such as photographic reconnaissance or telemetry. This may in part be because the test-ban technology is more directly related to scientific questions about earthquakes, while photo-reconnaissance is a much more sophisticated technology than its civilian-counterpart Landsat activities, and electronic espionage on telemetry signals via ferret satellites has no civilian parallels. Some verification problems may be too difficult to solve satisfactorily, such as the monitoring of a ban on chemical and biological weapons, and hence may attract less interest — and produce less literature.

The net effect is to make it difficult to collect good technical literature on verification; either it is too political, too superficial, or too little; or else it is too specialized and hence not directly related to the issues. Yet more information about verification capabilities and about their implications ought to be publicly available. Verification capabilities have often in the past limited what agreements could be reached. Preparation is needed now to be ready for future debates about arms-limitation agreements, so that the policy makers won't be as uninformed as during the SALT-II debate. In the technical area of verification, those who are technically knowledgeable may have had their own way too much; there may have been too little oversight by policy makers. Interpretative and evaluative aspects of verification may outweigh in importance the technical aspects. But if the technical aspects are not known and understood by a broader public, the interpretative aspects can be controlled in subtle ways by those who claim to possess expert wisdom.

GENERAL REFERENCES

In readings about verification a few sources are cited repeatedly because they provide extensive material, and a small group of journals contains a significant amount of relevant material. These references are listed here.

General References

Jasani, B. Ed. *Outer Space—A New Dimension of the Arms Race.* Cambridge, MA: Oelgeschlager, Gunn & Hain, 1982. Part II on space technology, crisis monitoring, and arms control has a series of articles that relate to verification.

Potter, Wm. C. Ed. *Verification and SALT: The Challenge of Strategic Deception.* Boulder, CO: Westview Press, 1980, and *Verification in Arms Control.* Cambridge, MA: Ballinger, 1985. Two useful collections of articles on various aspects of verification including technology, politics, as well as a bibliographic essay.

Scribner, R. A. and R. Scott, Eds. *An Annotated Bibliography of Strategic Nuclear Arms Control Verification.* Washington, DC: American Association for the Advancement of Science, 1984. An extensive collection of references, heavy on the political aspects of verification.

Scribner, R., W. Metz and T. Ralston. *The Verification Challenge: Problems and Promise of Strategic Nuclear Arms Control Verification.* Boston, MA: Birkhauser, 1985. A compilation of facts and policy written in a primer style for the general reader by the AAAS.

The Society of Photo-Optical Instrumentation Engineers (SPIE) has frequent meetings in which reconnaissance is discussed; the resulting *Proceedings* can provide up-to-date information on the technical capabilities of optical surveillance systems.

Stockholm International Peace Research Institute. *World Armaments and Disarmament: SIPRI Yearbook*, prepared annually by SIPRI, and most recently published by Oelgeschlager, Gunn & Hain, Cambridge, MA. Has a regular summary of space activities, including satellite launching dates, guesses as to their purposes, and a review of the state of activities in orbital space.

Journals

Arms Control Today. Newsletter of the Arms Control Association, obtainable from the ACA at 11 Dupont Circle, NW, Washington, D.C. 20036. Pro-disarmament view of arms-race issues, has brief reviews of some verification problems, and lists current publications.

Aviation Week and Space Technology. This is the trade journal for aviation and space technology and frequently gives some information about surveillance systems and their capabilities. It is often authoritative, but tends to be overly technologically optimistic and sometimes does not separate fact from speculation.

The Defense Monitor. The newsletter of the Center for Defense Information, obtainable from the CDI at 122 Maryland Ave., NE, Washington, D.C. 20002. A review of arms race issues, including verification.

Foreign Affairs. Discusses the policy implications of modern technology; sometimes includes concerns with verification.

IEEE Spectrum. Survey articles of contemporary technologies, including those useful in verification.

Journal of the Optical Society of America. Contains articles on optical sensors and image processing.

Public Interest Report. The newsletter of the Federation of American Scientists, obtainable from the FAS, 307 Massachusetts Ave., NE, Washington, D.C. 20002. Contains good summaries of current arms-race controversies, sometimes on verification issues.

Scientific American. Has arms-race articles with good scientific and technical content, some on verification. Unfortunately, it is largely qualitative, and the references are often not very helpful.

SALT-TYPE VERIFICATION

General Sources

Aspin, L. The Verification of the SALT II Agreement. *Sci. Am.* 240 (2) (February 1979):38–45. Does the U.S. have adequate "national technical means" to monitor a SALT treaty?

Bamford, J. *The Puzzle Palace*. Boston, MA: Houghton Mifflin, 1982. General journalistic overview of intelligence methods and hardware, some relevant to verification by national technical means.

Bennett, P. *Strategic Surveillance: How America Checks Soviet Compliance with SALT*. Cambridge, MA: Union of Concerned Scientists, June 1979.

Gray, C. Moscow is Cheating; and Krepon, Michael. Both Sides are Hedging. In *Foreign Policy* 56 (1984). Two views of the compliance issue.

Katz, A. H. *Verification and SALT: The State of the Art and the Art of the State*. Washington, DC: The Heritage Foundation, 1979; see also his The Fabric of Verification: The Warp and the Woof, Chapter 11 in Potter, *Verification and SALT*, op. cit., pp. 193–220. Critical of verification enthusiasts, enjoyable reading.

Lehman, J. F. and S. Weiss. SALT Verification. Chapter 6 of *Beyond the SALT II Failure*. New York: Praeger, 1981.

A plethora of journalistic exposés of space activities has been and is being published. These generally have a few tidbits related to satellite reconnaissance. See, for example: Beckett, B. *Weapons of Tomorrow* (1983); Karas, T. *The New High Ground* (1983); Ritchie, D. *Space War* (1982), and Stine, G. H. *Confrontation in Space* (1981).

Stockholm International Peace Research Institute. *Outer Space—Battle-*

field of the Future? London: Taylor & Francis, 1978. A general survey of satellite types, verification, etc.

Optical Reconnaissance: Sensors

Blair, B. G. Reconnaissance Satellites, in Jasani, *Outer Space*, op. cit., pp. 125–134.

Blair, B. G. and G. D. Brewer. Verifying SALT Agreements, in Potter, *Verification and SALT*, op. cit., pp. 7–48. Very nice semi-technical review of reconnaissance sensors and capabilities.

Brock, G. C. *Physical Aspects of Air Photography.* New York: Longmans, Green & Co., 1952. Basic "bible" on the photographic techniques of aerial photography; old but still valid explanations and frequently referenced.

Federation of American Scientists. National Technical Means: Imaging Reconnaissance Satellites, and Image Interpretation. *FAS Public Interest Report* 35 (7) (September 1982): 3–4, and 11.

Greenwood, T. *Reconnaissance, Surveillance and Arms Control.* London: International Institute for Strategic Studies, Adelphi Paper No. 88, 1972; see also his article in *Sci. Am.* 228 (2) (February 1973): 14–25. Old but good references, still heavily cited.

Hafemeister, D., J. Romm and K. Tsipis. The Verification of Compliance with Arms Control Agreements. *Sci. Am.* 247 (October 1982): 66–74.

Hudson, Jr., R. D. and J. W. Hudson. The Military Applications of Remote Sensing by Infrared. *Proc. IEEE* 63 (1) (January 1975):104–128. An excellent technical review of IR sensors and their military uses.

Jasani, B. Verification using Reconnaissance Satellites. *SIPRI Yearbook 1973*, pp. 60–101.

Jasani, B. Reconnaissance Satellites. *SIPRI Yearbook 1974*, pp. 287–302, *SIPRI Yearbook 1975*, pp. 378–401 and *SIPRI Yearbook 1976*, pp. 102–119.

Jasani, B. Military Satellites. *SIPRI Yearbook 1977*, pp. 103–179 and *SIPRI Yearbook 1978*, pp. 69–103.

Jasani, B. The Military Use of Outer Space. *SIPRI Yearbook 1979*, pp. 256–304, *SIPRI Yearbook 1981*, pp. 279–293, and *SIPRI Yearbook 1982*, pp. 291–315.

Jasani, B. A Role for Satellites in Verification of Arms Control. *SIPRI Yearbook 1980*, pp. 187–207.

Jasani, B. Military Competition in Space. In *The Impact of New Military Technology*, edited by Jonathan Alford. Cambridge, MA: Allanheld, Osmum and Co. for the IISS, Adelphi Library No. 4, 1981.

Jasani, B. Military Space Technology and Its Implications. In Jasani, *Outer Space*, op. cit., pp. 1–124.

Karkoszka, A. and O. Wilkes. Verification of the SALT II Treaty. *SIPRI Yearbook 1980*, pp. 285–315.

Kristian, J. and M. Blouke. Charge-Coupled Devices in Astronomy. *Sci. Am.* 247 (4) (October 1982): 66–74.

Lintz, J., Jr. and D. S. Simonett, Eds. *Remote Sensing of the Environment*. Reading, MA.: Addison-Wesley, 1976. A textbook.

Myer, D. G. Strategic Satellites: Our Eyes in the Sky—Can They Save the World from Armageddon? *Armed Forces J. International* 120 (7) (February 1983): 30–40.

Perry, G. E. Identification of Military Components within the Soviet Space Program. In Jasani, *Outer Space*. op. cit., pp. 135–254.

Richason, B. F., Jr., Ed. *Introduction to Remote Sensing of the Environment*. Dubuque, Iowa: Kendall/Hunt, 1978. A good textbook by committee.

Richelson, J. The Keyhole Satellite Program. *Jour. Strategic Studies* (2), 121 (1984). An excellent history of KHs.

Simonett, D. S., Ed. *Manual of Remote Sensing*, Vol. 1: *Theory, Instruments and Techniques*. 2nd ed. Falls Church, VA: American Society of Photogrammetry, 1983. Has description of remote sensing technology, some relevant to verification.

Slama, C. C., Ed. *Manual of Photogrammetry*. 4th ed. Falls Church, VA: American Society of Photogrammetry, 1980. Good reference for data taking and analysis, including Chapter 17 on "Satellite Photogrammetry," edited by D. L. Light, pp. 883–977.

Swain, P. H. and S. M. Davis. *Remote Sensing: The Quantitative Approach*. New York: McGraw-Hill, 1978. Good review articles of instrumentation, pattern recognition, data processing, etc.

Thomson, G. H. Soviet Spy Satellites—What Can They See? *Brit. J. of Photography* 126 (10 August 1979): 774–775. A report on the types of satellites launched, and the deduced missions. See also Soviet Photo Reconnaissance Satellites—What Are They Used For? *ibid.*, 127 (21 November, 1980): 1164–1165.

Wilkes, O. The Arms Race in Space. *SIPRI Yearbook 1978*, pp. 104–130.

York, H. F. U.S. Air and Space Reconnaissance Programs. *SIPRI Yearbook 1977*, pp. 180–187.

Optical Reconnaissance: Transmission and Analysis

Estes, J. E., Ed. *Manual of Remote Sensing, Vol. 2: Interpretation and Applications*. 2nd ed. Falls Church, VA: Am. Soc. of Photogrammetry, 1983.

Lee, S. H., Ed. *Optical Information Processing: Fundamentals*. New York: Springer, 1981.

Lillesand, T. M. and R. W. Kiefer. *Remote Sensing and Image Interpretation*. New York: Wiley, 1979.

Orhaug, T. and G. Forsell. Information Extraction from Images, in Jasani, *Outer Space*, op. cit., pp. 215–228.

Pritchard, W. L. Satellite Communications — An Overview of the Problems and Programs. *Proc. IEEE* 65 (March 1977): 294–307.

Sakata, T. and H. Shimoda. Image Analysis and Sensor Technology for Satellite Monitoring, in Jasani, *Outer Space*, op. cit., pp. 197–214.

Schowengerdt, R. A. *Techniques for Image Processing and Classification in Remote Sensing*. New York: Academic Press, 1983. Very nice qualitative and quantitative techniques for analyzing images.

Walker, J. The Amateur Scientist. *Sci. Am.* 247 (5) (November 1982): 194–205. Simple optical experiments in which spatial filtering removes the "noise" from pictures.

York, H. F. Reconnaissance Satellites and the Arms Race. In *Arms Control and Technological Innovation*. edited by D. Carlton and C. Schaerf. New York: Wiley, 1976, pp. 225–231. Talks about data transmission rates.

Side-Looking Radar

Foster, L. E. *Telemetry Systems*. New York: Wiley, 1965. An old text with some parts on telemetry systems that are still quite useful.

Hovanessian, A. A. *Radar Detection and Tracking Systems*. Dedham, MA: Artech House, 1978 [1973]). Describes basic radar principles, probabilities of detection, new technologies like synthetic radar arrays, and specific applications such as missile tracking. It can be understood by senior-level physics students.

Jensen, H., L. C. Graham, L. J. Porcello, and E. N. Keith. Side-looking Airborne Radar. *Sci. Am.* 237 (4) (October 1977): 84–95. Radar observation is independent of the weather or time of day; its capabilities are improving rapidly.

Marcus, J. *Radio Remote-Control and Telemetry and Their Application to Missiles*. New York: Pergamon, 1966. Old, but still of some interest.

Toomay, J. *Radar Principles for the Non-Specialist*. Belmont, CA: Lifetime Learning (Wadsworth), 1982. A textbook for engineers who want to learn about radar.

Verification of SALT Treaties

Davis, P. K. Land-Mobile ICBMs: Verification and Breakout, in Potter, *Verification and SALT*, op. cit., pp. 143–162.

Federation of American Scientists. Verification. *FAS Public Interest Report* 36 (9) (November 1983): 13–16. On verifying ASAT treaties.

Humphrey, G. J. Analysis and Compliance Enforcement in SALT Verification, in Potter, *Verification and SALT*, op. cit., pp. 111–127.

Kaiser, R. G. Verification of SALT II: Art and Science. Three articles in the *Washington Post* (June 15, 16, and 17, 1979). The fact that these newspaper essays were sometimes cited as the best available literature about verification technologies during the SALT-II debate is symptomatic of the dearth of good analytical writings on this issue.

Pieragostini, K. Cooperative Verification. *Arms Control Today* 13 (5), (June 1983): 1–4.

Scoville, H. Verification of Soviet Strategic Missile Tests, in Potter, *Verification and SALT*, op. cit., pp. 163–176.

Sharp, J. Verifying a Warhead Freeze. *Arms Control Today* 13 (5) (June 1983): 1–7.

Steinberg, G. M. *Satellite Reconnaissance: The Role of Informal Bargaining*. New York: Praeger, 1982. Discusses the legality and tradition of satellite overflights and reconnaissance.

Wolfe, T. *The Salt Experience*. Cambridge, MA: Ballinger, 1979; and Talbott, S. *End Game: The Inside Story of SALT II*. New York: Harper and Row, 1979. Very good journalistic tales about the development of the SALT II agreements, and how verification entered into the discussions.

TEST BAN TREATIES

Monitoring Above-Ground Nuclear Tests

Hussain, F. *Impact of Weapons Test Restrictions*. London: International Institute for Strategic Studies, London, Adelphi Paper No. 165, 1981; e.g., Ballistic Flight Detection and Identification, pp. 39–47.

Latter, R., R. F. Herbst, and K. M. Watson. Detection of Nuclear Explosions. *Rev. Nucl. Sci.* 11 (1961): 371–418. Has equations for the decoupling phenomenon, for electromagnetic pulses from explosions, for x-ray fluxes and photon yields from nuclear tests in space.

Singer, S. The Vela Satellite Program for Detection of High-Altitude Nuclear Detonations. *Proc. IEEE* 53 (12) (December 1965): 1935–1948.

Monitoring of Underground Nuclear Tests

Bolt, B. A. *Nuclear Explosions and Earthquakes: The Parted Veil*. San Francisco, CA: Freeman, 1976. An excellent book on earthquakes and underground nuclear explosions, not only on the science but also on the history and politics of nuclear-test-ban efforts.

Dahlman, O., and H. Israelson. *Monitoring Explosion Seismology*. New York: Elsevier, 1977. More detailed than Bolt, but more difficult to follow.

Gilpin, R. *American Scientists and Nuclear Weapons Policy*. Princeton, NJ: Princeton University Press, 1962. A classic discussion of the role scientists can play in scientific-political debates.

Jacobson, H. K., and E. Stein. *Diplomats, Scientists and Politicians: The U.S. and the Nuclear Test Ban Negotiations*. Ann Arbor, MI: University of Michigan Press, 1966. Gives an indication of the role verification played in the test-ban debates.

Rodean, H. C. *Nuclear Explosion Seismology*. Springfield, VA: National Technical Information Service, TID-25572, 1971. Very sophisticated, yet understandable review of the generation of seismic signals by underground nuclear explosions, including the phenomenon of decoupling to minimize signals.

Stokes, P. A. The National Seismic Station. Albuquerque, NM: Sandia National Laboratory, Report SAND81-2134, 1982. Describes black boxes to be placed unattended in foreign countries for unobtrusive "in country" seismic monitoring for underground nuclear explosions.

Sykes, L. R., and J. F. Evernden. The Verification of a Comprehensive Nuclear Test Ban. *Sci. Am.* 247 (4) (October 1982): 47–55. Optimistic about the potential of seismic verification.

Sykes, L. R., J. F. Evernden, and I. Cifuentas. Seismic Methods for Verifying Nuclear Test Bans. In *Physics, Technology and the Nuclear Arms Race*. Edited by D. W. Hafemeister and D. Schroeer. New York: Am. Inst. of Phys., AIP Conf. Proc. No. 104, 1983, pp. 85–133.

NON-PROLIFERATION

De Volpi, A. *Proliferation, Plutonium and Policy: Institutional and Technological Impediments to Nuclear Weapons Propagation*. New York: Pergamon, 1979. Has very good and extensive discussion both of the technical aspects of critical yields, denaturing, and so forth, and of the political aspects of institutional safeguards—all relevant to monitoring the NPT.

Federation of American Scientists. Verifying a Model Freeze. *FAS Public Interest Report* 35 (7) (September 1979): 1–12.

Gallini, L. D. Nuclear Weapons Monitoring. *IEEE Spectrum* 18 (7) (July 1981): 48–51. A general survey.

Greenwood, T., H. A. Feiveson, and T. B. Taylor. *Nuclear Proliferation: Motivations, Capabilities, and Strategies for Control*. New York: McGraw-Hill, 1977. Still a good review.

CHEMICAL AND BIOLOGICAL WEAPONS

Stares, J. *Chemical Disarmament: Some Problems of Verification.* New York: Humanities Press for SIPRI, 1973.

Stockholm International Peace Research Institute. *Chemical and Biological Warfare: A Study of the Historical, Technical, Military, Legal and Political Aspects of CBW and Possible Disarmament Measures*, six volumes. New York: Humanities Press for SIPRI, 1971.

THE CRAFT OF INTELLIGENCE

Abdel-Hady, M., and A. Sadek. Verification Using Satellites: Feasibility of an International or Multinational Agency, in Jasani, *Outer Space*, op. cit., pp. 275–296.

Callaham, M., and K. Tsipis. *Crisis Management Satellite.* Cambridge, MA: Program in Science and Technology for International Security, MIT, Report No. 3, 1978. A publicly-controlled "crisis management satellite" with reconnaissance, surveillance, and possibly communications capabilities could have wide uses in verification, early warning, and reduction of international suspicions. Some discussion of Landsat capabilities.

Cohen, S. A. The Evolution of Soviet Views on SALT Verification: Implications for the Future, in Potter, *Verification and SALT*, op. cit., pp. 49–75.

Lowenthal, M. U.S. Organization for Verification, in Potter, *Verification and SALT*, op. cit., pp. 77–94.

THE REQUIREMENTS OF VERIFICATION

Freedman, L. *U.S. Intelligence and the Soviet Strategic Threat.* Boulder, CO: Westview, 1977. Shows how successes and failure in reconnaissance influenced policy decisions.

Harris, W. R. A SALT Safeguard Program: Coping with Soviet Deception under Strategic Arms Agreements, in Potter, *Verification and SALT*, op. cit., pp. 129–141.

Heckrotte, W., and G. C. Smith, Eds. *Arms Control in Transition: Proceedings of the Livermore Arms Control Conference.* Boulder, CO: Westview Press, 1981. A general survey of arms control, not focussing on verification per se; it is interesting to see how little emphasis even technically-oriented arms-control experts place on verification.

Prados, J. *The Soviet Estimate: U.S. Intelligence Analysis & Russian Military Strength.* New York: Dial Press, 1982. Describes the history of U.S. intelligence resources, and how intelligence estimates influence policy.

Index

411

About the Editors and Contributors

THE EDITORS

Kosta Tsipis is Director of the Program in Science & Technology for International Security at M.I.T.

David Hafemeister, Visiting Scientist at M.I.T. Program for Science & Technology for International Security 1983–1984, is Professor of Physics at California Polytechnic University.

Penny Janeway is Technical Editor at M.I.T. Program for Science & Technology for International Security.

THE CONTRIBUTORS

Jerome B. Wiesner, President Emeritus of M.I.T., was Presidential Science Advisor from 1961 to 1964.

Noel Gayler, USN (ret.), is Chairman of the Deep Cuts Campaign, American Committee on East–West Accord. He was Commander, U.S. Forces in the Pacific (1972–76); Director, National Security Agency (1969–72); Deputy Director, Joint Strategic Target Planning Staff, Joint Chiefs of Staff (1967–69).

William E. Colby, Senior Advisor, International Government Counselors, Washington, D.C., was Director of the Central Intelligence Agency (1980–81).

Ralph Earle II is Managing Partner, Baker & Daniels, Washington, D.C. He was Director, U.S. Arms Control and Disarmament Agency (1980–81) and U.S. Ambassador and Chief Negotiator for the SALT II talks (1978–80).

Michael Krepon is a Senior Associate at the Carnegie Endowment for International Peace, where he directs the Verification Project. He was Director of defense program and policy reviews at ACDA in the Carter administration.

Joseph J. Romm is a Research Associate at M.I.T. Program for Science & Technology for International Security.

Ronald Ondrejka is an advanced planning consultant to government and industry in the area of remote sensing systems for aircraft and satellite applications.

J. Richard Vyce is Director of Advanced Program Development at Litton/Itek Optical Systems.

John W. Hardy is a Principal Engineer at Litton/Itek Optical Systems.

Morley Blouke is Principal Scientist, CCD Engineering, at Tektronix, Inc.

James R. Janesick is an engineer in the Space Photography Section at the Jet Propulsion Laboratory, Pasadena.

B. R. Hunt is Professor of Electrical Engineering and Optical Sciences at the University of Arizona and Chief Scientist for Image and Signal Processing with Science Applications International Corp. in Tucson.

Eli Brookner is Consulting Scientist for the Raytheon Company Equipment Division. He was a technical consultant on the Cobra Dane, Cobra Judy and PAVE PAWS radars.

James C. Fraser is Manager, Advanced Sensors, at New England Research Center, Inc. He was Assistant Director for Surveillance for the Strategic Technology Office of DARPA.

Robert J. Bell is Professor of Physics at the University of Missouri-Rolla and consultant for the Naval Research Laboratories.

Herbert H. Scoville, Jr. was Deputy Director for Science & Technology of the Central Intelligence Agency (1955–63).

Richard L. Garwin is IBM Fellow, Thomas J. Watson Research Center; Adjunct Professor of Physics, Columbia University; Adjunct Research Fellow, Center for Science & International Affairs, Harvard University; and Andrew D. White Professor-at-Large, Cornell University. He is a former member of the President's Science Advisory Committee and of the Defense Science Board.

Jack F. Evernden is Research Geophysicist, U.S. Geological Survey, Menlo Park, California. He is former Professor of Geophysics, University of California, Berkeley, and was a seismologist at the Air Force Applications Center, ACDA and ARPA.

Charles B. Archambeau is Adjunct Professor of Geophysics, University of Colorado, with the Cooperative Institute for Research in Environmental Sciences and the Center for Seismic Studies of the Department of Defense.

Paul A. Stokes is Manager, Systems Research Department, Sandia National Laboratory.

Eystein Husebye is Director of Scientific Research at NORSAR, Kjeller, Norway.

Shane Ingate is a Research Associate at the Earth Resources Laboratory at M.I.T.

Harold V. Argo was Head of the Global Positioning Satellite Program at the Los Alamos National Laboratory.

E. V. Weinstock is a physicist in the Instrumentation Division at Brookhaven National Laboratory and Deputy Head of the Technical Support Organization, which provides technical advice on safeguards to the Department of Energy.

A. Fainberg is a physicist in the Instrumentation Division at Brookhaven.

G. Robert Keepin is Safeguards Advisor to the Deputy Director, International Atomic Energy Agency; and Program Manager and Group Leader, Nuclear Safeguards Affairs, at Los Alamos National Laboratory.

Frank von Hippel, a theoretical physicist, is Professor of Public and International Affairs at Princeton and an affiliated faculty member at the University's Center for Energy and Environmental Studies.

Barbara G. Levi is a research physicist at Princeton University's Center for Energy and Environmental Studies.

Philip Morrison is Institute Professor at M.I.T. (Physics) and a student and author on nuclear weapons and nuclear warfare since Manhattan Project days.

Dietrich Schroeer, Professor of Physics at the University of North Carolina at Chapel Hill, spent 1984–1985 working on directed energy weapons and arms control at the International Institute for Strategic Studies in London.